Portland Community College Library

Korea's Future and the Great Powers

THE NATIONAL BUREAU OF ASIAN RESEARCH

The National Bureau of Asian Research (NBR) is a nonprofit, nonpartisan institution that conducts advanced research on policy-relevant issues in Asia. It also serves as the global clearinghouse for Asia research conducted by specialists and institutions worldwide. NBR is uniquely positioned to promote informed and effective U.S. policy toward the region.

- NBR sponsors projects that examine the economic, political, and strategic questions affecting U.S. relations with East Asia, South Asia, and the former Soviet Union.

- NBR efficiently draws upon the world's premier specialists to develop and carry out its research agenda.

- Through its advisory board, programs, and print and electronic publications, NBR integrates its research into the policymaking communities of the United States and Asia.

NBR's operations are governed by its Board of Directors, a nationally prominent group of leaders with long-term interests in Asia. NBR's research agenda is developed in consultation with its Board of Advisors, which consists of experts from research centers, universities, and corporations, and of more than sixty U.S. Senators and Representatives. Guidance is also provided by leading American companies through NBR's Corporate Council.

Korea's Future and the Great Powers

Edited by

Nicholas Eberstadt and Richard J. Ellings

 NBR The National Bureau of Asian Research

in association with

University of Washington Press
Seattle and London

To Mary and Marta,
our vital interests

Library of Congress Cataloging-in-Publication Data

Korea's future and the great powers / edited by Nicholas Eberstadt and Richard J. Ellings.
   p. cm.
   Includes index.
   ISBN 0-295-98129-6 (alk. paper)
   1. Korean reunification question (1945-). 2. Korea (South)--Economic policy. 3. Korea (North)--Politics and government. 4. East Asia--Politics and government. 5. World politics--1945- I. Eberstadt, Nicholas, 1955- II. Ellings, Richard J.

DS917.444 .K685 2001
951.904--dc21   2001018305

The paper used in this publication meets the minimum requirements of American National Standard for Information Sciences--Permanence of Paper for Printed Library Materials, ANSI Z39.48-1984.

Contents

ECONOMIC CONTEXT

STRATEGIC IMPLICATIONS

Acknowledgments

Widely unexpected and even startling events, reflecting significant policy shifts or mistakes by the two Koreas and the surrounding powers, took place during the writing of this volume. To name but a few of these: South Korea, newly admitted to the OECD for its great economic success, in December 1997 negotiated a $58 billion emergency loan with an IMF-led international consortium to avert a looming debt default; North Korea fired a multi-stage rocket over the Japanese archipelago in August 1998; South Korea's Kim Dae Jung and North Korea's Kim Jong Il held a summit in Pyongyang less than two years later, in June 2000; and in October 2000, a top North Korean official was received by President Clinton in the White House, occasioning a reciprocal visit by Secretary of State Madeline Albright to Kim Jong Il in Pyongyang. These dramatic and surprising milestones had the immediate effect of complicating our analytical task—but we felt that they also under-scored the importance of this project, and to our relief and appreciation, so did our fellow authors.

Because this volume is the culmination of much work by many very talented people, our debt runs wide and deep. Our American team exceeded the roster of authors. Contributing mightily in our lengthy discussions and meetings in Washington were Bob Zoellick, Jim Lilley, Kent Harrington, and Ken Lieberthal (who had to resign from the project when appointed as Special Assistant to the President and Senior Director for Asian Affairs on the National Security Council). We hope that this volume reflects at least some of their remarkable insights and wisdom. Above all, we thank our authors for their acuity, hard work, and patience beyond the call of duty.

The project commenced, and then was punctuated for mid-course correction, with helpful meetings in Washington: the first set on October 29–30, 1997, and the next 24 months later, on October 12–13, 1999. On those occasions we met key officials from the National Security Council, the Departments of State, Defense, and Treasury, and the intelligence community. For generously taking time out of their demanding schedules we owe thanks to, among others, Jack Pritchard, Ken Lieberthal, Russ Deming, Chuck Kartman, Jack Merrill, Jeff Baron, Bob Carlin, Ken Quinones, Bill Newcombe, Kurt Campbell, Wallace Gregson, Jr., Rick Finn, Todd Harvey, Daniel Zelikow, and Jason Singer.

In addition to meeting with U.S. government officials, we held a series of bilateral meetings with counterparts from the Republic of Korea, Japan, and China. These were convened in Washington from October 19–22, 1998, for the purposes of exploring conceptions of national interest with regard to Korean reunification and of obtaining views on possible futures of North Korea. We are particularly indebted to the Sejong Institute, which under the direction of Hahn Bae Ho and later Kim Dalchoong agreed to support the U.S.-Korea bilateral with funding and assistance in assembling the Korean delegation. Led by Ha Young-Sun, the Korean group was composed of Kim Byung-Kook, Kim Suk-Woo, Lee Tai Hwan, Park Se Il, Yang Changseok, Yang Un-Chul, and Youn Miryang. For our bilateral with Japan we wish to thank Ichiro Fujisaki, Kan Kimura, Masao Okonogi, Yasunori Sone, and Tsuneo Watanabe. Joining us for the excellent U.S.-China bilateral were Liu Ming, Long Guoqiang, Ren Xiao, and Wu Xinbo.

The staff of The National Bureau of Asian Research (NBR), especially Jen Linder, was responsible for the extraordinary logistical support and cat herding required for this ambitious undertaking. Bill Abnett, tremendous friend and colleague, provided many pages of critical background research. NBR Vice President Brigitte Allen adeptly helped raise the funding upon which we depended. Through the publication phase, whose difficulty was so compounded by the events of 1997–2000, Jen Linder (again), Erica Johnson, Meira Meek, Bruce Acker, and Michael Wills collaborated in a superb editing and indexing effort. We owe the University of Washington Press, and especially our editor Michael Duckworth, our sincere appreciation for patience and masterful publication expertise. Along the way other

NBR staff and several interns provided invaluable research assistance and organizational "heavy-lifting." They include Toby Dalton, Mark Frazier, Monica Ghosh, Bryan Krekel, Jonathan Perkins, Vanessa Preisler, and Tu-Uyen Tran.
Financial support for the project was wide and deep as well. We wish to thank the Smith Richardson Foundation, which provided our lead grant, The Lynde and Harry Bradley Foundation, the Center for Nonproliferation Studies of the Monterey Institute of International Studies, the American Enterprise Institute for its support of Nicholas Eberstadt, and, again, The Sejong Institute. We gratefully acknowledge the inspiration and steadfast support of Marin Strmecki, Samantha Ravich, Allan Song, and Diane Sehler.

Had we foreseen the challenges that eventually confronted us in this project, we're not sure we would have possessed the courage to tackle it. In the event, we were tremendously fortunate to enjoy the support of all the aforementioned, and their help was indeed necessary to bring us this far. These colleagues are responsible for what good has come from this project and we alone are responsible for its shortcomings.

Nick Eberstadt
Rich Ellings
January 2001

Commonly Used Abbreviations

ABM	Anti-Ballistic Missile (Treaty)
ADB	Asian Development Bank
APEC	Asia-Pacific Economic Cooperation
ARF	ASEAN Regional Forum
ASEAN	Association of Southeast Asian Nations
BOK	Bank of Korea
CBM	confidence building measure
CCP	Chinese Communist Party
CIA	Central Intelligence Agency
CPRF	Communist Party of the Russian Federation
CSBM	confidence and security building measure
DMZ	Demilitarized Zone
DPRK	Democratic People's Republic of Korea
DSPJ	Democratic Socialist Party of Japan
EBRD	European Bank for Reconstruction and Development
GDP	gross domestic product
GNP	gross national product
IAEA	International Atomic Energy Agency
ICBM	inter-continental ballistic missile
IFI	international financial institution
IMF	International Monetary Fund
ITC	investment trust sector
KEDO	Korean Peninsula Energy Development Organization
KPA	Korean People's Army
KWP	Korean Workers' Party

LDP	Liberal Democratic Party
NAFTA	North American Free Trade Agreement
NATO	North Atlantic Treaty Organization
NMD	national missile defense
NPT	Nuclear Nonproliferation Treaty
NSC	National Security Council
OECD	Organization for Economic Cooperation and Development
PLA	People's Liberation Army
PRC	People's Republic of China
ROK	Republic of Korea
SEATO	Southeast Asian Treaty Organization
SNCC	South-North Coordination Committee
TMD	theater missile defense
UNC	United Nations Command
UNTCOK	United Nations Temporary Commission on Korea
USSR	Union of Soviet Socialist Republics
WMD	weapons of mass destruction
WTO	World Trade Organization

Korea's Future and the Great Powers

1

Introduction

Nicholas Eberstadt and Richard J. Ellings

KOREA'S FUTURE AND INTERNATIONAL SECURITY:
THE IMPERATIVE OF FORWARD THINKING

For over a century, the Korean Peninsula has figured fatefully in the international strategies of all the major powers of the Pacific region: China, Russia, Japan, and the United States. A small, secluded, and impoverished kingdom—as Korea most assuredly was not so long ago—might not seem like an obvious prize for great powers to struggle over. But Korea is at the crossroads where the national interests of these Pacific powers converge: and their policies for protecting and promoting their interests have impelled their involvement in this once-remote region.

Thus Korea became a stage upon which the drama of great power competition was played out—often to a tragic script. When the Pacific powers assessed their interests in Korea accurately, they were on occasion brought into bloody conflict with one another (as at the turn of the twentieth century). If a Pacific power neglected or misassessed its interests in Korea, however, this too could lead to war between great powers—as the United States learned in 1950.

In the half-century since the outbreak of the Korean War, Korea has undergone a monumental transformation; so has the character of great power politics in the Pacific. With South Korea's ascent to affluence and its emergence as an open, competitive democracy, and North Korea's simultaneous descent into mass starvation in the midst of a focused campaign to develop weapons of mass destruction under a dynastic socialist dictatorship, the political and economic contradictions within the Korean Peninsula itself have perhaps never been so great. By contrast, with the end of the Cold War, political hostilities between the Pacific powers have been vastly diminished. Though by no means impossible, it is far more difficult to envision a strategy-driven military confrontation between these Pacific powers today than it would have been just a few years ago.

At the dawn of a new century, these local and international developments seem to lay the foundation for a dramatic and indeed historic change in the Pacific powers' interplay with the Korean Peninsula. Heretofore, in much the manner that Poland long served as "God's playground"[1] in European power politics, Korea has been akin to an anvil upon which the great powers of the Pacific have wielded their hammers to forge world history. In the strategic environment that is currently evolving, however, Korea looks to be increasingly positioned to act—deliberately or inadvertently—as a driver of international events.

Today, indeed, developments emanating from the Korean Peninsula stand to have a serious impact on the national interests of each of the Pacific powers. The prospective developments are poised not only to affect the security and well-being of these powers directly, but also to challenge fledgling attempts to construct a durable regional order characterized by concerted cooperation among them. On the immediate horizon, North Korea's quest to develop an arsenal of nuclear, biological, and chemical weapons—and the ballistic missile systems to target distant countries with these deadly devices—threatens to alter the security calculus that has maintained stability and peace in the North Pacific region for the past five decades. Moreover, still greater Korean challenges to international peace and stability may lie in store.

Divided Korea's two-state structure is under mounting internal pressures due to South Korea's successes and systemic North Korean failures. Indefinite continuation of the now-familiar two-state arrangement on the Korean Peninsula is no longer a foregone conclusion. Yet quite clearly termination of that arrangement could entail terrible upheavals, with repercussions reverberating well beyond the confines of the Korean Peninsula. Coping with radical change in Korea, and devising a new architecture for peace and prosperity in a very different Korea from the one we know today, may be urgent tasks confronting the Pacific powers and the international community in the uncertain years ahead.

To date, unfortunately, such prospective tasks have been afforded precious little attention. Instead, in the capitals of the four Pacific powers—China, Japan, Russia, and the United States—policymakers and strategists seem to be more comfortable today positing a continuation of the Korean status quo than contemplating what alternative Korean futures might portend for their own national interests.

The factors accounting for a lack of forward thinking about Korea at this relatively calm juncture in world affairs are, on the whole, quite understandable—indeed, all too understandable. To explain the phenomenon, however, is not to excuse it. For policymakers are always at a disadvantage when they are taken by surprise by the rush of events. When they have not considered well in advance the range of plausible problems they may have to confront, they are more likely to commit costly errors. Given Korea's importance in contemporary world affairs, and some of the plausible problems that the peninsula could face in the not-too-distant future, the costs of Korean "surprises" for inadequately prepared governments with interests in the region could prove to be especially high.

This volume is intended as a small step toward redressing this large lacuna in policy planning about Korea. It is part of a larger project led by The National Bureau of Asian Research (NBR) initiated in 1997. Convinced that the Korean *problematik* and its post-Cold War geopolitical ramifications deserved intensive strategic consideration, and concerned that decisionmakers in the U.S. government had apparently not yet committed themselves to any sustained agenda of forward thinking about Korea, NBR began a project to assess the bearing of Korea's future upon U.S. national interests—and the manner in which America's economic, political, and security interests might be protected and championed in the face of a hypothetical but not unreasonable array of alternative futures for the Korean Peninsula.

The project assembled an American study group with the sweeping expertise requisite for this wide-ranging undertaking, including: specialists in Korean affairs; eminent students of Chinese, Japanese, and Russian history and government; authorities on the Korean economies, international trade, and global finance; seasoned analysts of Asian defense and security questions; and a number of distinguished practitioners of U.S. diplomacy, national security policy, and intelligence assessment.[2]

Forward-looking strategic analysis requires not only a solid grounding in historical realities and an informed appreciation of the workings of national and international political and economic structures, but also up-to-date knowledge about the expectations and intentions of the major actors who stand to shape the international strategic environment—the official outlooks that frame state calculations—and set the scene for possible miscalculations. For this reason, the group conferred repeatedly with officials responsible for current U.S. defense, security, and economic policy toward Northeast Asia to share in the latest U.S. government thinking about the Korea question. To plumb Japanese, Chinese, and South Korean perceptions of their countries' respective national interests in the evolving Korean situation, and to appraise possible strategies and approaches by Beijing, Tokyo, and Seoul in the face of potential future changes on the Korean Peninsula, the group held separate conferences with leading foreign policy and area specialists from each of the countries in question. In addition, members of the study group consulted with counterparts from the Russian Federation to take a closer measure of Moscow's current perceptions of interests and options. The rigorous discussions and confidential conversations of these national and international meetings enhanced the study group's appreciation of the complex terrain upon which future Korean policy might have to be charted by the United States and the other Pacific powers.

The contributions in this volume offer scholars and policymakers a textured, contemporaneous context from which to assess the strategic challenges that face the Pacific powers, individually and collectively, in making the choices that lie ahead for their respective Korea policies. While this volume examines the constraints and options facing all the Pacific powers—and facing the two current Korean states as well—the focus of analysis leans toward possibilities and problems for American policy.

KOREA AND THE PACIFIC POWERS
UNDER BYGONE REGIONAL ORDERS

In world affairs, a country's location has consequences—profound, far-reaching, and enduring consequences. In modern times, Korea is one of the spots on the map to provide vivid—indeed, searing—illustration of the point. By an utter accident of geography, Korea occupies precisely the space where the great powers of the Pacific happen to adjoin. The Korean Peninsula shares land borders with both China and Russia. It is separated from Japan by the narrow Korea Strait (at their closest points, the Japanese island of Tsushima lies just 21 miles from Korean soil). And with the Pacific Ocean for now an "American Lake"[3] (to recall a phrase coined by critics of Washington's international reach), the United States is also a de facto neighbor of Korea—actual physical distances notwithstanding. Neighboring Korea as they do, each of these four political giants has tended to regard the Korean terrain as falling "naturally" within its own ambit. Koreans, for their part, have long recognized geographical circumstance as their people's own special predicament. In fact, in the words of a famous Korean folk saying, the nation's fate is to suffer as a "a shrimp among whales."

Those "whales" have not frolicked gently in and around Korea. Since the spheres of influence (putative or genuine) of the four Pacific powers overlap in Korea, the peninsula has been the site over the past century and a half of recurrent collisions between great-power interests. Given the dramatic changes in the fortunes of these major international actors over that long sweep of history, those collisions of interests have portended extraordinary and repeated upheaval for Korea, as successive regional political orders devised by these Pacific powers collapsed—or were displaced.

With the demise of Imperial China's "East Asian World Order"[4] in the late nineteenth century and the coalescence of what a revisionist Japanese state eventually termed its "Greater East Asian Co-Prosperity Sphere," Korea was wrenched from its status as a tributary kingdom in a Sino-centric universe and transformed instead into a subject colony beneath Japanese imperial rule—a condition it endured for almost four decades.

Then, with the immolation of the Japanese imperium in 1945 and the dawn of a "Cold War era," the Korean nation was involuntarily partitioned into Soviet and American zones of occupation—zones, of course, that laid the foundations for the current Republic of Korea (ROK) in the south of the peninsula and the Democratic People's Republic of Korea (DPRK) in the north (states whose ongoing hostilities, ironically, have outlasted the clash of the international political orders that begat them).[5]

Great power competition in Korea also exposed that land to risks extending far beyond the prospect of sudden, momentous, and involuntary changes in the local political system. Given the contentious temperaments and radical ideologies that possessed some of the Pacific powers for long interludes over the past century and a half—and the grave, virtually irresolvable differences at the heart of the Korea policies these powers often pursued over that interim—violent conflict between the great powers over Korea was a perpetual possibility. And on three separate occasions between 1894 and 1954, Korea served not just as a field of contest, but as a field of battle amongst the Pacific's great powers.

The 1894–95 Sino-Japanese War was directly sparked by Beijing and Tokyo's contention for dominance in Korea and fought out by them largely on Korean soil and waters (with considerable loss of Korean life—both civilians and Tonghak rebels—in the process). Thereafter, Japan's struggle with Imperial Russia for mastery over Manchuria and Korea culminated in the Russo-Japanese War of 1904–05; the knockout blow in that war—the naval Battle of Tsushima, wherein Moscow lost virtually its entire Baltic Fleet—was launched from the Korean port of Chinhae (where the Japanese navy had been harbored, near the present-day metropolis of Pusan). And following Korea's 1945 partition, the cataclysmic Korean War of 1950–53 erupted, drawing all of the Pacific powers into confrontation against one another in either leading or supporting roles. In that bitter and devastating struggle, troops from China and the United States engaged in prolonged combat; the Soviet Union provided materiel and covert military assistance for the communist side, while Japan offered rear bases and logistical support to the U.S.-led United Nations Command.

The Korean War, to be sure, was fueled by deep and manifestly explosive political tensions within Korea itself, as some recent scholarship has emphasized.[6] But the Korean War was not simply a civil conflict in which interested foreign powers happened to intervene. Rather, the Korean War was, in a meaningful and indeed defining sense, a great power conflict: for it was not only authored, planned, and financed by Pacific powers, but largely soldiered by them as well.

In its scale and portent, this great power clash overshadowed all previous international skirmishes on the Korean Peninsula. Millions of casualties were sustained by combatant forces and hapless civilians (almost all of the latter, of course, Koreans). The cities and industrial infrastructure of divided Korea were laid waste. And the fearful but inconclusive fighting in that ultimately stalemated conflict brought the world perilously close to the use of (American) nuclear weapons. Indeed, in the sober assessment of one historian, the Korean War effectively served for the international powers as a "surrogate for World War III"[7]—a sort of "limited experiment" that demonstrated just how easily an annihilating global war could be waged, given the killing force of modern technologies, the inimical stances of the opposing camps that held claim on them, and the worldwide scope of their contest for dominance. Certainly it is true that over the following three and a half decades, the remainder of the Cold War was conducted with the "lessons of Korea" (as those were collectively understood) borne very clearly in mind by all concerned powers: perhaps foremost among them the imperative of avoiding a direct military confrontation between what were called the "superpowers," and the correlative urgency of managing "superpower" competition in regions like Korea, places at once strategically important and potentially volatile.

KOREA AND THE NATIONAL INTERESTS OF
THE PACIFIC POWERS IN THE POST-COLD WAR ERA

With the end of the Cold War, one era in global politics has just concluded and another has just begun. Typically the shape of things to come is obscure at the end of an international era—and so it may be today. Nevertheless, there are important preliminary indications that may be divined about international relations in the Asia Pacific. With the end of the Cold War, a new and very different dynamic governs the interplay of the great powers of the Pacific. Thanks to the dissolution of the Soviet Empire and the earlier categorical rejection by the Chinese leadership of the Maoist path in favor of a more pragmatic augmentation of national economic and political power, it would appear that the prospects for military confrontation among the Pacific powers have been immediately and remarkably reduced, and the scope for cooperation among them looks to be greatly magnified.

This is not to romanticize the general character of power politics in the nascent post-Cold War era—much less its specific characteristics in East Asia and the Pacific. The end of the Cold War has not ushered geopolitics into the Elysium. Some high initial expectations notwithstanding, international relations in the post-Cold War era do not promise to approach Hegel's conception of the "End of History" or Kant's conception for "Perpetual Peace" any time soon. "National interests" have hardly been brought into full consonance in the world arena—much less eliminated from it altogether. In East Asia more specifically, as one recent study has persuasively argued, the post-Cold War horizon may well be "ripe for rivalry"[8] among great and not-so-great powers; subsequent analyses have warned of some of the challenges to peace, stability, and prosperity that may arise in the decades ahead as a result of tensions—or failures—within the region's post-Cold War order.[9]

The structural troubles inherent in the Pacific's emerging international arrangements are not difficult to identify. They are cast in relief by even cursory consideration of the circumstances of the three great powers surrounding Korea.

China, after generations of relative decline, is now a rising regional power with steadily growing economic and military capabilities. Today, Chinese governance is by no means as monolithic, or its international posture as harshly ideological, as during the era of Maoist rule. But Beijing's continuing and doctrinal antipathy to the precepts of political liberalism, in tandem with its unconcealed ambition to exert a greater influence over regional and international affairs,[10] would seem to introduce to the East Asian scene most of the familiar elements witnessed in the classic revisionist power's challenge to an existing order.[11]

For its part, Russia may indeed have decisively and conclusively repudiated its legacy of Marxist-Leninist political power under Boris Yeltsin's presidency[12]—yet while the repudiation of Soviet communism may be a necessary condition for a stabilizing and constructive Russian presence in the Pacific theater, it is hardly a sufficient one. The Russian Federation's political "growing pains" are palpable today. At the center, western-style rule of law is not yet firmly established, while at the periphery, regional separatist conflicts tug at the integrity of the state. Russia's present leadership is keenly aware of the country's straitened circumstances, and the immediate response has been to issue a new "National Security Concept" that explicitly lowers the threshold at which Moscow might decide to unleash nuclear weapons.[13]

And then there is Japan. Japan is, to be sure, a securely grounded and prosperous liberal democracy. Moreover, Tokyo's alliance with Washington incontestably qualifies as the most important single link in the U.S. security system in the Pacific region. Yet in a fundamental sense, one may suggest, what was memorably termed the "Japanese question"[14] still remains to be answered. A great power in a not always pacific region, Japan's defense capabilities are conspicuously confined—one might even say unnaturally limited. This is, of course, no accident. Six decades after the end of World War II, Japan—unlike Germany—awaits the day when it can conduct sovereign defense and security policies "like a normal nation" (in the striking formulation of Ichiro Ozawa).[15] Japan cannot yet do so in no small part because its government and society have not fully come to terms with the nation's militarist past—widely noted and ongoing movement in that direction notwithstanding. Japan's struggles with the past have consequences for Pacific security at present. For not only is Japan itself ill-positioned to assume the regional responsibilities one might ordinarily expect a democratic country of its size to shoulder, but lingering concerns about the "Japanese question" on the part of other American allies throughout the Pacific region have thus far frustrated the development of the sorts of multilateral security networks that contributed so much to stability and peace in Europe after 1945.

But if it would be unwise to exaggerate the promise of international comity that attends the end of the Cold War, we would be equally amiss in minimizing its moment for international relations in general, and for relations among the Pacific powers in particular. The collapse of the Soviet Empire, the political and economic transformation of the Russian system, China's determined embrace of a controlled but market-driven modernization, and America's abrupt elevation to the status of a world power without peer competitor have recast the calculus of both confrontation and cooperation in East Asia quite profoundly. Great power competition, of course, can be expected to continue within the region—but the parameters of that competition have been fundamentally altered. On the one hand, the Cold War logic that previously fueled system-based conflict between the Pacific powers has been thoroughly undermined. On the other hand, the incentives for mutually beneficial intercourse between the Pacific powers have been magnified and reinforced by regional and global changes in the decade since the end of the Cold War.

Yet despite these heartening trends, the structure of international relations in Northeast Asia remains fundamentally asymmetrical and reflects profound, and unresolved, conflicts. For over two decades now, each of the great powers of the Pacific has maintained diplomatic relations with the other three—but Tokyo and Moscow have yet to settle territorial claims from the World War II. Although talk of a "strategic partnership" with Beijing has in recent years echoed through policy corridors both in Washington and Moscow, the only true security relationship between any of these Pacific powers binds Japan and the United States (formalized by their Mutual Cooperation and Security Treaty, now entering into its fifth decade). On the Korean Peninsula, the asymmetries are still more pronounced. Neither Pyongyang nor Seoul formally recognizes the legitimacy of its counterpart Korean state—but the Republic of Korea has, since 1992, enjoyed diplomatic relations with all four Pacific powers, while the DPRK is only recognized by Beijing and Moscow (a circumstance unchanged since the start of the Korean War half a century ago). With respect to security linkages, the DPRK's treaty of "Friendship, Cooperation and Mutual Assistance" with Moscow, initiated in 1961, was allowed to lapse in 1996, after the end of the Soviet

Union. In the year 2000, Moscow and Pyongyang signed a treaty of "Friendship, Good Neighborliness and Cooperation," but that agreement evidently lacks any specific provisions for mutual defense in the event of crisis. Pyongyang and Beijing still recognize their 1961 treaty of "Friendship, Cooperation and Mutual Assistance"—yet it is by no means clear that Beijing would today "immediately render military and other assistance" if the DPRK were to find itself "in a state of war," even though the treaty stipulates precisely that. The ROK, on the other hand, enjoys increasingly close military cooperation with Japan and is bound to the United States by a "Mutual Defense Treaty," under whose provisions over 35,000 American troops continue to be stationed in South Korea.[16]

In the current post-Cold War world, all great powers now perforce inhabit an international order dominated by a reluctant but singular superpower, the United States. That order is also strongly shaped by American rules. Those rules are, in essence, the precepts of political and economic liberalism writ globally; and "globalization" is the current code word for the worldwide process they are promoting. The worldwide boom in international financial and commercial transactions since 1989 (a boom in which China has participated fulsomely, while post-communist Russia has been largely bypassed) is entirely characteristic of the spread of this America-dominated order. The economic and political arrangements of that order strongly favor and reward enterprise among countries (in accordance, to be sure, with the unforgiving "creative destruction" of market forces). As the demonstrated benefits and vested interests from commercial cooperation increase, the costs of dislocations caused by political conflict mount commensurately.

Of course, "globalization" does not forestall the possibility of international conflict—or even major conflict between significant economic actors. (One may recall that in early twentieth-century Europe, interstate commerce was flourishing and political liberalization was much in evidence—up until the eruption of World War I.) Yet it may be fair to venture that there has been no previous period in modern history when animosities between *all* of the great powers of the Pacific were as attenuated as they are today—or when the international structure of security and economic relations so encouraged national advance through commercial cooperation and international economic integration.

Ironically, it is at this seemingly more harmonious juncture that instability from Korea, generated within the peninsula itself, could pose serious challenges to the security of each of the Pacific powers and could also strain relations between them. Three factors account for this incipient reversal of historic roles.

The first is that Korea is no longer the "shrimp" it once was—and some of the "whales" no longer qualify as such imposing behemoths. Economic yardsticks make the point. Thanks to decades of rapid growth in the ROK and years of stagnation and decline in the USSR and Russia, South Korea today appears to produce just about as much output as the entire Russian Federation.[17] Furthermore, estimated total trade turnover for contemporary South Korea is roughly 75 percent greater than for Russia,[18] and per capita productivity is estimated to be roughly three times the Russian level.[19] South Korea's material achievements over the past generation and a half have increased the region's weight in world affairs tremendously. Simply put, what happens to Korea matters intrinsically to other countries much more today than in the past.

Second, North Korea's program for developing weapons of mass destruction (WMD) currently appears to be on the verge of bestowing upon Pyongyang a capability for adversely affecting the security and stability of areas far beyond the Korean Peninsula. And as the recent review of U.S. policy toward the DPRK by former Defense Secretary William Perry (the October 1999 "Perry report") detailed, these WMD capabilities would permit North Korea to endanger international security in a variety of ominous new fashions:

Acquisition by the DPRK of nuclear weapons or long-range missiles, and especially the combination of the two … could undermine the relative stability [of the strategic situation on the Korean Peninsula]. [It] … might weaken deterrence [in Korea] as well as increase the damage if deterrence failed.… Acquisition of such weapons by North Korea could also spark an arms race in the region and would surely do grave damage to the global nonproliferation regimes covering nuclear weapons and ballistic missiles. A continuation of the DPRK's pattern of selling its missiles for hard currency could also spread destabilizing effects to other regions, such as the Middle East.[20]

The report's somewhat oblique reference to a "weakening of deterrence in Korea," security specialists will note, is a warning about the consequences of North Korea's prospective ability to threaten the Pacific powers directly. The unspoken argument is that if the United States, Japan, and other concerned countries were confronted with the possibility of a North Korean WMD strike at a moment of Pyongyang's own choosing, their credibility as coercive peacemakers in Korea at some future point of crisis would unavoidably be degraded.

Pyongyang, in short, appears today to stand on the threshold of success in what can be understood as its longstanding campaign to elevate the "North Korean problem" from a local to a global concern. If that campaign is successful, it will require significant responses by the Pacific powers to safeguard their own vital national interests—but those responses may inflame tensions with other Pacific powers. Beijing's and Moscow's sharp criticisms of Washington's newly proposed system of "national missile defense"—a program American policymakers expressly justify as a shield against the gathering North Korean WMD threat—is only a foretaste of such potential tensions.

Third, and perhaps most portentously, the tense standoff between the two states in divided Korea—an unstable balance that has held since the 1953 ceasefire in the Korean War—is under mounting pressure, owing to the utterly divergent fortunes of the peninsula's two polities. Those pressures raise the possibility that Korea's unstable balance may finally fail, as competition between the two contesting Korean states loses all viability. Such a dramatic turn of events would likely unleash volatile local forces, precipitating an uncertain but wrenching process that would ultimately result in a radical reconfiguration of the Korean Peninsula's political structure. Needless to say, the onset, trajectory, and end point of such a departure for the Korean status quo would all be fraught with extraordinary consequence for every one of the Pacific powers.

Today the contrast in the performance of divided Korea's two systems could hardly be starker.[21] Over the past decade, the ROK—once an unstable autocracy—has firmly secured its claim as a legitimate constitutional democracy. Moreover, that recently impoverished society has managed an amazing economic ascent and now ranks as a member of the Organization for Economic Cooperation and Development (OECD), the club of affluent western aid-dispensing countries.[22] North Korea, by contrast, has suffered continuing political repression and severe economic decline since the end of the Soviet experiment.

In the 1990s, despite a worldwide wave of political liberalization, the DPRK stubbornly resisted all pressures for a relaxation of its internal controls—and, if anything, appeared to grow even more illiberal. In 1998, for example, "Great Leader" Kim Il Sung, the state's then-four-years-dead founding figure, was officially proclaimed to be the country's "eternal president"; Kim's reclusive son, "Dear Leader" Kim Jong Il, effectively assumed the role of all-powerful ruler, yet did not become the country's "head of state."[23]

Political involution coincided with a drastic and perhaps still unchecked downturn in the country's economy. Although reliable data on all North Korean conditions are amazingly scarce thanks to Pyongyang's remarkable policies of information control, the DPRK's hyper-militarized economy was evidently already faltering before the end of the Cold War, staggering under the extreme distortions caused by official policies and practices. North Korea's economic failure in the 1990s was so profound that a country-wide food crisis erupted. In 1995, despite its officially extolled self-reliance (*juche*) doctrine, Pyongyang issued an international humanitarian appeal for emergency food relief. The magnitude of North Korea's food crisis remains a state secret: Pyongyang has steadfastly refused to reveal its precise dimensions even to the international agencies that are currently engaged in alleviating it. But the fact that intensive international relief operations for the DPRK are at this writing entering their sixth consecutive calendar year suggests that the country has, for all intents and purposes, lost the capacity to feed its own population. This is an unprecedented and indeed unique instance of systemic economic failure in the modern era: nothing like this has ever before befallen an urbanized, industrialized society during peacetime.

It is not clear how the North Korean leadership can check the economy's downward spiral. To rejuvenate their economic system would require far-reaching policy changes—but to date Pyongyang has insisted that such measures are out of the question since they would risk the destabilization of the country's political system. (In Pyongyang's oft-repeated evaluation, "'reform' and 'opening' ... are a honey-coated poison."[24]) At the moment, North Korea is obtaining concessional food aid from the international community, energy aid from the U.S.-led Korean Peninsula Energy Development Organization (KEDO), and some additional assistance from official and private South Korean sources. These transfers, however, mitigate only the symptoms of North Korean economic decline—not the sources.

North Korea's leadership, naturally, is intent upon state survival, and displays a confidence that it will weather the treacherous shoals it must currently traverse. With Kim Jong Il's assumption of the "top position of state" in 1998, the DPRK officially ended its "arduous march" of the mid-1990s and embraced instead the proclaimed goal of building a "strong and prosperous nation" (*Kangsong Taeguk*) on the pillars of "ideology, gun barrel, and science and technology" through a "military-first policy."[25]

In the year 2000, the DPRK embarked upon an unparalleled, and heretofore entirely uncharacteristic, burst of international diplomacy. Over the course of that year, Pyongyang established, re-established, or moved to establish diplomatic relations with a number of western countries, including Australia, Canada, France, Italy, New Zealand, and the United Kingdom. Pyongyang also revitalized its relations with China and Russia through an "unofficial" visit to Beijing by Kim Jong Il and by hosting a state visit for President Vladimir Putin in Pyongyang. But most significantly, it launched a new phase of relations with both the Republic of Korea and the United States. In June 2000, Kim Jong Il received ROK President Kim Dae Jung in Pyongyang for a three-day summit—the first meeting of divided Korea's top leaders since the peninsula's partition in 1945. Later in the year, a high-level North Korean delegation—led by Marshal Jo Myong Rok, vice chairman of the DPRK's National Defense Commission and possibly the second highest-ranking official in Pyongyang's hierarchy—traveled to Washington and, in another diplomatic first, met with President Clinton. Soon thereafter, Washington reciprocated by sending a delegation led by U.S. Secretary of State Madeleine Albright on a two-day visit to Pyongyang, where they conferred with Kim Jong Il about issues of mutual concern. Nothing like that year's tempo or scope of diplomatic activity had ever been witnessed in the DPRK's history.

It is unclear how these developments should be interpreted. From the very inception of the North Korean state, the DPRK has manifested an ability to surprise outside observers—a talent that speaks in part to the deep importance of strategic deception in the government's posture toward the outside world. But the new signs of motion in North Korean diplomacy ineluctably beg fundamental questions about the future of the North Korean system. If these stirrings presage a truly new direction in North Korean policy, they leave unanswered questions of how the DPRK will withstand much more intensive interactions with the world beyond its borders—hardly a peripheral matter in light of Pyongyang's decade-long declamation that "cultural and ideological infiltration" (of precisely the sort that such a new North Korean direction would augur) led to the downfall of the Soviet and Eastern European systems. If, on the other hand, these new activities are simply temporizing measures to provide the beleaguered DPRK system with a bit of "breathing room," they amount to nothing more than palliatives for a direly ill political economy. The specter of systemic failure haunts the Democratic People's Republic of Korea—and the recent maneuverings of the North Korean government have by no means banished that ephemera from the realm of plausible consideration.

It goes without saying that a failure by the North Korean government to maintain its competition with the South Korean government would have massive repercussions. Ever since the formation of the two current Korean states, both Seoul and Pyongyang have laid claim to suzerainty over the entire Korean Peninsula. But if North Korea's decline continues unabated, South Korea—and all of the Pacific powers—will eventually be faced with pressures that could militate for a reconfiguration of the Korean political order. Furthermore, the pressures in question might entail the risk of major military conflicts and could propel Korea toward new political and security arrangements that would bear directly upon the interests of all the Pacific powers.

Enunciating some of the plausible scenarios for failure of the North Korean system lays out the challenges that concerned states might have to shoulder. There is, of course, the perennial risk of a North Korean "explosion"—a failure of deterrence that culminates in DPRK aggression against the ROK. Given the current balance of military forces on the peninsula and within alliance systems, such an explosion would likely result in defeat of the North Korean forces and eradication of the North Korean state. Alternatively, North Korea's system could suddenly be convulsed by internal turmoil unpredicted by outside analysts, with heretofore unknown regional warlords commanding fractions of the formerly integral territory and possessing weapons of mass destruction that would focus attention upon their particular claims and interests. Additionally the DPRK could experience systemic exhaustion and collapse, recalling the denouements of the Soviet Bloc states and forcing the question of what would fill the political vacuum suddenly created in this strategically central Pacific meeting point.

PROSPECTIVE CHALLENGES TO THE NATIONAL INTERESTS OF THE GREAT POWERS OF THE PACIFIC

A forward-looking assessment of the risks and opportunities that significant changes on the Korean Peninsula could presage for the United States and other Pacific powers requires: (1) a careful analysis of the current policies of the major actors that engage in the Korean *problematik* (including the underlying thinking and domestic or international constraints that frame these distinct national approaches); (2) an appreciation of the economic realities and international economic forces that would shape any new role for Korea within the global market and financial structure; and (3) rigorous reflection upon the strategic implications of a radically different Korean political architecture for the Pacific powers in general and (given the vantage point of this project) the United States in particular. The eleven contributions to this volume present the separate components that together permit such an overall assessment.

The first five chapters lay out the historical and political context that informs, and also confines, the approaches of the state actors that must now contend with the possibility of a very new situation on the Korean Peninsula. In chapter two, Chae-Jin Lee paints a panoramic overview of the Pacific powers' interactions concerning the Korean Peninsula since World War II and outlines some of the major issues that could join these powers in cooperation, or divide them in conflict, if the peninsula's political order undergoes dramatic restructuring.

Initially, as Lee writes, "The two Korean governments were fully integrated into the Cold War framework. Neither the North nor the South exercised a significant degree of policy autonomy apart from its powerful external patrons." However, with the heightening of a Sino-Soviet rift and the impending failure of America's war to contain communism in Vietnam in the early 1970s, the United States, the USSR, and China embarked upon an exploration of paths for possible bilateral cooperation. During this Cold War "search for cooperation" among the Pacific powers, the two Korean states—now far more autonomous than they had originally been—made their own tentative gestures toward inter-Korean reconciliation, most importantly in 1972 and 1990–91, though actual movement toward reconciliation proved impossible. With the end of the Cold War, Lee emphasizes, great power "military conflicts, diplomatic disagreements, and ideological differences" over Korea "are less critical than before.... The present international environment is generally conducive to promoting the goals of peace, stability, and reconciliation on the Korean Peninsula."

In the present post-Cold War environment, Lee explains, all four great powers in the Pacific region favor the Korean status quo—or some meliorated variant thereof—over radical peninsular changes. Moreover, the overlap of their concerns and interests about maintaining Korean security is now considerable. With respect to immediate issues, "all four Pacific powers share a common interest in discouraging military confrontations and nuclear proliferation on the Korean Peninsula" and are making efforts to "engage" North Korea to opt for a less confrontational posture toward the outside world. The most visible manifestations of these efforts include the 1994 Agreed Framework between the United States of America and the Democratic People's Republic of Korea (the "Agreed Framework") and the U.S.-ROK-Japan "Trilateral Consultation and Oversight Group," organized for multilateral support of the "Perry process" and the Kim Dae Jung administration's "sunshine policy."

Less welcome possibilities in Korea also face the Pacific powers. Lee warns that "the probability of another war in Korea is not entirely unthinkable." The course and conclusion of such a conflict would raise fundamental questions about Korea's future—and troubling questions about relations between the United States, China, and Russia.

Reunification of the Korean Peninsula through absorption of North Korea by the South—analogous to German reunification—could also lie in store. Today, however, "all four Pacific powers seem to share serious concerns about the absorption scenario." First, given the great financial expense that German reunification has entailed, underwriting a similar expense for Korea, which has much more modest domestic resources, might result in unwelcome international burdens. Second, rapid reunification of Korea might "have a destabilizing effect on the balance of power in the Asian Pacific region.... Whereas Germany after unification is anchored in and integrated with the European Union and NATO, a unified Korea is likely to be a freestanding entity with no effective structure of regional economic integration or collective security." Third, the Pacific powers "may have a greater sense of uncertainty toward a unified Korea than toward a divided Korea." Because "South Korea's political institutions and democratic practices remain fragile and vulnerable ... the weakening of a unified Korean government may ... intensify the conflict among the major powers." The spillover problems for the surrounding powers might be of a very different nature from those that attended Germany's unification.

If a Korean reunification is consummated, Lee concludes, the Pacific powers will have to deal with the question of the new power's international orientation. Since a united, ROK-governed Korea would be most likely to choose the United States as its main ally, a nonaligned or "neutral" Korea might appear preferable to some of the other Pacific powers. Nonalignment, however, would invite security risks of its own—most importantly the prospect of "a 'power vacuum' that leaves Korea vulnerable to outside interference." At the end of the day, viable nonalignment for a united Korea would presuppose "a reasonable degree of national consensus in Korea and a substantial congruence of interests and capabilities among the Pacific powers"—quantities that cannot yet be taken for granted. By contrast, Lee argues that a post-unification alliance between the United States and a new Korea would serve a multiplicity of important interests: "it would facilitate a smooth process of Korean national integration, stabilize the regional order, protect Japan's security interests, and enhance America's economic benefits." But for such an arrangement to truly succeed, Lee emphasizes, both Beijing and Moscow would have to regard themselves as "stakeholders" in it; and to do that, both China and Russia would have to see themselves as beneficiaries of that new order. Consequently, Lee surmises, it would be imperative for the United States and Korea to "make every concerted effort to ensure that China, Japan, and Russia not only receive 'absolute gains' from the U.S.-Korean alignment, but also perceive no significant asymmetries in their respective 'relative gains.'"

Where chapter two offers a panoramic sketch of issues and contingencies with which the Pacific powers may have to contend in Korea in the years ahead, the third chapter focuses narrowly upon North Korean affairs. That narrow focus is critical, for the Democratic People's Republic of Korea—its system and government—lie at the epicenter of the Pacific powers' anxieties over the future of Korea. Despite its relatively small population (roughly the size of Romania's) and tiny economy (with an estimated trade turnover in the late 1990s only slightly above Nepal's), North Korea commands deep and serious consideration from all the surrounding powers due to the uncertainties that could be generated within the region by the DPRK's capabilities (for provoking conflict—or alternatively, suffering collapse) and its intentions.

Divining Pyongyang's true strategic intentions has, quite understandably, been a continuing priority for the U.S.-ROK-Japan alliance—and a task that has not become notably less challenging for the allies with the passage of time. Some presume that Chinese and Russian policymakers should have an inherently deeper grasp of the strategic intentions of this sometime ally than their western counterparts; but while that presumption may be reasonable, it is not self-evidently correct. After all, Beijing and Moscow themselves often seem to be taken by surprise by North Korean maneuvers.

So long as the North Korean state manages to survive and function, its strategic intentions will critically shape the landscape for competition or cooperation between the great powers of Northeast Asia. In chapter three, Chuck Downs ventures to elucidate some of those North Korean intentions.

By restricting his analysis to Pyongyang's intentions in its dealings with South Korea, Downs is able, first, to evaluate North Korean intentions by drawing upon the extended evidentiary record of North-South negotiations, rather than by resorting to some more speculative or inferential methodology. Second, since the outcome of North Korea's protracted duel with Seoul is intimately and inexorably affected by the actions of the great Pacific powers, any insight into Pyongyang's intentions toward Seoul will necessarily reveal important features of a broader international calculus.

Although the North Korean government deliberately cloaks itself in secrecy and relies heavily upon "strategic deception" to keep its adversaries off balance, Downs maintains that there is, in actuality, little mystery surrounding Pyongyang's fundamental intentions toward the ROK. "Logic alone," he writes, "would suggest that North Korea desires to extend its system throughout Korea, and the North's ideological commitment to a unified Korea under communist control has often been stated…. But that goal has been so elusive for so many years and appears so impossible today that analysts outside the regime often persuade themselves that the regime has disposed of it."

Detailing the record of the initial North-South diplomatic interactions in the early 1970s and the landmark summit in Pyongyang in June 2000 between ROK President Kim Dae Jung and the DPRK's Kim Jong Il, Downs discerns strong and consistent patterns. "Dialogue in the past," he writes, "has advanced few, if any, concrete steps toward unification, but it has served the North's interests by aggravating political instability in the South, exciting Korean nationalistic zeal, portraying the Republic of Korea as incapable of advancing reunification, and characterizing the presence of American troops as the single most important obstacle to patriotic objectives." Notwithstanding hopes buoyed by the recent Pyongyang summit, Downs cautions that "review of past periods of illusory progress in North-South talks suggests that the euphoria brought on by the June 2000 summit in Pyongyang … will in all likelihood end in frustration … for the South but

... substantial economic assistance to the North."

If Downs' assessment is correct, this would mean, at a minimum, that the Korean option preferred by all four Pacific powers—namely, peaceful coexistence and rapprochement between the peninsula's two governments, gradually leading to the transformation of the DPRK—is unlikely to come within the grasp of the international actors involved in the Korean drama.

The implications for the United States of Downs' analysis are direct. According to his reading, so long as the DPRK is intent upon and capable of a hostile competition with the ROK, attenuating—or severing completely—the security ties that bind Seoul and Washington must be a paramount objective for North Korean strategy. Downs sees that very objective faithfully reflected in inter-Korean deliberations: "North Korea's persistent effort to turn the focus of dialogue to the question of withdrawal of American troops is entirely consistent with an intention of making the entire peninsula vulnerable to Leninist methods of taking power."

The development of North Korean weapons of mass destruction capable of reaching the United States, one may note, would be a logical extension of a North Korean strategy to weaken the American security commitment to South Korea. In this regard, Downs's essay stresses the importance to the United States not only of maintaining solid security relations with the ROK in the years ahead, but of encouraging other Pacific powers to appreciate exactly how those security ties advance their own national interests as well.

Japan—a great Pacific power in its own right—also happens to be the United States' most important partner in East Asia. In chapter four, Ambassador Michael Armacost and Kenneth Pyle analyze Japanese interests in Korea's future, and Tokyo's options for promoting its interests. What they describe is the predicament of a colossus (despite the past decade of stagnation, Japan is the world's second or third largest economy[26]) with vital concerns next door but remarkably little leeway for independent action, given its historical legacy, its postwar polity, and the narrow international channel that contemporary Japanese policymakers wish to navigate. While Japan manifestly "has critical interests at stake" in the resolution of nearby Korea's deep problems, write Armacost and Pyle, Tokyo "labors under constraints that make it unlikely to take the lead in resolving the complex issues involved ... [and]

more likely to be reactive and adaptive ... cautious and incremental" in response to changing Korean circumstances.

In a sense, Japan's present international policy dilemmas—in Korea and elsewhere—speak to the great success of the country's past international strategies. The so-called Yoshida doctrine of concentrating on the nation's economic growth while studiously eschewing collective security commitments, Armacost and Pyle argue, "worked brilliantly in the circumstances of the Cold War"—but "the abrupt end of the Cold War left Japan disoriented." Thanks in no small measure to the Yoshida doctrine, Japan has entered the post-Cold War era with a "weak prime ministership and [a] lack of crisis management practice and intelligence capability"—institutional deficiencies that limit the government's ability to formulate and implement international policy. The Yoshida doctrine, observe Armacost and Pyle, had the further effect of "encourag[ing] the persistence of isolationist and pacifist sentiment in the populace"—a legacy that continues to proscribe Tokyo's international options.

Tokyo's approach to Korean questions is complicated more specifically by the tortured history of the relationship that entwines Korea and Japan. While relations between South Korea and Japan have unmistakably improved over the past decades, a reservoir of apprehension and mistrust still colors the South Korean public's reading of Tokyo's diplomatic moves in the Korean theater. The likelihood of sharp criticism from South Korean quarters against *any* assertive policy toward Korea, regardless of its substance, has in Armacost and Pyle's estimate reinforced Tokyo's inclinations to "keep a low profile" in Korean affairs.

For Tokyo, write Armacost and Pyle, the overriding security imperatives in Korea are that the Korean Peninsula be both nonnuclear and peaceful. "Given the difficulty of peacefully achieving the kind of united Korea that they favor," they continue, "most Japanese policymakers have quietly concluded that their wisest course is not to hasten unification, [but rather to pursue] a course that maintains the status quo for as long as possible, all the while supporting American policies of deterrence, hoping to contain tensions and foster cordial ties with South Korea, and favoring policies to promote a gradual reconciliation rather than a rapid and potentially violent reunification which might produce new problems for Japan." Yet Japan's "customary circumspection" toward thorny international disputes, they argue, seems especially appropriate for engaging the Korean security problem at this moment in time, considering the current tempo and temperature of that ongoing drama.

Although Armacost and Pyle assert that American and Japanese interests in the Korean Peninsula fundamentally coincide, they also point out that "Tokyo and Washington do not have identical agendas" with respect to the North Korean problem. They note the "natural tension between the approach that each instinctively takes," with Washington "normally seek[ing] to dominate management of grand strategy toward Korea while maximizing Japan's support for its implementation," and Tokyo "seek[ing] to extend Washington's responsibility for managing security issues on the peninsula while retaining maximum flexibility as to how it will respond to specific requests for help"—and they underscore the "asymmetry in their involvement in negotiations on Korea's future," insofar as the United States always stands as a central figure in such deliberations, whereas Japan (like China, and even more so, Russia) cannot count on always being included. Until such time as Japan itself can enunciate, outline, and pursue a more comprehensive strategy toward the Korean Peninsula, this Pacific power will have to rely heavily upon a foreign government—the United States—to safeguard and advance its own national interests in the region.

Looking toward the future, Armacost and Pyle highlight a key long-term issue that reunification would raise for Japan—the future of U.S.-ROK security arrangements. In their judgment, "a post-unification U.S.-Korean alliance and a continued U.S. military presence on the peninsula would reassure Japan that a reunified Korea would be disposed to improve ties with Japan." Implicitly, a strong U.S.-ROK alliance would also serve as reassurance that bilateral U.S.-Japan security ties would also remain vibrant and strong.

Armacost and Pyle also identify the critical importance of a continued deepening of the Japanese-ROK relationship. A strengthening of that bilateral bond may be the prerequisite for developing a genuinely multilateral security framework for Northeast Asia—and such an architecture could help

Tokyo better cope not only with Korean questions, but perhaps no less importantly with looming and as yet unanswered questions about Japan's future relationship with China.

In chapter five, Robert Scalapino elucidates Beijing's interests in, and approaches to, the Korean question. Scalapino reminds us that for China, Korea historically has played two roles. The first was as "tributary state" into which—and beyond which—Chinese influence flowed; the other was as a "source of threat unless it could be controlled or neutralized since it was a potential entry point for rival powers." These contending roles, he intimates, continue to shape China's involvement in Korea today.

With calculated understatement, Scalapino observes Chinese policies toward divided Korea "have gone through many stages." In fact, over the past half century, China has managed an almost breathtaking repositioning of its presence on the Korean Peninsula. In 1950 China was a militant and menacing revisionist power: at war on the peninsula against American and South Korean forces, protecting Kim Il Sung's regime against the consequences of its own dangerous military gamble to upset the regional balance. By 1999 China's reputation was that of regional conciliator, with intimate diplomatic relations, and even military exchanges, with *both* Seoul and Pyongyang. On the economic front, while cultivating a thriving and profitable commerce with South Korea, China was also bestowing foreign aid on North Korea, enhancing that beleaguered state's prospects for internal stability and survival. Moreover, by the late 1990s both Washington and Seoul were soliciting Chinese participation in the Korean "peace process." China's assent to "four-party talks" with Pyongyang, Seoul, and Washington was a source of hope rather than distress for U.S. and South Korean diplomats—and an indication of just how far China's communist government had progressed toward cementing an international reputation as an agent of constructive stability in Korean affairs.

China's success in restoring its influence in Korea speaks to skillful diplomacy pursued under highly complex conditions. Not the least of these complications center upon Beijing's relations with the DPRK. Incumbent in China's current role as what Scalapino calls "Pyongyang's sole (more or less) ally" is the obligation of supporting a state whose actions not infrequently reverberate against Beijing's interests. (North Korea's 1998 test-firing of a ballistic missile over Japan, for example, predictably pulled Japanese policy closer to approval of the very theater missile defense (TMD) system that China so adamantly opposes.) China must also fulfill its newly valued role as a purveyor of unwelcome advice to Pyongyang (on issues including economic reform and nonproliferation, but hardly limited to them) without alienating the North Korean government and thus losing leverage in Korea— and with the other Pacific powers. "Living with contradictions" is a precept of both Taoist philosophy and Leninist doctrine; China's present policymakers are heirs to both of these traditions, a fact that may aid them in managing today's "negotiations with Korean characteristics."

Although policymaking by the Chinese Communist Party and government remains opaque in fundamental respects, Scalapino argues that "certain facts are clear" about Beijing's intentions in Korea. China does not want a nuclear DPRK, heightened tension on the Korean Peninsula, nor a collapsed North Korea. DPRK state failure would set in motion a train of events potentially inimical to Beijing's security: refugee flows, major new foreign economic obligations, and an unsettling of China's Korean minorities in Manchuria, among other immediate worries. Furthermore, security policies of a reunified Korea could confront Beijing with fundamental questions (and possibly major exertions) that it would just as soon defer—or avoid altogether.

In the final analysis, Scalapino emphasizes, Washington and Beijing's "views on the Korea issue are by no means identical," but "the United States and the People's Republic of China have basic interests in common. Hence, cooperation has been possible on key matters." He warns, however, that the possibilities for future cooperation in Korea will depend crucially upon the overall tenor of relations between the two governments—which is to say that tensions between Washington and Beijing over seemingly unrelated issues could seriously limit the prospects for constructive Sino-American cooperation on the Korean Peninsula.

This insight is absolutely critical. Teamwork in addressing Korean problems will be vastly more difficult to elicit if other disagreements are poisoning the Chinese-American relationship—and it is all too easy to imagine how such disagreements could arise in the years ahead. If a future Sino-American dispute over Taiwan (or some other issue) were to take on a life of its own, even mutually beneficial agreements concerning Korea might prove hard to secure. At the same time, however, Scalapino suggests that for China and the United States, "Korea may be one area where continued interaction of a positive nature can take place—if a chasm in U.S.-China bilateral relations can be prevented."

Russia, of course, is the other Pacific power with longstanding interests in Korea. With the collapse of Soviet communism, the breakup of the USSR into fifteen independent republics, the deliberate demobilization of the once-mighty Red Army, and the ongoing travails of economic transition, both the tenor of Moscow's foreign policy and the capabilities for conducting it have changed radically in recent years. But while Moscow's political disposition may have changed, its land border with the Korean Peninsula has not. As Herbert Ellison emphasizes in chapter six, Moscow still has important interests in Korea. Moreover, the Russian Federation's concern about the future of what Ellison terms this "vital region with great potential for dangerous conflict" can only be heightened by Moscow's recognition of its newly limited potential for influencing the outcome of events in Korea that may bear directly on Russian security.

One might presume that Korea's strategic importance to the Russian Federation, together with Moscow's suddenly diminished foreign policy capabilities, would concentrate state attention upon crafting a careful and consistent approach to advancing Russian interests in the Korean Peninsula. Yet as Ellison demonstrates, postcommunist Moscow has been something less than a consummate promoter of its own diplomatic advantage in the region. Rather, he writes, Russia now suffers "marginalization," not just in Korea but in the entire East Asian diplomatic arena—and "much of the explanation for this predicament lies in Russian foreign policy" itself.

Ill-advised gambits by Moscow on the Korean board, of course, predate the end of the Cold War. The manner in which the USSR's 1990 diplomatic normalization with Seoul was handled—without previous consultation with Pyongyang and with a sudden, ostentatious cutoff of almost all Soviet aid to the DPRK—virtually precluded the sort of working relationship with North Korea that China's communist government maintained after its official recognition of the ROK in 1992. With the liquidation of the USSR, the new Russian government was free to chart a different course in Northeast Asia, but quickly encountered difficulties—some born of domestic political constraints, others more clearly of its leadership's own devising.

In 1992, as Ellison recounts, Russian Federation President Boris Yeltsin delivered a dramatic speech to the ROK National Assembly in which he declared "that the focus of Russian policy had shifted to Asia and that South Korea would be Russia's leading partner in that region." That surprising pronouncement may have sounded impetuous—like many Yeltsin proclamations—but it also reflected a troubling reality for Moscow's new foreign policymakers. In Northeast Asia, Japan should have been the obvious candidate to be the leading regional partner for a democratic Russian state, but dramatic improvements in Russia's chilly relations with Japan were not a realistic prospect—then or now—due to the lingering dispute over islands off Hokkaido held by Moscow since World War II but considered sovereign soil by Japan. For a liberally-oriented Russian Federation, building a partnership with Seoul clearly constituted a second-best solution to the problem of East Asia policy—but it looked to be the best option viable at the time, given other constraints. And in itself, the intention to lean toward the ROK was not necessarily a miscalculation (although as Ellison intimates, the actual execution of the Russian Federation's overtures may have inadvertently fueled the North Korean nuclear drama of the early 1990s). But in the event, a vibrant Russian-South Korean partnership did not emerge.

Domestic political constraints within the new Russia accounted in part for this failure. As Ellison emphasizes, "the postcommunist political system in Russia ... is not, in the full sense of the expression, postcommunist. A substantial part of the legacy of communist governmental structure and personnel remain in place...." Moreover, communism still retains considerable popular appeal—so much so, in fact, that the Communist Party of the Russian Federation won working control of the country's parliament during Yeltsin's first term in office. Thereafter, the politics of democratic compromise impelled the Yeltsin government to abandon its original Korea policies and to embrace an approach much more redolent with "old thinking." The resultant twist in Russian Federation foreign policy—away from its initial, enthusiastically pro-western precepts—has, in Ellison's estimate, further frustrated Moscow's hopes of enhancing its influence in Korean (and more broadly, East Asian) affairs.

The Russian Federation's revised foreign policy orientation is closely associated with the thinking of ex-Prime Minister Yevgeny Primakov, who criticized his immediate predecessors for naive neglect of Russian international interests and advocated instead an unsentimental pursuit of Russian interests through cold-eyed balance of power diplomacy. Yet paradoxically, Ellison argues, the seeming pragmatism of this approach has in practice actually *weakened* Russia's role in Korea and its environs.

The centerpiece of that approach is the concept of "multipolarity"—which, Ellison explains, is essentially "code language for opposition to the single 'pole' (i.e., to U.S. global and regional dominance)." Ironically, rather than consistently promoting Russian interests, Moscow's "multipolar" policy became increasingly "focused on resisting American hegemony"—often at the direct expense of its own interests. For given the distinct limits of the bilateral Russo-Japanese relationship, and the still-fanciful notion of a Sino-Russian "strategic alliance," "multipolar" diplomacy toward Korea has meant grasping for nonexistent counterweights to American-led efforts to ensure the region's security—effectively excluding Russia's voice from the decisionmaking process involving Washington and its Northeast Asian allies.

Ellison concludes: "[T]o the extent that [the policy of multipolarity] aims to reduce the American leading role" in Korea and Northeast Asia, it "is destined to fail—unless the American side unilaterally undertakes such a reduction." The "multipolar" approach, moreover, fails to appreciate the overlap of Russian and American interests on the Korean Peninsula. "The reality," Ellison emphasizes, "is that Russian security interests require close cooperation with the United States, Japan, and South Korea, as well as China, and recognition of the necessity of American leadership in the regional security structure." Resentment of American power does not in itself constitute a strategy—and may dispose Russian decisionmakers to champion objectives that would redound to their own disadvantage.

The next two chapters in this volume examine some of the potentially powerful economic ramifications that a departure from Korea's familiar "Cold

War architecture" could presage. Apart from a posited continuation of the peninsular status quo, virtually every vision of a future Korea supposes—at some stage and in some manner—an economic reconstruction of the North. Such an undertaking, of course, would promise to be a monumental task— and how it is approached and implemented would, almost certainly, have an impact not only on the material well-being and economic prospects of Korea's population, but on the political stability of the peninsula and the region.

The prospective economic reconstruction of North Korea, it may be necessary to emphasize, is not a specter to be contemplated with pure and unreserved foreboding. To be sure: great sums of outside capital may be required to revitalize northern Korea's industrial base and to bring the skills and qualifications of the North Korean labor force up toward world standards. But a dynamic, productive northern Korean economy could generate high rates of return on those same funds—enriching outside investors as the area begins to prosper. Moreover, the economic rejuvenation of northern Korea would surely provide an impetus for economic integration, sparking the growth of trade and investment ties between northern Korea and all major economies of the region. Such commercially driven economic integration would not only help to sustain northern Korea's prosperity—and to spread prosperity beyond its boundaries—but might also contribute to political stability in Northeast Asia by reducing social tensions on the Korean Peninsula and increasing the incentives for the great powers of the Pacific to engage in peaceful cooperation in the Korean economic theater. Insofar as a "successful" economic reconstruction of the North would generate a maximum of international benefits and impose a minimum of international costs, it would seem that all four Pacific powers could share an interest in promoting such an outcome—if and when overhaul of the economy of northern Korea becomes a politically feasible proposition. Chapters seven and eight elucidate some of the critical economic issues that Korean policymakers, foreign governments, and international investors would have to face in the event of such an overhaul.

In chapter seven, Marcus Noland examines policy options for stimulating an economic revitalization of the Korean north. He begins by considering the prospects for an economic upswing through a homemade North

Korean variant of "reform socialism." Even if a genuinely "reformist" indigenous leadership were to take power in Pyongyang, he warns, the obstacles to successful economic reform would be more formidable for North Korea than they were for either China or Vietnam—Asia's extant exemplars of reform socialism. "At the time they initiated reforms," Noland reminds us, "China and Vietnam had more than double the share of population employed in the agricultural sector than North Korea apparently has today, and their reform strategies were made possible by the existence of this enormous pool of low-productivity labor." Moreover, given North Korea's relatively small size, the fate of any outward economic opening would depend upon the state of its political relations with South Korea, Japan, and the United States—countries that would "naturally" be major trade and investment partners, but with whom economic relations are problematic and minimal today. Even if Pyongyang's leadership were totally committed to the process, managing a successful economic reform under socialist rule in the northern half of a divided Korea would be an extraordinarily daunting task.

Calculations by Noland and his colleagues highlight the enormity of the potential tradeoffs. With open North-South borders, "North Korea would be nearly depopulated before equilibrium was attained." "Conversely," he writes, "incentives for migration could be reduced through the maintenance of employment and wage increases, though the necessary investment could be enormous—as much as $1 trillion—if the incentive to migrate were eliminated solely by capital investment."

In the wake of Germany's enormous post-unification budgetary subsidies to the regions of the former German Democratic Republic, many analysts and policymakers are filled with apprehension by the prospective costs of a Korean unification. Noland maintains, however, that some of this *angst* results from muddied thinking. "The key point overlooked in most discussions of 'the costs of unification,'" in his view, "is that efficiently allocated investment yields returns, not just costs." In fact, Noland and his colleagues use figures derived from the German experience to conclude "that in a scenario with relatively small amounts of private capital investment combined with relatively high levels of North-South migration, South Korea actually would come out ahead: the present discounted value of future consumption would be $35 billion higher with unification compared to the no unification baseline."

A poorly selected unification strategy, on the other hand, could cost the South Korean economy very dearly: "in the worst-case scenario—large grant transfers combined with low levels of migration—South Korea [would be] approximately one half trillion dollars worse off."

Given the extraordinary range of prospective benefits and costs from a Korean unification under various policy approaches, Noland argues that the distributive implications of unification strategies must be carefully thought through. A reunification with the North would inescapably affect the absolute and relative economic standing of every segment of South Korean society—and the allocation of unification's benefits and costs among northerners and southerners could take on a fateful ethical and political salience.

Ultimately, Noland believes, the most important distributive decisions devolving from unification would be determined by whether or not North Koreans were accorded full citizenship in a post-DPRK Korea. As he explains it, "A whole host of unification issues [will] have enormous implications for the economic welfare of current residents of the DPRK. ... Policies that deny North Koreans some of the economic gains of unification (such as proposals to maintain the DMZ and administer North Korea as a special administrative zone, which would prevent the equilibration of wages and rates of return on capital between the North and South) would only be sustainable if North Koreans were denied political rights. Thus the key economic question is to what extent North Koreans will be full participants in the political system of a unified Korea."

A successful economic strategy for Korean unification, of course, presupposes wholesale institutional-legal change in the North. In this regard, Noland notes, for example, that one of the lessons "of other transitional economies is that one must privatize quickly—not because private managers are uniquely competent, but because without clear property rights and privatization, there will be no investment, and without investment there cannot be economic rehabilitation." He further observes: "There will be a need for well-functioning capital markets to channel investment into the North." That very need, however, underscores the importance of institutional, legal, and policy reforms in *South* Korea. Noland alludes to problems that were all too vividly exposed by the ROK's financial crisis of 1997–98, emphasizing that "South Korea needs to restructure its banking system, improve the operation of its bond market, create a better climate for foreign direct investment, and better integrate foreigners into its financial market." Noland indicates that continued economic reform in South Korea remains a virtue in its own right, but today also qualifies as necessary preparation for any future unification of the two Koreas.

In chapter eight, Gifford Combs takes up where Noland leaves off, appraising possibilities for international financing of a future economic reconstruction and reunification of Korea.

Combs's approach to the problem differs somewhat from Noland's: Noland's métier is economic theory and research whereas Combs voices the practical concerns of a financier, alert to the very real possibilities of gain or loss in situations where private capital will be placed on the line. Combs, however, fully shares Noland's misgivings about the capabilities of the current ROK financial system to attract and allocate the foreign capital that would be needed in the great venture of a North Korean economic reconstruction. In Combs's judgment, the need for economic reform in South Korea is, if anything, even more pressing than Noland's chapter would suggest. According to Combs's analysis, unbankable practices and expectations are rife throughout the ROK business community—and so deeply seated that the great financial crisis of 1997–98 (when South Korea's inability to meet international obligations was only narrowly averted thanks to an International Monetary Fund (IMF)-led commitment of over $50 billion in standby funds) has not yet prompted the necessary corrections.

"If South Korea is to integrate the North's population and economy into its own," Combs argues, "it will need to bear the entire burden of the increased population by itself." Whereas Germany was able to pass on some of the "adjustment" pressures generated by its unification process thanks to its central economic role in the European Union and the importance of the deutschemark to world currency markets and the then-European Monetary System, "South Korea lacks the economic clout to socialize the cost [of unification] and spread it implicitly across the globe through economic policymaking as Germany did. Instead, the Korean government will require explicit grants and loans from international sources—large amounts of capital."

But how can South Korea attract that capital? Combs believes that public channels—international financial institutions like the IMF or the World Bank, or governments such as the United States and Japan—will be able to supply only a small fraction of the sums that may prove necessary. The preponderant share of the foreign funds that might be mobilized for a prospective reconstruction and economic unification of Korea lies in private hands—and consequently will have to be attracted by convincing foreigners to invest or lend their resources to the project.

The Korean business climate, Combs indicates, will be critical in determining the magnitude of the capital flow that may be enticed from overseas. But despite South Korea's great economic advances and consistently strong performance in export markets over the past four decades, Combs depicts the ROK's business climate as surprisingly harsh and unwelcoming to outside purveyors of capital. "The Korean distrust of the foreign investor" he writes, "is real, palpable, and present at all levels of society.... If reunification is to be successful, this must change."

Combs sees "a rampant distrust of the free market" in contemporary Korea—South as well as North. A distrust of market forces, he argues, was embedded in South Korea's formula for national economic progress. As he describes it, "Korea, Inc." was an edifice riddled with *dirigiste* weaknesses— weaknesses especially obvious in the country's financial structure: "Under the traditional South Korean model, there was competition only for resources. Once those were obtained, everything else was secondary.... [The model] depended heavily on two features: (1) the closed nature of the Korean financial system and (2) the ability of Korean industry to make investments that could generate at least some cash.... Korea's [formal] financial system was [characterized by] bank lending at preferential interest rates. Certain borrowers were extended credit on a virtually unlimited basis, to a point where they became too big to fail."

Though the South Korean economy rebounded rapidly in the years immediately following the crisis of 1997–98, recovery did not necessarily signify the advent of an institutional-legal framework adequate to address the flaws that brought the old system to the verge of bankruptcy. Although the crisis forced "at least a plurality of the country's elite" to recognize that "the economy needs some form of dramatic and immediate reform," Combs asserts, "progress has been slower in the past year than most observers had predicted because *chaebol* [South Korea's major business conglomerates] ... have proved very resistant to change and have successfully stymied efforts ... to rationalize and deregulate." In his assessment, "The government's efforts to open markets and unfetter pricing by fiat in areas such as telecommunications or insurance have been very successful.... Less successful to date have been efforts to reform the institutional framework of financial markets." Yet the latter task, he reiterates, "remains a crucial element to be addressed if Korea is to attract large amounts of foreign capital, especially in light of any effort to rebuild the North."

Combs' low estimate of the ROK's efforts to date in financial sector restructuring, it is worth noting, is widely shared within the international financial community. In late 1999, for example, Moody's Investor Service "rated the financial stability of Korea's banks forty-third out of forty-six countries—hardly the sort of performance," in Combs' ironic formulation, that "one would associate with the 'poster child of Asian economic reform.'"

Combs cautions: "It is not enough anymore for a country to offer low-cost land and large numbers of 'docile' low-wage workers (the inducements usually cited in optimistic pronouncements about the process of rebuilding North Korea). Western investors simply have too many other options...." Investing in Korea's future, in other words, will *not* be the irresistible proposition that some Koreans today tend to assume—unless the appropriate preparations are made.

Chapters seven and eight should impress the reader with the central importance of *Korean* decisions to the peninsula's future economic outcomes. The Pacific powers cannot directly participate in those Korean decisions, but they may be able to influence them: through government-to-government dialogue, multilateral consultations, transnational "public education" conversations, and more extensive but less formal interactions between respective private sectors. And in considering the international agenda that these distinct forums could promote, it is immediately apparent that the four Pacific powers would not be coequal participants.

Given its own domestic economic troubles and its highly fragile international economic position, Russia's prospective contribution could only be negligible. China's contributions might be greater than Russia's—but given China's still limited role in international financial institutions, international commerce, and international intellectual exchange, decidedly marginal nonetheless. Clearly Japan is better poised than either Russia or China to contribute to the process of helping Korea prepare for its economic future. But without doubt it is the United States that would have the most to offer—through bilateral, multilateral, and informal private channels alike—and not only today, but over the foreseeable future. Assisting Koreans to think clearly about the economic paths that lie before them would appear to be very much in the interest of all Pacific powers—and if that engagement is to be successfully consummated, it is a process in which Americans must be prepared to take a leading role.

The final four chapters reflect upon the strategic implications of fundamental change on the Korean Peninsula for the great powers of the Pacific—but with a special emphasis upon their implications for the interests of the United States. In chapter nine, Admiral Michael McDevitt begins this thematic discussion with a wide-ranging contemplation of the potential consequences of a Korean unification for the East Asian security environment—and for American security policy in Korea and elsewhere.

McDevitt laments that, despite the "outpouring of high quality speculation" in recent years about a possible Korean reunification, "the focus of the published intellectual effort has been only on the scenarios per se and the reactions of the interested regional powers, and not on the time-line and associated processes." Those time-lines and processes, he argues, would have a decisive impact on the security landscape—and on options for post-unification security arrangements in the Pacific. "A quick reunification set in motion because of a North Korean collapse," he maintains, "would have the least impact on the avowed aims of Seoul and Washington to preserve the U.S.-ROK alliance and on the continued presence of some U.S. forces on the peninsula. On the other hand, a slow, evolutionary process of reunification that involves negotiation, with its attendant compromises, probably dooms chances for sustaining U.S. forces in Korea, and makes a continuation of any type of U.S.-ROK alliance highly problematic."

"Even if [Seoul] really wanted to embark on an independent course," McDevitt reasons, a rapid collapse of the DPRK would greatly increase the pressures for the ROK to "maintain the current trajectory of its national security strategy.... If the nation were consumed by the crisis of absorption, it is hard to imagine that Seoul would decide to increase uncertainty, at home and regionally, by choosing to walk away from its alliance with the United States...." Perhaps paradoxically, in this assessment radical discontinuity in the Korean Peninsula's political arrangements would most likely result in continuity in ROK national security strategy.

Whereas rapid collapse and absorption of the North would, in McDevitt's analysis, militate for a preservation of the current U.S. security framework for Korea, a prolonged, gradual movement toward a peaceable reunion of the two Koreas is viewed as likely to undermine that familiar architecture. Since peaceful unification would only be achieved after a long series of Seoul-Pyongyang negotiations—first for a peace treaty, then for the successive stages of a political integration of the two states—U.S.-ROK ties would fall under unending scrutiny and criticism. McDevitt senses that South Korean public support for that security relationship would eventually erode under this scenario: "If the tradeoff is between a U.S. alliance and reunification, unification most likely would be the choice of the people of South Korea." Thus "despite the best intentions and desires of leaders and policymakers today, the process of making peace and then working toward reunification would almost certainly make the extension of the Republic of Korea's current national security strategy too difficult to achieve." Instead, McDevitt concludes, a unified Korea would be most likely to choose either "strategic independence"—by which he means a unified Korean state with sufficient military strength to establish a large measure of autonomy—or neutrality—in which the security of a relatively weak Korean state is dependent upon security guarantees from the surrounding Pacific powers.

In an earlier chapter, Chae-Jin Lee strongly intimated that an alignment with the United States for a post-unification Korea would be preferable to alternative security arrangements—and not just for Korea and the United States. McDevitt, by contrast, is relatively sanguine about the security outlook for an Asia in which Korea has been reunited by free and peaceful means and for which a U.S.-Korea military alliance is a thing of the past. "None of the factors that created an unstable past" for the region, McDevitt hypothesizes, would "be present when a united Korea becomes part of Northeast Asia's future.... China will not be weak; [neither will] Korea.... Both Russia and Japan have left their imperialist predilections in the past.... By and large, all the states in the region will be territorially intact and reasonably well satisfied with their existing frontiers. In other words, there is a very good chance for this historically troubled region to be free of the prospect or reality of war for the first time since the mid-nineteenth century." (In this relatively calm and reassuring security environment, he continues, a united but unaligned Korea would have little motivation to opt for nuclear power status, since such a move would cause the state more problems than it could solve.)

Because an end to the U.S.-ROK alliance would precipitate a reconfiguration of the U.S. military presence in East Asia, the new rationale for an American forward presence in Asia, McDevitt writes, would be to forestall what he calls "militarily induced instability," and thereby help preserve a regional balance of power. And in reality, such a rationale would not really be so new. "The record of U.S. diplomatic history," he writes, "is clear: throughout the twentieth century, the United States has been willing, diplomatically or militarily, to frustrate attempts by others to achieve hegemony [in East Asia]." McDevitt argues that his envisioned role for American military forces—to sustain strategic equilibrium in Asia—would be widely welcomed in the region. McDevitt acknowledges, however, that sustaining regional stability would be more difficult for the American public to accept as a motive for the involvement of troops than the objectives of Cold War deterrence or containment.

With this new envisioned mission, the structure and size of the U.S. force permanently assigned to East Asia would look very different than it does today. "To sustain stability in the future," McDevitt suggests, "U.S. force structure [would] have as its primary combat focus defeating power-projection anywhere beyond the East Asian littoral.... By the very nature of the mission and the geography of East Asia, it would necessarily be composed primarily of air and naval forces.... The first thing to appreciate about this hypothetically reshaped U.S. presence in the region is that the return of most of the soldiers and marines to the United States would greatly reduce its overall size, perhaps by as much as 60 percent."

McDevitt's vision of an American military strategy for Asia, of course, begs the profound question of China's future role in Asia's security calculus. As he puts it, "When the prospect of another Korean War no longer poses a threat, any discussion about stability in East Asia must start with China." Yet he is cautiously optimistic about the prospects for living with a "rising China." "China's continental dominance," he points out, "is a fact of life today—an accepted feature of the East Asian strategic landscape that is *not considered destabilizing*.... [In fact, it] generally is greeted with equanimity— certainly in the United States." American security policy, he further argues, need not be overly exercised by Chinese military predominance on continental East Asia: "a U.S. force structure whose mission is to sustain stability need not have a capability to preserve stability on the Asian mainland. Because so many of Asia's most important nations lay beyond both China's and one another's reach, the action that would most upset this [potential Sino-American security] condominium would be an attempt by China or any other power to become militarily superior on both the continent and the rim of Asia."

McDevitt's essay raises a myriad of questions germane to forward thinking for American interests in Korea—and in Asia more broadly. One of these merits particular mention—the political viability in *prospective host countries* of the redefined mission for American forces in Asia that McDevitt spells out. If American forces were to leave the Korean Peninsula, Japan would then be the only country in East Asia with an American forward military presence on its soil. Would such a unique designation be acceptable to the Japanese public? One may entertain doubts. And if, due to local political considerations, forward deployment of American forces in East Asia proved in practice to be a "two countries or none" proposition, what places would stand out as logical candidates to join Japan in the basing of America's military presence?

In chapters ten and eleven, Ambassador Robert Gallucci and Douglas Paal offer, respectively, a consideration of some of the diplomatic issues that might arise in negotiations for peaceful and voluntary Korean reunification and a proposed American policy agenda for helping to achieve Korea's ultimate unification.

Both Gallucci and Paal implicitly agree that any practical effort in forward thinking about Korea's future must be tightly tethered to an appreciation of the *current* North Korean problem—that is to say, to a careful and unromantic reading of the behavior and possible motives of the "real existing DPRK," as opposed to the possible dispositions of some subsequent (as yet only notional) leadership configuration in Pyongyang. Their analyses of the North Korean *problematik,* however, lead the authors to stress somewhat different priorities in the quest for a new and better Korean security architecture.

Gallucci begins by asking "whether there is a way forward to serious talks between North and South that could lead to reunification over time." He argues the affirmative—but warns that the path to such talks cannot be reached unless three immediate obstacles are surmounted. First, he writes, the DPRK "will have to accept on-site inspections as necessary and resolve the nuclear question whenever it is raised"; second, ballistic missile talks will have to result in an end to testing and exports; and finally, "the U.S. Congress will have to be persuaded to continue support for KEDO and the Agreed Framework."

Such steps (Gallucci terms them "preliminaries") are necessary for genuine progress in North-South talks, he maintains—but are not sufficient. A "new atmosphere" would have to be created—and most of the requisite actions for creating it would fall to Pyongyang. (Cessation of DPRK military provocations, implementation of existing but currently unfulfilled North-South agreements, and a credible North Korean commitment to confidence- and security building measures are the milestones Gallucci identifies for this road toward a new North-South atmosphere—a rather imposing list of preconditions at this writing.)

Ambassador Gallucci, readers will recall, served as the principal American negotiator for the 1994 Agreed Framework between the United States of

America and the Democratic People's Republic of Korea. But he guides his readers "away from the expectation that the Framework or KEDO will be a model or vehicle for serious political talks between North and South." Any successful diplomatic talks on reunification, Gallucci continues, would have to involve not only the two Korean governments, but all four Pacific Powers. He emphasizes that if a negotiated Korean reunification is to "stick," it "should emerge from an inclusive process. No matter what format reunification talks might assume, we can expect the objectives of the parties to differ substantially, in geopolitical as well as other terms."

Gallucci stresses that a negotiated international end to Korea's division is not yet remotely in the offing—and that for now American policy and diplomacy should focus on immediate problems on the Korean Peninsula. His proposed agenda: "(1) contain the North Koreans ...; (2) prevent ballistic missile exports and tests from doing more political damage; (3) avoid circumstances that could lead to conventional war on the peninsula; (4) continue to push a negotiating track—four-party talks or whatever works; and (5) continue looking for economic openings in the North that will help produce ... economic and political evolution."

Where Gallucci sees the Agreed Framework as a possible starting point for a prolonged process of "engagement" with North Korea that could culminate in peaceful Korean reunification, Douglas Paal takes a more skeptical and pessimistic view. Paal argues that the policies of engaging Pyongyang championed in the late 1990s conjointly by Seoul, Tokyo, and Washington have not promoted their stated objective of enhancing security on the Korean Peninsula, and wonders whether the Agreed Framework may not also have been a misstep in coping with the North Korean problem. Paal's proposed approach to the North Korean problem advocates a mix with fewer carrots and more sticks, for in his estimate the key to lasting stability in Korea is regime change in the North—and regime change is more likely to be achieved through deterrence and external pressure than through subsidies to the DPRK government.

Paal discerns a pattern of "conditional appeasement" in U.S.-ROK-Japan policy toward North Korea in the mid- and late-1990s and warns that the tendency to reward North Korea for desisting from menacing behavior has only increased Pyongyang's incentive to generate still greater menace. Western governments fell into de facto appeasement of North Korea, he writes, because Pyongyang managed to reclassify itself in western eyes as a "proliferation problem" rather than the "deterrence problem" it had been treated as since the 1953 Korean ceasefire. Paal argues that U.S. and western policy toward North Korea should de-emphasize proliferation concerns and return to its previous emphasis on "effective deterrence" for the sake of immediate regional security and ultimate Korean reunification.

Paal concedes that "from a nonproliferation perspective" his proposed policy might appear "less than optimal." He counters that "from the perspective of regional security, however, this approach would leave the North unrewarded for its proliferation activity. [Pyongyang's] isolation and economic weakness would continue to diminish its conventional military threat. Reasonable people can certainly disagree about whether even a relatively small number of nuclear weapons can be tolerated in the hands of the Pyongyang leadership, given the assumption of worsening circumstances in the North. [Yet] even with a successful Agreed Framework, it will be years before a scientifically based judgment can be made on the possible number of nuclear weapons North Korea may already possess."

China might resist a stricter western policy toward the DPRK, but Paal does not view this as an insuperable problem. "Being North Korea's last backer," he counters, "will carry the unappetizing burden of taking responsibility for Pyongyang's actions, something Beijing would presumably be loath to do for long." He stresses, however, that "entering a new phase in dealing with the DPRK" will be easier for Washington "if the U.S. posture toward China is not uniformly confrontational. As a general rule in East Asia, regional problems are easier to work out when the United States and China have an effective relationship." Here Paal echoes a theme already highlighted by other contributors to the volume—Chae-Jin Lee and Robert Scalapino among them.

In Paal's view, "over time ... most regional states should be prepared to let North Korea live or die by its own efforts to reform itself, not by its capacity to threaten its neighbors." To encourage the reform process, Paal recommends "reduc[ing] nonstrategic barriers to trade and investment with

North Korea at the outset. Among the goals of doing so up front would be to set as much pressure for regime transformation in motion as possible, rather than doling it out bit by bit. Better to undermine those military priorities with an alternative incentive structure founded on economic survival." And "in anticipation of regime transformation," he urges that "allied policy should lay the groundwork for eventual reunification."

Paal agrees with Gallucci that "reaching an international agreement to guarantee the security of the Korean Peninsula after reunification will require at least the six powers concerned: North and South Korea, China, Russia, Japan, and the United States." He suggests, however, that while "a new forum will be required" for those deliberations, it "probably [will prove] not ... acceptable until the last possible moment." Therefore, Paal reasons, "extensive preliminary consultations will be necessary at various official and unofficial levels, to establish common vocabularies and test the concerns of the various parties. Some of this has begun, but there is considerable scope for more."

Paal complements Gallucci's discussion of possible negotiating frameworks for an international Korean settlement with observations about some of the practical preparations that would be required for such talks. "The United States will need to have done serious thinking," he comments, "at home first, then among its allies, then with the Chinese and Russians, about what it views as its vital interests on the peninsula and in the region.... Washington will need to listen equally carefully to what the other capitals say and be prepared to accommodate them to some extent.... Beijing, for example, may have objections or conditions it would insist upon.... Washington will do well to know [Beijing's] bottom line beforehand."

The final chapter is the editors' overview on Korea's future and the national interests of the neighboring powers. This chapter concludes the volume by distilling some of the book's recurrent themes and highlighting some of the issues that may facilitate cooperation or exacerbate conflict between the major state actors with a stake in, and some influence over, Korean affairs. Exactly how events will unfold in Korea in the years ahead is impossible to foretell, but the interests and perspectives of the Pacific powers in the shape that future takes are surprisingly enduring. Indeed, in the final analysis, it is precisely the "embedded" nature of so many of these interests and perspectives that permits forward thinking about the Korean question.

NOTES

1. Norman Davies, *God's Playground: A History of Poland* (New York: Columbia University Press, 1982).

2. Members of the study group included Ambassador Michael Armacost, President, The Brookings Institution; Gifford Combs, Managing General Partner, Chemin de Fer Limited; Chuck Downs, Senior Foreign and Defense Policy Advisor (Retired); Herbert Ellison, Professor of History and Russian Studies, Jackson School of International Studies, University of Washington; Robert L. Gallucci, Dean, School of Foreign Service, Georgetown University; Kent Harrington, Chairman, Harrington Fauver, LLC; Chae-Jin Lee, Director, Keck Center for International Studies, Claremont McKenna College; Kenneth Lieberthal, Special Assistant to the President and Senior Director for Asian Affairs, National Security Council; Ambassador James R. Lilley, Resident Fellow, American Enterprise Institute; Admiral Michael McDevitt, Senior Fellow, Center for Naval Analyses; Marcus Noland, Senior Fellow, Institute for International Economics; Douglas H. Paal, President, Asia Pacific Policy Center; Kenneth B. Pyle, Founding President, The National Bureau of Asian Research, and Professor of History and Asian Studies, Jackson School of International Studies, University of Washington; Robert A. Scalapino, Robson Research Professor of Government Emeritus, Institute of East Asian Studies, University of California, Berkeley; and Robert B. Zoellick, Former Undersecretary of State, and Senior Fellow, German Marshall Fund.

3. Peter Hayes, Lyuba Zarsky, and Walden F. Bello, *American Lake: Nuclear Peril in the Pacific* (New York: Penguin Books, 1986).

4. For an exposition on the system and the events that led to the disintegration of China's "East Asian World Order," consult Key-Hiuk Kim, *The Last Phase of the East Asian World Order: Korea, Japan and the Chinese Empire, 1860–1882* (Berkeley, Calif.: University of California Press, 1980).

5. For a concise, informative, and opinionated recounting of this story, see Bruce Cumings, *Korea's Place in the Sun: A Modern History* (New York: W. W. Norton, 1997).

6. See, for example, John Merrill, *Korea: The Peninsular Origins of the War* (Newark, Del.: University of Delaware Press, 1989).

7. William Stueck, *The Korean War: An International History* (Princeton, N.J.: Princeton University Press, 1995).

8. Aaron L. Friedberg, "Ripe For Rivalry: Prospects For Peace In A Multipolar Asia," *International Security*, vol. 18, no. 3 (Winter 1993), pp. 5–33.

9. For one particularly imaginative example, see Rajan Menon and S. Enders Wimbush, "Asia In The 21st Century: Power Politics Alive And Well," *National Interest*, no. 59 (Spring 2000), pp. 78–86.

10. Such ambitions are impressed into official text as well as revealed in official policies. Perhaps the most important recent pronouncement on China's strategic thinking is the "White Paper on China's National Defense," issued by the State Council of the People's Republic of China. For an English language version, see *Xinhua*, July 27, 1998; republished as "China: 'Text' of Defense White Paper" in U.S. Foreign Broadcast Information Service (hereafter, FBIS), FBIS-CHI-98-208, July 27, 1998 (electronic version); and "China's National Defense in 2000," White Paper issued by the Information Office of the PRC State Council, broadcast by *Xinhua* Domestic Service, October 16, 2000; translated as "'Text' of PRC White Paper on National Defense in 2000," FBIS-EAS-2000-1016, October 17, 2000.

11. For two careful recent considerations of the geopolitical consequence of China's recovery and ascent on the world stage, see Zalmay M. Khalilzad et al., *The United States and a Rising China: Strategic and Military Implications* (Santa Monica, Calif.: RAND, 1999); and Michael D. Swaine and Ashley J. Tellis, *Interpreting China's Grand Strategy* (Santa Monica: RAND, 2000).

12. A proposition perhaps most powerfully and persuasively outlined in Leon Aron, *Yeltsin: A Revolutionary Life* (New York: St. Martin's Press, 2000).

13. Russia's new "National Security Concept" was approved by President Vladimir Putin on January 10, 2000; its text was first published in *Nezavisimoe voennoe obozrenie*, no. 1 (174), January 14, 2000. For a translated text of the main passages of the document, see "Russia's National Security Concept," *Arms Control Today*, vol. 30, no. 1 (January/February 2000), pp. 15–20.

14. Kenneth B. Pyle, *The Japanese Question: Power and Purpose in a New Era* (Washington, D.C.: AEI Press, 1992).

15. Ibid.

16. The text of Moscow's new treaty with Pyongyang has evidently not yet been publicly released (a perhaps telling indication of the opacity with which the Russian

Federation's foreign relations are currently being conducted). For all other treaties mentioned in this paragraph, consult the University of Tokyo's web site for "Basic Documents on Postwar International Politics" <http://www.ioc.u-tokyo.ac.jp/in-dex-ENG.html> (accessed November 20, 2000).

17. World Bank, *Entering The 21st Century: World Development Report 1999/2000* (New York: Oxford University Press, 1999), pp. 230–31. Estimates are for 1998 GNP. At current exchange rates, the Republic of Korea's economy is estimated to be somewhat larger than Russia's; when "purchasing power parity" (PPP) adjustments are attempted, it is calculated to be slightly smaller than Russia's.

18. In the year 1999, the Russian Federation's exports of goods and services were estimated at about $85 billion, versus about $144 billion for the Republic of Korea; Russian imports totaled an estimated $52 billion, while South Korea reported $120 billion in imports. Data drawn from International Monetary Fund (IMF), *International Financial Statistics Yearbook 2000*, (Washington, D.C.: IMF, 2000), pp. 823-25; and ROK Bank of Korea web site <http://www.bok.or.kr/index_e.html> (accessed November 20, 2000).

19. *World Development Report 1999/2000*, pp. 230-231. Estimates are for 1998 GNP per capita, adjusted for PPP. The 2000/2001 edition of the *World Development Report* revises this estimate somewhat, indicating that the ROK's PPP-adjusted per capita GNP is "only" 2.3 times greater than Russia's. World Bank, *World Development Report 2000/2001: Attacking Poverty*, (New York: Oxford University Press, 2000), pp. 274-275.

20. William J. Perry, "Review of United States Policy Toward North Korea: Findings and Recommendations" (Washington, D.C.: U.S. Department of State, Office of the North Korea Policy Coordinator, October 12, 1999 [unclassified]), p. 3.

21. The following several paragraphs draw upon Nicholas Eberstadt, "North Korea," in *Present Dangers: Challenges And Opportunities in American Foreign and Defense Policy*, William Kristol and Robert Kagan, eds. (New York: Encounter Books, forthcoming).

22. The ROK formally applied for membership in the Organization for Economic Cooperation and Development (OECD) in late 1994, and acceded to the OECD in late 1996.

23. Kim Jong Il's top governmental post is chairman of the DPRK National Defense Commission. According to the September 1998 DPRK constitution, however, the National Defense Commission is merely "the highest *military* leading organ of State power " [emphasis added]. The question of who actually serves as head of state

for North Korea—or whether this extraordinarily centralized system even *has* a head of state—is now constitutionally ambiguous.

24. *"Rodong Sinmun* and *Kunroja* Call for Maintaining Independent National Economic Construction Line," *Korean Central News Agency,* September 17, 1998.

25. *Minju Choson,* August 10, 2000, translated as "DPRK: Cabinet Adopts Decision on Party Central Committee Slogans," FBIS-EAS-2000-0823, August 28, 2000.

26. *World Development Report 2000/2001,* p. 274f. GNP calculations based on foreign exchange rates rank Japan as the world's second largest economy, after the United States. "Purchasing power parity" calculations suggest that Japan generates the world's third largest GNP, after the United States and China.

HISTORICAL AND POLITICAL CONTEXT

2

Conflict and Cooperation:
The Pacific Powers and Korea

Chae-Jin Lee

Even though we have witnessed the dramatic dissolution of the Soviet Union, the peaceful reunification of Germany, and the unmistakable passing of the Cold War in recent years, it is an unfortunate fact that the Korean Peninsula still remains a serious source of mistrust and conflict in the Asia-Pacific region. Indeed, the basic structure of Korea's national division has not changed much for half a century. The two heavily-armed rival Korean states clearly remember the bitter legacy of their earlier war, and tensely face each other across the thirty-eighth parallel and the Demilitarized Zone (DMZ). In spite of the tremendous euphoria generated by the inter-Korean summit meeting held in Pyongyang in June 2000, it is uncertain whether that summit would eventually pave the road for genuine national reconciliation and peaceful reunification.

The tortuous development of inter-Korean relations has been intimately linked with the complex interests and policies of four major Pacific powers—the United States, the Soviet Union (Russia), China, and Japan—which have exhibited a mixture of conflictual and cooperative relations in the region. This dynamic hexagonal linkage contains both continuities and discontinuities in military, diplomatic, political, and economic realms. At the height of the Cold War, both Koreas conceived and executed their respective policies in the context of a relatively simple bipolar system of opposing military and diplomatic coalitions. While the Soviet Union and China concluded mutual defense treaties with North Korea and showed an extreme degree of hostility toward South Korea, the United States embraced the Republic of Korea as one of its pivotal client-states and adopted a rigid framework of containment and isolation against the Democratic People's Republic of Korea. Japan conducted limited economic transactions and people's diplomacy with North Korea, but it did not deviate from the U.S.-led containment strategy on the Korean Peninsula.

As the Cold War ended, however, the four major powers not only restructured their own relationships but also modified their approaches toward the peninsula. The Soviet Union and China abandoned their one-Korea policy and recognized South Korea in 1990 and 1992, respectively. At the same time, the United States began to relax its traditional containment and isolation policy toward North Korea. In October 1994 the United States and the DPRK agreed to exchange semi-diplomatic liaison offices and to work toward full diplomatic and economic normalization. In tandem with the improvement of U.S.-North Korea relations, Japan is cautiously exploring the possibility of establishing diplomatic relations with the North. As the era of confrontation gives way to a promise of accommodation in the region, all four major powers are expected to cooperate, as well as compete, in the process of Korea's reunification.

PATTERNS OF CONFLICT AND COOPERATION

National Division

The sources of Korea's national division stem from political developments at both the international and national levels: the policy cleavage between the United States and the Soviet Union and the irreconcilable conflict among indigenous Korean political forces. The origin of these developments can be traced to the joint declaration of President Franklin Roosevelt, Prime Minister Winston Churchill, and Generalissimo Chiang Kai-shek at the Cairo

Conference (December 1, 1943), which expressed their intention to "restrain and punish the aggression of Japan," and declared: "The aforesaid three great powers, mindful of the enslavement of the people of Korea, are determined that in due course Korea shall become free and independent."[1] The ambiguous phrase "in due course" did not specify a precise time frame, and those leaders who participated in the Cairo, Tehran, Yalta, and Potsdam Conferences during World War II assumed that a period of multipower trusteeship over Korea would be required immediately after Japan's defeat. They felt that Korea would not yet be ready for self-rule.

General Secretary Joseph Stalin surprised the Americans by promptly accepting their proposal that the United States and the Soviet Union make the thirty-eighth parallel a temporary line for dividing the responsibilities of receiving the Japanese surrender on the Korean Peninsula.[2] This suggestion, made in the last days of the Pacific War by President Harry S Truman, was designed to further U.S. interests in the Asia-Pacific region. At that time, Soviet troops were strategically positioned to rapidly sweep across the entire Korean Peninsula, and the United States decided upon the thirty-eighth parallel as a means to claim its influence in Korea and to protect its postwar control of Japan. The issues of Korean unification and independence became inevitably intertwined with the postwar unfolding of U.S.-Soviet relations when the de facto division of Korea into two zones of foreign occupation occurred. China and Japan were in no position to become directly involved in Korea at that time: Japan's 35-year colonial rule in Korea ended with its defeat by the Allies, and China was deeply embroiled in an emerging civil war and unable to influence the Korean situation.

The United States and the Soviet Union, along with Great Britain and China, agreed in Moscow in December 1945 to set up a provisional and democratic Korean government, a U.S.-Soviet joint commission, and a four-power trusteeship over Korea for a period of up to five years. Throughout 1946 and 1947, however, the joint commission failed to carry out the Moscow agreement. This failure was a reflection of the increasing conflict between the two global powers in Korea and elsewhere. Moreover, intense rivalries among Korean political forces thwarted efforts for compromise between Korea's communist and nationalist leaders across the thirty-eighth parallel, and Syngman Rhee led the movement to oppose the imposition of trusteeship on Korea.

The United States regarded the Korean Peninsula as an important buffer zone in Northeast Asia and decided to remove the Korean question from the deadlocked joint commission by referring it to the United Nations General Assembly, where Washington enjoyed a voting majority. Although the General Assembly called for free elections on the peninsula under the supervision of the new, nine-nation United Nations Temporary Commission on Korea (UNTCOK) in November 1947, the Soviet Union refused to allow UNTCOK to enter North Korea. The Republic of Korea, under President Syngman Rhee, was proclaimed on August 15, 1948, after UNTCOK-supervised elections were held in the U.S.-occupied zone only. In the Soviet-controlled zone, the Democratic People's Republic of Korea under Premier Kim Il Sung was established a few weeks later. Although the United States and the Soviet Union legally terminated their three-year occupation of Korea and withdrew their troops by mid-1949, the coexistence of their respective client-states ensured the continuation of the U.S.-Soviet conflict on the peninsula.

The Era of Conflict

Kim Il Sung, intent on unifying Korea by military force, sent North Korean troops into South Korea on June 25, 1950. The invasion had been sanctioned by the two major communist nations: Stalin had explicitly approved and Mao Zedong had given his direct blessing. Kim's invasion was not regarded by the Truman administration as a civil war for national unification, rather as an integral part of Stalin's global military designs against the United States and its allies. Secretary of State Dean Acheson concluded that the war was "an open, undisguised challenge to our internationally-accepted position as the protector of South Korea, an area of great importance to the security of American-captured Japan."[3] The United States responded to North Korea's swift move southward with the direct deployment of its own troops in Korea, and with resolutions by the United Nations Security Council.

Kim seized control of the entire peninsula, save for a small southeastern coastal perimeter that stretched from Tageu to Pusan, after the full-scale military commitment of the United States and other UN member-states failed to stop the North Korean armed forces. The tide of the war did not turn until General Douglas MacArthur's successful landing at Inchon in September 1950. At that point, the U.S. war strategy shifted from the defensive goal of repulsing North Korean aggressors to the offensive goal of seeking total military victory and Korean unification. An overconfident MacArthur told Truman at Wake Island on October 15, 1950 that within a very short period of time total victory would be achieved. MacArthur dismissed the possibility of Chinese or Russian intervention in Korea, but assured Truman that even if the Chinese did intervene, they would suffer "the greatest slaughter."[4] History proved that he made a fatal mistake in his drastic underestimation of China's intentions and capabilities.

Viewing the advancing U.S. forces as a direct threat to their own security and determined to reassert their traditional role on the Korean Peninsula, the Chinese espoused a revolutionary solidarity with their beleaguered North Korean comrades. Although Stalin reneged on his promise to provide Soviet air cover for Chinese troops in Korea, Mao dispatched a large number of "Chinese People's Volunteers" across the Yalu River in mid-October.[5] The Kim Il Sung regime was rescued from territorial extinction after this massive Chinese intervention reversed the U.S. advance. By the summer of 1951, after a series of military campaigns, China and the United States reached a stalemate along a line adjacent to the thirty-eighth parallel. Mao realized that his initial goal of total military victory was unattainable. Meanwhile, the United States and the Soviet Union cooperated in arranging a negotiation for ceasefire, and preliminary negotiations started at Kaesong on July 10, 1951. It was two years, however, before both sides ironed out the terms of a ceasefire.[6] On July 27, 1953, an armistice agreement that averted a larger international conflict in the region was signed, and subsequently the status quo ante bellum in Korea was restored. As a result of the three-year war, mistrust and hostility between North and South Korea intensified, creating a powerful obstacle to the opening of dialogue and reconciliation.

Despite its costly participation in the war, China was able to enhance its international revolutionary status, and it joined the United States and the Soviet Union in assuming a legitimate role in the management of Korean affairs. The Chinese took part in the Military Armistice Commission at Panmunjom. They attended the Geneva Conference on Korea and Indochina in 1954 and kept their forces in North Korea until 1958. If the Soviet Union was the founder of the North Korean regime, China was its savior. The involvement of both the Soviet Union and China in North Korean affairs created an opportunity for Kim Il Sung to negotiate a delicate balance between the two communist giants and to extract maximum benefits from each. Although Japan had no significant role in the Korean War, it was a "godsend" for Japan's economic recovery, mainly because of U.S. military procurements in Japan.

Upon the conclusion of the Korean War, Washington adopted a general policy of military containment, diplomatic isolation, and economic sanctions against North Korea and China. In order to deter another war, the United States signed a mutual security treaty with South Korea in 1953. Article Three stipulated:

> Each Party recognizes that an armed attack in the Pacific area on either of the Parties in territories now under their respective administrative control, or hereafter recognized by one of the Parties as lawfully brought under the administrative control of the other, would be dangerous to its own peace and safety and declares that it would act to meet the common danger in accordance with its constitutional processes.[7]

In addition to this legally-binding security guarantee, the United States continued to deploy its forces in South Korea and to render military assistance to the ROK.

To implement its anticommunist containment policy in the Asia-Pacific region, the United States erected a chain of bilateral and multilateral security arrangements—defense treaties with South Korea, Japan, the Philippines, Taiwan, Australia, and New Zealand, as well as the Southeast Asia Treaty Organization (SEATO). The United States also actively persuaded its two Asian allies—Japan and South Korea—to improve their relationship. In 1965 the two sides agreed to set aside their history of mutual animosity and to normalize diplomatic relations. Japan offered South Korea an economic assistance package of $500 million in government loans and grants and $300 million in commercial loans. While the Japanese government hoped to assist South Korean economic development and further stabilize the peninsula, the Soviet Union, China, and North Korea vehemently attacked the Seoul-Tokyo diplomatic rapprochement as a conspiracy to revive Japanese militarism and to sabotage Korean reunification.

The U.S.-led coalition with Japan and South Korea faced a counter-alliance of the Soviet Union, China, and North Korea. In the 30-year Treaty of Friendship, Alliance, and Mutual Assistance signed in February 1950, the Soviet Union and China agreed to use "all necessary measures" to prevent the revival of Japanese imperialism and the resumption of aggression on the part of Japan or "any other state that may collaborate with Japan directly or indirectly in acts of aggression." China used the treaty to safeguard its security interests, while the Soviets used the agreement to tie China to their bloc.

The Sino-Soviet treaty served as a model for North Korea's mutual defense treaties with the Soviet Union and China that were signed in 1961. The two treaties had a few minor semantic and procedural differences, but both China and the Soviet Union were equally committed to the protection of North Korean security. Article two of the Sino-North Korean treaty declared:

> The two Contracting Parties shall collectively take all measures to prevent either Contracting Party from being attacked by any other country. If either of the Contracting Parties should suffer armed attack by any country or coalition of countries and thus find itself in a state of war, the other Contracting Party shall immediately extend military and other assistance with all means at its disposal. [8]

In spite of growing signs of a Sino-Soviet dispute, an essentially bipolar strategic system prevailed on the Korean Peninsula during the 1950s and 1960s. The two Korean governments were fully integrated into the Cold War framework. Neither the North nor the South exercised a significant degree of policy autonomy apart from its powerful external patrons. Any maneuver for inter-Korean negotiations was unthinkable at that time.

In Search of Cooperation

The first major breakthrough in easing the Cold War confrontation in the region took place in 1971 when the United States changed its policy of military containment, diplomatic isolation, and economic sanctions against China. President Richard Nixon wanted to employ détente with China as a strategic counterweight to the Soviet Union and as an instrument to address a number of regional issues involving Vietnam, Japan, and Korea. This "Nixon shock" stimulated Sino-Japanese diplomatic normalization and the beginning of the inter-Korean dialogue.

On July 4, 1972, the two Koreas issued a joint communiqué in which they agreed to seek the peaceful and independent unification of Korea without foreign interference and to realize national unity by transcending differences in ideologies and systems. They promised to end armed provocations, to promote various exchange programs, and to establish a hotline between Seoul and Pyongyang. The South-North Coordinating Committee was set up to implement the joint communiqué. The four major powers applauded this unprecedented thaw in inter-Korean relations, but the euphoria was short-lived. The Coordinating Committee was stalemated in August 1973, and each side blamed the other for the failure. The détente between opposing international coalitions encouraged inter-Korean contacts, but in the end it proved insufficient to resolve the deep-seated mistrust and the fundamental policy cleavage between Seoul and Pyongyang.

The second major breakthrough occurred in May 1989 when Mikhail Gorbachev and Deng Xiaoping held a historic summit in Beijing and agreed to normalize all aspects of relations between the two countries. In a joint communiqué, the two sides promised to develop their relations on the basis of five "universal principles"—mutual respect for sovereignty and territorial integrity, mutual nonaggression, noninterference in each other's internal affairs, equality and mutual benefit, and peaceful coexistence.[9] They expressed readiness to resolve all disputes through peaceful negotiation and to refrain from using or threatening to use arms against each other. Russia and China shared the view that "peace and development are the two most important questions in the world of today" and indicated their desire to alleviate military confrontations and to peacefully settle regional conflicts. The joint communiqué did not make specific reference to the Korean question, but it was clear that both China and the Soviet Union wished to see the easing of tensions as well as the continuation of dialogue between Seoul and Pyongyang.

The Sino-Soviet reconciliation deprived North Korea of some of its leverage to play off one communist ally against the other, and furthered South Korea's ambitious northern diplomacy, which was designed to improve its relations with the Soviet Union, China, and East European countries. After his meeting with Gorbachev in San Francisco in June 1990, President Roh Tae Woo spoke of his goal:

> The ultimate objective of our northern policy is to induce North Korea to open up and thus to secure stability and peace on the Korean Peninsula. The road between Seoul and Pyongyang is now totally blocked. Accordingly, we have to choose an alternative route to the North Korean capital by way of Moscow and Beijing. This may not be the most direct route, but we certainly hope it will be an effective one.[10]

To North Korea's chagrin, the Roh administration was able to establish diplomatic relations with the Soviet Union and East European countries by the end of 1990 and to exchange resident trade offices with Beijing. At their Moscow summit meeting in December 1990, Roh and Gorbachev ruled out the likelihood of armed confrontation between Seoul and Moscow, in effect nullifying the application of the Soviet-North Korea defense treaty against South Korea.

After the decisive U.S. victory in the Persian Gulf War in early 1991, the Soviet Union and China felt it all the more imperative to improve their bilateral relations to counter American ascendancy in world affairs. At their May 1991 Moscow summit meeting, Gorbachev and Jiang Zemin noted with satisfaction that the friendly and cooperative bilateral relations in political, economic, scientific, cultural, and military areas were developing steadily.[11] They attached special attention to the question of security and stability in the Asia-Pacific region and observed that "hot spots and unsettled conflicts" still remained. The two leaders declared that both countries were ready "to make joint efforts for turning the Asian-Pacific region into a zone of openness, cooperation and prosperity." They also stated:

China and the Soviet Union hold that relaxation of the situation on the Korean Peninsula is of great importance for security and stability in Northeast Asia. Both sides welcome the positive changes that have recently taken place on the peninsula, and reaffirm their support for the realization of a peaceful reunification of Korea through dialogue and consultations between the North and South. They express the hope that the North and South will continue their dialogue for further improvement of mutual relations, and call for both sides to refrain from taking any acts that might impede détente on the peninsula and a peaceful reunification of Korea.[12]

It is possible that while meeting in Moscow, Gorbachev and Jiang attempted to persuade Kim Il Sung to accept the separate admission of the two Korean governments to the United Nations; eight days after Jiang's Moscow visit, Kim announced North Korea's decision to join the United Nations together with South Korea.

Most important in view of the passing of the Cold War, the two Korean governments reached a milestone in December 1991 when their prime ministers signed a comprehensive 25-article Agreement on Reconciliation, Nonaggression, and Exchanges and Cooperation (the "Basic Agreement"). Among other provisions, they declared that "both parties shall not use armed force against each other and shall not make armed aggression against each other" and that "differences of opinion and disputes arising between the two parties shall be peacefully resolved through dialogue and negotiations."[13]

Furthermore, the two governments issued the "Joint Declaration on the Denuclearization of the Korean Peninsula" on December 31, 1991. This declaration stated that both sides would not test, produce, receive, possess, store, deploy, or use nuclear weapons. In order to verify the denuclearization, the two governments promised to conduct nuclear inspections under the auspices of the South-North Nuclear Control Commission.

The inter-Korean accords obtained enthusiastic support from all four major powers and facilitated North Korea's diplomatic contact with the United States and Japan. Yet tensions on the Korean Peninsula escalated in March 1993 when North Korea announced its intention to withdraw from the Nuclear Nonproliferation Treaty (NPT). In the summer of 1994, former U.S. President Jimmy Carter was successful in reaching a broad outline of a settlement on nuclear issues with North Korea and bringing about an agreement for a summit meeting between Presidents Kim Young Sam and Kim Il Sung. However, the death of Kim Il Sung thwarted the summitry. After a series of bilateral negotiations and multilateral maneuvers, the Agreed Framework between the United States and the Democratic People's Republic of Korea at last was signed in Geneva on October 21, 1994.[14] In return for the North Korean pledge to freeze its nuclear programs, to remain in the NPT regime, and to resume inter-Korean talks, the United States agreed to provide alternative energy supplies (light-water nuclear reactors and heavy oil) to North Korea, to exchange liaison offices between Washington and Pyongyang, and to reduce barriers to trade and investment with North Korea. The agreed framework stipulated that "as progress is made on issues of concern to each side, the U.S. and the DPRK will upgrade bilateral relations to the ambassadorial level."

This brief historical review illustrates the dramatic transformation of conflict and cooperation among the two Koreas and the four Pacific powers. Gone is the Cold War era when the two sets of military and diplomatic coalitions— U.S.-Japan-South Korea vs. Soviet Union-China-North Korea—dictated the substance and direction of Korean affairs. The four Pacific powers have appreciably expanded the scope of their cooperation in military, diplomatic, and economic fields from the 1960s to the 1990s. While South Korea has significantly increased the level of cooperation with all four powers during the same period, North Korea has seen a mixed result—a difficult readjustment of its alliance with China and Russia and a gradual improvement of its relations with the United States and Japan. Yet military conflicts, diplomatic disagreements, and ideological differences are less critical than before, and pragmatic economic pursuits are increasingly important to all parties concerned. Hence the present international environment is generally conducive to promoting the goals of peace, stability, and reconciliation in the Korean Peninsula.

PROCESSES OF KOREAN UNIFICATION

It remains uncertain whether the two Koreas can take advantage of their favorable external environment, realize the two accords signed in December 1991, and cooperate toward their peaceful and democratic reunification (although the prospects for these events appear to be greater following the historic summit between Kim Dae Jung and Kim Jong Il in June 2000). In the next few years the relationship between Seoul and Pyongyang will probably follow one of four contrasting scenarios—status quo, constructive engagement, war, or absorption. Whereas the first two scenarios continue Korea's national division, the second two may lead to its eventual unification.[15]

Status Quo

The possible scenario for sustaining the status quo in intergovernmental relations between Seoul and Pyongyang may include a number of distinctive features. First, both Korean governments fail to carry out the Basic Agreement and the Joint Declaration on the Denuclearization of the Korean Peninsula and continue to stay in an unstable state of heavily-armed peace. Second, the two sides are unwilling to arrive at any substantive change in their hostile relations except for a limited degree of governmental contacts, food aid, commercial transactions, tourist industries, and cultural exchanges. Third, no tangible progress is made in improving Korea's security environment; the four-party talks for Korean peace (the attempts of the United States, China and both Koreas to transform the Korean Armistice Agreement into a more permanent peace mechanism) do not bear fruit.

There is no doubt that the zero-sum mentality—a legacy of the Cold War—lingers in both Korean capitals. Moreover, both sides are presumably influenced by the logic of realist or neorealist orientations. Even though both states can expect absolute gains from cooperation, they are reluctant to engage in mutually beneficial cooperative activities because of their persistent preoccupation with relative gains in an essentially anarchic situation which lacks central authority or enforcement mechanisms. Kenneth Waltz states:

When faced with the possibility of cooperating for mutual gain, states that feel insecure must ask how the gain will be divided. They are compelled to ask not "Will both of us gain?" but "Who will gain more?" If an expected gain is to be divided, say, in the ratio of two to one, one state may use its disproportionate gain to implement a policy intended to damage or destroy the other. Even the prospect of large absolute gains for both parties does not elicit their cooperation so long as each fears how the other will use its increased capabilities. [16]

Joseph Grieco, a leading realist theorist, further explains that "states fear that partners may achieve relatively greater gains; that, as a result, the partners could surge ahead of them in relative capabilities; and, finally, that these increasingly powerful partners in the present could use their additional power to pressure them or, at the extreme, to become all the more formidable foes at some point in the future."[17] So long as either North Korea or South Korea cannot overcome the dilemma of relative gains, especially in regard to national security issues, it will be hard for either side to pursue a genuine policy of mutual cooperation.

The North Koreans were hesitant to respond favorably to their southern partner's proposals for direct governmental dialogue and cooperation until recently. The subministerial meetings between the two sides in Beijing broke down in April 1998 and in July 1999. As suggested by neorealist theory, North Koreans were indeed afraid that even if cooperation would give them absolute gains, the inter-Korean balance might be tilted decisively in favor of South Korea and force the North to accept an open-door policy and economic reforms more rapidly than they would like. They preferred to bypass South Korea and deal primarily with the United States, and in the process attempted to drive a wedge between the United States and South Korea so as to undermine South Korea's advantageous status.

If the North Koreans were to adopt an ambitious reform program, their *juche* ideology might be undercut and their political system threatened. They might also suffer from inertia; since they have managed somehow to muddle through their difficult condition, it was not easy for them to take the initiative or even to consider a conceptual transformation in their policymaking processes. Most important to North Korea's uncooperative behavior was the increasing influence of military leaders after the death of Kim Il Sung. The "hard-line" forces appeared to enjoy the upper hand over the "moderate" or "pragmatic" forces, as indicated by the defection of top-level ideologue Hwang Chang Yop in February 1997.

The status quo scenario in inter-Korean relations is not necessarily adverse to the national interests of the United States, China, Japan, and Russia. Even though all four major powers publicly commit themselves to a policy of peaceful Korean reunification, there is no compelling reason for them to take the bold initiative in breaking up the status quo or to replace it with another formulation.

Constructive Engagement

Since the status quo scenario contains uncertainty and risk, it is important to look at an alternative scenario—that of constructive engagement or peaceful coexistence between Seoul and Pyongyang. In this respect, neoliberal institutionalists dispute the neorealist assumptions of relative gains and assert that the constraints of relative gains that inhibit cooperation are mostly applicable to a two-player game and a finite number of interactions.[18] Robert Axelrod concludes that cooperation can emerge in a situation with an infinite number of interactions.[19] Given the "shadow of the future," a tit-for-tat strategy of reciprocity for mutually reinforcing interactions can replace a strategy for mutual defection even in an anarchic situation because "defection is in the long run unrewarding."[20] Other scholars propose that states focus primarily on their absolute gains and are not constrained by the gains of others, and that there is a possibility of decentralized enforcement of cooperation, particularly with the assistance of international institutions.

As applied to the Korean situation, neoliberal institutionalism supports the proposition that since the two Korean governments can conduct an infinite number of interactions, they could surmount the fear of relative gains and mutual defection and engage in mutually beneficial cooperative activities. Even if North Korea expects to gain less than South Korea would in a two-party game, it may be persuaded to cooperate with South Korea so that improvement in inter-Korean relations can lead to absolute gains for North Korea in multinational settings such as those involving the United States,

Japan, and other countries. The two Korean governments may work together for common interests with the assistance of international institutions—including the Korean Peninsula Energy Development Organization, the United Nations Development Program, the Food and Agriculture Organization, the International Atomic Energy Agency, the ASEAN Regional Forum, and the Asian Development Bank—and with mediation by the United States or China.

Moreover, an increasing level of inter-Korean functional transactions and communication in nonpolitical fields can draw the Korean people's beliefs, motives, and perceptions of each other closer together and may facilitate the formation of a unitary community. The growing linkages and shared interests of particular groups— such as "moderate" forces and economic bureaucracies in both states—are anticipated to have positive spillover effects on other aspects of inter-Korean relations. Hence the growth of "moderate" or "pragmatic" forces in both Koreas increases the likelihood of constructive engagement and a gradual, cumulative, and functional process of national integration. This scenario requires a restoration of the 1991–92 phase of inter-Korean cooperation. For this purpose, the two Korean sides should faithfully fulfill both the letter and the spirit of the Basic Agreement and the Joint Declaration on the Denuclearization of the Korean Peninsula as well as the U.S.-DPRK Agreed Framework. If the four-party talks can replace the Korean Armistice Agreement with a more stable system for peace and stability, the door could be opened widely for genuine cooperation in Korea and for a favorable external environment in Northeast Asia.

Compared with his predecessor, Kim Young Sam, President Kim Dae Jung presents a distinctly conciliatory and liberal approach toward North Korea. In his inaugural address, he explicitly declared that "we do not have any intention to undermine or absorb North Korea" and that "we will actively pursue reconciliation and cooperation between the South and North" on the basis of the Basic Agreement.[21] In spite of North Korea's provocative activities, Kim Dae Jung promised to separate economic issues from political considerations and expressed his interest in exchanging special envoys with Pyongyang and in reviving the agreement for a summit meeting. His "sunshine policy" allowed Chung Ju Yong (founder of the Hyundai Corporation) to meet with Kim Jong Il in Pyongyang in November 1998 and October 1999 and to undertake a number of cooperative economic activities with North Korea with special emphasis on tourist industries and joint ventures. President Kim has urged the United States and Japan to improve their relations with North Korea. His ideas are incorporated in William Perry's comprehensive report, *Review of United States Policy Toward North Korea: Findings and Recommendations* (the "Perry report"), issued on October 12, 1999. The summit that took place between Kim Dae Jung and Kim Jong Il in June 2000 may suggest that this policy is working. If North Korea continues to respond positively to Kim's forward-looking policy, the scenario for constructive engagement between the two Korean governments will have a good chance to be realized.

War

If the hard-line forces continue to dominate North Korean decisionmaking under Kim Jong Il and fail to prevent further deterioration of Pyongyang's economic conditions and international standing, it is conceivable that they will become increasingly frustrated with the status quo of inter-Korean relations and will assume a more militant and radical posture toward South Korea. While it is highly unlikely that South Korea would initiate actions that North Korea could interpret as armed threats (except for arms acquisitions and military exercises), the North Koreans are capable of undertaking provocative actions toward South Korea. They have already challenged the legitimacy of the Korean Armistice Agreement, violated the DMZ, deactivated the Military Armistice Commission and the Neutral Nations Supervisory Commission, and provoked a naval clash with South Korea in June 1999.

South Korea and the United States take the North Korean threat seriously, and believe that the Korean Peninsula is one of the world's potential military flashpoints. They surmise that North Korea allocates about 25 percent of its GNP to national defense and has a substantial number of ground troops, commando forces, and critical military supplies, including jet fighters, bombers, tanks, artillery, armored personnel carriers, attack submarines, and amphibious craft. The two allies also conclude that North Korea poses a potential threat to South Korea by deploying its forces offensively near the

DMZ, by developing weapons of mass destruction and missiles, and by basing its aircraft less than six-minutes flight time from Seoul.

For all practical purposes, it is highly unlikely that North Korea would launch an all-out offensive against South Korea in the next few years. First, despite its recent financial difficulties, South Korea enjoys economic and financial superiority over North Korea. Second, the U.S. military presence in South Korea and the Combined Forces Command present an effective deterrence against North Korea's military actions. In the Gulf War the United States clearly demonstrated its political will and sophisticated military strategy to defend its vital interests. Third, the success of South Korea's northern diplomacy has significantly eroded the political basis of North Korea's conventional alliance system. The North Koreans cannot expect to rely upon assistance from China or Russia in the event of war—as was the case during the Korean War. Most important, despite the formidable extent of North Korea's military preparedness, its quality has suffered in recent years because of shortages of fuel, food, and supplies; outdated military technology; limited opportunities for training and exercises; heavy involvement in non-military activities; and the overall economic downturn. Hence it is widely assumed that the leaders of North Korea are primarily interested in survival, not suicide.

Yet the probability of another war in Korea is not entirely unthinkable. A few analysts suggest that North Korea's deteriorating economic conditions can prompt or necessitate armed provocations against South Korea. Bruce Bennett anticipates war not as a purposeful North Korean act of expansion, but rather as an act of desperation.[22] While the commander of the U.S. forces in Korea, General Gary Luck, refers to the possibility of "a cornered rat syndrome,"[23] Edward Olsen applies the "Masada Complex" to the North Korean leadership.[24] Makoto Momoi, a leading Japanese military expert, notes: "Histories of wars are full of cases in which ill-prepared, poorly equipped military all too often resorted to wars in desperation and failed after prolonging the conflict, pathetically disregarding the maxim, 'every war must end.'"[25] Moreover, Michael Green asserts that "A decision in Pyongyang to unleash all of the North Korean military's destructive power on the South remains a dangerous possibility in the event of a regime crisis in the North."[26]

The South Korean government has noted the possibility of North Korean aggression, and states in a 1998 Defense White Paper:

North Korea's military strategy toward the South is short-term blitzkrieg, which aims at creating great panic in the South in the early stage of a war by launching simultaneous attacks in the forward and rear areas, plunging quickly and deeply into the South with maneuver forces armed with tanks, armored vehicles and self-propelled artillery to take the initiative in the war, thus sweeping the entire South before USFK reinforcements come. Considering the US military capability, South Korea's human and material potential, the ROK-US alliance and their joint military posture, and the sentiment of the UN and the international community, blitzkrieg is regarded as the only strategy it could use for a war.[27]

According to veteran journalist Don Oberdorfer, the United States has a contingency plan—Operations Plan 50-27—which in response to North Korean aggression would authorize a massive American and South Korean counterattack that would cross the DMZ, take Pyongyang, proceed toward the Yalu and Tumen Rivers, and reunify the country.[28] No doubt another Korean War would profoundly upset the existing regional order and enormously complicate the dynamics of relations among the Pacific powers. To be sure, it would escalate tensions, conflicts, and mistrust among them to the extent that any framework for regional cooperation would be severely strained or even destroyed. It is most unlikely that the United States (and South Korea) could obtain a UN Security Council resolution which would authorize them "to repel the armed aggression and to restore international peace and security in the area" (as it did at the outbreak of the Korean and Gulf Wars). At the UN Security Council, China and/or Russia may veto such a resolution, call for a ceasefire, or maneuver to dispatch a UN peacekeeping force to Korea.

In order to justify retaliatory measures against North Korea, the United States and South Korea could invoke their mutual security treaty, claim the inherent right of self-help as recognized by the UN Charter, and enforce the principle of hot pursuit of the aggressor. In the event of North Korean aggression, the two allies should take the following steps so as not to provoke China and Russia:

(1) Establish that North Korea unmistakably initiated an unprovoked aggression so that China would not feel it necessary to invoke Article Two of the Sino-North Korean treaty;

(2) Let South Korean troops operate north of the DMZ with America supplying only air, naval, and logistical support;

(3) Ensure that in the event that U.S. ground forces are committed north of the DMZ they stay away from the Chinese and Russian borders or perhaps stop at the Pyongyang-Wonsan line; and

(4) Make it clear that as soon as the war is over, U.S. ground forces will withdraw from Northern Korea.

It is unclear whether the above-mentioned steps and assurances would be sufficient to persuade China (or Russia) not to take a direct part in the war or to issue an ultimatum against U.S. and South Korean military advances. Confronted with such an agonizing dilemma, however, the Chinese would be most likely to refrain from repeating their costly experience in the first Korean War and seek a negotiated settlement, preferably via the United Nations. Vice Minister of Foreign Affairs Tang Jiaxuan indicated in March 1997 that if North Korea starts a war, China would not honor its security treaty with Pyongyang and would not automatically intervene in the war.[29]

Unlike China, Russia has neither a treaty obligation for automatic assistance toward North Korea nor an enduring attachment to the legacy of the Korean War. As it did during the Gulf War, however, Russia may take advantage of the war by attempting to reassert its role in the management of the Korean question. There is a possibility that Russia and China would form a diplomatic united front to counter the U.S. military ascendancy in the region. In April 1997 Russian Defense Minister Igor Rodionov expressed his readiness to support China in the event of armed conflict in Korea.[30]

As mandated by the Guidelines for U.S.-Japan Defense Cooperation approved in June 1997, Japan is fully expected to provide "rear area support" to U.S. forces fighting in Korea: to conduct such activities as intelligence gathering, surveillance, and minesweeping; to help protect lives and property; and to undertake relief activities, treatment of refugees, and search and rescue operations.[31] As in the Gulf War, Japan would be asked to share the cost for U.S. and South Korean military operations. The Japanese would be concerned with the potentially adverse spillover effects of the war—such as North Korean missile attacks on U.S. bases in Japan, an influx of refugees, and agitation by the pro-Pyongyang Federation of Korean Residents in Japan (Chosoren or Chochongnyon). The nature and extent of Japan's reaction to the war would depend on its internal political and economic conditions as much as on its relations with the United States, China, and Russia.

In spite of the horrendous human and economic destruction, it is almost certain that North Korea could not win the war and that South Korea, in cooperation with the United States, may have an opportunity for a military conquest of North Korea in accordance with Operations Plan 50-27. Hajime Izumi, a Japanese specialist on Korea, is "one hundred percent sure" that North Korea would eventually lose the war.[32]

Absorption

The reports of severe food and energy shortages in North Korea, beginning in the aftermath of the demise of the Soviet Union, East Germany, and other Eastern European socialist systems, touched off an intense debate over North Korea's viability and advanced a Germany-type scenario for Korean reintegration—South Korea's peaceful but abrupt absorption of North Korea, an event to be endorsed by the major powers. While the South Korean government publicly disavows any intention to absorb North Korea, the North Koreans contend that the United States and South Korea have conspired to bring about a "peaceful evolution" and system collapse in North Korea. No doubt "hard-line" forces in South Korea and the United States wish to apply this Germany-type scenario to the Korean Peninsula so that the root cause of all the vexing problems, including North Korea's conflict escalation and nuclear development, could be removed once and for all. More moderate forces in South Korea and in the United States argue, however, that this scenario may not necessarily serve the long-term interests of a unified Korea, nor maintain the balance of power in Northeast Asia.

In his testimony before the Senate Select Committee on Intelligence (February 1996), Director of the CIA John Deutch stated:

Without deep cuts in military outlays, market-based reform, or significant new economic aid, the economy will probably continue to deteriorate and the decline in living standards will further undermine social stability. The North will find it harder to maintain military capabilities, and to insulate the armed forces from worsening economic problems. If food shortages should spread to front-line military units, it could undermine regime stability.[33]

Moreover, General Gary E. Luck, commander of U.S. Forces in Korea, told a subcommittee of the House of Representatives in March 1996: "We worry that, in a very short period, this country [North Korea] will either collapse or take aggressive actions against the South in a desperate attempt to divert attention from its internal situation." The question, he said, is not "Will this country disintegrate?" but rather, "How will it disintegrate—by implosion or explosion? And when?"[34]

In an article in *Foreign Affairs*, Nicholas Eberstadt argues:

The North is more likely to implode. The cherished vision of a gradual and orderly drawing together of the two Koreas is today nothing more than a fantasy. As time goes on, North Korea will only grow economically poorer and militarily more dangerous. For all parties affected, from the peoples of northeast Asia to the powers of NATO, the faster reunification takes place, the better.[35]

Eberstadt predicts that the early absorption of the DPRK by the ROK would be beneficial in economic and military fields and that a free, democratic, and united Korea would become a "force for stability and prosperity" in the region. Hence, he favors a rapid absorption scenario à la Germany.

Likewise, Edward Olsen writes that it is only a matter of time before the DPRK will cease to exist because of the incremental erosion of its economy, enervation of its polity, and obsolescing of its military.[36] Even if North

Korea adopts a policy of reform, Aidan Foster-Carter contends, all roads lead to collapse in North Korea because "North Korea's leaders face a Catch-22: damned if they do [reform], and equally damned if they don't." He maintains that "gradualism too will lead to collapse by unleashing political conflicts that will be impossible to contain."[37]

Contrary to these predictions of collapse, Selig Harrison believes that North Korea may not collapse easily due to: (1) the presence of a quasi-religious nationalist mystique; (2) totalitarian discipline; (3) the Confucian tradition of political centralization and obedience to authority; (4) the memory of a fratricidal war; and (5) tight insulation.[38] He favors a "soft-landing" scenario—a prolonged process of Korea's peaceful integration. James Laney and Jason Shaplen also argue that pursuing a policy of North Korean collapse is "futile" because the Kim Jong Il regime is not likely to disappear in the near future.[39] And Marcus Noland assumes that North Korea will neither reform nor collapse but will manage to muddle through.[40]

In general, economic determinism has had a limited applicability to Leninist states; popular uprisings or political demonstrations in Hungary and Poland (1956), Czechoslovakia (1968), and East Germany and China (1989) did not directly spring from economic crises. The widespread famine and death in the Soviet Union during the 1930s and in China during the late 1950s did not threaten Stalin's or Mao's repressive systems. Hence economic factors alone may not directly cause collapse, but they may trigger inter-elite cleavages or weaken the state's control mechanisms.

There is no doubt that China's support and assistance are indispensable to economic survival and system maintenance in North Korea. In the spring of 1996 the Chinese evidently decided to rescue North Korea from its severe economic predicament: on May 22, Vice Premiers Li Lanqing and Hong Song Nam signed an agreement on economic and technological coopera-tion.[41] This agreement reportedly specified that China would give North Korea 500,000 tons of grain per year (half free of charge and half at a cut-rate "friendship price") and 1.3 million tons of petroleum and 2.5 million tons of coal in the next five years. Nevertheless, the gap between the economic ori-entations of China and North Korea will widen as China outgrows its ideo-logically prescribed economic policy and adopts a "socialist market economy."

China cannot afford to sustain its increasingly burdensome economic relationship with North Korea for long. The continued decentralization of China's economic policymaking authority and the privatization of its large enterprises have limited Beijing's ability to dictate prices and timetables for economic transactions between local Chinese governments and North Korea. It is conceivable that China's economic assistance will not remain available to North Korea free of obligation, as pragmatic Chinese technocrats such as President Jiang Zemin and Premier Zhu Rongji, who no longer have revolutionary and personal ties with North Korea, make economic policy decisions. Beijing may require that in return for China's food aid, North Korea adopt an open-door economic policy and institute sweeping structural reforms in its agricultural sector.

The North Koreans, however, hesitate to fully follow the Chinese example of economic modernization precisely because they fear that it might compromise their *juche* ideology and ignite political problems similar to those that led to the Tiananmen Square incident. They are well aware of the potentially adverse social consequences of a capitalistic system in China's Shenzhen special economic zone. They are likely to undertake only highly selective and cautious experiments along the lines of the Chinese model.

If, however, North Korea verges on collapse, it is not at all clear how China would react. A number of Chinese, Korean, American, and Russian specialists suggest that China will not allow North Korea to collapse economically, will not be a mere bystander in the event of nation-wide disorders in North Korea, and will probably send troops into the North either to support the Pyongyang regime or to keep its own borders stable.[42] While Alexander Zhebin asserts that China would find North Korean collapse intolerable because it would result in Beijing's losing face, confidence, authority, and security,[43] Victor Cha, too, argues that China would not pass lightly over the adverse security implications of the absorption scenario following North Korea's collapse.[44] A task force organized by the Council on Foreign Relations reports that China is prepared "to do whatever is required to avert a North Korean collapse and to do so unconditionally."[45] However, even though China will continue to assist North Korea to a reasonable extent, it will be neither willing nor able to "do whatever is required to avert a North Korean collapse" because, as Banning Garrett and Bonnie Glaser report, China will prefer to take a pragmatic, flexible, and peaceful approach toward the Korean question.[46] They conclude that China will not intervene politically and militarily in the event of a North Korean internal crisis, such as a power struggle, civil war, or popular demonstrations. At the same time, both the United States and Japan, unlike Russia, have sufficient economic capacity to prevent or delay an economically induced collapse of North Korea, but they do not have the political will to do so because of internal and external constraints.

Yet all four Pacific powers seem to share serious concerns about the absorption scenario for several reasons. First, drawing an analogy with the German reunification model, the four powers are afraid that a precipitously unified Korea would adversely affect their economic interests because it would be too great a financial burden for them to support a viable economic system on the peninsula. Even though West Germany had a distinctly robust economy with a GDP five times larger than that of South Korea, and it only absorbed a relatively small East German population of 16 million (compared to the 60 million West Germans), the unified German government continues to suffer from a "double economic crisis"—the burgeoning problem of incorporating and restructuring the former East Germany and the crisis of the former West Germany's "social market economy." The financial crisis in South Korea, which required massive bailout assistance from the International Monetary Fund (IMF) and other foreign financial institutions in 1997 and 1998, demonstrates the underlying vulnerability of the South Korean economic system.

Second, the four powers are concerned that a rapid reunification of Korea may have a destabilizing effect upon the balance of power in the Asia-Pacific region. A RAND Corporation study argued that the reunification process in Korea would prove far more tumultuous within the region than German reunification did in Europe. It explained that "the emergence of a unified, economically strong Korea could bring on a new era of competition to replace the tensions of the Cold War, centered on the possible advent of intense economic and diplomatic rivalry with Japan and the revival of historical suspicions of China and Russia."[47] Whereas Germany after unification is anchored in and integrated with the European Union and NATO, a unified Korea is likely to be a freestanding entity with no effective structure of regional economic integration or collective security.

Third, the four powers may have a greater sense of uncertainty toward a unified Korea than toward a divided Korea due to the possibility that a unified Korean government may adopt an excessively nationalistic international outlook, a destabilizing foreign and military policy, and a protectionist economic posture, while even an authoritarian political system cannot be rejected as a possibility. Unlike the long existence of mature and stable political institutions in West Germany prior to unification, South Korea's political institutions and democratic practices remain fragile and vulnerable. The weakening of a unified Korean government may also intensify the competition among the major powers.

However, if the two Korean governments agree to unify by peaceful and democratic means, the four Pacific powers may not be in a position to resist or veto the reunification. In an attempt to help with the difficult transition to a unified Korea, the four powers may invoke the "one-plus-four" formula so that they agree to guarantee Korea's unity and viability. If the absorption scenario is carried out in Korea, there will be a fundamental difference between Germany and Korea in managing the problems after unification. Whereas a unified German government has dealt with the relatively peaceful and constructive process of military integration and political democratization, but has faced an enormous obstacle to economic equalization, a post-absorption Korean government is likely to face a greater degree of difficulties in the process of military demobilization than that of economic integration and political assimilation.

POLICIES AFTER KOREAN UNIFICATION

Alignment

Even though the prospects for Korean reunification by war or by absorption are relatively low at the moment, it is useful to consider how the government of a unified Korea would make a choice among competing options for its foreign policy (notably, between alignment and nonalignment), and how the Pacific powers and Korea would manage the changing dynamics of conflict and cooperation among them. This policy choice will reflect a combination of several factors, including: (1) Korea's domestic situation; (2) its relations with each Pacific power; and (3) the new regional environment, especially the relationship between the United States and China.

Conventional wisdom assumes that a unified Korea under Seoul's control would prefer to maintain its traditional and familiar policy of close military and political alignment with the United States, at least until such a time as the initial stages of Korea's national integration are satisfactorily completed. This preference would be particularly acute if the process of Korean reunification is extremely tumultuous and if the United States continues to enjoy an influential status in world politics. The aforementioned task force of the Council on Foreign Relations recommends that "a residual U.S. military presence" in post-unification Korea would make a meaningful contribution to the peace and stability of the region as a whole.

Viewed from the realistic perspective of a unified Korean government, a military and political alignment with the United States would be advantageous for a variety of reasons:

(1) To obtain Washington's support and cooperation, which would serve as a source of political legitimacy and internal stability;
(2) To rely upon its alliance with the single remaining superpower to counterbalance the actual or imagined ambitions of other major powers;
(3) To use its stable relationship with the United States as an effective means for securing international economic cooperation; and
(4) To seek U.S. "good offices" as leverage to settle international disputes and disagreements.

In pursuing alignment with the United States, however, the Korean government may face a number of potential disadvantages and challenges because this relationship could:

(1) Provide an opportunity or excuse for U.S. interference in Korea's internal affairs;

(2) Become a source of anti-U.S. sentiment and agitation;

(3) Complicate Korea's relations with China and Russia and, to a lesser extent, with Japan;

(4) Encourage a strategic alliance or partnership between China and Russia against U.S. hegemony in the region; and

(5) Involve Korea in disputes between the United States and other Pacific powers.

It would be in the best interests of the United States to sustain its alliance with a unified Korea in order to facilitate a smooth process of Korean national integration, stabilize the regional order, protect Japan's security interests, and enhance America's economic benefits. Moreover, the United States can utilize its effective alignment with Korea as a symbol of its global leadership and commitment. It would be necessary for the U.S. government to carefully persuade the general public and Congress about the continuing importance of U.S. alignment with Korea.

In order to address the concerns and misgivings that other Pacific powers may have in regard to the U.S. alignment with a unified Korea, it will be advisable for the United States and Korea to recognize each of the Pacific power's unique interests and sensitivities. In particular, they should ensure that no U.S. troops will be deployed in northern Korea; if they are dispatched there for military campaigns, humanitarian intervention, or peacekeeping operations, they should be withdrawn as soon as the situation permits. They also would need to modify the U.S.-South Korea Mutual Security Treaty, the Combined Forces Command, and the United Nations Command so that the United States would have a lower military profile in Korea. Additionally, the United States should encourage Korea to accept a "one-plus-four" treaty with all four Pacific powers in the manner of the "Treaty on the Final Settlement with Respect to Germany"[48] and to conclude bilateral treaties of peace, friendship, and cooperation with China, Russia, and Japan. In multilateral settings, a regional or global consortium would need to be formed to assist Korea's economic reconstruction—as exemplified by the Korean Peninsula Energy Development Organization (KEDO) and by the IMF-led rescue program for South Korea. The Asia-Pacific Economic

Cooperation (APEC) forum and World Trade Organization (WTO) trade agreements would also have to be adjusted in consideration of a unified Korea. Significantly, the international arms control and disarmament regimes (such as the Comprehensive Nuclear Test Ban Treaty, Missile Technology Control Regime, and Nuclear Nonproliferation Treaty) would have to be applied to the entire Korean Peninsula. Confidence-building measures would need to be expanded in the region and a nuclear-weapons free zone established. Finally, the Pacific powers should institutionalize a new regional security forum or amplify the ASEAN-Regional Forum (ARF) so that all four powers share a sense of participation as well as responsibility in guaranteeing Korea's security and in promoting regular consultations and policy coordination among the major powers. In this connection it is important to heed the neorealist proposition about the questions of absolute and relative gains. The United States and Korea should make every concerted effort to ensure that China, Japan, and Russia would not only receive "absolute gains" from the U.S.-Korean alignment, but also perceive no significant asymmetry in their respective "relative gains."

Although the Chinese would be disappointed by Seoul's "victory" over Pyongyang, they are likely to assume a pragmatic and adaptive posture toward the alignment between the United States and Korea. In the immediate post-unification period, they can be persuaded to accommodate the U.S.-Korean alignment as a necessary transitional arrangement to support Korea's internal order and to promote regional stability. Banning Garrett and Bonnie Glaser report that a Chinese specialist of Korean affairs expects U.S. troops to serve as a buffer or reassurance against any armed animosity between Korea and Japan.[49] Moreover, it can be argued that the U.S.-Korean alignment would discourage nuclear proliferation in East Asia, lessen Japan's need for rearmament, and weaken Russia's desire for military assertiveness in the region.

It is possible that China and Korea, as any other contiguous dyad, would have tensions and disagreements (especially if the process of unification is not completely satisfactory to China), but both states are likely to be attentive to each other's national interests and to develop a peaceful, friendly, and interdependent relationship. More specifically, the Korean government would be well advised to deal with a number of bilateral issues (such as the security and usage of the Yalu and Tumen Rivers, the status of ethnic Koreans in China, protection of China's vested economic interests in Northern Korea, the joint hydroelectric power plants, border trade, and repatriation of Korean refugees) in the most conciliatory and constructive fashion.

Although Japan has not favored Korea's unification by military or peaceful means, it would be in Japan's interest to support the U.S.-Korean alignment, to offer substantial financial assistance to Korea, to overcome the legacy of colonialism, and to nurture a mutually beneficial relationship.[50] Tied to U.S. military alliance, both Japan and Korea are expected to cooperate in regional security affairs and to resolve a number of sensitive matters, including territorial disputes, fishing and other economic issues, the status of Koreans in Japan, and the disposition of the pro-Pyongyang Federation of Korean Residents in Japan.

So long as Russia is preoccupied with its internal problems, it may not play an important role in post-unification Korea, but it opposes a world dominated by any one power and favors a multipolar system. The United States and Korea should attempt to obtain Russia's understanding and cooperation in regard to their alignment policy.

Nonalignment

If the United States and Korea mismanage their political and military alignment and alienate Korea's important internal forces and/or major external players in such a way that tension and instability dramatically escalate in and around the peninsula, it is conceivable that there would emerge a movement to swing the pendulum of Korea's foreign policy from alignment to nonalignment (namely, neutralization). As Cyril Black and other scholars suggest, neutralization is attractive to relatively minor states that "by reason of strategic position or symbolic political value, have become or threaten to become the focal points of contests for control or dominant influence between principal regional or global rivals."[51] It is regarded as a method of conflict management and diplomatic compromise in a situation where the struggle for control of minor states is dangerous and destructive.

In fact, the United States applied this concept in the top-secret National Security Council document (NSC 170/1), "U.S. Objectives and Courses of

Action in Korea," approved by President Dwight Eisenhower on November 20, 1953.[52] The document specified that the United States should seek a "unified and neutral Korea" under a "free, independent and representative government" and with a "self-supporting economy." To this end the United States was prepared to accept:

(1)   A unified Korea friendly to the United States, without U.S. or other foreign forces or bases in Korea;

(2)   U.S. and communist assurances of the territorial and political integrity of Korea under the ROK but foregoing all rights granted to the United States under a U.S.-Korea mutual assistance pact; and

(3)   A level of Korean armed forces sufficient for internal security and capable of defending Korean territory short of an attack by a major power.

Whereas the Joint Chiefs of Staff opposed Korea's neutralization at the NSC meetings, the Department of State argued that the neutralization of Korea would remove it as a political and military problem, favor the security of Japan, reduce the U.S. military and economic burden, and "make possible a strengthening of the military position of the free world in other areas."[53]

If its initial policy of alignment with the United States or any other Pacific power(s) were about to collapse, the government of a unified Korea may find neutralization an attractive policy option. Like Switzerland and Belgium, Korea has indeed been a focal point of contests and conflicts among its more powerful neighboring states and a *casus belli* of three major wars from the 1880s to the 1950s. In his influential essay "On Neutrality" written in 1885, Yu Kil Jun, a leading advocate of reform and modernization, viewed the United States as a distant and unreliable power that could not help Korea at a time of crisis. Yu proposed a collective agreement on Korean neutrality as a strategy for guaranteeing its political independence and territorial integrity and for developing "a more congenial, friendly diplomatic relationship among the nations."[54] Faced with an extreme predicament both at home and abroad, Korea's King Kojong first sought assistance from the United

States, but to no avail, and then pursued a policy of neutrality in the early 1900s. However, this did not save his dynasty due to Japan's aggressive moves and America's benign neglect.

Admittedly, the internal and external conditions of a unified Korea will be vastly different from those that prevailed a century ago. Nonetheless, if a unified Korea is confronted with a chaotic and volatile situation analogous to that of the 1880s and 1890s, or becomes disillusioned with the United States, the arguments advanced by Yu Kil Jun and his contemporaries suddenly may become persuasive to the troubled Korean leaders. They could expect to obtain a host of positive advantages from Korea's neutralization since it would protect Korea's political independence, territorial integrity, and diplomatic flexibility; avert potentially explosive debates and cleavages among Korean leaders over the country's foreign policy orientation; establish Korea's equidistant relations with all four Pacific powers without prejudice and seek a balance of power among them; and reduce conflicts among the Pacific powers over Korea and promote peace and stability in Northeast Asia.

At this time it is not quite clear as to how the Pacific powers individually or collectively would respond to a movement for Korea's neutralization. In general, as demonstrated in the case of Laos, China and Russia are likely to welcome and endorse Korea's neutralization because it would limit the pre-eminent influence of the United States, provide an "equal" opportunity for their activities, and establish a buffer zone for their respective security interests. While the Japanese prefer to see the continuation of the U.S.-Korean alignment, they may have no serious objections to the neutralization of Korea so long as a neutralized Korea prevents the ascendancy of Chinese or Russian influence and pursues a peaceful and friendly policy toward them.

The United States is most likely to encounter a dilemma between its desire to preserve alignment with a unified Korea as long as possible and the necessity not to veto Korea's neutralization if it is unavoidable. It would be painful for the United States to shift its traditional posture toward Korea, but neutralization would still be better than other possible alternatives, such as Korea's alignment with other Pacific powers, a region-wide counter-alliance against the United States, and/or a rapid escalation of international conflicts over Korea. As NSC document (170/1) suggests, the United States believes it could live with a unified, neutral, and friendly Korea that can protect U.S. national interests in the region.

If a unified Korea is neutralized by international agreements (as were Switzerland and Laos) or by self-neutralization (as in the case of Austria), it may encounter a number of potential disadvantages and pitfalls. It may have limited flexibility and dynamism in foreign affairs, lack an effective system of checks and balances among the major powers, bring about a "power vacuum" that leaves Korea vulnerable to outside interference, or lose the rationale for substantial foreign economic assistance. Ultimately, however, the viability of a unified and neutralized Korea will depend upon a reasonable degree of national consensus in Korea and a substantial congruence of interests and capabilities among the Pacific powers.

CONCLUSION

The changing relationships among the Pacific powers, which are bound together in a closely intertwined hexagonal linkage on the Korean Peninsula, will undoubtedly continue to exert a significant impact on the probability of Korean unification. In the post-Cold War era, all four Pacific powers have adopted a generally conciliatory and cooperative posture toward each other and have recognized the importance of protecting peace and stability in the Asia-Pacific region. In this context, the four powers share a common interest in discouraging military confrontations and nuclear proliferation on the Korean Peninsula, supporting peaceful cooperation between Seoul and Pyongyang, and ensuring that the process and consequences of Korean unification will not cause irreparable tensions and conflicts among them. Sustaining a concert of the Pacific powers, especially between the United States and China, will be crucial to the peaceful evolution of the Korean situation.

Yet to a great extent it is ultimately incumbent upon the leaders of both Koreas to determine which of the four scenarios will be appropriate for their relationship. It appears that they will overcome the status quo, seek peaceful coexistence, and attempt to avert both war and absorption in the near future. If the peninsula were to unify by war or absorption, however, a unified Korean government would be hard-pressed to adopt the painful measures that would be necessary to promote genuine national integration and to chart a peaceful, constructive, and assertive foreign policy. Even though one cannot completely rule out nonalignment (neutralization) as a potential policy choice for a unified Korea, it is widely believed that Korea would prefer to uphold the basic framework of Seoul's traditional alignment with Washington.

Speaking to the South Korean National Assembly in July 1993, President Clinton declared:

As the Cold War recedes into history, a divided Korea remains one of its most bitter legacies. Our nation has always joined yours in believing that one day Korea's artificial division will end. We support Korea's peaceful unification on terms acceptable to the Korean people. And when the reunification comes, we will stand beside you in making the transition on the terms that you have outlined.[55]

This statement reflected his hope or expectation that the Korean Peninsula would be unified sooner rather than later.

As promised by President Clinton, the United States is expected to facilitate the transition to a unified Korea and to support Korea's political independence and national security. In order to make sure that a unified Korea will enjoy economic prosperity and democratic practices, develop an appropriate self-defense capability, and assume a pivotal role in the Asia-Pacific region, the United States can take the lead in nurturing an effective system of cooperative relations among the Pacific powers and in promoting a set of regional institutions for economic interdependence and security coordination. As a country deeply involved in the initial division of Korea and in the prolonged maintenance of the rival Korean states, the United States at last will have an opportunity to help Korea become a united, viable, and peaceful state.

NOTES

1. For a historical survey, see Chae-Jin Lee and Hideo Sato, *U.S. Policy Toward Japan and Korea* (New York: Praeger, 1982), pp. 6–7.

2. See Dean Rusk's recollection in *Foreign Relations of the United States, 1945,* vol. 6 (Washington, D.C.: USGPO, 1969), p. 1039.

3. Dean Acheson, *The Korean War* (New York: W. W. Norton, 1971), p. 20.

4. On the Truman-MacArthur meeting, see *Foreign Relations of the United States, 1950,* vol. 7 (1976), p. 953.

5. For Mao's decisionmaking process, see Sergei N. Goncharov, John W. Lewis, and Xue Litai, *Uncertain Partners* (Stanford, Calif.: Stanford University Press, 1993); and Chen Jian, *China's Road to the Korean War* (New York: Columbia University Press, 1994).

6. For the armistice negotiations, see Rosemary Foot, *A Substitute for Victory* (Ithaca, N.Y.: Cornell University Press, 1990).

7. See Lee and Sato, *U.S. Policy Toward Japan and Korea,* p. 20.

8. Cited in Chae-Jin Lee, *China and Korea: Dynamic Relations* (Stanford, Calif.: Hoover Institution Press, 1996), p. 60.

9. See the text of the Sino-Soviet Joint Communiqué in *Beijing Review* (May 29–June 6, 1989).

10. Roh Tae Woo, *Korea: A Nation Transformed* (Elmsford, N.Y.: Pergamon Press, 1990), pp. 47–49.

11. See the text of the Sino-Soviet Joint Communiqué in *Beijing Review* (May 27–June 2, 1991).

12. Ibid.

13. See the English text in *Peace and Cooperation: White Paper on Korean Unification* (Seoul: Ministry of National Unification, 1996), pp. 200–207.

14. See Robert L. Gallucci, "The Agreed Framework: Advancing U.S. Interests with North Korea," *U.S. Department of State Dispatch* (December 12, 1994). On U.S. nuclear diplomacy, see Leon V. Sigal, *Disarming Strangers* (Princeton, N.J.: Princeton University Press, 1998).

15. For a discussion of the four scenarios, see Chae-Jin Lee, "The Future of Inter-Korean Relations," in *Patterns of Inter-Korean Relations,* ed. Bae Ho Hahn and Chae-Jin Lee (Seoul: Sejong Institute, 1999), pp. 253–71.

16. Kenneth Waltz, *Theory of International Politics* (New York: McGraw-Hill, 1979), p. 105.

17. Joseph Grieco, *Cooperation among Nations* (Ithaca, N.Y.: Cornell University Press, 1990), p. 40.

18. See Robert Powell, "Absolute and Relative Gains in International Relations Theory," *American Political Science Review* (December 1991), pp. 1303–20; Duncan Snidal, "Relative Gains and the Patterns of International Cooperation," *American Political Science Review* (September 1991), pp. 701–26; and John C. Mathews III, "Current Gains and Future Outcomes: When Cumulative Relative Gains Matter," *International Security* (Summer 1996), pp. 112–46.

19. Robert Axelrod, *The Evolution of Cooperation* (New York: Basic Books, 1984).

20. Robert A. Keohane, *After Hegemony* (Princeton, N.J.: Princeton University Press, 1984), p. 75.

21. For the text, see *Korea Herald*, February 26, 1998.

22. Bruce W. Bennett, "The Prospects for Conventional Conflict on the Korean Peninsula," *Korean Journal of Defense Analysis* (Summer 1995), pp. 96–127.

23. As cited in Don Oberdorfer, *The Two Koreas: A Contemporary History* (Reading, Mass.: Addison-Wesley, 1997), p. 314.

24. Edward A. Olsen, "Coping with the Korean Peace Process: An American View," *Korean Journal of Defense Analysis* (Winter 1997), p. 167.

25. Makoto Momoi, "The Improvement of US-North Korean Relations," *Korean Journal of Defense Analysis* (Winter 1996), p. 176.

26. Michael Green, "North Korean Regime Crisis: US Perspectives and Responses," *Korean Journal of Defense Analysis* (Winter 1997), p. 16.

27. *Defense White Paper 1998* (Seoul: Ministry of National Defense, 1999), p. 56.

28. Oberdorfer, *The Two Koreas: A Contemporary History*, p. 312.

29. As quoted in Banning Garrett and Bonnie Glaser, "China's Pragmatic Posture toward the Korean Peninsula," *Korean Journal of Defense Analysis* (Winter 1997), p. 75.

30. As cited in Alexander Z. Zhebin, "Russia and Four-Party Talks on Korea," *Korean Journal of National Unification,* vol. 6 (1997).

31. For a detailed explanation of the guidelines, see *Boei Hakusho [Defense of Japan]* (Tokyo: Defense Agency, 1998), pp. 231–51.

32. See Hajime Izumi, "The Present North Korean Situation and Its Implications for Japan," *Korean Journal of National Unification*, vol. 6 (1997), pp. 63–75; and Michael O'Hanlon, "Stopping a North Korean Invasion: Why Defending South Korea Is Easier than the Pentagon Thinks," *International Security* (Spring 1998), pp. 135–70.

33. As quoted and discussed in Chae-Jin Lee, "U.S. Policy Toward North Korea," *Korea and World Affairs* (Fall 1996), p. 375.

34. *Los Angeles Times*, March 30, 1996.

35. Nicholas Eberstadt, "Hastening Korean Reunification," *Foreign Affairs* (March/April 1997), p. 79.

36. Olsen, "Coping with the Korean Peace Process: An American View," p. 161.

37. Aidan Foster-Carter, "North Korea: All Roads Lead to Collapse," in *Economic Integration of the Korean Peninsula*, ed. Marcus Noland (Washington, D.C.: Institute for International Economics, 1998), pp. 27–38.

38. Selig S. Harrison, "Promoting a Soft Landing in Korea," *Foreign Policy* (Spring 1997), pp. 57–75.

39. *Los Angeles Times*, June 12, 1998.

40. Marcus Noland, "Why North Korea Will Muddle Through," *Foreign Affairs* (July/August 1997), pp. 105–18.

41. Chae-Jin Lee, "The Evolution of China's Two-Korea Policy," in Bae Ho Hahn and Chae-Jin Lee, eds, *The Korean Peninsula and the Major Powers* (Seoul: Sejong Institute, 1998), pp. 115–46.

42. See Kyongmann Jeon, "The Likelihood and Implications of a North Korean Attack on the South," in *Economic Integration of the Korean Peninsula*, ed. Noland, pp. 9–26. A leading Chinese specialist of Korean politics asserts that "aiding North Korea is aiding us because its downfall will be disastrous to our interests." Interview with author, August 3, 1998.

43. Alexander Zhebin, "Russia and Korean Unification," *Asian Perspective* (Fall–Winter 1995), p. 186.

44. Victor D. Cha, "Korean Unification: The Zero-Sum Past and the Precarious Future," *Asian Perspective* (Winter 1997), p. 82.

45. See Council on Foreign Relations, *Managing Change on the Korean Peninsula* (June 1998).

46. Garrett and Glaser, "China's Pragmatic Posture toward the Korean Peninsula."

47. James A. Winnefeld et al., *A New Strategy and Fewer Forces: The Pacific Dimension* (Santa Monica, Calif.: RAND, 1991), p. 13.

48. For the text, see Konrad H. Jarausch and Volker Gransow, ed., *Uniting Germany* (Providence, R.I.: Berghahn Books, 1994), pp. 204–08.

49. Garrett and Glaser, "China's Pragmatic Posture toward the Korean Peninsula."

50. For a discussion of close alignment between Korea and Japan, see Wolf Mendl,

Japan's Asia Policy: Regional Security and Global Interests (New York: Routledge, 1995).

51. Cyril E. Black, Richard A. Falk, Klaus Knorr, and Oran R. Young, *Neutralization and World Politics* (Princeton, N.J.: Princeton University Press, 1968), pp. v–vi.

52. *Foreign Relations of the United States 1952–1954*, vol. 15, part 2 (Washington, D.C.: USGPO, 1984), pp. 1620–24.

53. On discussions at the NSC, see Donald Stone Macdonald, *U.S.-Korean Relations from Liberation to Self-Reliance: The Twenty-Year Record* (Boulder, Colo.: Westview Press, 1992), pp. 16–19.

54. For the English text, see In K. Hwang, *One Korea Via Permanent Neutrality: Peaceful Management of Korean Unification* (Cambridge, Mass.: Schenkman Books, 1987), pp.146–51. For Yu's publications and activities, see Young Ick Lew, *Hanguk konhyondaesa* [Treatises on Modern Korean History] (Seoul: Ilchogak, 1992), pp. 82–86, 129–47, and 159–61.

55. William Clinton, "Fundamentals of Security for a New Pacific Community," *U.S. Department of State Bulletin* (July 19, 1993).

3

Discerning North Korea's Intentions

Chuck Downs

A peculiar feature of political analysis concerning the Korean Peninsula is the debate over the intentions behind North Korea's proposals. Inductive logic alone would suggest that North Korea desires to extend its system throughout Korea, and the North's ideological commitment to a unified Korea under communist control has often been stated. In 1975, Kim Il Sung wrote that North Korea's "objective is to carry out a people's democratic revolution against U.S. imperialism and fascist rule in South Korea, over-throwing the corrupt colonial and semi-feudal social system and setting up a people's democratic regime on its grave."[1] But that explicitly stated goal has been so elusive for so many years and appears so impossible today that analysts outside the regime often persuade themselves that the regime has disposed of it.

The scholarly debate over the intentions behind the North's unification proposals rages—even though few governments have ever pursued an objective so consistently and openly as North Korea has in its struggle to bring South Korea under communist control, with violence if that would bring success. Both the history of the North's aggression and its ideological foundations reveal that violence is considered a legitimate, and indeed necessary, means of extending communism. Leninism, which Kim Il Sung called the "powerful weapon for all revolutionary people," posits violent revolution as a necessary stage in progress toward true communism. Lenin said that the existence of communist states side by side with capitalist states for a protracted period was "unthinkable" and "collisions" were "inevitable."[2]

Kim Il Sung theorized that eventual unification under communism would progress through stages, with the final stage being a violent clash. He believed the people of the South would shoulder the major portion of the burden for the revolution against their leaders: "The South Korean people cannot expect to win genuine freedom and liberation," Kim asserted, "...except by sweeping away U.S. imperialism and its stooges and seizing power by revolutionary and violent means."[3] Naturally, he saw the removal of American troops as a necessary step in the process toward the Communist Party's success in the South: "The peaceful unification of our country," he wrote, "can be materialized only after the U.S. imperialist aggressor army has been forced out of South Korea, and the South Korean people have overthrown the present puppet regime, and the progressive forces have come into power."[4]

Before the ultimate violent stage of Kim's theoretical revolution, North Korea sees the intervening periods of peace as opportunities to build up strength "to meet the great revolutionary event in full readiness."[5] Peaceful gestures, such as talks with the South, are useful to help create an environment conducive to North Korea's longer-range objectives.

North Korea has occasionally presented enticing proposals for unification that stir hopes and raise expectations. Patterns in this behavior, however, indicate that interests other than unification motivate the proposals. The North has rushed to conclude agreements with the South in order to reclaim control over the reunification issue when international initiatives were building momentum, especially in 1972 when the United States and China discussed their views on Korean unification during the Nixon-Zhou talks. It has made major proposals to take advantage of political instability and civil unrest in the South, from 1960 to 1962 and again in 1979 and 1980. North Korea has also generated North-South dialogue when it has needed to deflect international attention from acts of terror, following such attacks as the 1976 Panmunjom axe murders, the 1983 Rangoon bombing, and the 1987 downing of Korean Airlines flight 858. This chapter will explore how North Korea's intentions were revealed in three such instances.

In each of these situations, the North's proposals were designed to take advantage of specific opportunities. There is a pattern not only in the timing of North Korea's pursuit of dialogue, but also in the proposals themselves. When its control over unification measures was challenged by the momentum behind international initiatives, the North portrayed itself as an emerging anticolonialist nation struggling to maintain its sovereignty. It rushed to sign on to unenforceable arrangements, knowing it would benefit from illusory gestures and could not be held to compliance. During periods of political instability in the South, the North sought to portray itself as more genuinely democratic than the South in an effort to attract support among South Korea's disenfranchised opposition. Its proposals therefore focused on convening "grand national assemblies" comprising thousands of participants, seemingly affording an opportunity for broad-based political participation. When the objective was to distract the world's attention from its acts of terror, the North portrayed itself as eager to resolve tensions, not from remorse, but in order to escape accountability. It deflected attention from its crimes to its grievances, suggesting that the rationale for its acts of violence would end when national division ended and foreign troops withdrew.

THE SOUTH-NORTH COMMUNIQUÉ OF 1972

In 1972, a dramatic shift in the relationship between China and the United States prompted North Korea to change its tactic of refusing direct North-South talks on reunification. The Nixon-Zhou talks resulted in the Shanghai Communiqué of February 28, 1972, which seemed to usher in a new era in multilateral management of Northeast Asian security issues. The Shanghai Communiqué stated that "the United States will support efforts of the ROK to seek relaxation of tension and increased communication in the Korean Peninsula" and that China "firmly supports the eight-point program for the peaceful reunification of Korea put forward by the Government of the Democratic People's Republic of Korea on April 12, 1971."[6]

Both the United States and China sought not to offend their ally's sensitivities with this reaffirmation of standing policies, but the leaders of the Koreas were nevertheless motivated to bring Korean matters under their own control.

Secret meetings were accordingly arranged in Pyongyang and Seoul. Director of the ROK Central Intelligence Agency Lee Hu Rak met Kim Il Sung in Pyongyang on May 2–5, 1972. In a reciprocal exchange, Pak Song Chul, the vice premier of the DPRK, visited President Park Chung Hee in Seoul from May 29 to June 1. These secret meetings led to the startling public announcement on July 4 of the "South-North Communiqué."

These first South-North secret talks produced agreement on two principles that were essentially identical to the subsequent agreement reached between Kim Dae Jung and Kim Jong Il nearly 30 years later in June 2000. The principles stipulate that "unification shall be achieved through independent efforts without being subject to external imposition or interference" and "through peaceful means, and not through the use of force against each other."[7] These terms set aside demands that North Korea had previously made regarding political representation that would have given the North's smaller population disproportionate power. They also substituted the North's calls for removal of foreign forces with a general commitment to nonaggression.

South Korea's chief negotiator, Lee Hu Rak, obtained three specific concessions. At his initiative, Kim Il Sung agreed that the two sides would not: (1) slander or defame each other; (2) make unilateral unification proposals for propaganda purposes; or (3) use their militaries to harass the other side. Lee also drove home the point that the Red Cross talks should be handled exclusively as a humanitarian matter, divorced from political manipulation.

The North wanted an agreement that would restore its claim to having advanced a method of reunification, thereby deflecting mounting pressure from international, and perhaps even domestic, sources clamoring for advancement of long-sought Communist-Party objectives. The South wanted progress on the question of reuniting family members and agreed to an acceptable North-South declaration in the process. The North got what it wanted.

Kim Il Sung proposed that to implement the objectives of the communiqué reductions should be made in the militaries on both sides and a "South-North Coordinating Committee" (SNCC) should be established, ostensibly to carry out the objectives of the agreements.[8] As would happen again in 2000, two authorized structures for discussions between North and South were to implement the 1972 Communiqué: the higher level, official South-North Coordinating Committee (SNCC) and Red Cross discussions. In the thirteen-month period following the communiqué, the two Koreas convened six North-South Coordinating Committee meetings, seven Red Cross plenary meetings, and numerous related subgroup meetings.

Despite the electrifying momentum behind the communiqué and the succeeding months of contact, however, both sets of talks failed. The North eventually returned to its long-term intractable demand—the removal of American troops from the South. Although the initial stages of these negotiations appeared so promising as to raise expectations, raising expectations seems to have been part of the North's longer-range strategy.

PHASES OF NORTH KOREAN NEGOTIATING BEHAVIOR

Two participants from the South's delegations, Lee Dong Bok, and Song Jong Hwan, wrote insightful analyses of what transpired during the talks. They identified phases in the negotiations during which the North made grand initial gestures, then hardened its posture, and ultimately condemned its opponents for not accepting its demands.

Lee Dong Bok perceived five negotiating stages—from the North's initial eagerness to conclude arrangements to the South's efforts to bring the North back to the table. He identified the five stages chronologically from November 1971 to the time of his writing in 1977, but the stages could also be characterized as: (1) getting to the table; (2) setting preconditions and terms for an agreement; (3) disputing the agreement's terms; (4) disavowing the agreement; and (5) fixing the blame on South Korea for the collapse of negotiations.

Song Jong Hwan's studies simplified these gradations to three phases of North Korean behavior during the period of active negotiation itself. As he described it:

In the first phase, the North Korean side induced its counterpart to negotiations and tried to reach "agreements in principle," the details of which could be worked out later. In the second phase, the North tried to secure advantageous detailed agreements by interpreting the above "agreements in principle" in arbitrary ways. In the last phase, in the case of disagreements, North Korea discontinued the talks unilaterally while blaming the failure of agreements on the South Korean side."[9]

The pattern Lee and Song described has appeared in numerous negotiations with North Korea before and since.

Phase One: Agreeing in Principle

In the opening stage of dialogue following the 1972 communiqué, the North's negotiators were "very friendly to the South Korean delegation members."[10] "The first round of meetings in Pyongyang and the second round in Seoul were held in a festive mood," South Korean observers noted, "because of the emotions arising from the fact that for the first time since the territorial division, large delegations from the South and the North crossed the boundary line. Various congratulatory events prevailed over the conference itself."[11]

"During the first period every meeting produced an agreement," Song Jong Hwan observed. "The two sides came to speedy conclusions on such matters as agenda, venue, date, and other procedural matters."[12] Throughout this phase, Kim Il Sung showed a personal interest in the dialogue. When the South Korean delegations visited Pyongyang, he met with them and hosted a luncheon in their honor.

The North "tried to disguise its image of a closed society as well as its violent revolutionary line," Song noted, "by proposing principles of freedom and democracy and showing a positive attitude on peaceful unification."[13] The session in Seoul actually concluded with the delegates agreeing to "adhere to the principles of democracy and freedom, the spirit of the South-North Joint Communiqué, brotherly love and the Red Cross humanitarianism in solving all problems envisaged in the agenda."[14]

Phase Two: Reinterpreting the Agreement

For North Korea, the task that follows the conclusion of an agreement may be to guarantee that it is not implemented, or to pursue a more advantageous arrangement. The second phase, in which the North reverses its approach and puts obstacles in the path of negotiations, began to emerge in the December 1, 1972 plenary meeting of the implementing structure—the SNCC. Even though the ink on the implementing procedures agreement was barely dry, the North demanded that the SNCC be reorganized.

By the time of the next SNCC plenary session, the reversal in the North's attitude was undeniable. Lee Dong Bok observed that North Korea became increasingly reluctant to hold the SNCC plenary meetings on schedule. The second meeting was to have been held in Pyongyang some time before the end of February, but North Korea postponed it until March 14–16, 1973.[15]

A week before the SNCC session in Pyongyang, the North created an incident that would undermine the negotiations and bring attention to their claim that the United States was responsible for Korea's continued division.

On February 27, 1973, the United Nations Command had informed North Korea, in accordance with long-standing practice, that a South Korean work party would replace military demarcation line markers—a routine maintenance detail—in the central sector of the DMZ. The task had been discussed with North Korea in advance, as has been standard practice. On March 7, North Korean guards fired on the work party. Attacking from a North Korean guard post in broad daylight, the North Koreans killed a South Korean Army officer and a sergeant and wounded a third soldier. The killings occurred while the South Korean delegation to the second SNCC plenary session was near the DMZ—transiting through Panmunjom on its way north for the talks.

When the South's delegates arrived for the second SNCC plenary session, North Korea did not supply the customary helicopters to ferry the delegates from Kaesong to Pyongyang. Furthermore, Kim Il Sung declined to meet them. "Without Kim Il Sung's personal participation," Lee Dong Bok noted, "the second meeting was destined from the outset to be merely a 'talk show.'"[16]

At the conference table, the North, having lost interest in trying to straighten out the functions of the SNCC, dismissed the South's efforts to develop implementing procedures. Contending that "unless the state of military confrontation between the two sides is removed first, no genuinely trustworthy dialogue can take place," the North's chief delegate, Pak Sung Chul, set out a five-point proposal dealing with military issues and demanded that his proposal be discussed before any other matters.[17] The points included well-worn propaganda from the North Korean playbook: limitations on South Korea's military size, weaponry, and operations; a demand for the withdrawal of American forces; and a call for a peace treaty to replace the armistice agreement.

North Korea also demanded that a new institution be established with responsibilities duplicating the functions of the SNCC. It called for a North-South Political Negotiation Conference "to resolve the problem of unification." Alternately calling it a "General National Congress" and a "Joint Meeting of Representatives of Political Parties and Social Organizations in the North and South of Korea," the North envisioned an assembly attended by an equal number of delegates from both sides representing "all political parties, social organizations, and individuals of various classes." Its size alone would have made it unwieldy; it was to have between 700 and 3,000 members.

To drive home the propaganda that South Korea's government was not truly democratic, the North demanded that a reputed underground communist network in South Korea be recognized as a legitimate political party and fully represented at the proposed assembly. Furthermore, the North argued that anticommunist parties did not genuinely support true unification and therefore should be barred from participation.[18]

The Red Cross talks were similarly distorted to focus on North Korea's demands. At the Red Cross meeting in Seoul, May 9–10, 1973, the North Korean Red Cross demanded that the South abrogate its anticommunist law and its national security law, and disband its anticommunist agencies and organizations. The North insisted that North Korean "expounders" should be sent South "to every ri or dong" (the lowest administrative units) to engage in "publicity activities." The North's proposal would have meant that some 36,000 North Korean cadres would travel into the South, while 4,300

South Korean officials could visit the North.[19]

The chief South Korean Red Cross delegate, Lee Bom Sok, told the North Koreans that their "unreasonable and unrealistic" proposals were "outright interference in the internal affairs of the Republic of Korea." The North was not only intruding into matters of the South's domestic policy, but was demanding that alterations in policy be made "as conditions for dialogue." "It is ironic," Song Jong Hwan observed, "that a country so resistant of outside influence would feel it could recommend settlement of military problems, improvement of legal conditions and social circumstances in South Korea,..." [20]

Phase Three: Blaming South Korea for the Failure of the Talks

By the time of the third plenary meeting of the SNCC, June 12–15, 1973, North Korea had unalterably hardened its approach. In an effort to revive North Korea's interest, South Korea proposed an extensive program of economic exchanges. On June 13, President Park Chung Hee issued a "Declaration for Peace and Unification" that might reasonably have been expected to reignite North Korea's interest in dialogue.

The declaration was meant to reassure the North of the South's devotion to peaceful unification as "the supreme task," its commitment to noninterference and nonaggression, and its general pursuit of "peace and good neighborliness." In a major gesture to the North, the declaration also offered the provision that "South Korea will not object to North Korea's dual admittance in the United Nations, provided that it does not hinder national unification; [and] even before North Korea's admittance into the United Nations, South Korea will not be opposed to its also being invited to attend the United Nations General Assembly's deliberations on the Korean question." [21]

For the North, however, the dialogue had outlived its usefulness. It refused to receive incoming calls over the South-North direct telephone line, so additional meetings could not be scheduled.[22] The executive council was suspended in June after three meetings. There was little hope that even the humanitarian objectives dreamed of in July of the previous year—reuniting families from North and South—would ever occur. At the seventh plenary session of the Red Cross delegations, held July 11–13, the South put forward a new proposal for groups from both sides to visit tombs in the South and North, but the North declined this overture as well.

What North Korea Gained by Halting Talks

North Korea ended dialogue with the South when everything seemed to be going its way. In 1975, international tours by its highest-ranking officials resulted in formal diplomatic recognition of the DPRK by many emerging third world countries at the expense of the ROK. Its entrance into the Nonaligned Movement was unanimously approved while the ROK's application was rejected. A declaration adopted at the Lima, Peru meeting of foreign ministers of the Nonaligned Movement called for withdrawal of foreign forces from South Korea and replacement of the armistice with a peace treaty.[23]

More significantly, the 1975 debate in the United Nations advanced the notion that each of the Koreas had an equivalent claim to political legitimacy. In November, the UN General Assembly adopted two contradictory resolutions. The pro-DPRK resolution called for the parties to the armistice agreement to replace it with a peace agreement, the dissolution of the United Nations Command, and the withdrawal of all foreign troops stationed in South Korea under the UN flag. The pro-ROK resolution urged the four parties directly concerned with the Korean armistice agreement to initiate talks by January 1, 1976, aimed at dissolving the United Nations Command.[24]

During the period following the joint communiqué, North Korea had been able to deflate notions of "peaceful coexistence" advocated by the Soviet Union, isolate the Korean question from the rapprochement being pursued between Beijing and Washington, seize the initiative from the ROK for advancing reunification, portray the ROK as incapable of negotiating in its own right, and demand withdrawal of American forces as its single most important precondition for continued dialogue.

The DPRK had succeeded in establishing a new context for the international debate: the international community had expressed its desire for the termination of the UN Command; the ROK could no longer cite the UN declarations of 1949 as recognizing its exclusive political legitimacy; the ROK government, heir to deeply held anticolonial convictions, was being portrayed as a colony itself and ridiculed by the emerging anticolonialist majority at the UN; and finally, pressure to conclude a permanent peace arrangement had been applied equally to all parties, despite the fact that it was the DPRK's refusal to accept the UN's role in guaranteeing peace that had stymied peace from the start.[25]

TAKING ADVANTAGE OF INSTABILITY IN THE SOUTH

Periods of domestic instability in South Korea are not the wisest times for the ROK to enter into North-South dialogue. Yet when President Jimmy Carter visited South Korea on July 1, 1979, he persuaded Park Chung Hee to offer North Korea the opportunity for three-way talks. Park reluctantly agreed, believing that the North would dismiss the idea, and that he might win some leverage with President Carter, whom he was trying to dissuade from proceeding with American troop withdrawals.[26] Park was right about the North's reaction; it seized the opportunity to say that the key issues, withdrawal of U.S. forces from South Korea, and replacement of the Korean armistice agreement with a peace agreement, were matters to be resolved between the United States and North Korea "who are the actual parties to the armistice agreement."[27] Those North Korean arguments against North-South dialogue are standard components of their international propaganda, yet North Korea sets them aside when it perceives an advantage in doing so. In the case of the June 2000 summit, much has been made of Kim Jong Il's willingness to demure on the question of American troop presence, but past North Korean performance suggests such lapses in ideological rigidity are often temporarily pursued when North Korea so wishes.

On October 26, 1979, South Korea's political situation became more unstable when the head of the South Korean CIA, Kim Jae Kyu, assassinated President Park at a private dinner party. An interim government under Prime Minister Choi Kyu Hah was formed under martial law but was replaced in December when Major General Chun Doo Hwan emerged as the leading power in the ROK Army. Half a year later, South Korean protests against Chun Doo Hwan's martial law continued to inspire violent protests in a number of South Korean cities. North Korea saw these developments as an opportunity to propose talks on reunification. On January 12, 1980, it sent letters to eleven prominent political, military, and religious leaders across South Korea offering new opportunities for dialogue between the North and South including a meeting of prime ministers. South Korean Prime Minister Shin Hyon Hwak agreed to hold working-level meetings in Panmunjom to work out the details for the proposed meeting.

In keeping with the pattern noted by Lee and Song, the North Koreans moved from proposing, to disrupting, and then terminating the talks. Preparatory meetings were held from February until they broke down in August 1980. By that time, President Chun had suppressed much of the protests in the South and held firm control. Although it had initiated the talks when South Korea was unstable, by September the North decided it would rather distance itself from the Chun regime than negotiate with it. The North Koreans refused to host the eleventh meeting in Panmunjom on September 26, 1980, saying they would not deal with Chun's "military fascist clique."[28] In other words, while the North initially exploited instability as an opportunity to push their objectives and probe conditions in the South, when they discovered another means to exploit the South's instability, they pursued that instead. Their intention was to promote instability, not dialogue.

DEFLECTING INTERNATIONAL OPPROBRIUM

In an effort to undermine the 1988 Seoul Olympics, two North Korean agents posing as Japanese tourists planted a time bomb in an overhead compartment on Korean Airlines flight 858. The agents disembarked in Abu Dhabi and the plane continued on to Seoul. The bomb exploded in flight on November 29, 1987, killing the plane's 115 passengers. The North Korean agents were unexpectedly detained in Bahrain, where their forged travel documents came under scrutiny. When arrested, the two attempted to commit suicide, consistent with North Korean special operations training. The elderly male terrorist succumbed. A policewoman, however, slapped the poison from the mouth of the 25-year old female terrorist, Kim Hyun Hui, and Kim lived to tell the story of North Korea's treachery. Under interrogation, she reportedly explained that the attack had been ordered and directed by Kim Il Sung's son and successor, Kim Jong Il, in frustration over the North's unsuccessful attempt to block the holding of the Olympic games.[29]

Having committed an act of terror in midair against innocent civilians, and having lost face to South Korea's success, the North returned to the table for dialogue in order to refurbish its international image. It attended six preparatory North-South contacts to lay the foundation for parliamentary talks and a planning session for a North-South summit.

THE RECONCILIATION AND DENUCLEARIZATION AGREEMENTS OF 1992

In the late 1980s, North Korea's communist allies began to see that their own interests were more closely connected to South Korea's burgeoning economy and diplomatic openness than to the North's unproductive reclusiveness. The Soviet Union formally recognized South Korea in September 1990 and China followed suit in 1992. In spite of Kim Il Sung's condemnation of cross-recognition for almost two decades, when it became clear that its allies would no longer enforce Pyongyang's objections, North Korea took a seat in the United Nations simultaneously with South Korea on September 17, 1991.

Dialogue between North and South yielded some success in the years immediately following the Seoul Olympics. After a series of six meetings between ROK Prime Minister Chung Won Shik and DPRK Premier Yon Hyong Muk, two agreements were signed in 1991: (1) the Agreement on Reconciliation, Nonaggression, and Exchanges and Cooperation between the South and North, and (2) the Joint Declaration of the Denuclearization of the Korean Peninsula. Both entered into force on February 19, 1992, after endorsement by Presidents Roh Tae Woo and Kim Il Sung.

Like most forward movement in negotiations with North Korea, the agreements of the early 1990s came about only after North Korea recognized that its alternatives were considerably less attractive. Even still, they would stand only as long as it suited North Korea's objectives.

FURTHER PROBLEMS OF IMPLEMENTING THE AGREEMENTS

The agreements negotiated in 1991 and signed in 1992 addressed an extensive list of major issues between the two rival states and generated substantial enthusiasm among those who sought peace. In dealing with North Korea, however, the appearance of progress cannot be construed as evidence of progress.

The Joint Declaration of the Denuclearization of the Korean Peninsula, like the South-North Communiqué 20 years earlier, generated considerable fanfare and excitement. North and South agreed not to "test, manufacture, produce, receive, possess, store, deploy or use nuclear weapons" and to "use nuclear energy solely for peaceful purposes." Both sides agreed they would "not possess nuclear reprocessing and uranium enrichment facilities," and would verify denuclearization of the Korean Peninsula through mutual inspections. The agreement seemed to hold great promise for tension reduction on the Korean Peninsula; its terms and coverage were even more comprehensive than the agreements that emerged from the June 2000 summit. Unfortunately, in retrospect, it appears that the 1992 agreements merely provide another example of "phase one" behavior in North Korea's negotiating tactics. Trying to implement the much-heralded agreement would, unfortunately, pass through the familiar stages of reinterpretation and disavowal within the next year.

The denuclearization declaration stated that South and North Korea would "establish and operate a South-North Joint Nuclear Control Commission within one month."[30] Lee Dong Bok, who had been involved in the frustrating effort to implement the 1972 agreement, would find himself in a similar position two decades later when, in the capacity of special assistant to South Korean Prime Minister Chung Won Shik, he tried to persuade North Korea to agree to nuclear inspections by the Joint Nuclear Control Commission.[31] Like the implementing arrangements of the 1972 communiqué, the implementing arrangements of the 1992 agreements came to naught.

The agreement also stated that inspections would be permitted of "objects selected by the other side and agreed upon between the two sides, in accordance with procedures and methods to be determined by the South-North Joint Nuclear Control Commission." That provision requiring mutual agreement would effectively bar enforcement, just as similar provisions of the armistice agreement had in the 1950s.

CRISIS CAN BRING NORTH KOREA TO THE TABLE, BUT DOES IT CHANGE NORTH KOREA'S INTENTIONS?

The DPRK pursues its diplomatic objectives in North-South dialogue skillfully. At various times it seems accommodating or unyielding, belligerent or peaceful, bombastic or pleading. But in every instance, after North Korea obtains benefits simply by agreeing to engage in talks, the process of dialogue itself ends on terms dictated by North Korea, in stalemate, or in an unenforceable agreement. In almost every standoff, the issues are brought to focus on one final point: the North's precondition that American troops withdraw and foreign military assistance to the South cease.

The consistency with which U.S. troop withdrawal is used by North Korea as the deal stopper in North-South dialogue reveals two intentions: the North's objective is not so much to proceed toward unification as it is to focus attention on its singular demand; and the North wishes to make the South vulnerable more than it wishes to make Korea unified. Dialogue could have encouraged progress toward reunification under many of the arrangements that were discussed in North-South talks: South Korea has been extraordinarily flexible, but North Korea has repeatedly chosen to terminate dialogue because the South will not agree to undermine its own security.

The DPRK's approach may also demonstrate something far more ominous. North Korea's persistent effort to turn the focus of dialogue to the question of withdrawal of American troops is wholly consistent with an intention of making the entire peninsula vulnerable to Leninist methods of taking power. While the rest of the world dismisses with patient, patronizing, confidence North Korea's objective of sparking revolution in the South, the regime in the North nevertheless clings to this objective and designs its negotiating strategy accordingly.

North Korea's rhetoric on reunification objectives is published in plain sight, but its meaning is not always apparent. As recently as June 13, 2000, the first day of the inter-Korean summit, Pyongyang's news service said, "Struggle against the U.S. strategy for world supremacy is the only way for ensuring global peace and security and building a free and prosperous, new world."[32] And on June 19, North Korean papers stated, "The United States should pull its aggression troops out of South Korea unconditionally and immediately for the sake of peace and reunification of Korea and peace and security in Asia and the rest of the world."[33]

After the summit, Pyongyang media intoned: "If all the Koreans firmly unite as one on the basis of patriotism, guided by the principle of national independence, they can successfully solve the issue of national reunification, the cherished desire of the nation. The principle of peaceful reunification is the basic way of solving the issue of national reunification in conformity with the unanimous desire of the whole nation and the world's peace-loving people."[34]

It should not be surprising that North Korea would moderate its rhetoric to take full advantage of different circumstances. What is surprising is how frequently and how easily analysts forget North Korea's past performance and lull themselves into a false impression that the North's more reassuring gestures actually constitute genuine steps toward peaceful reunification.

The current explanation of the North's intentions, in vogue in Washington and Seoul, posits that North Korea is a desperate nation willing to accommodate foreign interests in order to obtain economic benefits. The Clinton and Kim Dae Jung administrations therefore conclude that North Korea has changed its intentions in light of its desperate circumstances and can be given economic assistance without adverse consequences. Yet North Korea has published this view of its dealings with nations that give it economic assistance: "The imperialists' 'aid' which they term 'greatly helpful' to the progress of other countries and nations is nothing but a noose for plunder and subjugation. . . . Any attempt to solve issues with the help of imperialists is little short of leaving one's own destiny to a herd of ferocious wolves."[35]

A review of past periods of illusory progress in North-South talks suggests that the euphoria brought on by the June 2000 summit in Pyongyang between South Korean President Kim Dae Jung and North Korea's Chairman of the Defense Commission Kim Jong Il will in all likelihood end in frustration. That is, frustration for the South, but only after the South has provided substantial economic assistance to the North.

Dialogue in the past has advanced few, if any, concrete steps toward unification, but it has served the North's interests by aggravating political instability in the South, exciting Korean nationalistic zeal, portraying the Republic of Korea as incapable of advancing reunification, and characterizing the presence of American troops as the single most important obstacle to patriotic objectives. Dialogue has also served to quiet complaints and help the DPRK obtain economic assistance. Logic and experience alike suggest the regime's intention is not to surrender its founder's Leninist approach, but rather to attain these short-term goals and await "the great revolutionary event in full readiness."[36]

NOTES

1. Kim Il Sung, *For the Independent, Peaceful Reunification of Korea* (New York: International Publishers, 1975), p. 132.

2. Song Jong Hwan, "How the North Korean Communists Negotiate: A Case Study of the South-North Korean Dialogue of the Early 1970s," *Korea and World Affairs*, vol. 8, no. 3 (Fall 1984), p. 621, citing V. I. Lenin, *Selected Works*. Hereafter cited as Song, "How the North Korean Communists Negotiate."

3. *Kim Il-Sung Biography*, vol. 3, pp. 464–68, cited in Hak Joon Kim, *The Unification Policy of South and North Korea* (Seoul: Seoul National University Press, 1977) p. 250.

4. Kim Il Sung on the occasion of the Centenary of the Birth of V. I. Lenin, April 16, 1970, in Li Yuk Sa, ed., *Juche! The Speeches and Writings of Kim Il Sung* (New York: Grossman, 1972), p. 223.

5. Kim Il Sung, *For the Independent, Peaceful Reunification of Korea*, p. 133.

6. "The Shanghai Communiqué," February 28, 1972, in *Public Papers of the Presidents of the United States: Richard Nixon 1972* (Washington, D.C.: Government Printing Office, 1974), pp. 376–79.

7. "White Paper on South-North Dialogue in Korea," December 31, 1988 edition

(Seoul: National Unification Board, 1988), p. 59.

8. Song, "How the North Korean Communists Negotiate," pp. 637–38.

9. Ibid., p. 634.

10. Ibid., p. 614.

11. "White Paper on South-North Dialogue in Korea," p. 76.

12. Song, "How the North Korean Communists Negotiate," p. 636.

13. Ibid., p. 637.

14. "White Paper on South-North Dialogue in Korea," p. 85.

15. Lee Dong-Bok, "South-North Coordinating Committee of Korea: An Analytical Review of How It Was Originally Designed to Function and How It Has Failed to Function as Originally Planned," in Hak Joon Kim, *The Unification Policy of South and North Korea* (Seoul: Seoul National University Press, 1977), p. 313.

16. Ibid., p. 313.

17. "White Paper on South-North Dialogue in Korea," pp. 72–73.

18. Lee, "South-North Coordinating Committee of Korea," p. 315.

19. Song, "How the North Korean Communists Negotiate," p. 643.

20. Ibid., p. 655.

21. Hak Joon Kim, *The Unification Policy of South and North Korea* (Seoul: Seoul National University Press, 1977), pp. 353–54.

22. "White Paper on South-North Dialogue in Korea," p. 103.

23. Barry K. Gills, *Korea Versus Korea: A Case of Contested Legitimacy* (New York: Routledge, 1996), pp. 134–36.

24. Record of the UN General Assembly, 30th Session, Doc. No. A/10327.

25. Gills, *Korea Versus Korea*, p. 174.

26. Don Oberdorfer, *The Two Koreas: A Contemporary History* (Reading, Mass: Addison-Wesley, 1997), p. 105.

27. FBIS, Pyongyang KCNA International Service in English, July 10, 1979.

28. FBIS, KCNA, "DPRK Prime Minister's Statement," in Pyongyang Domestic Service, September 24, 1980.

29. A full account is provided in Oberdorfer, *The Two Koreas*, pp. 182–86. A United States Government publication gives the number of passengers killed as 135. U.S. policy analysts viewed the bombing as an ominous change from North Korea's attacks on prominent political personages and military personnel to civilians, but in fact civilians had been killed in numerous North Korean incursions, notably the Ulchin-Samchok raid of 1968. See Andrea Matles Savada, ed., *North Korea: A Country Study* (Washington, D.C.: Federal Research Division, Library of Congress, June

1993), p. 262.

30. "Text of Joint Declaration of the Denuclearization of the Korean Peninsula," in Young Whan Kihl, *Korea and the World* (Boulder, Colo.: Westview Press, 1994), Appendix C, pp. 347–48.

31. *South-North Dialogue in Korea*, No. 56, October 1992, p. 15.

32. Korean Central News Agency (KCNA), Pyongyang, June 13, 2000.

33. KCNA, Pyongyang, June 19, 2000.

34. KCNA, Pyongyang, June 23, 2000.

35. KCNA, Pyongyang, June 10, 2000.

36. Kim Il Sung, *For the Independent, Peaceful Reunification of Korea*, p. 133.

4

China and Korean Reunification—
A Neighbor's Concerns

Robert A. Scalapino

From the beginning of recorded history, China has figured prominently on the Korean Peninsula. Historically, Korea played two roles from a Chinese perspective. On the one hand, Korea was a tributary state into which Chinese culture flowed, and beyond that, a bridge enabling the transmission of that culture to Japan. On the other hand, Korea was a source of threat unless it could be controlled or neutralized, since it was a potential entry point for rival powers. China's recent involvement in Korea has lengthy antecedents, and will continue for the indefinite future.

At the onset of the twentieth century, Japan established its supremacy on the Korean Peninsula by defeating first China and then Russia. This left China on the outside and, more seriously, unable to defend Manchuria against Japanese expansion. However, World War II dramatically altered this situation. In the final months of the war, Chiang Kai-shek and China's allies proclaimed the independence of Korea as one of the commitments to follow Japanese defeat. Yet China was not in a position to play any role in the events that immediately followed the war. The division of Korea at the thirty-eighth parallel was a product of Soviet-American concurrence, intended to be temporary and possible only because the Cold War had not yet commenced. Korea might have been unified at the war's close, but it could have been unified only under Soviet aegis since the United States was no closer than Okinawa and thus without capacity to occupy any part of the peninsula immediately.

FROM WORLD WAR II TO THE END OF THE COLD WAR

The Korean War and its Aftermath

Chinese actions and policies toward the two Koreas have gone through many stages since World War II.[1] As is well known, no agreement could be reached on unification, and in 1948 two Korean states came into existence. With the communist victory in the Chinese civil war, it was inevitable that the Democratic People's Republic of Korea, established in August 1948, would be recognized as the sole legitimate state on the Korean Peninsula by the newly established People's Republic of China (PRC). In the heyday of its adherence to socialist international solidarity, Beijing found it natural to embrace its small communist neighbor. Kim Il Sung, after all, had been introduced to communism in China, having initially been affiliated with the Chinese Communist Party (CCP) as a youth.[2]

PRC leaders found very quickly that solidarity can exact a high price. Beijing was not centrally involved in the planning for the Korean War, although Mao and his colleagues were informed prior to the event. It remained for the Chinese, however, to rescue Kim and his comrades from looming defeat. The motives, to be sure, were not primarily those of comradely duty. Once again, as so often in the past, China's leaders saw the unity of Korea under an anticommunist government, with American power at its side, as a serious threat. Indeed, under those circumstances, Beijing's leaders feared that the Chinese nationalists would use this corridor to reopen the civil war.[3]

The Korean War cost Beijing heavily, with over 900,000 Chinese lives lost. It is not without reason that the Chinese subsequently referred to their relationship with the DPRK as one sealed in blood. Moreover, in the immediate postwar era, China contributed manpower and resources in the drive to rebuild North Korea, assisting in the construction of dikes, waterways, roads, and railways. Grants and credits for postwar rehabilitation reportedly totaled some $320 million between 1954 and 1957. This was the period when "as close as lips and teeth," the term used to describe PRC-DPRK relations, had its greatest relevance in modern times.

Yet even in these years there were problems. Waging a domestic struggle for political supremacy, Kim Il Sung purged both the Yenan and the Soviet factions of the Korean Worker's Party in 1956 and 1957. And it was in this period that *juche* (self-reliance) became the supreme symbol of the effort to achieve maximum DPRK independence.

The Rift in International Communism: North Korea Seeks Balance between China and the Soviet Union

After a few years, the international environment in the communist world changed dramatically. The cleavage between China and Russia that erupted toward the end of the 1950s and rapidly grew in intensity provided both a problem and an opportunity for North Korea. In which direction should it turn? Initially, Pyongyang tilted sharply toward Beijing, being critical of Russian overlordship and Khrushchevian revisionism. Yet the economic assistance of the Soviet Union and Eastern Europe had been enormously important to the DPRK. In addition, to place reliance solely on one external power was to run serious risks as well as to violate the North's code of conduct.

At a later point, therefore, North Korea opted for a strategy of attempting to play the two communist nations against each other, seeking a position as close to equidistant as possible. This strategy was abetted by the onset of the Chinese Cultural Revolution in 1965, a debacle that saw many of Pyongyang's old Chinese friends purged and Kim Il Sung himself denounced by Red Guards as an arch-revisionist. A border dispute further aggravated relations.

After Zhou Enlai regained control of China's Foreign Ministry, he made a visit to the DPRK in April 1970 and apologized for past misdeeds. Relations improved, and China continued to take positions on key issues in line with those of the DPRK. For example, Beijing regularly asserted that the Koreans themselves should resolve the Korean issue without outside interference. It was also critical of the presence of U.S. forces in South Korea—although some observers doubted that Beijing would really desire the risk of the two Koreas facing each other alone.

New complications, however, soon arose. The rapprochement achieved between the PRC and the United States beginning in 1971, together with signs that the United States would withdraw from Vietnam, troubled both Koreas and resulted in high level secret negotiations between North and South, from which came the July 4, 1972, South-North Joint Communiqué. That document pledged efforts by the two parties to achieve unification based upon independent actions without outside interference, by peaceful means, transcending differences, and seeking "great national unity."[4]

During the 1970s, however, Beijing made considerable efforts to maintain close relations with North Korea. China's crude oil shipments and other economic assistance were of great importance. Military exchanges were frequent, as was the sale of PRC military equipment (although Soviet military supplies remained vital). In April 1975 Kim Il Sung visited Beijing and in May 1978 Premier Hua Guofeng traveled to Pyongyang. Both trips emphasized the importance of the relationship at a time when the Soviet Union remained distrusted.

Yet the following decade saw North Korea again making a strenuous effort to achieve a balanced relationship with its two huge communist neighbors. In May 1984 Kim undertook his first trip to the USSR since 1961, just days after having received CCP General Secretary Hu Yaobang in Pyongyang. Economic and military pledges made in the 1961 USSR-DPRK Treaty of Friendship were fulfilled, and relations with Moscow seemed to advance. Kim made a second trip two years later to meet the new Soviet leader, Mikhail Gorbachev.

The Communist Powers Recognize South Korea

Unfortunately for the DPRK, however, both Russia and China were increasingly interested in advancing relations with a dynamic Republic of Korea, especially on the economic front. After 1985 Chinese trade with the South began to exceed that with the North. And Pyongyang had increasing problems in repaying its debts to the USSR for extensive military and other purchases. Using the 1988 Seoul Olympics as an opening wedge and taking advantage of the shifting economic balance, ROK President Roh Tae Woo pursued *Nordpolitik* with determination—and success.

The first shift was taken by the Gorbachev administration, which was increasingly anxious to avert an economic crisis by utilizing the ROK and other countries. In the fall of 1990, Soviet Foreign Minister Eduard Shevardnadze traveled to Pyongyang to tell the deeply angered North Korean leaders that Russia was preparing to establish diplomatic relations with the ROK, and would also abandon "friendship prices" in favor of the prevailing market rate in its trade with the DPRK. In the years that followed, DPRK-Russian relations remained minimal and largely frigid, with Gorbachev labeled an "arch-revisionist" and Moscow castigated for abandoning principles for money. Indeed, Pyongyang made it clear that it was disappointed in the failure of the abortive coup against Gorbachev in August 1991.

Despite repeated efforts, not until 1999 was there evidence that Moscow's efforts to reestablish a genuine two-Koreas policy were achieving some results. After 1990, the Russian government remained "outside" as far as DPRK leaders were concerned, although two Russians, Marshal Yazov and an official from the Russian Communist Party were able to meet Kim Jong Il separately after his father's death. Presumably "good" Russians—and especially those with military connections—were welcome.[5]

This situation provided China with clear advantages. It now remained Pyongyang's sole (more or less) ally and the principal source of certain economic supplies. Beijing, however, had no intention of catering wholly to the North's desires. The first major move was signaled in early 1991 when China indicated to North Korea that it could not veto the South's admission to the United Nations, thereby forcing the DPRK to accept dual Korean membership despite its earlier insistence that such a move would delay reunification. The establishment of PRC diplomatic relations with the ROK soon followed, and economic relations with the South flourished.[6] Indeed, a natural economic territory emerged as South Korean investors poured into China's Shandong Province, taking advantage of cheap labor and raw materials, with subsequent expansion to Jilin. By 1997 two-way trade between China and

South Korea topped $23.7 billion, a four-fold increase since 1992. In contrast, PRC-DPRK trade shrank to only $656.3 million in 1997. This represented 30 percent of North Korea's total trade.[7] For China, however, it was a very modest figure. Even at its height in the 1970s, PRC-DPRK trade represented only about 5 percent of China's total trade. Clearly, the economic factor was strongly favorable to the South in China's peninsular relations and it remains so despite the ROK's recent economic difficulties.

Nonetheless, PRC spokesmen were careful not to offend Pyongyang too egregiously. The old phrases "lips and teeth" and "sealed in blood" largely disappeared, but both sides formally reiterated their "friendship" and "cooperation" and sent messages to each other on key anniversaries. On occasion, spokesmen from each side spoke of their common opposition to "hegemonism" and the sanctity of national sovereignty. More importantly, as the economic crisis deepened in the North, China became ever more crucial to Pyongyang in terms of food aid and oil supplies. There were also rumors of Chinese assistance in space and related military programs, rumors vigorously denied by PRC authorities. Throughout the post-1978 period, Beijing arranged for certain North Korean visitors to tour its special economic zones and other reform sites, hoping to influence DPRK policymakers to emulate China's economic policies. However, the results were disappointing, at least initially.

CHINA SEEKS ROLE AS MODERATOR

Meanwhile, the period after early 1992 was marked by a renewed downward trend in North-South relations and in the general atmosphere relating to DPRK relations with the United States and the International Atomic Energy Agency (IAEA).[8] The December 1991 agreement between the ROK and DPRK and the accompanying agreement on denuclearization of the Korean Peninsula had offered the greatest hope for a reduction of tension since the Korean War. Moreover, the U.S. withdrawal of nuclear weapons from South Korea and its willingness to conduct a bilateral discussion with the North Koreans in New York in January 1992 suggested a new beginning on this front. Yet these hopes were short-lived. A combination of events, including growing tension over IAEA inspections, plans for renewed U.S.-ROK Team Spirit military exercises, and political divisions in both South Korea and the United States led to estrangement between the United States and the DPRK. All bilateral talks were suspended and on March 12, 1993, the DPRK announced that it was withdrawing from the Nuclear Nonproliferation Treaty.

During this period, China sought to serve as facilitator or moderator. Beijing made itself available as a point of contact, and after the breakdown in U.S.-DPRK discussions, PRC authorities supported bilateral contacts between the United States and the DPRK. It did not veto the UN resolution urging the DPRK to abide by the Nuclear Nonproliferation Treaty, but it warned against provocation and sanctions. Thus it was pleased when U.S.-DPRK negotiations got underway in 1994, with Robert Gallucci and Kang Sok Ju the key initial figures.

Recurrent crises occurred in the ensuing months. At a crucial point in early June 1994, China may have played a significant role in persuading the DPRK to resolve the nuclear problem by indicating privately to Pyongyang that despite its opposition to sanctions the weight of international opinion was such that Beijing might not be able to veto a UN sanctions resolution if the issue reached that stage. At the same time, moreover, China abstained rather than voting against an IAEA resolution to suspend technical assistance to the DPRK nuclear program.

As the food crisis grew more serious in North Korea, Beijing was used as a site for semiofficial North-South talks in June 1995, after which the ROK agreed to supply 150,000 tons of rice. While various contentious events disrupted the agreement, the promised aid was ultimately delivered. Subsequent reports from refugees, international relief agencies, and various other sources underscored the seriousness of the North's economic problems, although figures relating to human casualties, crop production, and factory closings are widely divergent. Different sources have reported that 900,000 to 2.4 million people died between 1995 and 1998 in the DPRK from starvation or malnutrition-related illnesses. Some figures are even higher.[9] Crop failures reduced yields by 30 to 60 percent, and numerous factories were closed or operated at a fraction of capacity. North Korean authorities blamed the crisis primarily upon adverse weather conditions, but the Soviet collapse was a major factor. Despite the constantly repeated claim of *juche*, the DPRK had depended heavily upon the Soviet Union for key materials and the acceptance of delayed payments. Above all, however, the crisis was a product of a deeply flawed economic strategy, one combining Stalinism and traditionalism, thus separating the country from the global scientific-technological revolution (except in the military realm) and providing the most limited incentives for individual initiatives.[10]

In this setting, China played a crucial role as relief provider, and from most accounts it made rice and oil available in substantial quantities, although some reports indicate that food assistance was reduced in 1998.[11] As the food situation worsened, the border between China's Yanbian Autonomous Prefecture, with its large Korean population, and the northernmost part of the DPRK became more porous. Thousands crossed the border, mostly on temporary forays for food and other provisions, but in some cases seeking permanent refuge. Estimates of the number of illegal Korean immigrants vary hugely, from thousands to tens of thousands, the great majority living with Yanbian Korean families. How was such an outward flow possible? The evidence indicates that by bribing the North Korean guards at the border, or arranging the trip through a "broker" for a fee, the passage could be navigated. Some individuals, including local DPRK officials, appear to make the trip regularly, and barter trade has become a standard operation. In recent times, the Chinese have been sufficiently concerned about the tide of refugees that they have conducted house-to-house searches in the border area and have raised the fine for anyone caught helping refugees.

Another embarrassing challenge for the PRC has been high-level defections from North Korea via China. The most prominent case was Party Secretary Hwang Chang Yop, the highest official to defect from the DPRK, who appeared at the ROK embassy in Beijing on February 12, 1997.[12] At first, the North charged that South Korean agents had kidnapped Hwang. China was publicly silent. When the defection became unmistakable, a compromise was worked out: Hwang was held in China one month, then sent to a third country, the Philippines, and transported to Seoul from Manila. In response, the DPRK closed the border with China on February 18, but later reopened it when it became apparent that such an action encouraged smuggling and other illegal acts.

FOUR-PARTY TALKS

A new issue arose in the spring of 1997. In conjunction with a Clinton-Kim meeting on Cheju Island in mid-April, a proposal for four-party talks on Korea was launched, with the talks to include the United States, the two Koreas, and China. It quickly became clear that the North did not relish this idea. Within days, it counterproposed a two-step formula, suggesting that North and South Korea and the United States meet first, with China coming into the dialogue at a second stage. The triangular concept had been proposed earlier, in the 1970s, both by the DPRK and the United States. However, plans for the four-party talks went forward with the knowledge that China had approved of the idea in advance despite its earlier insistence that the issue of unification be handled by the two Koreas alone. Once again, a reluctant North Korea was forced to accept a format not to its liking when its principal friend walked cautiously down a new path.[13]

The four-party talks have progressed with difficulty in the past two years. Agreement was finally achieved on establishing two committees—one to deal with achieving a peace agreement in place of the armistice; the other to deal with a reduction of tensions on the peninsula. In connection with these actions, the PRC put forth a series of proposals that included five points regarding the subcommittee for the establishment of a peace regime:

(1) any issue of concern to one of the parties should be accepted for discussion;

(2) the talks should progress from issues upon which agreement is easier to those more difficult;

(3) common ground should be sought while temporarily shelving issues upon which no agreement is possible;

(4) the principle of consensus should be observed; and

(5) as the talks progressed, some operational principles might be supplemented if necessary.[14]

Another five propositions were put forth with respect to the subcommittee for tension reduction:

(1) cooperation in confidence-building measures (CBMs) should encompass the broadest range of exchanges in all fields;
(2) relations should be improved among relevant countries, and specifically the gradual normalization of relations between the DPRK and the United States should be welcomed;
(3) multilayered and multiformed cooperation in CBMs in the military field should conducted;
(4) effective and feasible measures to prevent possible military conflict should be taken; and
(5) each party should refrain from taking any hostile or provocative military action against others.

As can be seen, these proposals were not likely to upset any of the four parties, and certainly not the DPRK, especially the mention of the right to raise any issue (U.S. troop withdrawal) and of normalization of U.S.-DPRK relations. In the recent past, bilateral and trilateral dialogues involving the two Koreas, China, the United States, and even Japan (unpublicized) have taken place, with separate negotiations on an array of issues—from further searches for American MIAs and the thorny question of inspection of DPRK underground facilities to numerous issues relating to North-South relations. Proposals for expanding the four-party talks by adding Russia and Japan have not been supported by China (or others), with Beijing taking the view that a six-party dialogue on a range of issues can be set up separately at a later point.

Small Steps toward Reform in the DPRK

Meanwhile, evidence has accumulated in the recent past that the DPRK is beginning to take more seriously the need for significant economic changes if it is to confront its failed economy effectively.[15] To be sure, certain words are taboo. One must not speak of "economic reform" since reform signifies system change. Nor should one challenge *juche*, that most sacred concept.

"The socialist path" is also the only acceptable road.

Yet the amendments to the North Korean constitution enacted in September 1998 signaled a friendlier attitude toward the market and entrepreneurship. In addition to the effort to create a special economic zone at Rajin-Sonbong—an effort still limping due to the North's limited economic competitiveness—a number of specific developments have taken place. The most dramatic has been the agreement with Hyundai via founder Chung Ju Yong in late 1998 to develop the Mount Kumgang area for tourism, and beyond this to jointly develop an industrial site in the region. It is significant, moreover, that publicity was given to an earlier Daewoo small textile-manufacturing plant investment in Nampo, with the North Korean announcement that, in 1998, a $20 million profit had been achieved.

Further, between 1997 and 1998, some 60 North Koreans were sent abroad to take courses in economics in various foreign countries. One group of five spent a year at Australian National University with funding provided partly by The Asia Foundation. Negotiations with the International Monetary Fund and the European Bank for Reconstruction and Development are ongoing to set up an economic training program staffed by IMF and EBRD personnel, among others, and located in China.[16] Meanwhile, a legal training program has been conducted in Beijing for North Koreans, with U.S. Professor Jerome Cohen in charge. The Rockefeller Foundation has funded a program in rice biotechnology, and the W. Alton Jones Foundation is supporting an energy-training program conducted in Shanghai. Small DPRK groups specializing in energy and agriculture have also paid visits to the United States, and in 1998 the Nautilus Institute facilitated the construction of seven wind turbines in the village of Unhira, near Nampo.[17]

The most prominent external agents in these activities thus far have been the United States and China, the former as funder, the latter as host. In the long run, it seems certain that if the DPRK is to recover from its lengthy economic catastrophe, it will have to expand its training programs and external contacts, broaden the scope of the private sector (peasant markets are already playing an important role in the North, although restraints have been reported recently), and pursue many of the reforms that China has undertaken during the past two decades and upon which Vietnam is now

somewhat unevenly embarking. No doubt there will be problems. The
DPRK elite is likely to be divided with respect to the pace and timing of
such changes, and Kim Jong Il will be compelled to make the critical decisions.[18] Further, corruption is already a serious problem, with some key
figures such as Kim Jong U, formerly in charge of promoting external investment and trade, reportedly purged on charges of taking bribes.

FRAGILITY IN CHINA-NORTH KOREA RELATIONS

Meanwhile, despite certain public utterances to the contrary, PRC relations with the DPRK have been fragile. Privately, Chinese leaders are very
negative about the North Korean economic and political system. They see
it as a relic of the past—both the Stalinist past and the Korean past. In their
view, worship of the leader takes an even more exaggerated form than at the
height of the Maoist era. And despite earlier opportunities, the old generation surrounding Kim Il Sung refused to accept modernity. While the slogan
"agriculture first, light industry first, foreign trade first" was initiated in 1994,
as far as the Chinese are concerned, little was done to effectuate that slogan.

Negative feelings are not exclusive to the Chinese side. Privately, North
Korean spokesmen make it clear that they do not trust China. Despite public support on some issues, too often they feel that China has pushed them
to take positions or make moves that they did not wish to undertake. After
China recognized the ROK and economic relations began to flourish,
Pyongyang established contact with Taiwan, and in addition to visitations,
an agreement was tentatively reached for the DPRK to be paid for taking
Taiwan's nuclear waste from its power program.[19] This was later abandoned
under international pressure, and DPRK-Taiwan relations were never taken
seriously by outsiders except as evidence that Pyongyang, irked by some of
China's actions, sought to demonstrate its independence and gain economic
advantage.

Despite the problems in PRC-DPRK relations, however, both sides have
good reasons for striving to keep their relationship as favorable as possible.
Thus, while ROK President Kim Dae Jung's visit to China in November
1998 was very successful—according to Kim, he and President Jiang agreed to

build "a comprehensive partnership" between the two countries for the twenty-first century—PRC sources were cautious about the terms. However, Jiang indicated his support for Kim's "sunshine policy" toward the North, pursuit of a direct inter-Korean dialogue, and further PRC-ROK economic cooperation. Yet he did not voice support for Kim's proposal to establish a multilateral security and cooperation forum in Northeast Asia.[20] Jiang does not wish to unduly antagonize the North through any policies taken toward the South.

RECENT CHINESE POLICIES TOWARD
THE KOREAN PENINSULA

The Chinese intend to maintain a two-Koreas policy, notwithstanding the favorable trends in relations with the ROK.[21] The Kim–Jiang summit and the agreements set forth in conjunction with the visit undoubtedly made Pyongyang unhappy. North Korean media gave the trip minimal attention. Yet China continues to supply economic assistance to the DPRK. Although according to certain sources this aid has been somewhat reduced, it has been critically important to the DPRK and will continue to be so. If further training programs develop for North Koreans in China, the potential for economic reform somewhat similar to the Chinese model will increase.

The visit of Kim Yong Nam, head of the DPRK Supreme People's Assembly, to Beijing in 1999 set the stage for a secret visit by Kim Jong Il in late May 2000 just prior to his historic summit with Kim Dae Jung in Pyongyang. In any case, high level visits have been resumed, with both military and civilian contacts possibly expanding.

In recent times, the Chinese have uniformly asserted that they have limited contact with and influence on North Korea. There is considerable truth in such statements, but it has generally been assumed that they have more influence than any other country. The recent visit of Kim Jong Il to Beijing in May 2000, prior to the June Summit, signals the importance of China to Pyongyang. It might be argued, however, that in a curious way the United States currently has the greatest influence, since Pyongyang is extremely anxious to improve its relations with Washington in order to have the economic sanctions completely removed and to be accorded diplomatic recognition. Hence, in the intensive negotiations that are taking place, American decisions may be the most critical determinant of DPRK policies.[22] The visit of U.S. Secretary of State Madeleine Albright to Pyongyang in October 2000 gives evidence of the current efforts of both sides to take major steps forward.

With respect to China's attitudes, certain facts are clear. First, Beijing does not want heightened tension on the Korean Peninsula or a collapsed North Korea. Collapse of the North could easily mean a huge flow of refugees into China and extensive economic costs for the ROK and others. Further, China would not view with pleasure a unified Korea bordering the Yalu River under the aegis of the South. This might lead to closer identification with a reunified Korea among the nearly two million Chinese Koreans in the Yanbian Autonomous Prefecture.

In addition, the issue of security with a reunified Korea could easily add new complications. Would the Korean government still desire a security commitment from the United States? If so, in what form? It is very unlikely that China would accept willingly an American military presence on its border. After nearly 50 years, the Korean War would have been lost. Perhaps a Korean-American security agreement that did not include ground forces in the area could be achieved—but even an adjustment of this nature would likely cause complications with the PRC.

Nor does China want a nuclear DPRK. Such a development could only stimulate further military expansion in Northeast Asia by the ROK and Japan. Indeed, there is strong evidence that Beijing was unhappy about the August 31, 1998, test by North Korea of its Taepo Dong missile. Chinese sources indicate that Beijing was not informed prior to the event, and when it raised questions, was told "rudely" that such an action was the prerogative of a sovereign state. There is some indication, however, that China sought successfully to discourage the North from test-firing a Taepo Dong-II missile in mid-1999.

China desires a DPRK that evolves in the fashion of China over the past 20 years: remaining "socialist" with the Communist Party (Korean Worker's Party) in command to preserve stability, but progressively advancing toward a "socialist market economy," with greater interaction with its neighbors through economic intercourse of various types. As noted, moreover, the PRC would like to see the United States and Japan establish diplomatic relations with the DPRK, thereby strengthening the prospects for these preferred economic and political changes.

For these reasons, China has been willing to participate in the four-party talks and to urge bilateral negotiations between the United States and the DPRK and also between Japan and the DPRK. Further, it has encouraged North-South talks on a variety of issues, generally hewing to the thesis that the two Koreas should solve the reunification issue by themselves. In this regard, China aligns itself with a long-held position of the North. It has refrained from participation in the Korean Peninsula Energy Development Organization, but gives verbal support to the program.

THE KOREAN PENINSULA AND
THE BALANCE OF POWER IN EAST ASIA

While their respective views on the Korea issue are by no means identical, the United States and the People's Republic of China have basic interests in common. Hence, cooperation has been possible on key matters. The possibility of a more conciliatory relationship between the United States and the DPRK that has emerged as a result of the Perry report and subsequent bilateral meetings, culminating in the high level Washington talks, which took place in October 2000, should strengthen that cooperation. In any case, China will continue to make its services available as a conduit, and on occasion facilitator, of compromise. In a period of heightened difficulty in U.S.-PRC relations toward the end of the Clinton administration over a series of problems, Korea may be one area where continued interaction of a positive nature can take place—if a chasm in U.S.-China bilateral relations can be prevented. Given the deep divisions in Congress and in the U.S. media over the Clinton administration's policies toward North Korea, however, much also depends upon the actions and attitudes of the DPRK.

This situation illustrates a broader fact regarding international relations in the Asia Pacific. We are in an era when multilateralism is assuming ever-greater importance, albeit with bilateralism still a vital element. Within the multilateral sphere, moreover, the most meaningful mechanisms in an immediate sense may not be such institutions as APEC or the ASEAN Regional Forum. Rather, the construction of coalitions devoted to handling specific problems currently represents an approach to peacemaking and peacekeeping that is the most promising, despite the complex difficulties posed and the lack of strong international institutions in this realm.

Thus, the Asia-Pacific region is likely to witness a combination of concert of powers and balance of power. The former will play upon the common national interests of various nations in supporting peace and development. The latter suggests a stable regional order in a period when nationalism is being revitalized, military modernization is a common commitment, and various issues, including that of divided states, remain unresolved.

Contrary to the views of some observers, these two approaches can coexist. Indeed, they are already in operation. It remains to make them effective by accepting complexity in all bilateral relations and avoiding policies governed solely by "threat" or divergences on certain specific issues. Can the major powers, and notably the United States, rise to this challenge?

NOTES

1. For a fine survey of recent relations up to 1996, see Chae-Jin Lee, *China and Korea: Dynamic Relations* (Stanford, Calif.: Hoover Institution Press, 1996). See also Hong Yung Lee, "China and the Two Koreas: New Emerging Triangle," in *Korea and the World—Beyond the Cold War*, ed. Young Whan Kihl (Boulder, Colo.: Westview Press, 1994).

2. Kim's early years are discussed in Dae-Sook Suh, *The Korean Communist Movement 1918–1948* (Princeton, N.J.: Princeton University Press, 1967) and *Kim Il Sung: The North Korean Leader* (New York: Columbia University Press, 1988). See also Robert Scalapino and Chong-Sik Lee, *Communism in Korea*, two volumes (Berkeley: University of California Press, 1972).

3. In addition to the works cited above, for an early account of China's role, see Allen S. Whiting, *China Crosses the Yalu: The Decision to Enter the Korean War*

(Stanford, Calif.: Stanford University Press 1960); and Sergei Goncharov, John Lewis, and Xue Litai, *Uncertain Partners: Stalin, Mao and the Korean War* (Stanford, Calif.: Stanford University Press, 1993). See also James Cotton and Ian Neary, ed., *The Korean War in History* (Atlantic Highlands, N.J.: Humanities Press International, 1989), especially the chapter by Hak Joon Kim, "China's Non-Involvement in the Origins of the Korean War." The Russian archives, recently made available, have revealed revisionist theses regarding the Korean War as a conflict opened by the South, or merely a "civil war," to be totally erroneous.

4. For more on the 1972 "South-North Joint Communiqué," see chapter 3, "Discerning North Korea's Intentions," by Chuck Downs.

5. A Russian source has indicated to this author that the North Koreans sought to obtain Russian military equipment during Yazov's visit—but they had no money to pay for such purchases. Hence, the effort failed.

6. A Chinese perspective on major power relations with the Korean Peninsula in this period is given by Chen Qimao, "The Role of the Great Powers in the Process of Korean Reunification," in *Korean Unification—Implications for Northeast Asia*, ed. Amos A. Jordan (Washington, D.C.: Center for Strategic and International Studies, 1993).

7. These figures are provided by the Korea Trade and Investment Promotion Agency in Seoul, presented in *A Handbook on North Korea*, Naewoe Press, Seoul, 1998, p. 33. DPRK trade with Japan was reportedly $489.3 million, or 22.5 percent of its total trade. That with Russia was only 3.9 percent of total trade.

8. For a recent, valuable account of the contemporary Korean scene, see Don Oberdorfer, *The Two Koreas—A Contemporary History* (Reading, Mass.: Addison-Wesley, 1997).

9. John Pomfret, a *Washington Post* correspondent, toured the China-Korea border region in early 1999 and provided reports on border crossings and related matters. He asserts that estimates of North Koreans in northeast China hover around 100,000, a figure higher than some other estimates. He also indicates that young North Korean girls are being sold to men in the region as brides. See "Portrait of a Famine" and "For Some Food, North Koreans Deal Daughters," *Washington Post*, February 12, 1999. For another journalist's account of a recent visit to the border town of Dandong, China, see Don Kirk, "A Border City Courts the North Korean Elite," *International Herald Tribune*, December 15, 1998, p. 2.

10. On economic aspects of the crisis, see Marcus Noland, "Why North Korea Will Muddle Through," *Foreign Affairs* (July/August 1997), pp. 105–18; and Marcus Noland, Sherman Robinson, and Monica Scatasta, "Reforming the North Korean

Economy," *Journal of Asian Economics*, vol. 8, no. 1 (1997), pp. 15–38.

11. For an account of China's trade with the DPRK up to 1995, see Nicholas Eberstadt, "China's Trade with the DPRK, 1990–1994," *Korea and World Affairs*, Winter 1995, pp. 665–85.

12. For one account of Hwang's defection, see Kim Yong-ho, "Hwang Jang-yop's Defection: Its Impact on North Korea," *Korea Focus*, vol. 5, no. 2 (March–April 1997), pp. 37–49.

13. See Bae Ho Hahn and Chae-Jin Lee, eds., *The Korean Peninsula and the Major Powers* (Seoul: Sejong Institute, 1998).

14. The official PRC proposals have been made available to the author via the Chinese embassy, Washington, D.C.

15. For an effort to categorize and evaluate the probability-improbability of future scenarios for North Korea, see my essay, *North Korea at a Crossroads* (Stanford, Calif.: Hoover Institution Press, 1997).

16. A brief account of the IMF-EBRD consultations with North Korea is given in "Going to School," *Newsreview*, February 13, 1999, p. 7. This is a weekly journal published under the auspices of *Korea Herald*.

17. *The People's Korea* featured the completion of the wind turbines in an article entitled "First American Windpower Village established in DPRK," October 17, 1998, pp. 1, 8.

18. For an excellent recent study of North Korean politics, see Adrian Buzo, *The Guerilla Dynasty—Politics and Leadership in North Korea* (London and New York: I. B. Tauris, 1999).

19. For a South Korean account of DPRK-Taiwan relations, see Kim Kyung-ho, "Pyongyang, Taipei Seen to Share Feeling of Diplomatic Isolation in Nuclear-Waste Case," *Korea Herald*, February 10, 1997, p. 1.

20. For the full text of President Kim's speech at Peking University, see *Korea Times*, November 13, 1998, p. 8. A Korean account of the trip, including the Kim-Jiang summit and the agreements reached is provided in *Newsreview*, November 14, 1998, pp. 6–7.

21. A recent perceptive essay on China's policies with respect to the ROK is Victor D. Cha, "Engaging China: Seoul-Beijing Détente and Korean Security," *Survival*, vol. 41, no. 1 (Spring 1999), pp. 73–98

22. See the essays in the work edited by Tong Whan Park, *The U.S. and The Two Koreas—A New Triangle* (Boulder, Colo.: Lynne Rienner, 1998).

5

Japan and the Unification of Korea: Challenges for U.S. Policy Coordination

Michael H. Armacost and Kenneth B. Pyle

The sudden, unanticipated end of the Cold War presented Japan with a new set of foreign policy challenges, among which the prospect of Korean reunification is one of the most problematic. In this essay we argue that although it has critical interests at stake, Japan labors under constraints that make it unlikely to take the lead in resolving the complex issues involved. Rather, it is more likely to be reactive and adaptive to the unification process, accommodating to the changing circumstances of unification in a cautious and incremental fashion. In some respects, because the nature of reunification is so uncertain in its implications for Japan's interests, Japanese policymakers may privately prefer a continuation of the status quo of a divided Korea. Nevertheless, Japan cannot afford to resist unification. Moreover, in the potential scenarios for unification that we examine, Japanese cooperation with the United States is essential. American leadership in resolving strategic issues on the Korean Peninsula remains indispensable, but successful American initiatives will require skillful policy coordination with Japan that takes account of its interests and sensibilities. The resources that Japan can bring to bear and the role it plays will go a long way toward determining an enduring settlement on the peninsula and achieving a stable new order in Northeast Asia.

JAPAN'S STAKE IN KOREAN UNIFICATION

Japan has an immense stake in the outcome of unification because it will determine the fundamental nature of its strategic relationship with its closest neighbor. As Masashi Nishihara, the president of Japan's National Defense University, sums up, "Japan seeks a united Korea that is friendly to Tokyo and Washington, that is economically viable and politically open, and that will allow token U.S. presence to remain."[1] If unified Korea retains nuclear weapons, is tilted toward China, refuses to countenance a continued security relationship with the United States that includes some residual American military presence, and/or is resolutely hostile toward Japan in its vision of the future, it would represent a major foreign policy defeat for Japan and a problem of immense concern for the nation's future. A reunified Korea with renewed animus toward Japan would have long-term unfavorable implications for Japanese security.

In addition to the strategic relationship, Japan's commercial interests will also be deeply affected by the outcome of the reunification process. Despite the prolonged political bitterness between Japan and the Republic of Korea since World War II, the two countries have developed close economic ties. Japan provided the model for growth and supplied many of the capital goods needed for South Korea's industrialization. It also provided official development assistance, sizable flows of private investment, increasingly significant technology transfers, and a market for some imports. By the 1990s, although Japan ran persistent trade surpluses with the ROK, South Korea nevertheless emerged as a fierce competitor with Japan in steel, consumer electronics, shipbuilding, and many other key areas. At the same time, Japan had become South Korea's second leading trade partner (after the United States) and its leading source of foreign investment.

The extensive interdependence of their economies was evident in the 1997–98 financial crisis in South Korea: Japan contributed billions of dollars to help rescue the ROK economy and thus also cover the exposure of

Japanese banks, which held more than a third of South Korea's foreign debt. At the same time, Japan's own economic troubles caused problems for South Korea. Japan's banks, burdened by a mountain of nonperforming loans, had to withdraw credit facilities from neighboring countries. The stagnation of Japan's economy dried up a major Korean export market. Japanese Finance Minister Kiichi Miyazawa proposed a $30-billion trade facilitation fund, which was well received by Koreans but barely offset the withdrawal of bank credits formerly available. All of this is testimony to the close economic ties that had developed and that will be influenced and shaped by the course of unification.

Reunification and Japan's Relations with Other Powers

But more is at stake than Japan's future relations with Korea. So central is the issue of Korean reunification to the future structure of international relations in the region that it will bear heavily on Japan's relations with the other major powers whose interests intersect on the Korean Peninsula. Of greatest concern is the future of relations with the United States. How and under what circumstances unification takes place, Japan's role in the process, and the outcome of unification will have great influence on the future shape of the U.S.-Japan alliance. A post-unification U.S.-Korean alliance and a continued U.S. military presence on the peninsula would reassure Japan that a reunified Korea would be disposed to improve ties with Japan. The post-unification status of American forces in Korea is bound to have ripple effects on the American military presence in Japan, which Japan is likely to wish continued—although inevitably reduced and reconfigured.

The course that reunification takes will also bear importantly on Japan's relations with China and Russia. A unified Korea that tilted toward China or even stood equidistant between China and Japan would complicate Japan's future strategic position. During the past decade China has developed a significant relationship with Seoul—and of course throughout much of Korea's history prior to the twentieth century it was part of the Sinocentric order—which adds to the complexity of Japanese policymaking. In some respects, this gives Japan an incentive to improve its relations with Russia, which may have a similar interest in diluting China's role in a unified Korea.

Japanese Policymaking

Japan therefore has a great a stake in the outcome of Korean unification, but what are its policies toward the peninsula? How is Tokyo pursuing its interests? What initiatives is it taking? The answers have not always been easy to find. Nicholas Eberstadt, one of the most knowledgeable Americans observing the prospects of Korean reunification, recently wrote that "Japanese foreign policy is more opaque than that of most other [countries involved]" and that divining its underlying rationale is a challenge.[2] There are many reasons for the "opaqueness" of Japanese policy on this issue. Partly it reflects attitudes and emotions. The Japanese have tended to be deeply ambivalent about Korean unification. A strong, united Korean state could offer political and economic problems and competition; on the other hand a continuation of a divided Korea extends the life of an unpredictable rogue state that presents a security threat. Moreover, as one of Japan's leading strategic thinkers acknowledges, South Koreans are widely suspicious of Japan's motives, whichever position it takes.[3] Koreans tend to feel that Japanese support for reunification is indicative of a desire to weaken the Korean economy. Conversely, lack of enthusiasm for reunification is seen as a desire to keep the Koreans from gaining political and military strength. Therefore, this Japanese strategist, who requested to remain unnamed, concludes that it is best for Japan to maintain a low profile.

A low profile may also be a manifestation of Japan's characteristic diplomatic style in periods of uncertainty and flux associated with transformation of the international system. At such times Japan historically has tended to be adaptive and reactive, moved not by transcendent principles but rather by strategic caution—observing trends and pursuing its national interests through pragmatic and opportunistic policies. In this case Japan's customary circumspection seems especially appropriate. Given the difficulty of peacefully achieving the kind of united Korea that they favor, most Japanese policymakers have quietly concluded that their wisest course is not to hasten unification. Instead, policymakers favor pursuit of a course that maintains the status quo of a divided Korea for as long as possible, all the while supporting American policies of deterrence, hoping to contain tensions and foster cordial ties with South Korea, and favoring policies that promote a gradual reconciliation rather than a rapid and potentially violent reunification that might produce new problems for Japan.

Such a flexible and accommodative approach to the course of events is even more likely because there are no longer the strong domestic constituencies that had once advocated Japanese policy initiatives toward the Korean Peninsula. The dramatic decline of the Socialists (DSPJ), their longtime sympathy with North Korea, and ties to the Korean Worker's Party (KWP)—particularly since the wholesale renunciation of long-held Socialist foreign policy positions by the DSPJ leader, Prime Minister Tomoichi Murayama, in 1994—has sharply reduced domestic controversy over Korea policy. The decline of the Chosen-soren, the pro-North Korean organization of Korean residents in Japan, since the end of the Cold War and the continued obduracy of the Democratic People's Republic of Korea at a time when other surviving communist regimes have seen fit to adjust to the post-Cold War era have also contributed to the diminished domestic controversy. Repeated DPRK affronts to normalization negotiations have largely exhausted the enthusiasm of Liberal Democratic Party (LDP) groups interested in improved relations. Following the DPRK missile firing over Japanese air space in August 1998, both houses of the Diet passed unanimous resolutions condemning it as an "unforgivable act." Finally, North Korea has done little to create conditions that Japanese firms would find attractive to investment and trade. The value of North Korea-Japan trade is negligible and largely limited to small Japanese companies owned by North Koreans resident in Japan. In sum, there is no substantial domestic constituency advocating new Japanese initiatives in regard to North Korea.

CONSTRAINTS ON JAPANESE POLICY

Japan's Political-Economic Framework

Above all, Japan's low-posture stance on Korean unification—the apparent "opaqueness" of its policy—is a reflection of the multiple constraints under which its policymakers must work. They find their policy options limited by a variety of historic legacies and complex strategic considerations. The most significant constraint on Japanese policy is the legacy of its post-World

War II political-economic framework. In many respects Japan's unique Cold War foreign policy, with its principal concentration on economic growth, left it poorly prepared to deal with this and other overseas political-strategic issues and crises of the new era. The abrupt end of the Cold War left Japan disoriented. The nation lost its bearings in the period of flux and uncertainty that ensued. While much commentary at the time the Cold War ended was wont to attribute all-out success to Japan's foreign policy ("the Cold War is over and Japan has won"), the first international crisis of the post-Cold War era, the Persian Gulf War, revealed the downside of this policy in the new context. Unable to muster a coherent policy and reluctant to share the risks of international coalition action (despite the fact that 70 percent of its oil came from the Gulf), the Japanese government ended up writing checks totaling $13 billion, for which it got little thanks and much derision. This sizable sum was scorned in many foreign quarters as "checkbook diplomacy" and as a failure of Japan to meet the responsibilities of a country deeply dependent on the stability of the international system.

A similar inability to meet the expectations of the new era was evident in 1994, when the showdown with North Korea over its nuclear weapons program made conflict appear imminent. Citing the great Japanese stake in dealing with the proliferation issue in its immediate region, the U.S. command in Japan asked the Japanese government to contribute fuel and material for American forces, to provide ships and planes for sweeping mines and gathering intelligence, and to cut off financial flows to North Korea, but Japanese officials equivocated and were obviously relieved when Jimmy Carter's trip to Pyongyang defused the confrontation and made it unnecessary for a coalition government to resolve tough choices. Defense Secretary William Perry later said that if conflict had ensued and American forces had not had access to Japanese bases " it would have been the end of the alliance."

As a result, inter alia, of American dissatisfaction with Japan's response to the Gulf War, to the confrontation with North Korea, and to the Taiwan Strait crisis in March 1996, Japan agreed to a revision of the Guidelines for U.S.-Japan Defense Cooperation. These revised guidelines provide for an increased but still modest role for Japan in the event of a regional crisis and contribute to a tighter, more integrated, more complementary, and therefore more effective operational alliance. Although the Diet in 1999 approved the legislation necessary to initiate these guidelines, it is likely to be some considerable time before this new, limited role is fully operational. Moreover, Japanese leaders have yet to address the unresolved issue of whether the constitution permits Japan to participate in "collective self-defense." The government continues to maintain the position that, while all nations possess the right of collective self-defense under the UN charter, Japan cannot exercise this right. So long as this position is maintained, Japan will not be able to contribute leadership on the key strategic issues facing Northeast Asia.

Japan's foreign policy since World War II of shunning international political-military commitments while concentrating on economic growth—the so-called Yoshida Doctrine, named after the prime minister who formulated the nation's postwar strategy—worked brilliantly under the unique circumstances of the Cold War. Japan avoided foreign entanglements; it became an *idée fixe* of postwar Japanese diplomacy to avoid any collective security commitments. Following World War II, the realist pursuit of national power that had characterized Japanese foreign policy strategy since the nation entered the modern world was redirected principally toward economic competition in which the instruments of power were productive efficiency, market control, trade surplus, a strong currency, ample foreign exchange reserves, advanced technology, foreign direct investment, and foreign aid. It has been observed that "Japanese strategists have been more willing to accept U.S. military on their soil than they have U.S. bankers or manufacturers."[4] Concentration on economic growth left many political-strategic institutions undeveloped, however. The weak prime ministership and the lack of crisis management practice and intelligence capability are noteworthy examples. In addition, Japan's postwar foreign policy encouraged the persistence of isolationist and pacifist sentiment among the populace.

Troubled History of Relations with Korea

Among other constraints on Japanese policy, one of the most severe is the long and troubled history of Japanese-Korean relations. The burden of history and the residual suspicion of its neighbors have precluded Japan from adopting a proactive leadership role in shaping a new order in the region. As Professor Akio Watanabe, who recently chaired a commission advising the Japanese government on the unification issue, has written: "China and Korea, especially, still remember the hard times under Japanese domination. One legacy from this period is a politically hamstrung Japan, which has not been able to play a leadership role in the region.... All we can do is wait [and] ... not be too concerned about grand architecture."[5] Despite new conditions, the burden of the past will continue to weigh heavily on the course that the relationship with Korea takes.

Geography dictated that the Japanese and Koreans shared a past, a culture, and an ethnic heritage, but it also made circumstances on the Korean Peninsula from the earliest times critical to Japanese security. In the seventh century it was the specter of an expansive Tang Empire in China and the Silla unification of Korea that spurred the adoption of Chinese institutions to create the first unified Japanese state. Later it was from Korea that Kublai Khan launched his invasion attempts against the Japanese; and then it was through Korea that Toyotomi Hideyoshi undertook his failed expedition to conquer China. The bitter memories of this expedition are still kept alive today. In the heart of Seoul stands a massive statue of Admiral Yi Sun Sin, one of the most revered Korean military heroes, whose armored warships repeatedly defeated Japanese naval forces. In Kyoto there is a macabre war memorial known as the "ear mound" (*mimizuka*) where the ears and noses of tens of thousands of Koreans slain by Hideyoshi's warriors are buried.

The western intrusion into East Asia in the nineteenth century increased the critical importance of the Korean Peninsula to Japan's security. To prevent it from falling under the control of a third country, the rapidly modernizing Japanese military was prompted to establish its paramount position there. Japan's colonization of Korea left an intense bitterness among Koreans for the brutal repression that they experienced. Korean leaders still speak of Japan's "cultural aggression," which required Koreans to take Japanese names, speak Japanese, and worship the Emperor. Antipathy for the Japanese became the bedrock of Korean nationalism; and celebration of liberation from Japanese rule, August 15, 1945, a great patriotic holiday.

During the Cold War, aside from trade contacts, Japan and the divided Koreas maintained a distant and correct rather than cordial relationship. A half-century passed with only limited progress in dealing with the historical legacy of bitterness. Following normalization of relations with South Korea in 1965—when Japan, under strong U.S. pressure, recognized it as the sole legitimate government on the peninsula and provided $800 million by way of compensation—the Japanese made repeated carefully scripted apologies for the colonial period. But they were never accepted as sufficient. The emperor's vague words in 1984 on welcoming the South Korean president suggest why: "It is indeed regrettable that there was an unfortunate past between us for a period of this century, and I believe that it should not be repeated." More forthcoming apologies were offered later, but they were frequently undermined by utterances of Japanese cabinet members insisting that annexation had been "legal" or "beneficial." Textbook accounts were unsatisfactory, and the visits of Prime Minister Yasuhiro Nakasone and other conservative politicians to the Yasukuni Shrine in Tokyo, which memorializes Japan's foreign wars and their heroes, have offended many Koreans.

A particularly emotional issue arose in the 1990s with revelations of the experiences of " comfort women," tens of thousands of Koreans and others who had been compelled to serve in military brothels for the imperial army. The Japanese government, after initially refusing to acknowledge the revelations, later established a private fund to compensate survivors, but resisted a United Nations Human Rights Commission's recommendation that it make an official apology and compensation.

In addition, the plight of 700,000 Korean residents in Japan, many of whom had been brought to Japan during the colonial period to do hard labor, aggravated the relationship. While some of the more demeaning aspects of their treatment, such as the requirement of periodic fingerprinting, have been eased in the 1990s, Korean residents are still generally excluded from job opportunities in the public sector and are not extended voting rights. In addition, graduates of Korean schools in Japan are not permitted to take entrance examinations for national universities.

It is true that beneath the nationalism and public recriminations that characterized Japanese-Korean relations throughout the Cold War period, close personal ties were forged among some Japanese and Korean political leaders. This is a complex story, for along with the bitterness that Koreans felt toward their former colonial masters, there existed a certain respect and understanding for the way Japan conducted its politics. Just as Japan provided a development model for the Korean political-economy, so the Japanese Liberal Democratic Party inspired Korea's emulation during the regime of Park Chung Hee. These relationships resulted in active exchanges between members of the Japanese Diet and the ruling party in the South Korean National Assembly that facilitated cooperative relations between their respective governing parties, belying some of the nationalist animosities that were so much a part of the public relations between the two countries. In more recent years, as the power of the governing parties has weakened and as a new generation of political leaders in each country has come to the fore, these exchanges languished (as indeed have American parliamentarian exchanges with Japan and South Korea), leaving the bilateral relationship less prepared to mitigate the recurrent expressions of anti-Japanese nationalism in Seoul.

Koreans have vented their animosity in many ways that reveal the anti-Japanese strain of their nationalism. Japanese popular culture has been excluded. The imposing imperial-style building that had housed the Japanese colonial administration in Seoul was razed at a ceremony marking the fiftieth anniversary of Korean independence. Tokyo and Seoul loudly contested each others' claims to a tiny, uninhabited island (Takeshima/Tokdo) in the Sea of Japan/Eastern Sea. Popular novels with anti-Japanese themes such as *The Rose of Sharon Has Blossomed* (1993), which describes the defeat of Japan by the combined forces of North and South Korea, have been bestsellers. Former South Korean President Kim Young Sam often used anti-Japanese sentiment to shore up his domestic support. Never was this so painful to Japan as when he held a joint press conference with Jiang Zemin in 1995 on the occasion of the first state visit to South Korea by a Chinese head of state. The leaders lectured Japan on adopting, as Jiang said, "a correct view of history." Jiang continued: "We must be vigilant against a Japanese militarist minority. Although a half century has passed since the end of a war between China and Japan, some Japanese politicians still have a wrong historical view." To which President Kim added, "We will correct Japan's bad habits." Such signs of Sino-Korean rapport based on growing trade relations and residual suspicion of Japan could only leave Japan deeply uneasy.

The U.S.-Japan Alliance

Yet another factor in Japan's policymaking is the U.S.-Japan alliance, to which Tokyo has generally assigned precedence in its foreign policymaking. At key times, such as the decision to normalize relations with South Korea in 1965, the alliance relationship with the United States was a central determinant of Japan's Korea policy. With strong encouragement from the United States, Japan acknowledged that the security of the ROK was, as the Sato-Nixon communiqué stated in 1969, "essential to Japan's own security." On those grounds President Doo Hwan Chun in 1982 requested a grant of $6 billion in credits from Japan in recognition of the contribution that the ROK's huge defense burden was making to Japanese security. Prime Minister Zenko Suzuki refused to link economic cooperation and security, but his successor, the forceful Yasuhiro Nakasone, determined to impress Ronald Reagan and reverse the policies of the Yoshida doctrine, made an unprecedented trip to Seoul in January 1983. Nakasone made the trip shortly after taking office and approved a long-term government loan of $4 billion, which he and the Koreans explicitly linked to the strategic defense of Japan. Nakasone sought with limited success to undo the impression of a free-riding, politically passive Japan. But the balance of power in Japanese politics was still with the adherents of the Yoshida strategy.

At the time of the 1994 crisis over North Korea's nuclear program, the political disarray that had ensued from the LDP's fall from power the previous year also contributed to Japan's immobilism. The weak domestic political base of the Japanese government accentuated its reflexive preference for a negotiated settlement. The Japanese, like the South Koreans and Chinese, encouraged the United States to explore an accommodation with North Korea that would obviate the necessity of confronting tougher options. Japan was subsequently stuck with a hefty bill for the U.S.-North Korean Agreed Framework, but that price tag was cheap compared with the political and budgetary costs of some of the alternatives. Under pressure from Washington, Japan acquiesced, but had little enthusiasm for the Agreed Framework that the Americans negotiated with North Korea. It requires Japan to make a financial contribution of approximately $1 billion to the Korean Peninsula Energy Development Organization to cover 20 percent of the cost of constructing two light-water nuclear reactors.

Following the North Korean missile launch over Japan in August 1998, Japan suspended this financial aid to KEDO. But, amply illustrating the constraints under which it labors, Japanese policymakers were at once under American pressure to resume aid. They were reportedly angered by the U.S. determination to continue engagement with the North following this affront to their sovereignty. In the face of American pressure (and the strong urging of the ROK), they subsequently resumed their financial commitment to KEDO.

The Japanese inertia at the time of the crisis with North Korea in 1994 was belatedly recognized as jeopardizing relations with the United States, and prompted Japan to agree to a revision of the security guidelines for Japanese military assistance to U.S. forces dealing with "situations in areas surrounding Japan that will have an important influence on Japan's peace and security."[6] The legislation implementing the guidelines was passed by the Diet in May 1999 and constitutes the first acknowledgment of Japan's responsibility for rear area support of U.S. military operations outside of Japan. Accordingly, whatever its ambivalence about the prospect of unification, Tokyo has felt constrained to follow the policies developed by the United States in the wake of the 1994 crisis. It has revised its interpretation of constitutional restraints and prepared to undertake expanded security obligations should the soft-landing policies fail and a renewed military confrontation with North Korea ensue. As the junior partner in the security alliance, Japan repeatedly has been compelled to defer to American policy leadership on Korean issues. In addition, the fact that Japan is not a party to the four-party talks on achieving a permanent peace settlement has meant that it is often confined to the margins of negotiations, prompting Japanese leaders to acquiesce to American leadership, though at times with discomfort.

The Need to Consult South Korea

Another feature of Japanese policy has been Tokyo's gradual realization that it has little choice but to coordinate its policy closely with South Korea and not attempt initiatives toward the North without consultations with the South. This position was confirmed in the aftermath of one of the more bizarre incidents in postwar Japanese diplomacy—the failed initiative in 1990 led by LDP elder Shin Kanemaru, the most powerful figure in Japanese politics, to try to normalize relations with Pyongyang. Anticipating that with the end of the Cold War the United States might be scaling back its presence in Asia, observing the success of South Korea's *Nordpolitik*, which had led to normalization of ties with the Soviet Union in 1990 and China in 1992, and believing that an effort was necessary to balance China's growing influence on the peninsula, Kanemaru undertook a dramatic initiative independent of Seoul and Washington—and to some extent even of his own Foreign Ministry. In North Korea Kanemaru' s large delegation, composed of representatives of both the LDP and the DSPJ, as well as an uneasy Foreign Ministry diplomat, was warmly received, but the initiative evidently got out of hand when Kanemaru dismissed the rest of the delegation and met alone with Kim Il Sung. The latter, furious with the Russians for deserting the cause, allegedly told Kanemaru that the "yellow skins" must stick together against the "white skins."[7] Kanemaru reportedly emerged from the meetings with tears in his eyes, convinced of Kim's sincerity. In what turned out to be an astonishing aberration, Kanemaru proceeded to make the kind of profuse apology for past Japanese sins that South Koreans had long demanded but never heard. Further, he indicated readiness to provide reparations not only for the colonial period, as had been done at the time of normalization with South Korea, but also inexplicably for the abnormal relations in the postwar period.

Seoul was at once in an uproar; Washington was stunned; and in Tokyo the Foreign Ministry and members of Kanemaru's own party were angered. One interpretation of Kanemaru's demarche suggests that he hoped to receive kickbacks for his faction from North Korea and from North Korean firms operating in Japan once the huge payments of compensation to the DPRK were under way. However that may be, the proposals were quickly abandoned, Kanemaru flew to Seoul to express his regrets for blindsiding the South Koreans, and went to the American embassy in Tokyo to apologize to the American ambassador for having acted without any prior consultation. The incident fed South Korean suspicions of Japanese duplicity and was interpreted as evidence of a two-Koreas policy designed to perpetuate the division on the peninsula.

As a result of this fall-out from the Kanemaru caper, Prime Minister Toshiki Kaifu was anxious to make amends for the damage done to relations with Seoul and to mollify the Americans, who were already exasperated with the sluggish Japanese response to the Persian Gulf crisis. Not wanting to continue another source of discord, Kaifu acted quickly to tie off the issue. He formally agreed the following year to a request from President Roh to approach Pyongyang only after prior consultation with Seoul, to agree that improved Japanese relations with North Korea must be preceded by meaningful progress in inter-Korean dialogue, and to provide economic compensation and aid to North Korea only after normalization was achieved. The agreement was of course a simple recognition of the fact that Japan had a lot more on the line with South Korea than with the North. This commitment to coordinate Japan's policy toward the DPRK closely with Seoul and make it dependent upon the progress of North-South relations has been repeated by subsequent Japanese prime ministers, and represents a further constraint on Japanese policymaking.

North Korean Disinterest

Another limitation on Japan's ability to offer forthright policy initiatives has been the apparent disinterest of North Korea since the Kanemaru incident in pursuing a consistent policy of improved relations. Kanemaru and his entourage had concluded an LDP-DSPJ-KWP Three-Party Joint Declaration, which provided for the two governments to initiate normalization talks. These talks, which were held between January 1991 and November 1992, foundered on the misunderstandings created by Kanemaru's blunders. Pyongyang demanded that Japan adhere to the commitments implied by Kanemaru for reparations for both the colonial and postwar periods, which it calculated, taking into account inflation and Japanese economic aid to the ROK, at between $5 and $10 billion. Foreign Ministry officials, now back in charge of negotiations, dismissed Kanemaru's commitments as an unofficial party-to-party communiqué and therefore insisted on adhering to the principles of the Basic Treaty of 1965, under which normalization with South Korea had transpired and which limited claims for compensation to property damage done during the colonial period. The Japanese, for their part,

raised a number of issues, including North Korean debt to Japanese companies, the whereabouts of Japanese citizens alleged to have been abducted by
North Korea since the 1970s, permission for Japanese-born wives of North
Koreans to visit their relatives in Japan, and most importantly—because Seoul
and Washington insisted on it—opening its nuclear facilities for inspection by
the IAEA. The talks reached an impasse over these issues and have not been
resumed. Efforts have been made to revive the talks, and visits of Japanese-
born wives did take place in November 1997 and January 1998, but an impasse was reached when the DPRK resolutely denied any knowledge of abducted Japanese, which Japanese public opinion had come to regard as a
precondition for successful normalization talks.

A high-ranking Japanese foreign ministry official concluded in mid-sum-
mer 1998 that the North was determined to negotiate only with the United
States, in accord with Kim Il Sung's legacy, and was not seriously interested
in pursuing normalization with Tokyo. The August 1998 missile launch
over Japanese airspace added a still more decisive obstacle to progress on
normalization. A mission to Pyongyang in December 1999 led by former
Prime Minister Tomiichi Murayama reached agreement on a formula to re-
start normalization talks by referring to the two countries' Red Crosses the
issues of abducted Japanese, home visits by Japanese wives of North Koreans, and food aid. The agreement appeared fragile as it left the missile program unresolved and was accompanied by harsh DPRK rhetoric regarding
Japanese charges about abduction of their citizens. In sum, Japan's economic
resources, which might be used in support of a peaceful reunification based
on a negotiated agreement, and the prospect of a huge Japanese compensation package at the time of normalization might have been thought to pre-
figure an increased Japanese role in the reunification process, but the prospect does not appear imminent.

Complicated Relations with China and Russia

Japan's relations with China and Russia offer complications of a different
sort. While Japan wishes quietly to balance the growing influence that China
has acquired on the peninsula, it is not eager to drift into a confrontation
with China over Korea. Japan has a delicate and complex role to play in its

relations with China, in part because it involves triangular relations with the United States. As much as possible, Japan has sought to separate economics from politics in its relations with China. Accordingly, the Japanese were unenthusiastic about punishing China with sanctions in the aftermath of the Tiananmen incident and were the first of the G–7 to abandon this punitive stance a year later. It was not just that there was a huge Chinese market to exploit. Japan hoped to use aid to gain leverage and to moderate Chinese foreign policy. Japan therefore resumed its economic engagement with China, and even when Beijing, heedless of Tokyo's protests, resumed nuclear testing in 1995, the Japanese response of freezing grant aid was minimal. Japan, not as concerned as the United States by a mounting trade deficit with China, urged early admission of China to the World Trade Organization, and on less demanding terms, in a clear departure from American policy.

In this and other ways, Tokyo has sought to differentiate its policy toward China from Washington's. Foreseeing the likely Chinese reaction, Tokyo policymakers were accordingly uncomfortable at being pressed by the Americans to revise the security guidelines and to join in funding and joint research for the theater missile defense program. As late as January 1996, in discussions between Japanese and Chinese officials over security matters, the Chinese told the Japanese that "continued friendly relations between the United States and Japan are in China's interests." Since then China has become deeply suspicious and at times openly hostile in its view of the U.S.-Japan alliance. Several Japanese leaders have gone to great length to persuade China that increased defense cooperation with the United States is directed at the Korea problem and does not apply to Taiwan. Others prefer to leave the impression of ambiguity. The upshot is that efforts to preserve maximum autonomy in its policy toward China, an approach that is consistent with maintaining the American alliance, will continue to cause Japan to move cautiously and with great circumspection in undertaking expanded defense roles within the alliance.

With regard to Russia, Japan has been actively pursuing a stronger connection as a way of diversifying its diplomatic options and cultivating the potential common interest the two countries may have in balancing Chinese influence on the Korean Peninsula. In an exchange of visits in 1997 and 1998, President Boris Yeltsin and Prime Minister Ryutaro Hashimoto struggled to find a formula to set aside the territorial dispute over the Southern Kurile Islands so that Japan would be free to engage much more deeply in Russia's economic recovery and especially in Siberian development. The persistent disarray in the Russian government followed by the unwillingness of the new Putin government to make concessions, however, continues to frustrate progress on the territorial issue and makes the prospect for a breakthrough to a new relationship in the near term dim.

Economic Constraints

Finally, one more constraint of recent origin deserves mention. The prolonged economic stagnation of the 1990s together with the long-range fiscal concerns raised by Japan's demographic problems have resulted in an overall decline in resources available for the pursuit of foreign policy objectives. For example, Japan' s overseas development assistance, which has been called its principal foreign policy tool, was cut by 10 percent during the 1998 fiscal year.

In sum, despite the fact that Korean reunification is so critical to its future, Japan is unlikely to play a proactive role. Rather, it is more likely to be cautious, reactive, and adaptive to the process of reunification as it develops. Still, it is well to remember that every country must act within constraints. For the Japanese, as for others, foreign policy involves tradeoffs. Their aims are legion; their resources scarce. They have to balance various equities. The existence of these widely recognized constraints can serve as a useful excuse for avoiding what they do not want to do. By and large, Japan's leaders retain the policy reflexes of a middle power more interested in minimizing risks than maximizing accomplishments. They covet the status of a major power, but not its obligations and burdens. Given that mindset, they have done rather well vis-à-vis their Korean policy aims. They have developed productive economic relations with South Korea while leaving the security responsibilities to others. Their policies toward the two Koreas have not thus far imposed an intolerable burden on their links with China, Russia, or the United States. And they have managed to accommodate the various pressures they confront at home. All in all, it has not been a bad arrangement, but in light of recent developments, the Japanese themselves are coming to recognize that it may not fit the changing circumstances.

A WINDOW OF OPPORTUNITY

Despite the multiple constraints and ambivalence that the Japanese have felt about Korean reunification since the end of the Cold War, an extraordinary confluence of events beginning in 1998 after the election of Kim Dae Jung as ROK president offered opportunities for diminishing these constraints. Kim's visit to Tokyo ushered in a period of good feelings in ROK-Japanese relations. Moreover, the launching of the DPRK missile over their air space prodded the Japanese to think more seriously about their security needs and responsibilities. In addition, the confrontational approach of Jiang Zemin, the first Chinese head of state to visit Japan, privately angered many Japanese leaders who had been seeking a way to draw closer to Beijing in the wake of President Clinton's cordial nine-day stay in China. As a consequence, the Japanese were in a mood to abandon some of their usual caution regarding political issues that have aroused the Chinese.

The election of Kim Dae Jung brought to power a remarkable new ROK leader determined to be a repairer of the North-South breach. In his inaugural address in February 1998 he declared his intention to improve relations not only with North Korea through his so-called "sunshine policy" but also with Japan. The Japanese were delighted by his willingness to resist nationalist demagoguery, in contrast to his predecessor, and to seek a new relationship. He at once made good on his intentions by conciliatory moves on a range of issues from the "comfort women" to the fisheries dispute. Koreans in turn were pleased with Japanese economic aid at a time of critical financial need and, recognizing the importance of economic cooperation, took steps to encourage greater Japanese investment and loans, particularly for medium-sized and small South Korean firms.

The visit of Kim Dae Jung to Tokyo in October 1998 stands out as a major event in Japanese-Korean relations. His willingness to address the Japanese in their own tongue delighted them. He met with Emperor Akihito, whom he referred to as "emperor" rather then *nikko* or "Japanese king," a term of little respect that Koreans had used since 1945. Moreover, Kim eased the bans imposed a half century earlier on Japanese investment and on the importation of Japanese movies, music, magazines, and other forms of popular culture. Addressing the Diet (in Korean), he accepted a comparatively forthright apology for Japanese colonial rule from Prime Minister Keizo Obuchi and added that "South Korea should also rightly evaluate Japan, in all its changed aspects. And search with hope for future possibilities." Reflecting the possibilities of generational change, groups of young Japanese and Korean scholars have initiated exchanges among themselves and their students at which they discuss issues of common interest, including especially the history of their national relations.

Kim's magnanimity stood in marked contrast to the confrontational approach of Jiang Zemin, who during his visit the following month pointedly told the emperor and other Japanese leaders that China was not yet ready to forgive the past. By making clear his determination to establish a new and positive relationship with Japan, Kim succeeded in attaining an explicit written apology for the past. The Chinese demanded the same kind of apology but were unwilling to prepare the ground as Kim had.

Seoul's initiatives to improve relations, together with the North Korean missile launch, set the stage for a new Japanese receptivity to consider modest measures of security cooperation with the ROK. More than any recent event, the missile crisis stirred Japanese recognition of their vulnerability and of the inadequacy of their defenses. Since the end of the Cold War, the Japanese had become increasingly conscious of their lack of preparedness to deal with security issues. The flap over how to contribute to the Gulf War coalition in 1991, the tensions over North Korea's nuclear program in 1994, and the growing assertiveness of China as manifested in the Taiwan Strait crisis in 1996 all contributed to this rising consciousness. But there was much else. The incompetence in crisis management apparent in the Kobe earthquake and the nerve gas attack in a Tokyo subway in 1996, in the 126-day Peruvian hostage crisis at the Japanese ambassador's residence the following year, and in the nuclear accident at Tokai-mura in 1999 added to the mounting public dismay over official lack of preparedness to manage crisis situations. The menacing North Korean behavior crystallized this consciousness. Following the 1998 missile launch over their airspace, the intrusion of two North Korean spy boats into Japanese waters near Sado Island in March 1999 was once again met with official uncertainty and confusion. While the ships, discovered by U.S. intelligence monitoring, were fleeing Japanese waters the prime minister consulted with cabinet members as to whether restrictions on firing on vessels infringing upon Japanese sovereignty could be lifted. Eventually Prime Minister Obuchi gave permission to fire warning shots but with no effect as the ships returned to a North Korean port. This incident gave impetus to the drafting of a new and less restrictive legal framework to cope with emergencies. Indicative of the growing unease about Japanese preparedness as it related to North Korea was the fact that the Japanese Defense White Paper released late in 1999 was the longest in postwar history, and the section on North Korea was five times the length of the section in the previous year's White Paper.

In response to the missile launch, the Japanese government became more assertive regarding the DPRK missile program. In fact, Japan adopted a harder line than either the United States or the ROK. The missile launch helped galvanize the languishing political support for legislation enabling revision of the Guidelines for U.S.-Japan Defense Cooperation and contributed to the emergence of an LDP coalition with the security-minded Liberal Party of Ichiro Ozawa. The cabinet quickly made a decision to put up intelligence satellites of their own, reinterpreting a 1969 Diet resolution against the military use of space. The government also announced a long-deferred and debated decision to participate in and provide modest funding for joint research on the U.S. theater missile defense program, despite anticipated Chinese opposition. Moreover, the Japanese alone stopped all food aid and the government banned charter flights to North Korea. Government spokesmen repeatedly asserted that aid to KEDO might be suspended if another missile were launched. Younger members of the Diet, across party lines, prepared legislation to make remittances to the DPRK more difficult and to tighten export controls should another missile test be undertaken. At the time the Diet deliberated approval of Japan's $1-billion contribution to KEDO, the Japanese also began to assert the right to have their voice heard in the talks regarding North Korea. In an address to the UN and in his meeting with Kim Dae Jung, Prime Minister Obuchi proposed six-power talks on Korea's future. Such meetings would thereby include Russia and Japan, which are not present in the four-party talks. Kim supported this proposal, while Jiang Zemin gave it a cold shoulder. The Trilateral Consultation and Oversight Group, a quarterly meeting of U.S., ROK, and Japanese representatives initiated by former Defense Secretary Perry as part of his review of U.S. North Korean policy, helped to assuage this Japanese request for consultation.

Finally, and in some ways most significantly, the missile crisis encouraged greater willingness to consider modest measures of defense cooperation between Japan and South Korea. Since the establishment of KEDO, the United States had promoted an informal trilateral security dialogue to foster greater coordination between its two allies. In 1999 Japan and the ROK conducted their first joint naval exercises, which were focussed on humanitarian search-and-rescue operations. After the missile launch this process moved a step further with discussion of a trilateral joint defense framework. During Kim Dae Jung's visit to Tokyo, the two governments agreed to increase defense consultations and to establish regular bilateral cabinet meetings.

In sum, reacting to the implications of the missile crisis, Japan is cautiously moving to address the glaring vulnerability and lack of preparedness that was a legacy of its postwar political-economic framework. It is also responding to the new leadership in South Korea. The two governments exchanged repeated visits of leaders and discussed their plans to co-host the 2002 World Cup Games, the possibility of an imperial visit to South Korea, market opening measures, investment facilitation, and common approaches to trade issues in the WTO negotiations. The substantial progress in improving bilateral relations was largely the initiative of Kim Dae Jung. The important question is whether this development will be sustained after he leaves office.

By most standards, these recent steps taken by Japan to enhance its security are modest. They are cautious but cumulative steps which the Yoshida doctrine and a narrow constitutional interpretation would have earlier proscribed. They are signs that Japan is moving toward a heightened awareness of its own security needs and responsibilities, and as such constitute a window of opportunity. For all the dangers of the present situation on the Korean Peninsula, this window offers possibilities for preparing the ground for a more stable future order in the region by building closer ties between Seoul and Tokyo. U.S. policy is a key dynamic in this movement. Having the bilateral alliances with South Korea and Japan, U.S. leadership in security areas is critical to advance the trilateral coordination that is now being explored.

UNIFICATION ISSUES IN U.S.-JAPAN RELATIONS

The reunification of Korea has long been an issue in U.S.-Japan relations. Throughout the Cold War, Washington and Tokyo shared an interest in deterring Pyongyang from attempting to unify the peninsula by force. U.S. military units deployed north of Seoul offered visible evidence of the American commitment; bases in Japan provided the strategic reserve and logistic infrastructure required to implement operational plans to assist in South Korea's defense. Meanwhile, Japan's economic model and assistance helped the ROK prevail in its political-economic competition with the North. The United States served as a "midwife" in the reestablishment of political ties between Japan and South Korea in the 1960s and 1970s; in the 1990s it urged Tokyo to utilize any openings it might develop with Pyongyang to discourage North Korea's quest for nuclear weapons, and to encourage a more productive relationship with Seoul.

In the post-Cold War era, strategic realities in Northeast Asia have been changing rapidly, giving a new "spin" to Korean issues in U.S.-Japanese relations.

* The atrophy of Pyongyang's economic power, the impressive strength of ROK military defenses, the durability of the U.S.-ROK alliance, the evident stake of all the major Asian powers in regional stability, and the recent improvement in North-South relations have reduced the dangers of military conflict on the peninsula. Other developments—including the disintegration of the Soviet Union, Seoul's openings to

Moscow and Beijing, and the upturn in South Korean-Japanese relations—have further tipped the local balance of power in Seoul's favor.

- Risks of conflict persist, however, though they now arise less from North Korea's military strength than from its economic stagnation and longer-term uncertainties about the stability of Kim Jung Il's regime. A breakdown of the Pyongyang regime—a contingency that now seems less likely than it appeared a few years ago—would obviously add a volatile note of uncertainty, and raise questions as to how civil or civil-military discord within the North might spill over into the South, and what would become of the DPRK's weapons of mass destruction.

- In the 1990s North Korea's political isolation and economic decline increased its determination to develop nuclear weapons as an "equalizer" against the growing conventional military strength of South Korea and/or a source of leverage to pry concessions out of the United States. While the U.S.-North Korean nuclear "Agreed Framework" concluded in 1994, served at least temporarily to freeze the DPRK's nuclear activities and to secure a pledge for the eventual dismantling of its nuclear facilities, the agreement has not dispelled all suspicions about Pyongyang's nuclear status and aspirations. Indeed, developments in 1998–99 allowed the inference, noted in a report by the United States Institute of Peace, that "North Korea may be pursuing a dual track strategy: cooperation with the United States in dismantling its overt nuclear program, while covertly developing medium- or long-range missiles capable of delivering weapons of mass destruction, and less visible nuclear facilities capable of producing warheads for these missiles."[8]

- Kim Dae Jung, who has long favored a more active quest for peaceful coexistence with the North, has sought as his proximate objective reconciliation rather than reunification with Pyongyang. Hoping to avert, or at a minimum defer, North Korea's collapse while getting South Korea's economy back on track, Kim "separated economics from politics" in pursuit of openings to Pyongyang. And he encouraged Japan and the United States to help draw the DPRK out of its self-imposed isolation.

• Between 1999 and 2000, Pyongyang, confident about Kim Jung Il's authority, determined to escape its desperate economic straits, dubious that either Washington or Tokyo will soon provide large-scale economic help, impressed by the staying power of Kim Dae Jung's "sunshine policy," and perhaps attentive to advice from Beijing, reopened the door to more normal North-South relations. Furthermore, it cultivated diplomatic links with a number of Asian and European powers, and encouraged Seoul to put greater pressure on the U.S. and Japan to exhibit a forthcoming response to North Korea's requests for assistance.

• Kim Dae Jung's historic summit meeting in June 2000 with Kim Jung Il dramatically altered the political atmosphere in South Korea, shifted the diplomatic initiative on the peninsula back into the hands of Seoul and Pyongyang, and increased hopes that North-South tensions will recede and that stronger foundations for peaceful coexistence can be laid. This in turn stimulated greater interest by Washington and Tokyo in normalizing ties with Pyongyang even though questions persist as to whether the North's new course represents a tactical ploy or more fundamental strategic adjustment.

THE CHALLENGES OF POLICY COORDINATION ON KOREAN ISSUES

The challenges of policy coordination with Japan have focused in recent years on two particular reunification scenarios: (1) the absorption of North Korea into the ROK as a byproduct of Pyongyang's "collapse"; and (2) a gradual movement from North-South confrontation toward peaceful coexistence, and then to unification through negotiations.[9] At present, the latter seems more plausible. Either of these logical possibilities could unfold with many variations; each would impose unique demands for policy cooperation on the United States and Japan. Pending progress toward reunification, of course, the most daunting shared challenge is in containing North Korea's nuclear and missile programs.

Collapse and Absorption

A "collapse" of the North Korean regime implies more than just the replacement of the current leadership through, for example, a coup d'etat. It suggests a loss of governmental legitimacy and authority, widespread political confusion, the possibility of major civil discord, and perhaps a massive humanitarian crisis. Needless to say, such an "implosion" seems much less likely in the near to mid-range future than many thought a few years ago. The DPRK regime has demonstrated surprising staying power; and Kim Jung Il unexpected resilience. North Korea's repressive apparatus remains intact and brutally efficient; the capacity of its people to endure hardship has proven to be quite extraordinary. And Pyongyang is now moving swiftly to reestablish stronger ties with erstwhile allies (Russia and China), accelerate normalization talks with the U.S. and Japan, and establish diplomatic links with others (e.g. Italy, France, Germany, etc.). All these steps should increase its ability to secure outside aid to ameliorate its economic crisis and ward off a political crisis.

Still, North Korea faces a tricky political dilemma. More normal ties with the outside world imply a greater openness of North Korean society to outside influences. Market-oriented reforms would help overcome economic stagnation, yet expose its political system to new dangers. Indeed, authoritarian regimes may be most vulnerable when conditions are improving, though not as rapidly as expectations. Thus, "collapse" scenarios while perhaps less likely, cannot entirely be discounted.

Major instability in the North—let alone its collapse—would test the U.S. and Japanese ability to cooperate to fortify deterrence and cope with a major humanitarian crisis. Such contingencies could include massive emigration arising from food shortages and/or a catastrophic breakdown of the food distribution system. North Korea's "implosion" would raise other questions—how to respond to possible South Korean moves to occupy the North, how to resist Chinese temptations to intervene, and how to finance the integration of Korea's disparate economic structures.

Reunification through Prolonged Peaceful Coexistence

A more plausible, more protracted, and less risky scenario for accomplishing Korean unity would involve an incremental process of peaceful engagement and negotiation between Seoul and Pyongyang, nudged along by the major powers in Northeast Asia. Such a scenario presumes a gradual accommodation between North and South and its corollary: a growing exposure of North Korea to the wider international community. South Korean authorities clearly favor this option. It likewise appeals to Washington and Tokyo, not to mention Beijing and Moscow. And North Korea now appears prepared to facilitate movement in this direction.

Engagement by Tokyo and Washington with Pyongyang to advance North-South reconciliation will benefit from parallel courses of action on such issues as food aid, the dismantling of economic sanctions toward North Korea, the utilization of our respective economic levers of influence to encourage progress in the renewed North-South dialogue, and the choice of appropriate venues for tackling Korean security issues. If reunification were to be achieved, Washington and Tokyo would need to wrestle with another set of daunting issues—how to help finance the integration of drastically different economic structures; how to nurture regional institutions that can cushion the shocks of such a far-reaching change in the regional geopolitical structure; whether to maintain a U.S. strategic relationship with a unified Korea; and how to relate such a commitment to our links with the region's other major powers.

The Nuclear and Missile Issues

Whatever Pyongyang's motives for seeking to develop nuclear weapons, it is clear that the United States cannot put together an effective nuclear nonproliferation strategy toward North Korea without Japan's active collaboration. A U.S. preemptive military response would require Japan's political and logistical support. Economic sanctions would be ineffectual without Tokyo's participation. Sustaining the 1994 Agreed Framework presupposes continuing Japanese financial contributions. Persuading Pyongyang to foreswear the development, testing, deployment, and export of longer-range missiles demands coordinated diplomatic efforts by Tokyo and Washington. If counterproliferation efforts should fail, the need for more effective theater ballistic missile defenses—which presumes U.S.-Japanese political and technical cooperation—is destined to grow.

North Korea's more conciliatory and open diplomacy should strengthen the Agreed Nuclear Framework. But just as Pyongyang's recent foreign policy shift took many observers by surprise, its highly centralized regime could reverse direction again with little forewarning. Hence, the underpinnings of the Agreed Nuclear Framework remain a bit fragile. Doubts in America and Japan about Pyongyang's fidelity to the agreement increased in 1998 and 1999 due to North Korea's missile launch over Japanese territory and mysterious excavations near Yongbyon.[10] Such concerns complicated at least temporarily the ability of the U.S. and Japanese governments to meet their own obligations under the Agreed Framework and diminished their incentives to do so. They also provided an inducement to forge a more intensive U.S.-ROK-Japanese consultative process to deal with the North and to consider proposals—i.e., the Perry plan—for testing Pyongyang's intentions.

NATIONAL INTERESTS AND POLICY OPTIONS

U.S.-Japan Policy Coordination

The United States shares with Japan a host of security, economic, and political interests in Korea. Both have a stake in a stable balance of power in Northeast Asia, in preserving South Korea's independence, in avoiding war on the peninsula, in keeping Pyongyang's nuclear weapons program frozen, and in restricting the development, testing, deployment, and export of ballistic missiles. Both also share interests in seeing South Korea overcome the effects of the Asian financial crisis, regain its economic health, and establish a sustained and constructive dialogue with Pyongyang.

To be sure, Japan and the United States may bring somewhat different perspectives to bear on the issue of Korea's reunification. For America, a unified Korea—presuming it could be accomplished peacefully—would be a blessing. A united Korea would not threaten to embroil U.S. troops in a fratricidal struggle; it would supply a powerful buffer between the major powers in Northeast Asia; and given the size of its neighbors and the bitter memories Koreans harbor of past major power encroachments, it would retain a strong interest in maintaining close ties with the United States—the most distant and disinterested of the major powers. For Japan, a united Korea could become either a powerful commercial and political rival, susceptible to Beijing's influence, or an even closer partner and ally. Tokyo is unlikely either to seek to block Korea's reunification or to hasten it for fear of evoking accusations of interfering in Korean affairs or of complicating its relations with the United States. For the moment it is content to develop closer links with Seoul, endorse Kim Dae Jung's sunshine policy, cultivate improved relations with other Northeast Asian powers, and pursue its own normalization talks with North Korea in a cautious, tough-minded way.

Between Washington and Tokyo, policy coordination on Korean issues is inherently complex and challenging:

- Each is largely in the dark about the motivations underlying North Korea's policy moves, and each must balance its stakes in developing closer ties with the North with the political risks of doing so in the absence of forthright and reciprocal responses from Pyongyang.

- There is a natural tension between the approach that each instinctively takes. The United States, which is allied to the ROK and maintains troops there, normally seeks to manage grand strategy toward Korea while maximizing Japan's support for its implementation. By contrast, Japan, which has shunned overseas commitments for half a century, seeks to extend Washington's responsibility for handling security issues on the peninsula, while retaining maximum flexibility as to how it will respond to specific requests for help.

- There is also an asymmetry in their involvement in negotiations on Korea's future. The United States has been directly engaged along with Seoul, Pyongyang, and Beijing in the currently moribund four-party talks. Japan is not.[11] Hence, along with Moscow, Tokyo tends to favor a broader six-power forum (the U.S., China, Japan, Russia, South Korea, and North Korea) through which it could participate in decisions that will affect its future security environment. U.S. officials occasionally acknowledge the logic of a larger forum but fear that an effort to construct it now would complicate current negotiations.

- Both Tokyo and Washington confront domestic political minefields on Korean issues. In the United States, a Democratic president has confronted a Republican congressional majority that is distrustful of the administration's instincts on Korean issues. In Tokyo, the governing coalition contains parties with potentially conflicting perspectives on policy initiatives toward Korea.

- And heretofore, Pyongyang has appeared to assign a higher priority to normalizing relations with Washington than Tokyo, hoping perhaps to "soften" Japanese negotiating tactics by manipulating its fears of being left behind.

These challenges notwithstanding, Japan and the United States have managed to preserve a fair degree of compatibility in their approaches to Korea policy, particularly since the appointment in 1998 of former Secretary of Defense William Perry as coordinator for U.S. policy toward North Korea. In broad terms the objectives of Washington and Tokyo include: (1) deferring Pyongyang's collapse while preparing on a contingency basis to cope with it, should it occur; (2) solidifying North Korea's commitment to a freeze of its nuclear activities while intensifying efforts to restrain its drive to develop, test, export, and deploy advanced ballistic missiles; and (3) encouraging the DPRK to undertake a serious accommodation with the ROK through peaceful negotiations.

In keeping with these objectives, neither the Clinton administration or the Obuchi or Mori governments has attempted to accelerate North Korea's collapse or to embrace the sort of unreciprocated engagement with the North that Kim Dae Jung has at times encouraged.[12]

Each government has calculated that conscious efforts to deepen the North's economic crisis or stimulate internal discord would raise the risk of conflict, put it on a collision course with Seoul, and complicate its relations with Beijing. Both fear that tougher economic sanctions would harm the North Korean people more than the DPRK government in the short- to mid-term. Moreover, food aid is particularly difficult for the U.S. government to wield as an economic weapon, since important segments of the American public are reluctant to withhold humanitarian assistance from a starving populace, even in a country as unpredictable and dangerous as North Korea.

Nor is the United States or Japan currently prepared to extend its economic engagement with Pyongyang very far without reference to the latter's security policies. Unreciprocated gestures to foster trade and investment with the North are regarded as substantively dubious and politically risky. To sustain a variant of South Korea's "sunshine policy" without clear and verifiable North Korean steps to accommodate Washington's and Tokyo's political and security concerns would elicit little support from the U.S. Congress or Japanese Diet; it would elicit sharp criticism from the press; and it might even provoke anxiety among the most ardent ROK proponents of Kim Dae Jung's policy.

Foreswearing a strategy to hasten the North's collapse, the Clinton administration reaffirmed a more modest, two-track approach. The first was to foster a united diplomatic front among the United States, Japan, and South Korea to encourage Pyongyang's restraint and to supply Beijing with incentives for urging caution on North Korea. Clear progress was achieved on this front. Japanese Diet approval of the revised U.S.-Japan Defense Cooperation Guidelines in May 1999 bolstered the U.S. deterrent posture and permitted Japan's cooperation in the event deterrence on the peninsula should fail. Additionally, North Korea's Taepo Dong missile test over Japan in August 1998 hastened expanded U.S.-Japanese research and development cooperation on theater ballistic missile defenses,[13] and prompted Tokyo to warn North Korea in unusually blunt terms that it would terminate its financial support for KEDO if Pyongyang conducted further missile tests. This in turn served to stiffen the U.S. negotiating stance toward North Korea—an unusual but felicitous reversal of roles between Tokyo and Washington.

The second track involved a more active pattern of engagement with North Korea, designed less to reform or undermine the Pyongyang regime than to moderate its external conduct. The approach relies on a series of reciprocal steps to satisfy U.S. and allied concerns about Pyongyang's nuclear and missile aspirations while responding more affirmatively to Pyongyang's desire for a dismantling of U.S. economic sanctions and the establishment of normal diplomatic relations.

Specifically, through the Perry proposals, which were the subject of negotiations between Washington and Pyongyang in Berlin in September 1999, the United States sought: (1) complete and verifiable assurances that the North Koreans did not have a nuclear weapons program; (2) a verifiable cessation of the testing, production, and deployment of missiles exceeding the parameters of the Missile Technology Control Regime; and (3) the termination of export sales of such missiles and equipment and the technologies associated with them. In return Washington offered to move in a step-by-step fashion to relieve bilateral economic sanctions and normalize diplomatic ties. Perry also conveyed to North Korean officials the prospect of considerably tougher measures in the event Pyongyang spurned a conciliatory approach.

Results of these negotiations were encouraging, albeit inconclusive. In the Berlin Agreement, Pyongyang proclaimed a unilateral suspension of missile tests while talks regarding the dismantling of U.S. economic sanctions and steps to develop more regular diplomatic links were intensified.

The South Korean and Japanese governments officially welcomed the Berlin Agreement. Republican leaders expressed misgivings, but Congress gave the Clinton administration some "running room" to explore possibilities. The agreement also earned the support of the wider international community. By demonstrating a readiness to develop more constructive ties with Pyongyang, moreover, the U.S. would find it easier to mobilize domestic backing and international support for a tougher response, if North Korea should return to confrontational tactics.

The "price" the U.S. paid to secure the test moratorium, moreover, was limited. A U.S. commitment to normalize diplomatic relations and begin dismantling economic sanctions—implemented in mid-2000 by partially lifting the Trading with the Enemy Act's ban of all trade and investment with North Korea—had already been promised in the 1994 Agreed Framework. The removal of barriers to trade and investment could not guarantee that significant trade and investment would develop; that required decisions by private companies, which have been understandably skeptical about investing scarce resources in so problematic an economic environment as North Korea's. The reciprocal establishment of liaison offices and even more formal diplomatic ties would permit more direct communications with North Korean authorities and perhaps greater understanding of developments in the North. Both could be regarded as advantageous to the United States rather than as "concessions" to North Korea.

These considerations notwithstanding, the Berlin Agreement should not be oversold. It put missile restraints on the negotiating agenda, but the suspension of North Korean tests was only temporary. Even the modest "concessions" that were offered in return for this suspension reinforced an impression that negotiations with Pyongyang invariably entailed elements of extortion, and such precedents inevitably fostered a degree of moral hazard. Nor did these steps, as potentially useful as they might be, address the security dangers arising from the DPRK's forward conventional military deployments, utilize U.S. leverage to encourage North-South talks, or address what many consider the heart of the nonproliferation problem, i.e. the nature of North Korea's totalitarian and highly secretive regime. At best, the United States faced months of hard slogging in further negotiations. Yet, Japan supported the effort.

Indeed, in the wake of the Berlin Agreement, Tokyo decided to resume charter flights to North Korea, which had been suspended following the August 1998 missile tests. Although reluctant to resume food aid or to remove a ban on fund transfers until North Korea went beyond a temporary suspension of missile tests and/or addressed other humanitarian issues of concern to the Japanese, Tokyo did provide additional food aid in mid–2000 as an "entry fee" to kick start the resumption of its own normalization talks with North Korea.

When those talks get serious, (as of November 2000 it seems they may), Japan possesses ample sources of leverage. A normalization of Tokyo's relations with North Korea would bring the latter significant economic assistance. It could also bring an end to Tokyo's opposition to Pyongyang's bid for membership in the Asian Development Bank, the IMF, and the World Bank. Japan remains a potentially major trading partner; its government influences the flow of remittances from the pro-North Korean Chosen-soren organization; and if the North ever creates a hospitable political and legal economic environment for economic intercourse with the outside world,

Japan would become a major source of foreign investment. All of these considerations reinforce the importance of close U.S.-Japanese collaboration in approaching negotiations with the North—particularly now that a serious North-South dialogue has been resumed.

The pace of U.S.-North Korean talks accelerated in the wake of Kim Dae Jung's summit meeting with Kim Jung Il in June 2000. In October 2000 visits by Vice Marshall Jo Myong Rok to Washington, and by Secretary of State Albright to Pyongyang even stimulated talk about a possible trip by President Clinton to North Korea before leaving office. And in Japan both LDP leaders and the Ministry of Foreign Affairs now exhibit greater eagerness for a breakthrough in their talks with Pyongyang. While the pace of bilateral exchanges is quickening, however, it is not yet clear how quickly expanded U.S. or Japanese cooperation with North Korea will take shape. Indeed, many American and Japanese officials continue to wonder whether Pyongyang's more conciliatory diplomacy represents a tactical ploy or a more fundamental strategic adjustment.

In any event changes in the political atmosphere on the peninsula are giving a new twist to the challenge of coordinating policy between Washington and Tokyo.

- The appearance of a less menacing North Korea, if sustained, will diminish the sense of urgency which has provided much of the rationale for U.S.-Japanese cooperation on the development of theater ballistic missile defenses.
- The less threatening security environment on the peninsula is already stimulating sharper criticism in South Korea of the size of the U.S. military presence there, as well as requests to change certain provisions of the U.S.-ROK Status of Forces Agreement—issues to which Japanese officials pay close attention.
- Since Pyongyang is currently conducting parallel negotiations with Seoul, Washington, and Tokyo, it will undoubtedly be looking for ways of playing us off against one another.
- As the initiative on Korean diplomacy shifts back to Seoul and Pyongyang, moreover, Japan's and America's stake in close trilateral

consultations with the ROK increases, though its influence over the frequency and content of such consultations may not.

* And with respect to negotiating priorities, Seoul will naturally push intra-Korean issues to the top of the agenda, while Tokyo and Washington remain principally preoccupied by concerns about Pyongyang's nuclear weapons program and missile delivery capabilities, its export of sensitive technologies, and other features of its external conduct. America's perspectives are not destined to diverge from Seoul's, but neither will its priorities automatically coincide.

Washington and Tokyo should welcome the fact that a serious North-South dialogue has been resumed. Encouraging such a dialogue has long been a strategic aim. Peaceful coexistence is possible only insofar as the parties most directly concerned can work out a durable accommodation. As outside powers, the United States and Japan can afford to approach the North with a more measured and prudent pace, exacting a measure of reciprocity for concessions we extend, while testing North Korea's readiness to open itself gradually to outside influences. It is politically wise for both of us to proceed in that fashion, for critics in the Congress and the Diet are watching for miscues. It would be counterproductive for the United States to cut deals with the North at a pace or on terms which would damage diplomatic cooperation with Seoul or Tokyo—or for that matter, divert Pyongyang's attention away from its need to come to terms with Seoul. William Perry's greatest legacy with respect to Korean policy was the scrupulous process of trilateral consultation, which he arranged among Japan, the United States, and South Korea on matters related to the North. In the period ahead that process will be more crucial than ever.

FUTURE ISSUES

Over the longer term, the United States should encourage the evolution of multilateral security institutions in Northeast Asia. The United States, China, and the two Koreas possess special responsibilities for peacemaking on the peninsula deriving from their roles in preserving the armistice arrangements. Yet Japan—and Russia as well—have stakes in the stable resolution of Korean issues. If unification or a North-South accommodation occurs, Japan will be called upon to play a major role in supporting the North's economic revival and integration into the regional economy. Alternatively, if Pyongyang were to collapse, Japan would immediately confront potentially costly and risky consequences. More broadly, a region in which the interests of the four major powers intersect needs multilateral institutions to cushion the shocks arising from the interplay among their policies. One could start with a subregional version of the ASEAN Regional Forum—for example, with a periodic six-power consultation devoted to encouraging greater transparency on defense matters, confidence-building measures, and preventive diplomacy. All are relevant to any serious effort to cope with the Korea issue in the long term.

Another long-term issue is the fate of U.S. security ties with a unified Korea. Reunification would, of course, require a rethinking of the logic of both the U.S.-ROK alliance and the U.S. military presence on the peninsula. Both have served largely as a deterrent against North Korean aggression. In a reunited Korea, many will ask, why would there be any further need for the alliance, let alone forward-deployed U.S. military forces? The question itself is not dispositive, for the same issue arose in connection with Germany. Yet, a united Germany sits within an expanded NATO even though the Soviet Union and Warsaw Pact are now history.

It is possible that nationalist sentiment in Korea would reject a post-reunification U.S. security role on the peninsula. The Chinese, moreover, have little self-evident incentive to acquiesce to an American security role in a unified Korea, and they have traditionally opposed foreign military bases on the Asian mainland. Some Japanese may consider the unification of Korea as an opportune moment to phase out the U.S. military presence in Japan as well as in Korea. And the American people could regard reunification as a timely moment to terminate security commitments to Korea.

All these eventualities are possible. They are not inevitable. Kim Dae Jung has already expressed his hope that a residual U.S. military presence—albeit one that was configured differently—would remain after unification. And he has asserted that Kim Jung Il acknowledged the logic of that view in their Summit Talks in June 2000.[14] Located between China and Japan, many Koreans regard a continued security connection with the United States a necessary means of fortifying their independence vis-à-vis powerful neighbors. While China will doubtlessly be wary of a continued U.S. presence, it might conceivably be persuaded to accept a modified U.S. military role in Korea if it were slimmed down and confined geographically to areas well away from China's borders. Much would certainly depend on the state of U.S.-China relations at the time.

If strongly requested by a democratic Korean government, the American people might be willing to perpetuate the alliance with Korea while modifying the supporting arrangements and reducing and perhaps relocating major U.S. military deployments on the peninsula. This could be viewed as a relatively low cost means of supporting a strong ally while helping forestall a future Korean bid for nuclear weapons. Japan should welcome such a decision. Continued defense links between Washington and Seoul could diminish the lure of more intimate security ties between South Korea and China. And even a modest U.S. military presence in Korea should help sustain political support in Japan for forward deployments in that country. Even China might eventually conclude that a Korea loosely aligned with the United States might be preferable to a free-floating Korea flirting with the nuclear option or drifting toward closer defense relations with Japan.

It will be especially important to see that a unified Korea is a nonnuclear state. Japan has a huge interest in encouraging this outcome, for despite its long-standing policy and the sentiments of its people, Tokyo would find it difficult to resist acquiring nuclear weapons of its own if a united Korea were to develop or obtain them—for example, from a failed North Korea. Such developments would cast a pall over Korean-Japanese relations and complicate the U.S. strategic position in Northeast Asia. For this reason, among others, it is essential for Japan to continue cultivating closer ties with Seoul, and to assure the Koreans that it poses no threat to them. This will not be an easy task, given the legacy of mistrust between them, but it is a practicable objective.

In summary, Japan's cooperation is essential to any serious U.S. effort to move developments on the Korean Peninsula toward peaceful coexistence and reunification. The U.S.-Japan alliance bolsters deterrence in Korea and provides reassurance to both Pyongyang and Seoul that Japan's military strength is anchored to the U.S. connection. If North Korea succumbs to acute political instability, Japan can help the United States and Seoul cope with uncertainties and humanitarian crises. If the North's collapse leads to its eventual absorption by the South, Japan's assistance will be critical to the growth and prosperity of a unified Korea. And if the outside world is to find ways of helping Seoul draw North Korea into a more constructive involvement in the affairs of the Northeast Asian region, Japan has a large role to play in that endeavor.

Japan may not take the lead in Korean diplomacy. But neither can it be taken for granted. If its support is to be earned, its representatives must be carefully and consistently consulted. The proposals advanced by the United States must be designed to defend Tokyo's interests as well as its own. Unless U.S. initiatives account for Japanese interests, Tokyo will not be able to muster the necessary domestic support to provide a helping hand. And unless Japan is helpful, it will be difficult for the United States to mobilize the requisite political support to sustain its own role.

As this chapter has demonstrated, U.S. and Japanese diplomacy toward Korea have reached a new and hopeful phase. North-South talks have resumed. Relations between Seoul, Washington and Tokyo are in solid shape, and trilateral consultations among them have become routine. The Berlin Agreement expanded opportunities for a more direct U.S. relationship with North Korea. The North-South Summit in June 2000 provided additional incentives for capitalizing on those opportunities. Subsequent bilateral talks between Washington and Pyongyang on missile restraints and terrorism issues have yielded substantive advances, though no definitive breakthroughs (as of early November 2000). Japan's discussions with North Korea over the terms of normalization have evidently again turned serious as well.

The North-South talks remain central; it is there that the key accommodations must be struck if peaceful coexistence is to be put on a secure and durable basis. History reminds us that this will not be easy. In 1972 and 1991 North-South detente proved short-lived. More contemporary evidence suggests that the North Koreans are irresistibly tempted to put their relations with the South on the back-burner as opportunities for securing assistance from major outside powers present themselves. Thus the basic challenge of trilateral cooperation between the U.S., Japan, and the ROK remains the task of aligning U.S. negotiating aims and diplomatic tactics in such a way as to induce or impel Pyongyang to come to terms with Seoul and provide more substantial underpinnings for peaceful coexistence between North and South Korea.

Defining the contents of future negotiations in a way that accommodates the concerns of Seoul, Washington, and Tokyo (not to mention Beijing and Moscow) while sustaining the interests of Pyongyang will be no simple job. Critics in Congress and the Diet are watching for miscues. Powerful political constituencies in the United States and Japan may well balk at the concessions tough negotiations usually bring. Even if politically defensible bargains with the North are struck, there is no guarantee that Pyongyang will be steadfast in executing its end of the deal. The development of more normal U.S.-North Korean ties will almost inevitably stimulate nervousness in Tokyo, even as a reconciliation between Japan and North Korea will prompt anxieties in Washington, however scrupulous the consultations. Still, the effort to test Pyongyang's readiness to meet the political and security concerns of Seoul, Tokyo, and the United States is clearly worth the risks, if we approach the task with prudence. And the possibilities of a successful result have never seemed more promising.

NOTES

1. Masashi Nishihara, "Japan's Receptivity to Conditional Engagement," in *Weaving the Net: Conditional Engagement with China*, edited by James Shinn (Council on Foreign Relations, 1996), p. 187.

2. Nicholas Eberstadt, "Hastening Korean Unification," *Foreign Affairs* (March/April 1997), p. 79.

3. In preparation for writing this report the authors conducted interviews with policymakers and advisors in Tokyo and Seoul during the summer of 1998.

4. Eric Heginbotham and Richard J. Samuels, "Mercantile Realism and Japanese

Foreign Policy," *International Security* (Spring 1998), pp. 199–200.

5. See Akio Watanabe and Tsutomu Kikuchi, "Japan's Perspective on APEC: Community or Association," *NBR Analysis*, The National Bureau of Asian Research, vol. 6, no. 3 (November 1995), pp. 35–36.

6. "Completion of the Review of the Guidelines for U.S.-Japan Defense Cooperation," Department of Defense News Release, September 23, 1997.

7. See Don Oberdorfer, *The Two Koreas: A Contemporary History*, (Reading, Mass.: Addison-Wesley, 1997), pp. 221–222.

8. "Mistrust and the Korean Peninsula: Dangers of Miscalculation," *USIP Special Report*, The United States Institute of Peace, (November 1998), p.1.

9. For a broader analysis of these reunification scenarios, see chapter 2 in this volume, "Conflict and Cooperation: The Pacific Powers and Korea," by Chae-Jin Lee.

10. Although an on-site inspection turned up no concrete evidence of violations of the agreement, neither have U.S. officials been provided a persuasive explanation of the purpose of these excavation activities.

11. Tokyo is, of course, in a position to exert influence on Pyongyang's thinking on such issues through its own bilateral talks.

12. Though both governments have supplied sizable quantities of food aid without much conditionality.

13. In an interview with the *Asahi Shimbun* in early November 1999, Perry noted that if the DPRK were to threaten Japan there would be strong incentives to deploy theater ballistic missile defenses. But in the meantime, the United States, Japan and the ROK were working to convince the DPRK not to make such attempts. *Agence-France Press*, "US Envoy Urges Japan to Weigh Deployment of Anti-Missile Defense," Tokyo, Nov. 5, 1999.

14. Other DPRK officials considered to be speaking for the record have offered similar views for several years.

6

Russia, Korea, and Northeast Asia

Herbert J. Ellison

Many of the high hopes that accompanied the Russian Revolution of 1989–91 have been shattered, and the vision of a new Russian role in Northeast Asia is among them. The dual expectations of full regional partnership with the United States, Japan, and South Korea and rapid Russian economic integration into the region have been mostly disappointed. A decade later, evidence of policy weakness or failure can be found in the meager Russian influence in the two Koreas; in the feeble development of economic ties, especially with the ROK and Japan; and in the absence of regional diplomatic and security partnerships with other major powers—particularly the United States and Japan—concerned with the maintenance of security in a vital region with great potential for dangerous conflict. Faced with a combination of huge conventional military forces positioned on either side of a border only a few miles from Seoul and the threat of a Stalinist North Korean state on the brink of starvation and economic collapse—yet busily developing nuclear weapons and delivery systems—the major powers have not found Russia a useful partner in responding to the dangers confronting them.

The questions posed in this chapter are why the results have been so disappointing and what, if any, are the prospects for improvement. Seeking answers to these questions requires comment not just on the course and motives of Russian diplomacy in Northeast Asia, but also on the turbulent political struggle within Russia which has often frustrated constructive change in both domestic and foreign policy. The answers lie as well in the policies of the other regional powers—policies that have sometimes thwarted development of a constructive Russian role in the search for stability and peace on the Korean Peninsula.

THE GORBACHEV LEGACY

The crucial turning point in Russia's Korea policy came near the end of the Gorbachev era. In no area of Soviet foreign policy was the famous "new thinking" more influential than in Asia policy, within which Korea policy was a central component. The creative diplomatic initiatives included the reconciliation with China by May 1989, overtures to Japan on the Kurile Islands issue, and major shifts in policy toward Russia's main East Asian client states, Vietnam and North Korea. For Mikhail Gorbachev there were three main motives for the policy shift on Korea: (1) the urgent need to reduce the cost of Soviet subsidies for economic and military aid, which the faltering Soviet economy could no longer bear; (2) the negative view of North Korea's brand of communism among the reforming leaders in Moscow; and (3) the tremendous appeal of economic cooperation with South Korea that was expected to contribute much to restructuring and expanding the Soviet economy.

The dramatic climax of the shift in Soviet policy toward the Korean Peninsula was the establishment of Soviet diplomatic relations with South Korea in September 1990, an action described by the North as a "betrayal of socialism." The speedy foreign policy reorientation of the DPRK during the following year virtually eliminated the special relationship with the Soviets as Pyongyang quickly sought accommodation or active cooperation with South Korea, China, Japan, and the United States.

North Korea made major concessions to achieve its goals: abandonment of the condition of withdrawal of U.S. military forces and reduction of ROK military forces prior to North-South talks; expanded cooperation with China, despite growing Chinese ties with Seoul; and signals to the United States and Japan that Pyongyang was prepared to ignore the U.S.-Japan security treaty and seek normalization talks with both. The most ominous consequence of the new Soviet ties with South Korea was evident in a statement from the North Korean Foreign Ministry in September 1990 that promised "to take measures to provide for ourselves some weapons for which we have so far relied on the [Soviet] alliance."[1] Soviet "betrayal" was offered as justification for pursuit of nuclear weapons.

THE TRANSITION TO YELTSIN'S LEADERSHIP

Such was the negative legacy in relations with Pyongyang inherited by the Yeltsin government when it assumed power a little over a year later. The traditional special ties had been severed—and the situation gravely complicated— by the determination of North Korea to pursue both a challenging new diplomatic course and a program for the development of nuclear weapons. The situation was further complicated by the failed coup of August 1991 and the formal end of the Soviet Union the following December. The new Yeltsin government was not just reformed communist but anticommunist, dedicated to the introduction of democracy and a market economy. It quickly received the predictable condemnation from Pyongyang, which described the events as a logical consequence of Gorbachev's "betrayal of socialism."

Before discussing the details of Russian policy toward the Koreas and Northeast Asia in the Yeltsin era, it is helpful to review briefly the major factors affecting policy during that crucial period. These include the evolution of the political system and political leadership, the experience of economic reform (including foreign economic policy), and the main phases of foreign policy, with emphasis upon policy leaders and policy ideas inside Russia and the relations of Russia with the other powers in the region.

The Political System and Political Leadership

A few basics about the postcommunist political system in Russia are essential to the discussion of foreign policy. The first is that it is not, in the full sense of the expression, postcommunist. A substantial part of the legacy of communist governmental structure and personnel remain in place, and though the party dictatorship had been consigned to "the dustbin of history" (to quote Trotsky on the Russian Provisional Government of 1917), the Communist Party of the Russian Federation (CPRF) and its allies have dominated the crucial lower house of the parliament through democratic elections. They have managed to block much of the legislation needed for the economic institutions and policies of a market economy and greatly retarded the economic transition and economic growth. They have also had a major impact on foreign policy.

Lack of Economic Reform

The impressive advances in economic reform at the national level, such as macroeconomic stabilization and ruble convertibility (until the August 1998 financial collapse) and privatization of industry, trade, and housing, were made possible by President Boris Yeltsin's reform of the inherited political structure. At the outset he used special temporary powers granted by the Russian Supreme Soviet shortly before Gorbachev's resignation. These were expanded and institutionalized in the new constitution of December 1993, which allowed the president to introduce major changes by decree. The simultaneous expansion of the powers of regional governments—including the right to elect their own leaders—has enabled some of them to become innovators in economic reform within their own jurisdiction.

Despite these achievements, however, the Yelstsin era was one of persistent conflict and delay in the reform effort, a situation resulting from the fact that fully committed reformers led the government for scarcely two years of the first decade of Russian independence. This situation has done a great deal of damage to Russian plans to achieve a major role in the dynamic East Asian economy. Despite its enormous resources, the Russian Far East, for example, has faced tremendous obstacles in attracting foreign investment.[2] Investors from many countries have eagerly entered the region hoping to play a major part in its development, only to discover an inadequate economic infrastructure, an obstructionist bureaucracy, widespread corruption, and government policies hostile to foreign investment. This is nowhere more evident—or more inimical to the integration of the Russian Far East into the

East Asian economy—than in the restrictive regulation of foreign investment in the mineral resources of the region.[3] Not only were foreign firms subjected to restrictive regulation, but in energy and mineral exports they found themselves paying heavy taxes that were waived for their Russian competitors.

Hence the tremendous opportunities for Russia to become a major factor in the Asian economy remain largely unexploited. Achievement of the immense potential of Russia's natural resources on world markets will require massive foreign investment: but policy has been dominated by a mix of communist objections to foreign investment in principal, nationalist insistence on defense of "strategic resources" from capture by foreign interests, and powerful domestic financial groups seeking to protect their own corrupt ownership and/or exploitation of valuable natural resources from foreign competition.

The failure of the resultant policies is evident in the fact that in 1997 foreign investment in China was roughly eleven times larger as a percentage of GDP than in Russia.[4] Economic development has been severely constrained, integration into the East Asian economy has been retarded, and the state has been deprived of desperately needed tax revenues. The dream of Russia as a major economic power in Asia remains just that. In its stead is a state nearly halved in population, territory, and economic product, and recently undergoing a general financial collapse of uncertain outcome. Yet economic weakness explains much—but by no means all—of the of the marginalization of Russia in the East Asian diplomatic arena. Much of the explanation lies in Russian foreign policy.

Russia Seeks a New Course

The Yeltsin era began with efforts by the president and the young foreign minister, Andrei Kozyrev, to stress Russia's intention to become, as Yeltsin put it in a June 1992 speech to the U.S. Congress, a "partner in the building of global democracy." Russia sought close alliance with the democratic states both to sustain its own political reform and to build economic ties conducive to economic restructuring and development. Hence the early courting of Japan and South Korea, the Asian countries which appeared most likely to provide the investment and economic assistance required for Russia's recovery and growth.

However, improved relations with Japan and Japanese economic aid were blocked by Tokyo's insistence on prior settlement of Japan's claims to the southern Kurile Islands. (Japan calls these islands its "Northern Territories.") Japanese pressure for return of the islands, a policy supported by the United States, showed little sensitivity to the achievements and plight of the Russian leader who had given sovereignty and the right of secession to the republics of the Soviet Union and faced constant communist and nationalist attack for his efforts. Though willing to concede the islands himself, Yeltsin was checked by these forces in the parliament, as well as by regional leaders in the Far East, who were categorically opposed to meeting Japanese demands.

The ostentatious shift of Russia's attention to South Korea in November 1992, when Yeltsin abruptly canceled a trip to Tokyo and visited Seoul instead, marked the beginning of an effort to make South Korea rather than Japan Russia's main economic and political partner in the region. The courting of South Korea included a proclamation of joint commitment to freedom, democracy, human rights, and a market economy; a formal expression of regret for the victims of the Korean War; and presentation of the black box from the Soviet-downed Korean Airlines flight 007. The policy course further increased tensions in Russian-North Korean relations and failed to make Japan more accommodating on the islands issue or more eager to invest in Russian economic development.

Response from Pyongyang

In addition to the policy shift, many of the statements and discussions during the Yeltsin visit to Seoul were bound to give deep offense to Pyongyang. These included criticism of communism and the North Korean regime and the announcement that the 1961 Soviet-North Korean defense treaty was defunct and that arms shipments had been suspended. To these offenses were added a speech to the South Korean National Assembly announcing that the focus of Russian policy had shifted to Asia and that South Korea would be Russia's leading partner in that region. There was also discussion during the trip of Russian-South Korean defense cooperation. The 1993 visit by Defense Minister Pavel Grachev to discuss defense cooperation included agreements on military exchanges. The subsequent Russian representation at Team Spirit exercises with the United States and a Russian offer to sell weapons to the ROK were sharply denounced by Pyongyang.

Clearly Russian policy played a major role in the events leading up to the North Korean withdrawal from the Nuclear Nonproliferation Treaty in March 1993. Russia unilaterally reduced defense cooperation with North Korea to support only in the event of an attack on that country and demanded repayment of the $3.5 billion North Korean debt to the Soviet Union—both of which merely added to the long list of other offenses and to the reasons for the North Korean reaction. The Russian response—a demand for North Korea to abandon plans to develop a nuclear bomb and a commitment to join international sanctions—hardened North Korean resistance and elicited reciprocal offenses, such as the extension of the North Korean military zone in the Sea of Japan/Eastern Sea and verbal attacks on the Russians for disposal of nuclear waste in that sea.

Policy Debate

These events were an important factor in the foreign policy debate in Russia from 1993 through 1995, a debate in which Foreign Minister Kozyrev was under attack both for a putative subservience to the West and neglect of Russian interests in Asia. The attacks on Kozyrev were important in rallying Russian opposition to the expansion of NATO and focused heavily on the claim that he had failed to appreciate that Russia was a Eurasian power. A significant role in the debate, and a major role in the clandestine mobilization against Kozyrev, was played by VSR (Foreign Intelligence) head Yevgeny Primakov, who became Kozyrev's successor in January 1996. Primakov would bring major changes to Russian foreign and security policy, including especially Russian policy in Northeast Asia.

The Russian critics' case against Kozyrev was based in part on the charge that he had been clumsy in dealing with North Korea and had created an unnecessary confrontation. The case was strengthened by the events following Pyongyang's announcement of withdrawal from the NPT, especially the exclusion of Russia from participation in the eventual settlement.

Kozyrev's critics pointed specifically to the Agreed Framework worked out between North Korea and the United States in Geneva in October 1994. North Korea agreed to suspend its nuclear weapons program in exchange for less dangerous nuclear reactors and fuel oil. The United States also agreed to ease economic sanctions against North Korea and to allow telecommunications links and some oil imports. A few months later, on March 9, 1995, the United States, South Korea, and Japan agreed in New York to establish the Korean Peninsula Energy Development Organization. The agreement called for financing and support of two light water reactors, worth $4.5 billion, and for the supply of 500,000 tons of heavy crude oil per year. Russia protested its exclusion from the agreement, offering to provide two of the light water reactors, but as South Korea was paying for the reactors the offer was rejected. Russia was left out of KEDO, though Australia, New Zealand, Indonesia, Canada, and Finland were included. Meanwhile, negotiations went forward providing in July 1996 for extension of the rights of KEDO in transportation and communications and guaranteeing special rights and privileges for its operations and personnel.

SEEKING A NEW POLICY: PRIMAKOV AND MULTIPOLARITY

The extensive debate in the Russian press, government, and foreign policy circles concerning East Asia policy in general, and Korea policy in particular, continued vigorously in 1995 and 1996. After the appointment of Primakov as foreign minister in January 1996, important changes began to appear in Russian policy toward East Asia, with Primakov as the key figure. The policy that emerged was dominated by Primakov's concept of "multipolarity"—code language for opposition to the single "pole" (i.e., to U.S. regional and global dominance). Primakov launched a series of policy initiatives which aimed to build a so-called strategic partnership with China, to expand and strengthen relations with Japan, and to readjust relations with the Koreas in order to reestablish Russian ties with the North that had been destroyed in the years since diplomatic recognition of the South.

In an interview in January 1997 Primakov referred to Russia's "mighty ally" (China) in a "trend toward the formation of a multi-polar world," and announced "this means the emergence of a broad field for maneuvering, for multivector diplomacy."[5] Elaborating on various examples of the trend, he made clear that he was referring to the resistance of individual states to the policies of the United States and its allies, and that he felt Russian policy should seek to organize and lead the opposition, using the resistance to support Russian opposition to NATO expansion, the creation of a U.S.-led security structure in East Asia, or other policies.

A few days after the interview, a prominent Russian journalist followed Primakov's lead and presented a view of Eurasian politics that portrayed the United States as pushing NATO eastward against Russia in Europe, and simultaneously applying pressure to China in Asia by "forming an anti-Beijing grouping in the Far East comprising South Korea, Taiwan and other U.S. allies in the Pacific."[6] He described the post-Cold War American role as that of "global policeman, prosecutor and bailiff" and noted approvingly that U.S. pressure on both Russia and China was forging a partnership in which the two sides were now holding annual meetings of their presidents and prime ministers "to form a multipolar world without leaders and followers."

The meetings also included defense ministers. In April 1997 Russian Defense Minister Igor Rodionov visited Beijing for discussions on military cooperation. The Chinese defense minister's comments noted that "NATO is a product of the Cold War. We understand Russia's position on NATO expansion." Rodionov's main speech focused on Korea. He noted that "provision could be made for replacing American troops in the demilitarized zone with troops from neutral countries." Even more pointedly, he remarked that "in the event of an armed conflict between the Koreas, China and the U.S., which have nuclear weapons, could be drawn into the conflict," adding that "Russia would not be able to remain aloof either."

The inference drawn by the reporting Russian journalist was that this "amounted to a pledge on Moscow's part to side with the North Korean-Chinese bloc in the event of any problem, something that, in fact, already happened during the war on the Korean peninsula...."[7] The speech was reported to have elicited "tumultuous and prolonged applause" from the Chinese military personnel present.

Russia and China

Bilateral contacts and statements on military cooperation between Russia and China increased impressively during 1997 and 1998. During a January 1998 visit to Beijing of State Military Inspector and Secretary of the Defense Council Andrei Kokoshin, an *Izvestiia* reporter commented that "analysts believe that, in the past few years, defense cooperation with China has reached a level surpassing China's military relations with any other country."[8] More significant was the trend toward public expression of joint positions on current issues of international policy. Only a few weeks after the Kokoshin visit to Beijing, Boris Yeltsin and Premier Li Peng issued a joint statement in Moscow saying that Russia and China, both permanent members of the UN Security Council, would not accept a forcible resolution of the conflict with Iraq.[9]

Russia and Japan

Primakov also undertook a variety of new initiatives with Japan. Not the least interesting was the suggestion of joint Russian-Japanese economic activities in the Southern Kurile Islands/Northern Territories. Primakov's assurances that this would in no way compromise the long-standing Japanese claim of ownership of the islands showed diplomatic skill, however unconvincing his Japanese counterparts might have found it. A Russian reporter may have captured Primakov's calculation in his comment that "Japan sees the...dialogue as one way to bolster its position in Northeast Asia in the unstable pentagon formed by Tokyo, Moscow, Beijing, Seoul and Pyongyang."[10]

Primakov had several objectives in dealings with Japan. One was to gain Japanese acceptance of Russian membership in the G-7, making it the G-8. The matter was confirmed in principle during Foreign Minister Yukihiko Ikeda's official visit to Moscow in May 1997, though the Japanese emphasized that their acceptance was based on a formula of "principles and exceptions" which would preserve some matters—for example, financial problems—for discussion only by the G-7. The Japanese emphasized that settlement of the islands issue was not a precondition for membership, but also noted that once membership was settled it would be important that the matter of the islands be confronted, and that they did not understand the meaning of Primakov's formula of joint possession.[11]

During Foreign Minister Ikeda's visit to Moscow, Russian Defense Minister Rodionov, on the same visit that took him to Beijing, was busy in Tokyo seeking to calm Japanese worries about growing Chinese-Russian ties by offering military collaboration with the Japanese. Most likely, the main policy purpose of the visit was to press the Primakov line on replacing the U.S.-dominated regional security structure based on bilateral treaties with Japan and South Korea with the more fluid Primakov formula for regional security based on Primakov's "multipolarity." The Russian reporter summarized his plan as one based on "existing bilateral relations between Russia and China, Japan and the U.S., and the U.S. and Russia...." These three bilateral relationships were to be "tied into a single knot."[12] The ambiguity of the noun appears to have escaped him.

Russia, Japan, and China

It might appear hasty to conclude from the Russian policy initiatives toward Japan that their central purpose was to undermine the Japanese-American security treaty, though it is difficult to discern any other purpose in Rodionov's remarks, and such a policy would be consistent with Primakov's stress on reduction of the American role in Asia and the world. In the Russian press, on the other hand, and in publications of leading foreign policy think tanks, there is evidence of concern about the growing economic and military power of China, and the importance of Japan not just for its assistance in Russian economic development but as insurance against an aggressive China. This was the opinion of a Russian reporter, Andrei Ivanov of *Kommersant-Daily,* who commented on the new guidelines for Japanese-American defense cooperation signed in New York on September 23, 1997. He noted that Chinese reaction was hostile, especially concerning the inclusion of Taiwan in the Japanese-American joint defense zone. But he expected a more neutral reaction from Moscow.

Analysts close to the foreign ministry believe that Russia will most likely take a "neutral" stance toward the basic guidelines in view of

Japanese support for Russia's admission to the Paris Club and Japan's new initiatives in relations with Russia. Moreover, Russia, which, unlike the USSR, is not regarded as the chief adversary of the US and Japan, could benefit from the Japanese-American defensive alliance considering China's rapidly growing economic and military power. [13]

In late 1997 and early 1998 the discussions between the Japanese and Russian foreign ministers made substantial progress. In addition to extensive economic agreements, both parties endorsed the objective of signing a peace treaty by the year 2000. As they have for so many years, the obstacles to effective discussions appeared formidable, and the Japanese were uneasy about Primakov's efforts to broaden the discussion group to include government officials, particularly those concerned with economic matters, and regional leaders from the Russian Far East.[14] During the spring and summer of 1998, however, discussions went forward at an increasing pace and a variety of important new agreements were signed. These included the creation in May of the first joint investment company in the history of Russian-Japanese relations and an agreement on joint Russian-Japanese naval maneuvers in June.[15] By late July, in the run-up to the Japanese elections, Foreign Minister Keizo Obuchi, soon to be prime minister, said repeatedly that the normalization of relations with Moscow was his "mission."

In the following month, however, the test-launch of a North Korean ballistic missile over the Sea of Japan brought a rapid reevaluation of Japanese security policy, going well beyond the discussions of the preceding year. The first shock for both Russia and China was U.S.-Japanese discussion of a theater missile defense shield. The Chinese reaction to the 1997 security guidelines had been sharply negative, the Russian much less so, but both reacted with alarm to the theater missile defense discussion. Both also reacted very negatively when, in May 1999, the Japanese parliament passed supporting legislation for new U.S.-Japanese security cooperation. The changes, inspired both by the growing military power of China and the expansion of Chinese and North Korean capacities in nuclear weapons and delivery systems, were described by the *Novosti* Japan correspondent as a fundamental transformation of U.S. security policy: "For the first time since

World War II Japan's armed forces are permitted to go outside their national borders...to participate in actual operations."[16] This change, he argued, "has almost as much symbolic meaning for Asia as Germany's participation in the bombings in Yugoslavia does for Europe."

Deeply concerned about these developments, Russian policymakers and analysts stressed the urgency of efforts at regional cooperation to discourage the North Korean nuclear weapons effort, which had precipitated expanded Japanese-American challenges to their own security. Their continued endorsement of an expanded "strategic alliance" with China appeared to ignore the evidence that China's growing conventional and nuclear weapons strength had also been a major factor in the Japanese-American thinking.

RUSSIA AND KOREA

In the summer of 1996, a specialist at the Institute of the Far East of the Russian Academy of Sciences, Vasilii Mikheev, reviewed the record of Russia's Korea policy since 1991 and concluded that Russia was finally prepared to take a pragmatic approach to Korea as part of the task of building "a zone of stability along its borders."[17] He noted the ideological rather than practical reasons that led to the hasty cutback of relations with North Korea and found the "exaggerated expectations pinned on cooperation with Seoul" equally misguided, chiefly because Russia's troubled economic conditions made it impossible to reap the benefits of active economic ties with South Korea.

Confronted with the failure of both policies and with demands from a vocal segment of Duma deputies for restoration of ties with the DPRK, the Foreign Ministry attempted to conduct separate relations with Seoul and Pyongyang, though often behaving as if the real intention was to offend South Korea by cultivating ties with the North. Meanwhile, Russia took offense at the fact that it was not invited to be part of the four-party talks among North and South Korea, the United States, and China proposed in April 1996, and responded with an old Soviet proposal that added Japan and Russia and possibly representatives from the International Atomic Energy Agency or the UN. Far better, countered Mikheev, to encourage the four-party initiative, hoping it might at last provide a peace treaty to replace a 43-year-old truce, stabilize the political situation, and open the way for peaceful unification in which Russia could participate, since neither Washington nor Seoul were opposed to Russian involvement in a unification settlement. Meanwhile, continued Mikheev, the proper course would be to seek an improved relationship with North Korea but in a fashion that would not provoke a negative reaction from the South. This should be combined with pursuit of promising collaborative economic development efforts, such as the development of the Tumen River basin along the borders of Russia, China, and North Korea and the construction of a gas pipeline from Siberia to South Korea via the DPRK. These initiatives could be combined with the effort "to create a multilateral mechanism to deal with security problems in Northeast Asia."

Neither the Primakov vision of "a multilateral mechanism" (he failed to note the deep differences among the intended partners) nor the subsequent experience of Russia's Korea policy, appear to support Mikheev's sanguine analysis, however admirable his purpose and however reasonable his un-Primakovian assessment of the intentions of Seoul and Washington. In the wake of Russia's deal to trade arms with South Korea in exchange for debt reduction, Seoul received, among other items, BMP-3 infantry fighting vehicles and T-80 tanks: in a deal struck at a time when North Korean border violations and submarine intrusion into South Korean waters had increased worries about border security. North Korea responded to the shipments on October 1, 1996, by asserting that Russia "is all but in the camp of forces hostile to the Democratic People's Republic of Korea. If Russia continues...we will have to settle scores with it...."[18] The Russian response that the weapons were purely defensive and that all states have the right to strengthen their defense capability did not change the mood in Pyongyang. And Russian efforts in November to shift attention to Russian economic interest in North Korea with a new cooperation agreement could not conceal the fact that bilateral trade was less than $100 million and declining.[19]

During 1997 there were several signs of improvement in Moscow's relations with Seoul. Meeting with President Kim Young Sam and Foreign Minister Yoo Chong Ha in late July 1997, Primakov planned a future summit meeting and signed bilateral agreements. One of these added South Korea to the growing list of Asian states (China, Japan, and India) having a Moscow hotline. They also settled a long-standing dispute over the property of the pre-1917 Russian Embassy.[20]

The most important question in the discussions was Seoul's approach to North-South relations. The Korean side was uneasy because of Russia's earlier criticism that it had been excluded from the four-power negotiating group. Primakov dispelled such concerns by asserting that Russia supported any effort to promote stability on the Korean Peninsula. He also sought repeatedly to reassure North Korea by stressing that the discussions in Seoul were "not directed at any third party."

Russian-South Korean relations experienced no major improvement during the following year, and hopes of improved economic relations were dashed by the East Asian economic crisis and the ensuing severe problems of South Korea. Even without such a crisis, the economic relationship had languished; with the crisis, Korean businessmen were often obliged to withdraw from Russia rather than expand their investments there.

But a serious blow to the relationship came with the eruption of a spy scandal in the summer of 1998 involving South Korean intelligence agents in Russia. The crisis began when Cho Son U, the deputy station chief for South Korean intelligence in Moscow, was caught meeting with an alleged Russian agent, Valentin Moiseev, deputy director of the Russian Foreign Ministry's First Asian Department, who was subsequently charged with treason. Shortly thereafter, Russia demanded that South Korea recall two more diplomats/intelligence operatives from Moscow and three from Vladivostok, effectively closing down ROK National Security Planning Agency operations in both cities.[21] Only a week later, however, the Koreans allowed a Russian diplomat, Oleg Abramkin, expelled from Seoul after the Russian revelations in Moscow, to return to Korea. Both sides agreed that intelligence personnel should not engage in prohibited intelligence gathering, and Russia dismissed Federal Security Service Director Nikolai Kovalev.[22]

By early 1999 relations between Russia and South Korea showed signs of improvement. Trade talks in Moscow promised continued dialogue both on the handling of Russia's nearly $2 billion debt to South Korea and on large-scale joint development of gas production in the Irkutsk region, together with a pipeline through China to South Korea and a railroad through Russia and North Korea to facilitate transport to the Pacific. The Russian approach presented by the Foreign Ministry was to tie economic development talks with efforts to secure South Korean support for Russian inclusion in international discussions of Korean issues. Russian commentary envisaged Russian participation in vast future projects with broad regional cooperation:

The groundwork for the implementation of large-scale infrastructure projects in the twenty-first century is essentially being laid in the subregion at this time. Among them one could list both bilateral Russian-Chinese electric power installations and sweeping economic plans that could encompass Russia, the People's Republic of China, Japan, South and North Korea and Mongolia.[23]

Russia also continued to seek improved relations with North Korea. In the diplomatic sphere, the agenda emphasized the Treaty of Friendship, Good-Neighbor Relations and Cooperation signed on March 17, 1999, Russian interest in greatly broadened relations with the DPRK, and the integration of Korean issues into the broader regional context—with Russia as a participant in the discussions. This agenda highlighted the fact that the purpose of official policy was to regain a Russian role in discussions of Korean policy.

Russian official commentary on the Korean situation became increasingly pessimistic in late 1998 and 1999. The central concern was that the 1994 framework agreement between the United States and the DPRK was threatened by differences over inspection, and that a breakdown could bring a resumption of Pyongyang's nuclear program. This concern was increased by the lack of an effective security structure in the region:

The de facto destruction of the mechanism for keeping peace in Korea based on the 1953 armistice agreement, the lack of clarity on how to develop a new security structure on the peninsula, the unsettled relations of the United States and Japan with the DPRK are destabilizing the overall situation in the region. [24]

The source of the problem, according to the Russian analysts, was that the United States and Japan had acted hastily in discussing development of a joint theater missile defense system for the region following the August 1998 North Korean missile launch. Russia joined China and the DPRK in denouncing the proposal.

Looking beyond the immediate threat, the commentary encapsulated the central elements of Russia's Korea policy: active and equal engagement and cooperation with both Korean governments in all important areas of policy; repudiation of the "errors" of the one-sided (pro-ROK) policy of the early 1990s; and renewal of the 1994 Russian proposal for development of a regional security structure with the involvement of all of the regional powers.[25] Russian policymakers were fully aware of the great danger that the Korean "knot" continued to pose for the Koreas, for Northeast Asia, and for the world.

A major barrier to the success of Russia's effort to regain an effective role in regional security decisions was the legacy of the Primakov "multipolar" policy, continued by Igor Ivanov, his protégé and successor at the Foreign Ministry. The policy focused on resisting American hegemony, and while vigorously cultivating relations with Japan, the Koreas, and China, constantly emphasized the "strategic alliance" with China. The NATO bombing of Yugoslavia and the expansion of U.S.-Japan security cooperation (combined with discussion of a regional theater missile defense system) were the central factors strengthening this policy during 1999. Russian commentators frequently emphasized the connection between the pressure from NATO expansion eastward in Europe and the pressure of expanding U.S.-Japanese military cooperation in East Asia.

Meanwhile, their Chinese interlocutors were at least equally sharp in their denunciation of both. For Russian and Chinese leaders it was a matter not just of the ambitions of "the sole superpower." Both were also greatly concerned about the specific policy of NATO intervention in Yugoslavia to halt actions of the Yugoslav government against an insurgent ethnic minority. In the Russian context such action implied future problems with the United States over its own domestic problems in Muslim regions of the Caucasus. For the Chinese, the possibility of nationalist insurrection in Xinjiang and the growing independence of Taiwan were parallel problems. The most bizarre manifestation of this connection was the meeting of Yeltsin and Jiang Zemin at the oddly named Bishkek "Summit" of the "Shanghai Five" (Russia, China, Kazakhstan, Kyrgyzstan, and Tajikistan) in late August 1999. Yeltsin had obviously made the trip at the urging of Jiang, who was much concerned about Uighur separatism in Xinjiang and the growth of Taiwanese separatism. For his part, Yeltsin was concerned about Islamic fundamentalism and political terrorism, the latter soon to spread widely with the bombings in Central Russia. Yeltsin's speech at the meeting was a repetition of the Primakov rhetoric on multipolar diplomacy. The Russian president noted that "certain countries" were determined "to construct a world order that suits no one but themselves."[26] His actions—acceptance of a Chinese proposal to include in the conference summary a repudiation of the use of human rights violations as a pretext for intervention in the domestic affairs of another country—attacked a particularly important element of that "order." A Russian diplomat noted that Yeltsin was repudiating principles Russia had accepted in the Treaty on Security and Cooperation in Europe a quarter of a century earlier to satisfy Kazakhstan and China, which "have some problems with human rights."[27]

RUSSIA'S POLICY DILEMMA

A review of Russia's foreign and security policy toward the Koreas and Northeast Asia at the end of the Yeltsin era suggests that the inherited Primakov policy of multipolarity, to the extent that it aimed to reduce the leading American role, was a failure. The distinguished Russian foreign policy specialist Andrei Kortunov, explained why:

At the present time the United States is the undisputed leader in the Asian Pacific Region. The states of the region look to Washington as the final arbiter of their disputes and conflicts. Even the DPRK preferred a direct dialogue with the United States to the possibility of an intra-Korean dialogue. No alternative multiple-member system can strengthen the position of the USA; it could only be attached to American diplomacy. In all likelihood Washington will attempt to preserve the military-diplomatic status quo in the Far East on the basis of the effectiveness of the bilateral treaties with Japan and South Korea and the firm containment of the military-political ambitions of China.[1]

This view, coming from a policy specialist with a profound knowledge both of U.S. policy and of the international situation in Northeast Asia, contradicted the views of former Foreign Minister Primakov, his successor, Igor Ivanov, and of President Yeltsin in his speech at Bishkek. It offered a needed dose of realism for a Russian policy discussion in which the mantra "multipolarity" did more to obscure than to clarify the issues in the troubled and unstable context of international relations in Northeast Asia.

Russia's economic and military weakness, which seemed to be worsening rather than improving, denied it a major independent role in the management of the Korean transition. The reality was that Russian security interests required close cooperation with the United States, Japan, and South Korea, as well as China, and recognition of the necessity of American leadership in the regional security structure. The other realities were that the most immediate danger to all the powers in the region was the instability of North Korea and its potential possession of nuclear missiles, and that the "military-political ambitions of China" to which Kortunov refers, were a more serious threat to Russian security in the long term than the U.S. superpower against whose aims the policy of multipolarity was intended to defend. Unfortunately, Primakov's inherited worldview and policy were those of the Soviet era, modified by the Gorbachev-era "new thinking." They had clearly become an obstacle to developing an effective Russian policy in Northeast Asia, most especially on the Korean Peninsula. The evidence of his early policy initiatives suggests that Yeltsin's young successor agreed.

PUTIN ARRIVES

Vladimir Putin has proven himself to be an extraordinarily vigorous foreign policy leader, representing Russia imaginatively and aggressively at major international meetings, and traveling widely, especially in Europe and Asia.

The essence of his foreign policy outlook was contained in the national security concept, which he signed in July 2000. In preparation for over 15 months, it reflected many of the changes in Russian policy since the liberal Kozyrev era, revealing much of the legacy of Primakov's ideas, as well as the impact of the Russian experience in the economic collapse of 1998, and the conflict with NATO over its policy in Kosovo.

The Primakov emphasis upon the dangers of U.S. "unipolarism" is clear, along with opposition to the further expansion of NATO and the justification of armed attack on Yugoslavia by the humanitarian motive of protection of the Kosovo Albanians, and Russian objections to modification of the ABM Treaty. At the same time, the document insists that "Russian-American cooperation remains an essential condition for efforts to improve the overall international situation and to ensure global strategic stability."[2]

Another very strong element is the emphasis upon Asia and "its critical and ever-growing significance in the Russian Federation's foreign policy." As with all of Putin's major foreign policy statements, the discussion of Asian policy emphasizes economic development: "the need to bolster the economies of Siberia and the Far East."

Despite Putin's vigorous courting of Japan, the document focuses only on the familiar problem of the Southern Kuriles—the search for "an internationally recognized border between our two states." Meanwhile, the main focus is to be on "the leading Asian states, primarily China and India...." Detailing the main "sources of tension and conflict" in the region it notes "the situation on the Korean peninsula gives rise to the greatest concern" and then reaffirms the policy of seeking good relations with both Korean states, and the importance of Russian cooperation with other Asian powers in the search for stability on the Korean Peninsula.

An impressive example of Putin's foreign policy initiative closely related to Korea was his participation in the G-8 summit in July 2000. Stopping en route to Okinawa in Beijing and Pyongyang (where he picked up support for Russia's opposition to US pressure for modification of the ABM Treaty to permit a regional nuclear missile defense) he arrived at the conference with word from Kim Jung Il that he sought Western assistance in its development of rockets for satellite delivery and had no intention of using his missiles to threaten Western interests. When the initiative was followed by Madeleine Albright's visit to Pyongyang in October 2000, one Russian journalist asserted that "it was our President Vladimir Putin who opened the door to North Korea for the world community..."[3] Another, noting the haste with which Beijing sent its emissary to Pyongyang following the visit by the American Secretary of State suggested Chinese fears of a radical political shift in North Korea comparable to that which transformed Vietnam's relationship with the West after its unification, bringing negative consequences for China.[4]

It is clear that President Putin intends to pursue an energetic and very flexible Russian policy toward the Koreas—and Northeast Asia more broadly. Compared with Primakov, his use of the term multipolarity is more descriptive than normative, a vision of broader opportunities for Rusian policy initiatives rather than a formula for U.S.-Russian confrontation. The pragmatic approach of his recent dealings with Pyonyang is indicative. Faced with the fact that North Korean missiles are the main threat that justifies an American nuclear missile defense, and convinced that such a system would shake the foundation of Russia's security concept—its remaining nuclear arsenal—he has convinced Kim Jung Il tó shift course.

It is not surprising that when Madeleine Albright visited Pyongyang in October, the Russian Foreign Ministry announced that it "welcomes an expansion of North Korea's circle of foreign partners" and that "the new level of contacts between the U.S. and the DPRK is consistent with Russia's policy in the region."[5] No mention was made of the fact that Albright had criticized Putin for his visit to the capital of the "rogue state" three months earlier.

Clearly Russia had found both a new leader and a new approach to its place in the politics of the Korean Peninsula. Putin had very deftly opened a new Russian access in Pyongyang, using it effectively to support his strategic goal of blocking the US defensive missile deployment. He had also opened new lines of communication with Japan and China. It was a promising beginning in a vital region where Russia's frustrations had greatly exceeded its achievements during the crucial first decade of transition from communist rule.

NOTES

1. Andrew Mack, "The Nuclear Crisis on the Korean Peninsula," *Asian Survey*, vol. 33, no. 4 (April 1993), p. 342.

2. Jae-Young Lee, "The Economic Situation and Foreign Investment in the Russian Far East, *Sino-Russian Affairs*, vol. 70 (Summer 1996), pp. 332–36.

3. See, for example, Herbert J. Ellison and David V. Alhadeff, "Russia's Foreign Economic Policy," *Russia: Political and Economic Development*, Claremont McKenna College Monograph Series, no. 9, pp. 61–89.

4. Yonghau Pu, "China isn't Russia," *ChinaOnline* <http://www.chinaonline.com /commentary_analysis/economics/currentnews/secure/c80921pueditfinal.asp> (June 28, 2000).

5. "Yevgeny Primakov's Year," *Rossiiskaia gazeta*, January 10, 1997, p. 2, in *Current Digest of the Post-Soviet Press (CDPSP)*, vol. 49, no. 2, p. 4.

6. "World without Leaders and Followers," in *Ibid.*, p. 22.

7. "Russian and Chinese Brothers in the 21st Century," *Kommersant-Daily*, April 15, 1997, p. 2, in *CDPSP*, vol. 49, no. 15 (1997), pp. 25–26.

8. "Andrei Kokoshin Establishes Closer Ties With Chinese 'Power Wielders,'" *Izvestiia*, January 24, 1998, p. 3, in *CDPSP*, vol. 50, no. 4 (1998).

9. "Russia Eager to Enter China's Skies," *Kommersant-Daily*, February 19, 1998, p. 5, in *CDPSP*, vol. 50, no. 7 (1998), p. 19.

10. "Tokyo is Prepared to Consider Joint Projects," *Sevodnya*, November 19, 1996, p. 3, in *CDPSP*, vol. 47, no. 46, p. 25.

11. Sergei Gavrilov, "Japanese Minister Will Help Russia Become No. 8," *Kommersant-Daily*, May 24, 1997, p. 4, in *CDPSP*, vol. 49, no. 21 (1997), p. 25.

12. Ilya Bulavinov, "For the First Time, A Russian Defense Minister Pays an Official Visit to Japan," *Kommersant-Daily*, May 20, 1997, p. 4, in *CDPSP*, vol. 49, no. 20 (1997), p. 22.

13. Andrei Ivanov, "Russia Hasn't Objected so Far," *Kommersant Daily*, September 25, 1997, p. 4, in *CDPSP*, vol. 49, no. 39 (1997), p. 19.

14. Vasily Golovnin, *Izvestiia*, November 15, 1997, p. 3, in *CDPSP*, vol. 49, no. 46 (1997), p. 20. Andrei Ivanov, "Keizo Obuchi Brings Credit for Boris Yeltsin," *Kommersant-Daily*, February 24, 1998, p. 5, in *CDPSP*, vol. 50, no. 8 (1998).

15. Viktor Sokolov, "An Investment Company is Good, but a Bank is Better," *Nezavisimaia Gazeta*, May 13, 1998, p. 6, in *CDPSP*, vol. 50, no. 19 (1998), p. 23; and Aleksandr Zorin, "Japan's No. 1 Military Man in Russia," *Novyye Izvestiia*, June 2,

1998, p. 3, in *CDPSP*, vol. 50, no. 22 (1998), p. 20.

16. "Japan Expanding Military Alliance with the U.S.," *Nezavisimaia Gazeta*, May 27, 1999, p. 6, in *CDPSP*, vol. 51, no. 21 (1999), p. 17.

17. Vasily Mikheyev, "Korean Peninsula: A New Policy for Russia," *Sevodnya*, August 16, 1996, p. 9, in *CDPSP*, vol. 48, no. 33 (1996), pp. 26–27.

18. "North Korea's Final Warning to Moscow," *Kommersant-Daily*, October 1, 1996, p. 4, in *CDPSP*, vol. 47, no. 39 (1996), p. 26.

19. Gennady Charodeyev, "Juche Day in Economics Ministry," *Izvestiia*, November 30, 1996, p. 3, in *CDPSP*, vol. 58, no. 48 (1996), p. 22.

20. "Kremlin Makes Friends With Blue House," *Kommersant-Daily,* July 25, 1997, p. 4, in *CDPSP*, vol. 49, no 30 (1997), pp. 23–24.

21. "Relations Between Moscow and Seoul Enter 'Off Season'," *Sevodnya*, July 9, 1998, p. 3, in *CDPSP*, vol. 50, no. 28 (1998), p. 19. See also Igor Korotchenko, "Five South Korean Intelligence Agents to be Expelled from Russia," *Nezavisimaia Gazeta*, July 21, 1998, p. 2, in *CDPSP*, vol. 50, no. 29 (1998), p. 22.

22. Andrei Ivanov, "Koreans Allowed to Spy in Russia," *Kommersant-Daily,* July 29, 1998, p. 3, in *CDPSP*, vol. 50, no. 30 (1998), p. 17. Ivanov reported that Russia would withdraw its demand for withdrawal of Korean intelligence agents from Primorskii Krai, where they gather information on the DPRK and also assist the Russians in combating the Russian, Korean, and Chinese mafias.

23. Deputy Foreign Minister Grigory Karasin, "Our Concept is Security through Economics," *Nezavisimaia Gazeta,* March 26, 1999, p. 6, in *CDPSP*, vol. 51, no. 12, (1998), p. 23.

24. G. Toloraia and P. Iakovlev, "How to Undo the Korean Knot," *International Affairs*, vol. 45, no. 3 (1999), pp. 91–92.

25. Ibid., pp. 93–94.

26. "West Gets Final Chinese Warning," *Sevodnya*, August 26, 1999, p. 2, in *CDPSP*, vol. 51, no. 34 (1999), p. 14f.

27. Anatoly Adamishin, "How to Become a Standard Bearer," *Vremya MN*, August 27, 1999, p. 6. Ambassador Adamishin supported the right of intervention but argued that it should be applied only under the auspices, and with the approval, of the UN.

28. A. V. Kortunov, "Rol' vneshnikh faktorov v protsesse ob"edineniia Korei," (The Role of External Factors in the Korean Reunification Process) *Rossiia i Koreia v meniaiushchemsia mire,* Nauchnyi doklad no. 48 (Moscow: Moskovskii Obshchestvennyi Nauchnyi Fond, 1997), p. 75.

29. "The Foreign Policy Concept of the Russian Federation," *Nezavisimaia Gazeta*, July 11, 2000, pp. 1, 6. (*CDPSP* translation).

30. Dmitry Kozyrev, "Campaign Trip to Pyongyang," *Nezavisimaia Gazeta*, October 26, 2000, p. 6.

31. Vladimir Mikheyev, "Albright Flirting with North Korea," *Trud,* Oct. 25, 2000, p. 4.

32. Andrei Ivanov, "Moment Rich in Opportunities," *Kommersant,* Oct. 13, 2000, p. 10.

ECONOMIC CONTEXT

7

Economic Strategies for Reunification

Marcus Noland

The past decade has witnessed a considerable deterioration in the North Korean economy. The country has been facing food shortages at least since the early 1990s and is well into a famine of unknown magnitude. Although the status quo is unsustainable, there are many possibilities for the future. The current regime (or some successor) could undertake the economic and diplomatic moves necessary to stabilize the economic situation and end the famine. Reform of the North Korean economy would have two profound effects: first, there would be significant increase in exposure to international trade and investment (much of this with South Korea and Japan, two countries with which North Korea maintains problematic relations); and second, changes in the composition of output would be tremendous, and would require literally millions of workers to change employment.[1] Both developments could be expected to have enormous political implications, or alternatively, these implications could present significant, perhaps insurmountable, obstacles to reform under the current regime.

Indeed, North Korea's reform path would be more difficult than the ones traversed by China and Vietnam, Asia's two other major transitional economies. At the time they initiated reforms, China and Vietnam had more than

Table 7.1   Distribution of Labor Force at Time of Reform

Country	Year	Agriculture	Sector Industry	Service
Czech Republic[1]	1989	11[a]	39	50
Slovakia[1]	1989	15[a]	34	51
Poland[1]	1989	7[a]	37	56
Hungary[1]	1990	15[a]	36	49
Soviet Union[2]	1987	19[a]	38[b]	43
Ukraine[3]	1990	20	40	40
Belarus[3]	1990	20	42	38
Romania[1]	1990	28[a]	38	34
Bulgaria[1]	1989	19[a]	47	34
North Korea[4]	1993	33	37	30
China[5]	1978	71	15	14
Vietnam[2]	1989	71	12	17

Notes: (a) Agriculture and forestry; (b) Industry and construction

Sources:

(1) Simon Commander and Fabrizio Coricelli, *Unemployment, Restructuring, and the Labor Market in Eastern Europe and Russia* (Washington, D.C.: World Bank, 1995), Tables 1.1, 2.2, 3.5, 5.1, and 6.11.

(2) Nicholas Eberstadt, *Korea Approaches Unification* (Armonk, N.Y.: M.E. Sharpe/ The National Bureau of Asian Research, 1995), Table 6.

(3) Barry P. Bosworth and Gur Ofer, *Reforming Planned Economies in an Integrating World Economy* (Washington, D.C.: Brookings Institution, 1995), Table 3-1.

(4) Nicholas Eberstadt, "Quantitative Comparison of Current Socio-economic Conditions in North and South Korea," paper presented at the Second Conference of the International Interdisciplinary Project conference on Nation-Building for Korean Unification, Honolulu, Hawaii, January 21-25, 1998.

(5) Jeffrey Sachs and Wing Thye Woo, "Structural Factors in the Economic Reforms of China, Eastern Europe, and the Former Soviet Union," *Economic Policy*, vol. 18 (1994), pp. 101-145, Table 2.

double the share of population employed in the agricultural sector than North Korea apparently has today, and their reform strategies were made possible by the existence of this enormous pool of low-productivity labor. The freeing of agricultural prices has caused a large rapid increase in productivity and supply which has permitted the release of excess labor to other activities, in particular to the emergent non-state-owned light manufacturing sector. (In theory, this sector could then be taxed to provide the resources necessary to cushion the restructuring of the old state-owned heavy manufacturing sector. In reality, little progress has been made in restructuring state-owned enterprises in either China or Vietnam.) This agriculture-driven transition path is simply not available to North Korea, which in economic terms more closely resembles some of the economies of Eastern Europe than it does China or Vietnam (see Table 7.1).[2]

The second hurdle that North Korea faces is ideological. This can be seen when considering the case of Vietnam. The North Vietnamese government and their Vietcong allies defeated the South Vietnamese government in a civil war, allowing them to claim an ideological monopoly in the united Vietnam. Likewise, while China has contended with the rump of Taiwan, no one seriously has claimed that the Taiwanese historically represented an ideological threat to the Chinese government. The point is that reformers in both China and Vietnam had been relatively free to construct tortured rationalizations about how their market-oriented reforms were what Marx, or Mao, or Ho really had in mind.

The ideological terrain faced by the current North Korean regime is very different. Rather than monopolist purveyors or dominant definers of national ideology, the North Koreans clearly are junior partners, both in size and achievement. Moreover, the dynastic aspects of the Kim regime make it even more difficult for the son to disavow the legacy of the father. And while the ideologues of Pyongyang can certainly try to reinterpret *juche* to mean market-oriented reform, the existence of a prosperous, democratic South Korea makes their task very difficult indeed. After all, why be a second-rate imitation South Korea when one can head south and be part of the real thing?

This, of course, raises a third point. Reform would mean vastly increased exposure to the outside world, in particular to South Korea and Japan.[3]

While today's North Korean economy has unexploited latent potential, its isolation means that there is no institutional mechanism to transform this latent potential into products that the rest of the world would want to buy. Even in the case of China, a significant part of the vitality of China's international trade sector can be attributed to foreign-invested enterprises, which account for as much as 40 percent of Chinese exports.[4] In prosaic terms, North Korean enterprises need blueprints, worldwide distribution, and marketing networks.

Foreign direct investment (and through it an infusion of new technology and management) would undoubtedly play a key role in creating this institutional linkage between potential output and world markets. However, the most likely investors in North Korea are South Korean and Japanese firms, two countries with which the North's relations are troubled. U.S. economic sanctions are a disincentive for potential investors in the DPRK of all nationalities. It is unlikely that either Japan or the United States would normalize relations with North Korea without significant improvements in North-South relations. Normalization with Japan would permit the Japanese investment guaranty agency to insure Japanese investments in North Korea and pave the way for mainstream Japanese firms to make large-scale investments. Normalization with the United States would permit the termination of the remaining sanctions and the disincentive it presents to potential investors. Even with the "right policies," a series of diplomatic tumblers would have to fall into place for such a reform strategy to work. As hard as it may be for an economist to admit, this analysis suggests a case for the primacy of politics over economics in resolving North Korea's crisis.

Moreover, the Asian financial crisis has made Pyongyang's tasks even more difficult. The decline in dollar production costs throughout Asia, together with rising bankruptcies, means that purchasing existing assets has become more attractive to foreign investors relative to establishing new greenfield facilities. In other words, if one wants to manufacture garments, there is no reason to build a factory in North Korea when you can buy an existing one in Thailand (where you are already familiar with local laws and customs) at fire-sale prices. Moreover, the primary potential investors in North Korea, namely South Korean and Japanese firms, are in dire straits themselves, and their banking systems are unlikely to want to lend to speculative ventures in North Korea.

Of course, this may simply mean that the crisis will not be resolved happily. Maintenance of North Korea as an independent state would involve varying mixes of domestic economic reform and external support and could imply varying degrees of national political autonomy depending on the degree of reliance on outside support. That is to say, one could imagine a range of outcomes from significant reform, and possibly successful transition into a market economy with enhanced national political status and capabilities, to the economic equivalent of life-support and reversion to the status of a Chinese tributary state.

Needless to say, this does not exhaust the possible range of outcomes. One must consider the possibility that the line of argumentation developed above is fundamentally wrong. In other words, the assumption that time is on our side, hence that the key issue is maintenance of the Pyongyang regime to buy time for some kind of "soft landing," may be incorrect. Instead, time may be on their side—the aversion of a military confrontation with the United States in 1994 has given the North Koreans an opportunity to develop more effective means of extorting resources out of the rest of the world and pushing for unification on their terms. North Korea's August 1998 public announcement of its missile exports and test of a multistage rocket, and possibly renewed nuclear-related activities, perhaps give some indication of the country's future course.[5] North Korea could continue to play a strategy of attempting to extort resources out of the rest of the world, offering to abandon weapons development and export, while continuing to make clandestine sales. The marriage of the rocket and nuclear programs would give the North Koreans impressive tools with which to intimidate their immediate neighbors and create proliferation nightmares for the United States. The truly frightening aspect of this reasoning is that this scenario would mean a continuation of the status quo. Ironically, given the previously noted obstacles to reform, such an externally high-risk strategy might be the path of least resistance to a weak and risk-adverse regime.

The DPRK's intentions are critical in this regard, and recent signals emanating from Pyongyang have been mixed at best. Beginning in August 1998 the DPRK began demanding monetary compensation for access to suspected nuclear-related sites and an end to missile exports. After lengthy public diplomacy characterized by brinkmanship on the North Korean side, the United States was granted access to a suspected nuclear site at Kumchangri in exchange for a large donation of food aid. During the summer of 1999 the DPRK made preparations for a second long-range missile launch while demanding compensation from Japan. (The settlement of Japanese post-colonial claims was reputedly the biggest carrot contained in the comprehensive proposal conveyed to the DPRK by former Defense Secretary William Perry during his visit to Pyongyang in May 1999.) In September 1999 the United States and the DPRK reached a tentative accord under which North Korea would suspend long-range missile testing in exchange for the removal of economic sanctions. The latter development could be interpreted as a move toward more consensual, less confrontational relations, or alternatively, as another iteration of the DPRK extortion game.

On the economic front, a constitutional revision promulgated in August 1998 mentions "private property" (Article 24), "material incentives" (Article 32), and "cost, price, and profit" (Article 33) in an otherwise thoroughly orthodox elaboration of a planned, socialist, self-reliant, *juche* economy. Similarly, in May 2000, while visiting Beijing, Kim Jong Il made statements praising Chinese economic reforms. However, shortly after the constitutional revision, *Rodong Sinmum*, the newspaper of the Central Committee of the Korean Worker's Party, and *Kulloja*, the body's politico-theoretical magazine, published a joint article that argued:

If one wants the prosperity of the national economy, he should thoroughly reject the idea of dependence on outside forces, the idea that he cannot live without foreign capital. ... Ours is an independent economic structure equipped with all the economic sectors in good harmony and with its own strong heavy industry at the core. It is incomparably better than the export-oriented economic structure dependent on other countries. ... We must heighten vigilance against the imperialists' moves to induce us to "reform" and "opening to the outside world." "Reform" and "opening" on their lips are a honey-coated poison. Clear is our stand toward "reform" and "opening." We now have nothing to "reform" and "open." By "reform" and "opening" the imperialists mean a revival of capitalism. The best way of blocking the wind of "reform" and "opening" of the imperialists is to defend the socialist principle in all sectors of the economy. ... We will never abandon the principle, but will set ourselves against all attempts to induce us to join an "integrated" world.

Likewise, Kim's remarks praising Chinese reforms have not been reported in the North Korean media. Moreover, it appears that some prominent "reformers" (I use this term advisedly) have been purged and the Committee for the Promotion of External Economic Cooperation, the body tasked with encouraging international trade and investment, has been dissolved in the recent governmental reorganization. While it is doubtful that a strategy of brinkmanship could generate enough resources to pull the DPRK out of its economic tailspin, the notion that Pyongyang might choose such a strategy as the path of least resistance cannot be dismissed.

In the end, it is quite possible, indeed, some would say probable, that the North Korean regime will prove incapable or unwilling to make the economic and diplomatic moves necessary to ensure its own survival. While South Korea, China, Japan, and others may act to sustain the North Korean regime, intention does not ensure outcome. History is replete with examples of countries and regimes that did not go the way their patrons desired. The fact of the matter is that events in North Korea may not follow the script that others have written. Recent actions by the North Koreans and U.S. Congressional antipathy toward funding obligations under the 1994 Agreed Framework appear to increase the likelihood that one party or the other will pull out of the agreement, creating an uncertain and potentially dangerous situation.

The remainder of this chapter embarks from the premise that the North Korean regime collapses in some noncataclysmic fashion and that North Korea is absorbed into South Korea. The obvious analogy is to German reunification, though history does not operate by analogy and there are many possible differences. To preview the conclusions, the single biggest issue that will shape economic outcomes in a unified Korea will be the political rights accorded to current residents of the DPRK. The reason is simple: a series of studies analyzing the economics of unification using conventional general equilibrium models found that a key variable affecting virtually every issue of interest is the magnitude of cross-border labor migration from North to South.[6] Migration acts as a substitute for capital transfer. The more labor is allowed to migrate, the lower the amount of capital investment necessary to reconstruct the North Korean economy. If no investment were undertaken and North Koreans were able to move south freely, North Korea would be virtually depopulated before differences in income levels were sufficiently narrowed to choke off the incentive to migrate. Conversely, if incomes in North Korea were raised solely by infusions of capital investment, the amount needed to choke off the incentive to migrate could be as high as $1 trillion. Presumably neither of these outcomes is acceptable to South Korea, so the real issue is the form of an intermediate solution that would involve a combination of cross-border movements in both labor and capital.

And, of course, efficiently allocated investment yields returns, not just costs. My colleagues, Sherman Robinson and Ligang Liu, and I in fact have identified a scenario based on cross-border factor flows derived from the German experience in which South Korea would benefit relative to the no unification base case: the present discounted value of the South Korean future consumption stream with unification exceeded that of the no unification baseline.[7]

In another study, Sherman Robinson, Tao Wang, and I reexamined this result using a model calibrated to 1996 and found that the earlier findings rested on two problematic foundations. First, the situation in North Korea had deteriorated more than originally thought, and as a consequence the income gap had grown appreciably. Second, the result rested critically on the rapidity of technological convergence between the North and the South. In the potentially Pareto-improving (i.e., everyone is made better-off) case, the North adopts South Korean technology over a decade, attaining not only the South Korean level of productivity but its input mix as well. This is a more rapid rate of technology upgrading than has been observed in the case of Germany. Even in the optimistic case in which North Korea attains the rates of technological convergence observed in the reunified Germany and attracts sufficient investment to equalize the rate of return on capital between North and South Korea, per capita incomes in North Korea would remain well below those in the South, creating an ongoing incentive for cross-border migration.[8]

The second important message of the Noland, Robinson, and Wang work is that unification could have significant distributional implications. Unification would cause income to shift toward capital and away from labor, and would result in greater income and wealth inequality in the South. Put crudely, the economics come down to this: South Koreans can send money North, or North Koreans can head South. The policies that are ultimately adopted will be a function of politics. A number of rifts could result, the most obvious being between North and South if the North Koreans are denied some of the economic gains of unification. But cleavages within South Korea (e.g., between capital and labor) are possible as well.

CURRENT STATE OF THE NORTH KOREAN ECONOMY

When entering into an examination of the North Korean economy, it is tempting to warn readers that they are about to enter Alice's Wonderland, or at least that the figures should be regarded as a reflection of rigorous speculation.

A typical economic overview begins with output or income figures. Output in North Korea is measured on a material product basis, which is basically incompatible with the system of national accounts used in market economies.[9] Moreover, North Korea has a huge military sector that is difficult to assess economically.[10] Eui Gak Hwang has made a valiant effort to transform North Korean figures into the standard system of national accounts, but the results are not fully convincing.[11] Other scholars have estimated North Korean per capita incomes using the physical indicators approach, obtaining estimates of the ratio of South Korean to North Korean per capita incomes in 1990 in the range of 3.61:1 to 4.48:1.[12] Updating these ranges on the basis of the Bank of Korea real GDP estimates, the ratio of South to North per capita income in 1997 would be between 8:1 and 11:1.[13]

Recently, with the assistance of the United Nations Development Program, North Korean authorities have attempted to make their own estimates of GDP, calculating that in 1996 GDP was $10.6 billion and per capita GDP was $480 billion, using the official exchange rate of 2.15 North Korean won per U.S. dollar. These estimates imply that South Korean incomes were more than 20 times higher than those in the North.[14]

Data compiled by the Bank of Korea and released by the National Unification Board indicate that from 1991 to 1998, the North Korean economy registered negative growth (see Figure 7.1).[15] In June 2000, shortly before the North-South summit, the BOK announced that the North Korean economy had grown by more than six percent in 1999. This announcement was greeted with considerable skepticism outside the South Korean government.[16] Data recently provided to the International Monetary Fund (IMF) by the North Korean government date the decline from 1994. Although the quantitative estimates contained in these two sets of figures differ significantly, qualitatively they are consistent—the North Korean economy shrunk dramatically in the past decade.

Figure 7.1   North Korean GDP Growth, 1986–1999

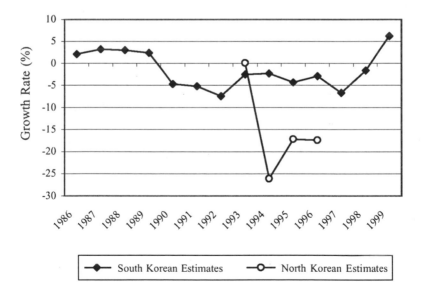

Some greater detail is provided in Tables 7.2, 7.3, and 7.4, which report figures the North Korean government provided to the IMF on the composition of output, government expenditures, and government revenues. In certain respects, this data is problematic, as will be discussed below. Nonetheless, it is worth examining, if for no other reason than because it is the official representation of the condition of the economy.

Table 7.2 Composition of Output, 1992–1996

(millions of US dollars at US$1 = won 2.15)

	1992	1993	1994	1995	1996
Agriculture	7,807	8,227	6,431	5,223	4,775
Industry	4,551	4,689	3,223	2,228	1,556
Construction	1,315	1,256	910	819	508
Other	7,160	6,762	4,858	4,532	6,478
TOTAL	20,875	20,935	15,421	12,802	10,588

Source: North Korean Submission to the IMF

Table 7.2 presents figures on the composition of output. What the data suggest is that the economy has collapsed around agriculture—that is, the fall in agricultural output is actually less dramatic than the decline in output in other sectors. According to these figures, industrial output fell by nearly two-thirds between 1992 and 1996, and construction activity declined by almost as much. Taking construction as a proxy for investment, it is possible that investment may well have fallen below replacement level and the capital stock may have been shrinking. This notion is supported by the government expenditure data reported in Table 7.3. Taking the economic development category as a proxy, investment has fallen by more than half from values the North Korean government announced in the early 1990s.[17] This point is further reinforced if one believes that certain military or military-related expenditures are hidden in the economic development budget. Estimates of North Korean military manpower and equipment do not show anything like this decline over the relevant period. Indeed, U.S. and South Korean defense ministry figures show a slight increase in North Korean military deployment during this period. This suggests that the non-military part of the economy is being severely squeezed.

Table 7.3   Government Budget Balance, 1994–1999

(billions of won)

	1994	1995	1996	1997	1998	1999
Revenues	41.6	24.3	20.3	na	19.8	na
Expenditures	41.4	24.2	20.6	na	20.0	20.4
Economic Development	na	na	12.4	na	na	na
Social and Cultural	na	na	5.0	na	na	na
Defense	na	na	3.0	na	3.0	3.0
General Administration	na	na	0.2	na	na	na
Balance	0.2	0.1	-0.3	na	-0.2	na
Memorandum item:						
GDP	33.2	27.4	22.7			

Source: North Korean Submission to the IMF; *The People's Korea* webpage.

Two other things stand out in Table 7.3. First, for 1994 the government reports expenditures and revenues far larger than GDP. This would seem to violate the basic precepts of national income accounting. Second, it reports expenditures on defense that are far smaller than normally cited. Indeed, data on labor force participation provided by the North Korean authorities appear to omit the military entirely. All in all, these figures should probably be taken with very large grains of salt.

Data on government revenues are reported in Table 7.4. The largest single source of revenue is turnover taxes, which is typical in centrally planned economies. These taxes present special problems for analysis because they are levied at differential rates depending on the legal status of the transacting parties. (For example, the tax wedge imposed on an exchange between two state enterprises is different from the wedge imposed on a transaction between a state enterprise and a cooperative.) Profit from state enterprises is the next largest source of government revenue. Excluding the problematic data for 1993, it appears that the government sector accounts for roughly 90 percent of national income.

Table 7.4 General Government Revenues, 1996

(billions of won)

Direct Taxes	
Profits from state enterprises	6,290
User fees for working capital	2,250
Profits from Cooperative farms	180
Indirect Taxes	
Turnover taxes	8,080
Social Insurance Revenues	90
Other Revenues	3,430
TOTAL REVENUES	20,320

Source: North Korean Submission to the IMF.

The North Korean regime's obsession with secrecy ought to be less of a problem in analyzing the countries' external economic relations. In principle, "mirror statistics" reported by North Korea's trade and investment partners can be used to deduce North Korea's external transactions. Aggregate trade figures derived from the IMF's *Direction of Trade Statistics* and other sources are shown in Figure 7.2.[18] Two points stand out. First, reported trade volumes have not been growing, reinforcing the impression of an economy in long-term decline. Second, North Korea has been running chronic trade deficits. These deficits must be financed in some way.

Figure 7.2   North Korean Trade, 1985–1998

One possibility is illicit commercial transactions. However, data reported by the State Department does not support the idea that clandestine arms sales are sufficient to cover the trade gap—indeed, this data, which is generally consistent with the findings of Nicholas Eberstadt, Marc Rubin, and Albina Tretyakova on DPRK-Russia trade, indicates that North Korea is now a net importer of military hardware (see Figure 7.3).[19] Other possibilities in this realm include drug trafficking and counterfeiting, and North Korean diplomats have been expelled from their host countries for both of these offenses.[20]

Another possibility is remittances from Japan, which are sometimes reported to be in the billions of dollars. However, recent research has concluded that these private aid flows are probably considerably smaller than claimed.[21]

A final possible explanation is that the trade deficits are implicitly financed by China, which has permitted North Korea to accumulate large arrears in its trade account. In reality, the North Korean deficit is probably financed by a combination of unrecorded transactions, private aid flows, and Chinese munificence.

As shown in Table 7.5, China is far and away North Korea's main trade partner, and has allowed the North Koreans to run annual bilateral deficits

Figure 7.3   North Korean Arms Trade, 1985–1996

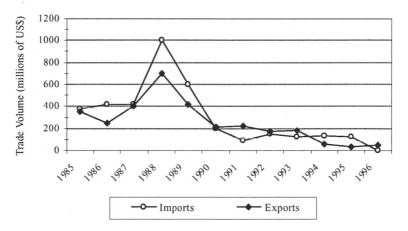

of approximately $500 million.[22] Indeed, China's prominence in North Korea's trade would be even larger if barter transactions and aid were counted in these figures. Following China, North Korea's largest trade partners are Japan, South Korea, Russia, and Germany. If North Korea's trade with China and South Korea are regarded as politically determined, these two countries are financing nearly two-thirds of the North Korean deficit.

The commodity composition of trade for 1997 is reported in Table 7.6. Again, interpretation is problematic. The data reported in Table 7.6 by commodity does not match the data reported in Table 7.5 by partner. Some countries may report overall trade with the DPRK but not its commodity composition, so the part of the sample underlying the Table 7.5 figures are omitted from Table 7.6, and it is unclear how the aforementioned arms trade is counted (if at all) in these figures.[23] Barter transactions are also omitted from these data. With these caveats in mind, the data in Table 7.6 indicate that natural resource products and light manufactures dominate North Korea's exports. On the import side, cereals, petroleum, and industrial intermediates are the largest categories.

Most recently, North Korea has obtained significant international assistance to deal with its food shortage from China bilaterally, and through the

Table 7.5 Trading Partners, 1997

(millions of US dollars)

	EXPORTS[a]	IMPORTS[b]	NET EXPORTS
CHINA (including Hong Kong)			
raw	147	556	
corrected	134	623	-489
JAPAN			
raw	296	179	
corrected	269	197	72
SOUTH KOREA[c]			
raw	193	115	
corrected	193	127	66
RUSSIA			
raw	17	74	
corrected	15	81	-66
GERMANY			
raw	43	43	
corrected	39	47	8
GLOBAL TOTAL[de]			
raw	954	1545	
corrected	993	1829	-836

Notes:
(a) DOTS export data (of partner country) adjusted for "missing" transportation and insurance costs.
(b) DOTS import data (of partner country) adjusted for transportation and insurance charges.
(c) NK-SK data from NUB. NUB data based on a customs clearance.
(d) NK-Iran and NK-Libya trade data from KOTRA. KOTRA data also adjusted.
(e) 1996 NK-Lebanon trade data used instead of 1997 numbers.

Sources: IMF, Direction of Trade Statistics (DOTS); Korea Trade Promotion Corporation (KOTRA); National Unification Board (NUB).

Table 7.6a   North Korean Exports by Largest Commodity Groups, 1997

INDUSTRY (SITC-4 Classification)	EXPORTS (US$1000)	SHARE (percentage)
Gold, non-monetary	161,225	15.1
Parts of telecommunications and sound apparatus	58,726	5.5
Other outer garments of textile fabrics	54,860	5.1
Crustaceans and mollusks, fresh, chilled, frozen, etc.	49,721	4.7
Hay and fodder, green or dry	47,467	4.5
Gramophone records and similar sound recordings	47,445	4.4
Machines & appliances for specialized particular industries	38,814	3.6
Overcoats and other coats, men's	36,241	3.4
Thermionic, cold & photo-cathode valves, tubes, parts	34,558	3.2
Other fresh or chilled vegetables	25,723	2.4
TOTAL - All commodities	1,066,182	

Table 7.6b   North Korean Imports by Largest Commodity Groups, 1997

INDUSTRY (SITC-4 Classification)	EXPORTS (US$1000)	SHARE (percentage)
Maize (corn), unmilled	96,430	7.7
Petroleum oils & crude oils from bituminous minerals	65,486	5.2
Meal and flour of wheat and flour of meslin	65,456	5.2
Res: Petroleum products, refined	53,790	4.3
Iron ore and concentrates, not agglomerated	53,063	4.2
Rice semi-milled or wholly milled, broken rice	47,555	3.8
Passenger motor cars, for transport of passengers and goods	38,929	3.1
Mineral or chemical fertilizers, nitrogenous	33,206	2.6
Fabrics, woven, containing 85% of wool/fine animal hair	26,549	2.1
Fabrics, woven of continuous synthetic textile materials	26,346	2.1
TOTAL - All commodities	1,259,134	

Source: Statistics Canada, World Trade Analyzer (1980-1997).

World Food Program from other countries.[24] The quantity, value, and concessional component of food coming from China is unclear.[25] Similarly, North Korea has been receiving energy assistance in the form of oil and nuclear reactor construction through the Korean Peninsula Energy Development Organization, a multinational consortium established as part of a 1994 nuclear agreement with the United States.

MODELING REUNIFICATION

North Korea is both larger in population and smaller in economic size (and hence poorer in per capita terms) relative to South Korea than East Germany was to West Germany, though by exactly how much no one really knows. The population of North Korea is roughly half that of South Korea. As noted in the previous section, enormous uncertainty exists as to the value of output and per capita income. Suffice it to say that in relative terms the North Korean economy is quite small.

Consequently, the impact of integration of product markets between North and South Korea, while critical to the North, would have trivial effects on the South.[26] The analogy would be to accession of a small central European economy to the European Union or to the formation of the North American Free Trade Agreement—tremendously important for the smaller economy (Mexico), but virtually imperceptible to the larger one (the United States).

The story changes enormously if factor markets are allowed to integrate. Cross-border movements in labor and capital potentially could have an enormous impact on the South Korean economy. As noted, migration can act as a substitute for investment: the more labor that is allowed to migrate, the lower the amount of capital transfer is necessary to reconstruct the North Korean economy. Using a model calibrated to 1990, we have conducted a thought experiment in which rehabilitation of the North Korean economy occurs solely through internal reallocation of factors of production, technology upgrading, and migration.[27] With no additions to the capital stock, nearly three-quarters of the North Korean population heads south. More recent work that incorporates the rapidly widening income differential since

1990 indicates that North Korea would be nearly depopulated before equilibrium was attained.[28] Conversely, incentives for migration could be reduced through the maintenance of employment and wage increases, though the necessary investment could be enormous—as much as $1 trillion—if the incentive to migrate were eliminated solely by capital investment.[29]

The key point overlooked in most discussions of "the costs of unification" is that efficiently allocated investment yields returns, not just costs. Figures derived from the German experience show that in a scenario with relatively small amounts of private capital investment combined with relatively high levels of North-South migration, South Korea actually would come out ahead: the present discounted value of consumption would be $35 billion higher with unification compared to the no unification baseline. (However, in the worst-case scenario—large grant transfers combined with low levels of migration—South Korea is approximately one-half trillion dollars worse off.)[30]

However, this result depends critically on the assumption that North Korea achieves full technological convergence with the South within a decade.[31] This would represent a more rapid rate of convergence than has been identified in the German case. Applying rates of technological convergence estimated from the German experience and assuming that the rate of return on capital in North Korea could not fall below that observed in South Korea, even under relatively optimistic conditions the North would not attain the 60 percent per capita income target within a decade. This suggests that North Koreans will face economic incentives to migrate south for a prolonged period of time.[32]

The second important message of this work is that unification could have significant distributional implications. With unification, income would shift toward capital and away from labor, and within labor toward higher skilled groups. To the extent that the highly skilled are the predominate owners of capital, this analysis suggests that absent some compensatory policies, unification would cause greater income and wealth inequality in the South.

Presumably these economic changes would have political implications as well. Several cleavages are likely: a regional one between the North and the South, and another within South Korea between capital and labor (capital owners viewing North Koreans as a new source of cheap labor, and labor regarding the North as a potential source of labor market competition). Cleavages within the South Korean labor force, between the highly skilled and the low-skilled are also possible. Depending on the macroeconomic policies applied, the internationally traded- and non-traded goods sectors could be affected in very different ways, opening up another cleavage.

A whole host of unification issues (conversion rate of the North Korean won to the South Korean won, assignment of property rights, etc.) have enormous implications for the economic welfare of current residents of the DPRK. The extent to which their interests are taken into account will be in part a function of the extent to which they participate in political decisionmaking. Policies that deny North Koreans some of the economic gains of unification (such as proposals to maintain the DMZ and administer North Korea as a special administrative zone, which would prevent the equilibration of wages and rates of return on capital between the North and South, or proposals for the South Korean government to retain rights to all assets in the North) would only be sustainable if North Koreans were denied political rights.[33] Thus the key economic issue is the extent to which the North Koreans will be full participants in the political system of a unified Korea.

GERMAN LESSONS FOR KOREA

German reunification is often thought of as a failure: nearly a decade and one-and-a-half trillion deutschemarks of transfers after the fact, unemployment in the former East Germany remains over 17 percent. Yet this judgement may be overly harsh: the Germans did, after all, achieve national unification through the peaceful, democratic liberation of a communist state. Alternatives matter. Faced with a starving, possibly nuclear-armed experiment in dynastic totalitarianism, would only the South Koreans be so lucky.

In two ways the Korean case could be worse than the German experience. As noted, North Korea is relatively larger and poorer in comparison to South Korea than East Germany was compared to West Germany, and North Korea is in more dire straits today than East Germany was in 1989.[34] In two ways Korea appears better off. Korea (the peninsula as a whole, and North

Korea in particular) is demographically younger than Germany was (and East Germany in particular).[35] Young people are presumably more adaptable than old, and with young people, the conventional education system can be used for retraining (reducing the need for new adult retraining institutions). The second advantage Korea has is that it can learn from German mistakes.

Monetary Union

Conventional wisdom has it that German monetary authorities made a fundamental (and easily avoidable) mistake in setting the conversion rate between ostmarks, the old East German currency, and deutschemarks. However, in reality the exchange rate was probably about right.[36] The mistake was in the subsequent wage policy, which pushed East German wages far above competitive levels—causing unemployment and necessitating large social welfare expenditures. Wages were driven up not because the Germans were stupid but because given the existing institutions, incentives, and the nature of the wage-setting negotiations, no one represented the interests of future owners of East German capital. To simply argue that the Germans set the exchange rate incorrectly, and that this situation could have been avoided, is inadequate.[37] If there is a concern about migration, and the South Koreans wants to give northerners an incentive to stay at home, the government should assign property rights to land and housing to current residents contingent on some period of continued residence.

Property Rights

The lesson from the cases of other transitional economies is that one must privatize quickly—not because private managers are uniquely competent, but because without clear property rights and privatization, there will be no investment, and without investment there cannot be economic rehabilitation.

The Germans made two related mistakes. First, they tried to bureaucratically restructure enterprises before putting them on the market, thereby slowing the process of privatization. Better to get the assets into private hands and let markets, not bureaucrats, handle restructuring. Second, they accepted the principle of restitution, whereby people could claim that they were the rightful owners of assets seized by the communist regime and demand restitution of the seized assets. This led to claims and counterclaims, leaving properties to deteriorate while in limbo and without clear ownership. Rather than restitution, if the South Koreans decide to compensate previous owners, it would be better for them to do so through monetary compensation not tied to the assignment of property rights to disputed assets. In other words, prioritize—privatize as quickly as possible, get assets into a responsible owner's hands, and begin the rehabilitation process. The secondary issue of whether someone should receive a payment from the state for an allegedly seized asset can be settled later. After all, if the asset was seized 40 years ago, another year or two wait for compensation is unlikely to be of critical importance.

Rapid privatization does not necessarily mean cash auctions, however. In the German case, East Germans had virtually no financial assets and certainly little buying power relative to the West Germans. The German government's demand for cash payment in exchange for assets formerly held by the East German state effectively excluded East Germans from the privatization process, and more than 90 percent of the assets eventually ended up in West German hands. To prevent this from happening in North Korea, other models, such as the Czech voucher system, should be considered.

Maintaining Production in the North

Maintaining production in the North will be a priority. There are at least two important issues here. First, there will be a need for well-functioning capital markets to channel investment into the North. The assumption that unification occurs through collapse and absorption inevitably implies an examination of the state of South Korean capital markets. The picture is not pretty. South Korea needs to restructure its banking system, improve the operation of its bond market, create a better climate for foreign direct investment, and better integrate foreigners into its financial market. In comparison to the German case, Korea could be facing a greater challenge under a vastly less efficient financial system. In this respect, the current financial crisis, which has spurred liberalization of South Korean financial markets, could be a blessing in disguise. In addition, the government of South Korea may want to consider fiscal incentives for investment in the North.

A second aspect of this problem involves the role of West German or South Korean firms in their respective new markets. In the case of East Germany, local production was temporarily depressed by a flood of West German consumer goods into the East German market. West German firms also attempted to take over potential competitors in the East, either shutting them down or turning them into sales offices, but the West German Cartel Office blocked these attempts. Similar dangers are obvious in Korea, but unlike the German case, South Korea does not have a strong state authority responsible for competition policy that would be capable of blocking anticompetitive actions by the *chaebols*.

EXTERNAL RELATIONS

North Korea is the world's most autarkic economy, and collapse and absorption would mean an enormous increase in trade, most of which would be with South Korea (which would presumably be treated as internal trade) and Japan. Likewise, the two primary sources of investment to rehabilitate the economy would presumably be South Korea and Japan. Other important partners would be the United States and China.

This could raise some thorny issues. First, fears have been expressed about Japanese economic "recolonization" of North Korea and the need for the Korean government to maintain property rights in order to prevent this from occurring. Frankly, given the gigantic needs for capital investment, such a stance would have a very high implicit price in terms of economic opportunities foregone—which would mainly fall on the current residents of North Korea. Second, both Japan and South Korea are members of the World Trade Organization and each have recourse to WTO dispute settlement procedures. Japan could file a case against Korea in the WTO if Korea were to discriminate against Japan in trade or investment relations. Third, Japan has never settled the issue of postcolonial claims with North Korea. Elsewhere, I have estimated these claims at $12 billion.[38] However, given the current state of Japanese finances, it would be astounding if Japan were to agree to transfers of this magnitude.

The point is that Korea and Japan have a number of issues to work through. It would not be at all surprising if the solution reflected the typically nontransparent and illiberal character of international economic relations in Northeast Asia. The same cannot be said for the United States, however. Because of the character of U.S. trade policymaking institutions, it will be much more difficult for the U.S. government to resist demands that Korea "play by the rules."

The same may not hold in the case of China, which as yet is not a member of the WTO, and whose public diplomacy may not be as subject to political capture by narrow special interests as is the case in the United States.

A final set of actors will be the international financial institutions (IFIs). If there were a special facility at the World Bank for "Peace and Reconstruction on the Korean Peninsula" and the North Koreans were to receive the same per capita transfers that the Palestinians get, this would amount to more than $4 billion in loans annually.[39] Similar special programs might be available through other international financial institutions. But the fact of the matter is that due to budget constraints, it is highly unlikely that the Korean Peninsula could attract lending programs on this scale. As Danny Leipziger has noted, the IFIs are unlikely to play more than a supplemental or supportive role—private capital will be key.[40] (Four billion dollars annually would be a considerable share of World Bank lending. If Vietnam is used as a model, peak lending in the hundreds of millions from all IFI sources might be conceivable.) Moreover, the postunification political treatment of North Koreans could be an important determinant of the receptivity of the rest of the world to Korean requests for assistance.

INTERNAL INSTITUTIONS

Another issue that would arise in a collapse and absorption scenario is the transition from North to South Korean internal institutions. First, there would be concerns about rapidity of change. Many commentators implicitly or explicitly subscribe to the notion that there is a dichotomy between "shock therapy" and "gradualism" and that policymakers can choose between these two approaches. This is illusory.

Choices and outcomes will always be constrained by economic conditions and political institutions. "Gradualism," as exemplified by China or Vietnam, has been made possible by the previously mentioned existence of an enormous pool of low-productivity labor in the agricultural sector—a path that is simply not available to North Korea. In the Korean case, the assumption that North Korea will be absorbed into South Korea means that policymakers have far fewer choices to make. North Korea will get the South Korean macroeconomic institutions. It will get South Korea's commercial code, judiciary, and so on. This will be de facto shock therapy, for better or worse.

Of course some adaptations or changes at the margin are possible. For example, in a collapse scenario, it is likely that the North Korean population will be physically weakened by prolonged deprivation. Since this will be a population with few, if any, assets, the immediate replacement of the DPRK's nonmarket, state-provided social service system with a market-oriented one (in the area of health care, for example) could have disastrous implications. Transitional institutions will be necessary.

THE STATE OF THE SOUTH KOREAN ECONOMY

A final consideration that could have enormous implications for outcomes is the state of the South Korean economy at the time of unification. After being rocked by a financial crisis in 1997, the South Korean economy contracted by nearly six percent in 1998.[41] In 1999, however, economic growth rebounded sharply and by year's end recovered the ground lost in the crisis. This remarkable turnaround is forcing a reassessment of the crisis and generating questions about the sustainability of the recovery.[42]

The crisis of 1997 had its roots in a development model characterized by considerable government intervention in the economy. The state encouraged the development of a state-dominated, bank-centered financial system which facilitated the channeling of capital to the state's preferred borrowers and projects. This policy of channeling government-directed capital effectively socialized risk. The result was the development of a symbiotic relationship between the state on the one hand and the giant conglomerates, or *chaebol*, on the other. This gave rise to moral hazard on a massive scale and encouraged the growth of the *chaebol*, whose economically unjustified agglomerations of unrelated economic activities were justified only by the owner-managers' relationship with the state.[43]

This system has been subject to periodic crises: one during the early 1970s; another during the early 1980s; and of course the recent crisis that plagued the country for two years. The 1997 crisis, if not its timing, was forseeable.[44] Indeed, the crisis would have eventually occurred regardless of events in Southeast Asia, although contagion exacerbated the situation.[45]

The South Korean economy rebounded remarkably in 1999. As economic conditions have improved however, there has been an understandable slackening of interest in reform: although beneficial to the economy as a whole in the long run, reform can be disruptive in the short run and can adversely affect the interests of those who are privileged under the status quo.

In part, the recovery appears to be illusionary. It has been driven in substantial part by traditional short-run Keynesian stimulus through government fiscal expenditure, recovery of private consumption from its extremely low levels of 1998, inventory restocking, and a trade surplus. None of these factors are sustainable in the long run. The government will eventually have to reign in spending, consumer buying habits will return to normal, firms will achieve their desired inventory levels, and a reduction of the trade surplus will act as a net drag on the economy. Indeed, the consensus among forecasters is a slowing of growth in 2000 and beyond.[46]

As a consequence, both the crisis and the recovery may prove more ephemeral than anticipated. In the long run, South Korea will need to come to terms with the underlying problems that contributed to the crisis in the first place. Not to put too fine a point on it, but if the South Korean banking system is insolvent and the nonfinancial firms are so leveraged that no prudent banker would loan them another won, then it will be hard for these institutions to rehabilitate the North Korean economy. In this regard the 1997 crisis, which may lead to structural rehabilitation of the South Korea economy, could be a blessing in disguise. As Nietzsche wrote, "what does not destroy me, makes me stronger."

RECOMMENDED POLICIES

While a process of gradual, peaceful integration may be desired, abrupt and possibly violent disintegration and collapse might occur. Moreover, while trends are positive, it is not clear that today South Korea is a *Rechtsstaat* in the same way Germany is. The government of a unified Korea will have to confront troublesome issues of respect for the law, the role of the judiciary, and local government autonomy.[47] Something will have to be done with the gigantic North Korean military. (Even accepting the "shrimp among whales" metaphor, one would have to expect a significant demobilization of forces in a unified Korea.) Beyond these fundamental issues of government organization, the Koreans will have to confront a legacy far more poisoned than the one faced by the Germans in 1989. The preceding analysis suggests a number of recommendations for policy, including those that will be important to implement in South Korea prior to unification.

Pre-unification

The focus at this stage should be to strengthen the South Korean economy in anticipation of the shock of unification. In the financial sector, personal and corporate tax changes are needed to reduce the favorable treatment of debt and thereby encourage equity finance. In debt markets, greater differentiation of risk should be encouraged. This can be promoted through the creation of benchmark issues to encourage a secondary market, as well as through the promotion of rating activities by both South Korean and foreign ratings agencies. A high-yield bond market should be fostered for firms that have traditionally not been among the government's preferred borrowers and that suffered disproportionately in the 1998 credit crunch.

With a greater emphasis on direct finance, there is a parallel need to promote the activities of independent institutional investors who are capable of monitoring corporate management decisions and exerting capital market discipline on incumbent management. Indeed, a source of current concern is *chaebol* domination of the nascent mutual fund industry. Three reinforcing means of addressing this issue come to mind. One method is to create firewalls and separate the *chaebols* into financial and nonfinancial groups.

While this goes against trends elsewhere, the exclusion of industrial *chaebols* from participation in the financial sector is warranted, given the predominant role of the largest *chaebols* in the South Korean economy. Another strategy is to encourage foreign financial firms in fund management. They have expertise that South Korean firms currently lack and are unencumbered by the web of connections and obligations characteristic of the South Korean financial sector. A third approach would be along the lines of a recent proposal by Edward Graham for a swap of suitably written-down nonperforming loans for government bonds, followed by a mandatory corporate debt-for-equity swap, and then sale of government-held shares to the public.[48] This would in effect democratize the ownership of the *chaebols*. It could also be used to foster the development of independent institutional investors. Last but not least, there is a need to improve the functioning of South Korea's bankruptcy procedures.

In product markets, there is a real threat of anticompetitive behavior due to increased concentration coming out of the crisis—a development actually encouraged by the government's policy of promoting "Big Deals" and industrial consolidation. For example, Hyundai-Kia now holds 72 percent of the passenger automobile market, 77 percent of the bus market, and 95 percent of the truck market.

The standard remedy in this case is to strengthen the Korea Fair Trade Commission and to engage in cooperative international competition policies, either bilaterally or multilaterally. Yet the Korea Fair Trade Commission cannot be strengthened overnight. As a consequence, it is imperative that South Korea aggressively liberalize international trade in order to "import" competition, especially in sectors such as motor vehicle products in which the potential for abuse of market position appears the greatest. The idea would be to use the threat of imports to maintain the competitiveness of markets, while domestic pro-competitive forces are strengthened. In this respect, liberalizing international trade does not just mean cutting tariffs, which in the case of South Korea are often reasonably low—it also includes undertaking a variety of ancillary actions which facilitate the presence of foreign firms in the market.[49]

South Korea's labor markets have a reputation for rigidity, despite the fact that by standard indices, such as job turnover or real wage variability, economy-wide they are the most flexible in the Organization for Economic Cooperation and Development. The segment where rigidity is a valid concern is with respect to the labor forces of the largest *chaebols*. For them, current employment regulations make labor a quasi-fixed factor of production, discouraging hiring on the one hand and encouraging the adoption of inappropriately capital-intensive techniques of production on the other. In this regard, the appropriate response is a two-track strategy of reducing labor market regulation (making it easier to dismiss employees), while at the same time strengthening the unemployment insurance system and broadening the social safety net. This is a complex set of issues because under current practices a whole basket of benefits (including pensions and housing) are not entirely portable and are contingent on employment.

These reforms would generate changes in the South Korean economy—the democratization of finance, increased competition in product markets, and more flexible labor markets—making it more dynamic and entrepreneurial. Beyond the present crisis, it is also recommended that the government err on the side of a tight fiscal policy in anticipation of the future liabilities associated with unification.

Lastly, the South Korean government should support DPRK entry into the international financial institutions.

During Unification

At the time of unification, the Korean government will have multiple (and potentially conflicting) policy objectives. On the one hand, maintenance of economic activity in the North on market-consistent terms will be the top priority. At the same time, the government should seek to effect a one-time-only wealth transfer to the current DPRK population, which will have to adjust to market institutions with virtually no household wealth. One can imagine a multipronged approach that would include:

- The adoption of dual rate monetary conversion. The government should aim for slight undervaluation of the North Korean won to maintain competitiveness, thereby making North Korea an attractive location for investment. It should also convert personal savings at an overvalued rate (effecting a wealth transfer).

- Deeding land to the tiller and the housing stock to its occupants, contingent on maintained use for some specified period of time.
- Maintaining some kind of temporary, emergency, non-market social safety net in the North.

Having given the land to the tiller, one must confront the issue of property rights claims by past owners or their descendants and the more general issue of assignment of property rights to commercial or industrial assets. The experience of Germany and other former centrally planned economies is instructive in this regard. The government of a reunified Korea should:

- Avoid the policy of restitution for seized assets. Monetary compensation for seized assets might be considered, however.
- Privatize quickly and avoid the cash-up-front model. Abolish interenterprise debts.
- Emphasize investment, not consumption, transfers.
- Accept assistance from foreigners, including the Japanese.

Post-unification

An effort will need to be made to actively integrate North Koreans into mainstream society. In the long run, maintenance of the DMZ as a method of population control is not sustainable, and the perpetuation of significant differences between the North and South is not in the long-term interests of the current population of the South.

North Koreans should be given full political rights in the context of a process similar to "de-Nazification." Unlike the Germans, the Koreans fought a horrific civil war. For both substantive and cultural reasons, retribution will be a far more important issue in Korea than it was in Germany. Although it may go against political tendencies in South Korea, pre-announced amnesties for high-ranking North Korean officials may play an important role in defusing a potentially explosive situation. Truth and reconciliation commissions such as those used in Argentina and South Africa may play some role. The point is that the country will face an enormous task both in revitalizing the North Korean economy and in preserving and extending the emerging liberal political culture of South Korea.

CONCLUSIONS

This paper has been written from the premise that North Korea will collapse in some noncataclysmic fashion and will be absorbed into the South. Obviously there are many other alternative premises that cannot be dismissed.

The key finding is that the political rights afforded to the residents of North Korea are the main determinant of economic outcomes. Per capita income differences are large, the North Korean population is young, and Seoul lies just south of the DMZ, glowing like a beacon. Unless they are forcibly restrained, one must assume that large numbers of North Koreans will head south if given the opportunity. Even if they were temporarily restrained, pressures for cross-border migration would persist until the income gap was substantially reduced. This could require considerable capital investment and technological transfer.

Although the United States, Japan, China, and other countries and international institutions have important roles to play, what happens on the Korean Peninsula will largely be determined by Koreans. The appropriate role of the outside world will be to support the Koreans in their attempt to strengthen liberal democratic institutions in the face of what could be an enormous political and economic shock.

NOTES

1. On these points, see Marcus Noland, Sherman Robinson, and Monica Scatasta, "Modeling Economic Reform in North Korea," *Journal of Asian Economics*, vol. 8, no. 1 (1997), pp. 15–38; and Marcus Noland, Sherman Robinson, and Tao Wang, "Rigorous Speculation: The Collapse and Revival of the North Korean Economy," *World Development*, vol. 28, no.10 (2000) pp. 1767–87.

2. Some parallels with Romania are briefly discussed in Marcus Noland, "Why North Korea Will Muddle Through," *Foreign Affairs*, vol. 76, no. 4 (1997), pp. 105–18.

3. Using a gravity model, I have found that nearly two-thirds of North Korean trade would be with South Korea and Japan if North Korea behaved as a "normal" country. See my "The North Korean Economy," *Joint U.S.-Korea Academic Studies*, vol. 6, pp. 127–78.

4. Barry Naughton, "China's Emergence and Prospects as a Trading Nation," *Brookings Papers on Economic Activity*, vol. 2 (1996), Table 3.

5. There is considerable confusion (much of it due to bureaucratic and domestic politics) over the missile that North Korea launched in late August 1998. Some have claimed that this was a test of the Taepo Dong-1 missile, while the North Koreans and some others have claimed that it was a satellite launch. Robert D. Walpole, the U.S. Central Intelligence Agency's senior intelligence officer for strategic programs, has stated that it was a three-stage rocket possibly capable of delivering a small payload across the Pacific (*Washington Post*, September 25, 1998). The North Korean government has threatened to use the rocket as a military delivery system.

6. Marcus Noland, Sherman Robinson, and Ligang Liu, "Calibrating the Costs (and Benefits) of Unification," in *Economic Integration of the Korean Peninsula*, ed. Marcus Noland (Washington, D.C.: Institute for International Economics, 1998), "The Costs and Benefits of Korean Unification," *Asian Survey* (August 1998), and "The Economics of Korean Unification," *Journal of Policy Reform*, vol. 3 (1999), pp. 255–99.

7. Noland, Robinson, and Liu, "The Costs and Benefits of Korean Unification."

8. Marcus Noland, Sherman Robinson, and Tao Wang, "Modeling Korean Unification," *Journal of Comparative Economics*, vol. 28 (2000), pp. 400–21.

9. Net material product covers value-added in the material product sectors (manufacturing, agriculture, construction, commodity transportation, productive communication, productive commerce, and a few others). Material product multiplied by prices yields the gross output value of social production. There are three outstanding problems with this definition. First, produced intermediate products are double-counted. Second, non-material sectors (housing, health and welfare expenditures, education, science, art, personal services, state administration, etc.) are ignored. Third, the prices, which are calculated to reflect the labor theory of value, do not reflect true scarcity values. As a consequence, even under the best of circumstances (such as having a cooperative government), converting material product accounts to a na-

tional accounts basis is difficult. Given the secrecy of the North Korean government, concordance is virtually impossible.

10. North Korea is the most militarized society on earth, with more than one million men (and increasingly, women) under arms out of a population of around 22 million. It is difficult to quantitatively assess the military's role in the economy. In general, militaries are difficult to evaluate economically, since many of their transactions occur on non-market terms. In the case of North Korea this general difficulty is compounded by the distorted nature of the non-military economy and the regime's secrecy. Moreover, the military is outside the control of the central planners and appears to have been omitted from the figures provided to the IMF by the North Korean government. In addition, it engages in activities that would be performed in the civilian sector elsewhere. The conventional wisdom (as represented by the U.S. Department of State) is that the military accounts for roughly one-quarter of national income, though the derivation and interpretation of this figure is problematic. Some believe that as a consequence of the recent deterioration in the North Korean economy and the military's privileged position in it, the military's share of the economy has increased substantially.

11. Eui-Gak Hwang, *The Korean Economies* (Oxford: Clarendon Press, 1993).

12. Hong-tack Chun, "Estimating North Korea's GNP by Physical Indicators Approach," *Korea Development Review*, vol. 14, no. 1, pp. 167–225 (In Korean); Kap-Yeong Jeong, "Comparing the North Korean Level of Economic Development by Principal Components Analysis," in *North Korea's Reality and Unification*, ed. Young Sun Lee (Seoul: Center for East and West Studies, Yonsei University, 1993) (In Korean); and Noland, "The North Korean Economy."

13. The prize for precision, North Korean division, goes to Shishido and Hamada (1998), who, without revealing their methodology, report a PPP-adjusted estimate of North Korean per capita income in 1995 of $3,596.9, which given the South Korean estimate of $11,172.1, would yield a ratio of 3.106.

14. These figures are subject to a variety of qualifications. If one is interested in making broad comparisons of welfare, the more relevant figures are purchasing power adjusted comparisons. Presumably the price level (however distorted) in North Korea is relatively low compared to South Korea, so that a comparison of per capita incomes based on market exchange rates would exaggerate the differences in income levels. However, the official exchange rate is surely overvalued (and probably to a very large extent) which would tend to overstate North Korean incomes in a common currency, and push the bias in the opposite direction. One could argue that in

an economy as distorted as North Korea's with a huge military sector and an ongoing famine, income as shorthand for household economic welfare is of questionable relevance. If one is using GDP per capita as a measure of technological prowess, then other, more direct indicators are probably preferable.

15. These data are also of questionable accuracy. They are apparently calculated by taking measures of physical output and then calculating income using South Korean value-added weights, and then are subject to interagency bargaining within the South Korean government prior to public release. Given the collection methods, there is no way to verify the estimates of physical output. Furthermore, it is far from obvious that the South Korean value-added schema is the most appropriate. In other countries where such methods have been applied, the resulting estimates appear to overestimate the volatility of output, as industrial output exhibits greater variance than service activities.

16. See Marcus Noland, The Two Koreas: Prospects for Economic Cooperation and Integration, East-West Center Special Report No. 7, December 2000. Honolulu: East-West Center.

17. Data on capital goods imports from an earlier period reported by Eberstadt suggest that the decline in investment may be a secular phenomenon going back decades. See Nicholas Eberstadt, "The DPRK's International Trade in Capital Goods, 1970–1995: Indications from 'Mirror Statistics'," Journal of East Asian Affairs, vol. 12, no. 1 (1998), pp. 165–223.

18. Even here one must be careful. Partner coverage may be incomplete. Additionally, there is a venerable history of trade ministry clerks around the world mistaking North and South Korea. Such errors have occurred in the past decade in Mexico, Austria, and most recently Lebanon. Moreover, the IMF reporting convention counts transport and insurance as part of imports; when one calculates the "mirror statistics" one has to adjust the constructed North Korean figures for this accounting convention. Lastly, these figures will ignore barter trade. Although the existence of barter transactions would presumably not bias trade balance estimates in any particular way, barter could significantly distort analysis of trade volumes and composition. For a more complete discussion of these issues, see Marcus Noland, "The External Economic Relations of the DPRK and Prospects for Reform," in North Korean Foreign Relations, ed. Samuel S. Kim (Hong Kong: Oxford University Press, 1998).

19. Nicholas Eberstadt, Marc Rubin, and Albina Tretyakova, "The Collapse of Soviet and Russian Trade with the DPRK, 1989–1993," The Korean Journal of National Unification, vol. 4 (1995), pp. 87–104.

20. Raphael Perl, "North Korean Drug Trafficking: Allegations and Issues for Congress," Congressional Research Service, March 9, 1999, processed.

21. See, for example, Nicholas Eberstadt, "Financial Transfers from Japan to the DPRK: Estimating Unreported Flows," *Asian Survey*, vol. 36, no. 5 (1996), pp. 523–42; and Noland, "The North Korean Economy," and "The External Economic Relations of the DPRK and Prospects for Reform."

22. Some have questioned whether these figures accurately reflect China's trade with the DPRK. It may well be that DPRK-ROK processing on commission trade, which is mainly routed through China, could be double-counted in the Chinese figures. Even if this were the case, however, the double-counting would occur with respect to both imports and exports, and would so do little to boost the magnitude of China's trade imbalance with North Korea. Similar arguments could be made regarding smuggling and barter: if accurately counted, these activities would increase recorded trade *volumes*, but it is unclear how they would affect trade *balances*, if at all.

23. That the military has its own trading channels is prospectively of enormous importance. They potentially could continue to engage in arms trade for pecuniary or strategic reasons, even if this were opposed by other parts of the state on diplomatic grounds.

24. For a highly informative discussion of famine-related issues, see Heather Smith, "The Food Economy: Catalyst for Collapse?" in *Economic Integration of the Korean Peninsula*, ed. Marcus Noland, Special Report 10 (Washington, D.C.: Institute for International Economics, 1998).

25. For a discussion of North Korea's food problem and the extent of Chinese assistance, see Scott Snyder, "North Korea's Decline and China's Strategic Dilemmas," *USIP Special Report* (Washington, D.C.: United States Institute of Peace, October, 1997).

26. For substantiation of this claim using computable general equilibrium models, see Noland, Robinson, and Liu, "The Economics of Korean Unification," and Noland, Robinson, and Wang, "Modeling Korean Unification."

27. Noland, Robinson, and Liu, "The Economics of Korean Unification."

28. Noland, Robinson, and Wang, "Modeling Korean Unification."

29. Noland, Robinson, and Scatasta, "Modeling Economic Reform in North Korea"; and Noland, Robinson, and Liu, "Calibrating the Costs (and Benefits) of Unification," and "The Costs and Benefits of Korean Unification." It cannot be overemphasized that these figures are highly speculative in nature. Two key assumptions are

the extent to which North Korea is subject to an "obsolescence shock," in which the value of its capital stock declines when exposed to international competition, and to what extent it achieves gains in technical efficiency as foreigners transfer capital, technology, and management in the context of a reform and opening policy. In both cases a fairly broad set of outcomes would be plausible. It is probably prudent to assume the magnitude of cross-border factor flows in a plausible unification scenario would be on the order of millions of workers and hundreds of billions of dollars.

30. Noland, Robinson, and Liu, "The Costs and Benefits of Korean Unification."

31. Noland, Robinson, and Wang, "Modeling Korean Unification."

32. Of course, this line of analysis does not exhaust the economic effects of unification. Presumably there would be a "peace dividend" associated with military demobilization. Noland, Robinson, and Wang report estimates of economic efficiency gains associated with partial demobilization in the range of $1 billion to $3 billion annually. (These estimates were obtained under variations on the assumption that with unification (or at least peaceful coexistence) military expenditures on the Korean Peninsula as a share of national income could be reduced to some international benchmark such as the OECD average.) There may also be negative "congestion externalities" associated with migration of North Koreans south. I am unaware of any estimates of the potential magnitude of these costs. See Noland, Robinson, and Wang, "Rigorous Speculation: The Collapse and Revival of the North Korean Economy," and "Modeling Korean Unification."

33. For a proposal along these lines, see Soogil Young, Chang-Jae Lee, and Hyoungsoo Zang, "Preparing for the Economic Integration of Two Koreas: Policy Challenges to South Korea," in *Economic Integration of the Korean Peninsula*, ed. Noland.

34. For a more detailed analysis of the German case and its lessons for Korea, see Marcus Noland, "German Lessons for Korea: The Economics of Unification," in *The Korea-United States Economic Relationship*, ed. C. Fred Bergsten and Sa Kong Il (Washington, D.C.: Institute for International Economics, 1997); Christian Watrin, "Monetary Integration and Stabilization Policy: The German Case," in *Policy Priorities for the Unified Korean Economy*, ed. Sa Kong Il and Kwang Suk Kim (Seoul: Institute for Global Economics, 1998); and Holger Wolf, "Korean Unification: Lessons from Germany," in *Economic Integration of the Korean Peninsula*, ed. Noland.

35. For demographic analysis and projections for North and South Korea, see Hong-Tack Chun, "A Gradual Approach Toward North and South Korean Economic Integration," KDI Working Paper, no. 9311 (Seoul: Korea Development Insti-

tute, November 1993).

36. For extensive discussions of these issues, see Gerlinde and Hans-Werner Sinn, *Jumpstart* (Cambridge: MIT Press, 1992); and Rudiger Dornbusch and Holger Wolf, "East German Economic Reconstruction," in *The Transition in Eastern Europe*, vol. 1, ed. Olivier Jean Blanchard, Kenneth A. Froot, and Jeffrey D. Sachs (Chicago: University of Chicago Press, 1994).

37. Indeed, it is arguable that an overgenerous conversion rate may be desirable. The reason is that like the East Germans (even more so), North Koreans will enter the market economy with virtually no assets, financial or otherwise. Converting their meager savings to South Korean won at a generous exchange rate would be a one-time wealth transfer, and a means to provide them with working capital and a financial cushion against unforeseen contingencies.

38. Noland, "The North Korean Economy."

39. Ibid.

40. Danny M. Leipziger, "Thinking about the World Bank and North Korea," in *Economic Integration of the Korean Peninsula*, ed. Noland.

41. For a fascinating review of more than 100 banking and currency crises over the past 30 years, see Graciela L. Kaminsky and Carmen M. Reinhard, "The Twin Crises: The Causes of Banking and Balance-of-Payments Problems," *International Finance Discussion Papers*, no. 544 (Washington, D.C.: Board of Governors of the Federal Reserve System, 1996).

42. For a more detailed assessment of this history, see Marcus Noland, *Avoiding the Apocalypse: The Future of the Two Koreas* (Washington, D.C.: Institute for International Economics, 2000).

43. As Leipziger (1988) in an analysis of industrial restructuring presciently put it, "Korea had no 'exit policy' and no institutions capable of managing it." See Leipziger, "Thinking About the World Bank and North Korea," p. 124. The sad and disturbing thing about Leipziger's observation is that it could have been written a decade later— nothing really changed. I address the internal, domestic moral hazard issue in Noland, *Avoiding the Apocalypse: The Future of the Two Koreas*, Box 6.1.

44. For an example, see Marcus Noland, "Restructing Korea's Financial Sector for Greater Competitiveness," *Working Paper Series* 96-14 (Washington, D.C.: Institute for International Economics, 1996).

45. For an assessment of research on this issue, see Noland, *Avoiding the Apocalypse: The Future of the Two Koreas*, Box 6.2.

46. See, for example, the forecasts contained in *Blue Chip Economic Indicators*,

September 10, 1999; *Financial Times Currency Forecaster*, October 1999; Asian Development Bank, *Development Outlook 1999 Update*, September 1999; and the International Monetary Fund, *World Economic Outlook*, October 1999.

47. For a discussion of these issues, see David Steinberg, "South Korea: Preparations Awaiting Unification—The Political Components," in *Economic Integration of the Korean Peninsula*, ed. Noland.

48. Edward M. Graham, "A Radical but Workable Restructuring Plan for South Korea," *International Economic Policy Briefs* 99-2 (Washington, D.C.: Institute for International Economics, January 1999).

49. For an example, see the analysis of the automobile sector by the American Chamber of Commerce in Korea, *Improving Korea's Business Climate* (Seoul: American Chamber of Commerce in Korea, 1999).

8

The Role of International Finance in Korean Economic Reconstruction and Reunification

Gifford Combs

If, as Samuel Johnson once observed, nothing concentrates a man's mind like the prospect of a good hanging,[1] then in a market economy nothing concentrates a lender's mind like the imminent bankruptcy of a borrower. In December 1997, the South Korean economy was on the verge of bankruptcy, and the world's financial *glitterati* scrambled themselves out of Christmas revelry to converge upon Seoul and hammer out a solution to South Korea's liquidity crisis. The World Bank and the International Monetary Fund agreed to extend credit to the South Korean government on both a short- and long-term basis and convinced international bankers from around the world to roll over a series of loans. Later, in March of 1998, South Korea took advantage of a resurgence in market sentiment to sell long-term dollar-denominated debt that allowed it to weather the balance-of-payments crisis.

The patching together of a consensus to stave off the collapse of the South Korean economy has been heralded as a benchmark of cooperation among private and public sector lenders and governments and as a model for the role that international capital can and should play in effecting stabilization around the globe. Certainly, in comparison to the difficulties encountered elsewhere in Asia, the Korean example looks like a stunning success.

Does this mean that such a process should serve as a dress rehearsal for the financial markets following the reunification of North and South Korea? Probably not: or at least not without substantial and diligent forward thinking and planning. The nature of reunifying the Korean Peninsula is uncertain, but it will require a major mobilization of capital to integrate North Korea with the world economy and rebuild its society. What role should international financial institutions and organizations play in the reconstruction process, and what, if any, lessons can be learned from similar efforts in Germany and Russia?

Almost by definition, crisis management such as occurred from December 1997 through March 1998 in South Korea indicates a failure of policymaking. After all, better planning might have averted the crisis in the first place. In reality, given the structure of the South Korean economy at the time and the waves of "contagion" that were sweeping through the emerging markets in Asia, it is probably too much to hope that Korea could have escaped untouched. But it is important to plan for what might happen the next time around. Sadly, it seems the South Korean government and private sector have learned very few lessons from the economy's "near-death experience." Three years after the crisis, the emphasis continues to be on treating the symptoms rather than the causes of economic dysfunction. Such behavior does not bode well for the challenges Korean society will face if the peninsula is reunified.

In thinking about the reunification of North and South Korea, the example cited most often as a model is the unification of East and West Germany in the early 1990s. In what has sometimes been termed the largest leveraged buyout in history, the West German economy integrated the East German population and workforce into itself over a period of several years. Without question, the key decision in that process was the establishment of currency parity between the old East German currency, the ostmark, and the deutschemark. The creation of currency parity had the effect of driving up inflation in Germany as a whole. Inflation from Germany was rapidly exported to the rest of Europe in the form of higher interest rates and led eventually to the collapse of the European Monetary System.

In purely financial terms, parity was a disaster for the rest of Europe. Germany's leading economic position allowed it to socialize and spread the cost of parity across the continent. Viewed historically, in political and human terms it likely will be judged a triumph. Nevertheless, the territories of the former East Germany lag behind their western neighbors in productivity and efficiency nearly a decade after the fall of the Berlin Wall—though they are making progress.

Is a replay of this scenario likely on the Korean Peninsula? Not under any realistic set of assumptions. East Germany, while highly subsidized by the Soviet Union, was a viable economy, which fed its people and produced some goods (e.g., optics, machine tools) that were competitive on the world market. In 1989, the government quickly lost credibility and collapsed. The Korean example is bleaker: North Korea has a subsistence economy that barely keeps a small minority of its population fed and leaves others to forage for bark and grass. The capital stock is outdated and inefficient, and the only competitive exports are weapons purchased by other rogue states that do not have access to better supply channels. In contrast to East Germany, the North Korean government *is* viable, in the sense that any ruthless military dictatorship that brooks no dissent is a sustainable, if static, model.

If South Korea is to integrate the North's population and economy into its own, it will need to bear the entire burden of the increased population by itself. And whatever the South pays for the assets of the North's economy, it almost certainly will be too much.[2] Buying North Korea's economy may well prove to be the wisest course in human and geo-strategic terms; but South Korea will need a great deal of help and preparation to pull it off. South Korea lacks the economic clout to socialize the cost and spread it implicitly across the globe through economic policymaking, as Germany did. Instead, the Korean government will require explicit grants and loans from international sources—large amounts of capital. Estimates for the cost of rebuilding North Korea vary enormously (depending as they do upon data that is suspect and incomplete) but range as high as one trillion dollars, which on a per-capita basis does not seem out of line.[3]

The South will face two problems in rebuilding the North: stabilizing consumption and increasing investment. The first can and will be dealt with through large transfers of humanitarian aid from international sources including the United States, Japan, the European Union, and the United Nations. Whether China will choose to participate will probably depend on the degree of influence it can wield in a newly unified state and on the volume of trade it enjoys with South Korea. The major priorities will be to ensure that North Korea's population is properly housed, clothed, and fed; and to prevent the mass migration of refugees south of the thirty-eighth parallel. These are likely to take on the aspects of a military operation and, as such, perhaps the appropriate analogy should be the Marshall Plan and the postwar occupation of Europe by the Allied forces.

But if a united Korea is to move quickly from being a refugee and humanitarian problem to a growing and dynamic economic entity, then South Korea must immediately begin a process of planning and restructuring that will allow it to nearly double its population while gaining very little in productive capacity. The integration of North Korea will bring, at first, only a net drain of resources and is unlikely to begin generating wealth for many years. What can and should be done by South Korea today to prepare for the possibility of reunification tomorrow?

THE ROOTS OF THE PROBLEM

The most encouraging result of South Korea's "near-hanging" in the winter of 1997–98 has been the realization by at least a plurality of the country's elite that the economy needs some form of dramatic and immediate reform. To outside investors and observers the contrast with Japan could not be more dramatic: Korea has apparently grasped the nettle and begun the difficult process of restructuring both its private sector and the relationship between the government and the business sector. (In Japan, it has been much less clear that *any* consensus on reform has existed.) Korea did so because: (1) it almost went broke; and (2) it realized that the old economic model was no longer working. But, the reform has been more illusory than real—focused on form rather than on substance.

Since the 1953 ceasefire ended the Korean War, the South Korean economy has essentially existed on a wartime footing.[4] Both equity and efficiency were sacrificed in favor of growth and preparedness, and a system of *dirigisme* patterned loosely after the pre-World War II Japanese model became entrenched. Bureaucracy waxed fat, industries became bloated, and labor grew accustomed to full-employment—the price for remaining passive players in the drama. Through it all, the controlling families of the *chaebols*—the large industrial combines—grew wealthy, at least on paper.

The root of the problem in Korea (both North and South) is a rampant distrust of the free market by all parties. No businessman would ever willingly choose an unforgiving free market over a cozy oligopoly, and the South Korean economy has served up not just oligopoly but monopoly opportunities for over 40 years. It is hardly surprising that there is resistance to change. Oligopolies, according to orthodox microeconomic theory, need not be inefficient. They can generate output and consumer surplus identical to conditions of perfect competition. But reality rarely matches theory. If one is the direct beneficiary of such an oligopoly, it is a frightening prospect to be tossed into a competitive environment. In competition there are winners and losers, determined by luck, skill, resources, and hard work. Under the traditional South Korean model, there was competition only for resources. Once those were obtained, everything else was secondary, as the chances were good that the erstwhile competitor was simply outgunned. Such a system breeds complacency and spawns corruption—two traditional hallmarks of the South Korean economy.[5]

Until the 1997 crisis, South Korea's economy was driven by a system in which bureaucrats directed where and when capital was to be allocated. In general, capital was mobilized from consumers through a restrictive banking system that lent money as directed without regard to underlying economics or financial discipline. The bargain went something along the lines of: "I won't tell *you* that you aren't profitable if you don't tell *me* that you can't pay me back." Like all variants on Ponzi's original entrepreneurial venture,[6] this one thrived on growth. And it went on for a surprisingly long period of time. The bargain depended heavily on two features: (1) the closed nature of the Korean financial system; and (2) the ability of Korean industry to make investments that could generate at least some cash.

The system came crashing down largely because in their quest to expand the *chaebols* became ever more reckless in their disregard for return on investment and because South Korea had opened the door ever so slightly to international capital markets. Once Korean industry began to depend to any degree on international finance, it was clear that eventually industrial enterprises in Korea would be held to a much higher standard than had been applied domestically. As such, Korea's financial system required only one liquidity crisis to topple the house of cards.

Korea's financial system was undisciplined by the market because it was dependent upon bank lending at preferential interest rates. Certain borrowers were extended credit on a virtually unlimited basis—to a point where they became too big to fail because they were favored by the ministries that supervised the banks and directed bankers to make such loans. These private contractual arrangements were kept out of public view and never subjected to analysis by outside observers, to whom public disclosure by the banks was kept to a minimum. No loan is ever "bad" if payments are made on time. But if payments can be made only because new credit is being extended on a continuous basis, it is difficult to see how any of the loans could be construed as "good." Remarkably, that is how the banking system worked in Korea.[7] The advantage of such a system for a borrower should be obvious: if one can obtain capital on liberal terms for almost any project, then it pays to expand vigorously in any and all directions. Further, because all of Korean industry was financed so heavily with debt rather than equity, such a system worked well for the management and owners of the businesses. Equity in Korea represented little more than the residual claims on highly leveraged enterprises—"equity stubs" in current financial parlance—and constituted a "heads I win, tails you lose" gamble for the holders. In such a world, it becomes almost impossible to say with any certainty whether a person is a billionaire or bankrupt.

It is easy to see why management preferred the old way. But what of bureaucrats and labor? Leaving aside the small minority of corrupt officials, Korean economic planners must have derived immense psychic income and satisfaction watching industry and the country grow.[8] As its part of the bargain, labor won some implication of lifetime employment with steadily rising real wages.

This equilibrium is no more. What will replace it is still unclear. Korea has no choice now but to engage much more completely in the world economy if it is to continue to benefit from free trade and attract capital. Foreign lenders and investors will only be willing to pour money into projects if they feel they can get a fair deal and if they feel the system is not stacked against them. The bankruptcy system in Korea is still primitive, making it difficult to drive inefficient operators out of business and recycle capital into the hands of more efficient and dynamic entrepreneurs.

OPENING MARKETS AND ATTRACTING CAPITAL

It is not hard to structure individual transactions to treat foreigners fairly—but it is difficult to reform an entire system overnight. Of course, in the short term at least, capitalists, being economic animals, will be attracted even if they do not quite like the system in place.[9]

Nevertheless, to build confidence among foreign investors and attract capital over the longer term, Korea's economy needs help in three very specific areas: (1) increasing labor mobility and training; (2) deregulating markets for both goods and services; and (3) restructuring the banking system. Each is a complicated process, but South Korea should be encouraged to draw expertise from abroad and try to avoid mistakes others have made.

Labor market mobility is a difficult problem even in the most economically advanced countries. South Korean industry has just begun the process of slimming down to compete effectively on world markets. Labor unions are rightfully frightened of what is to come. Yet cuts must be made and management must have the right to staff appropriately. The months of negotiations over the sale of the bankrupt KIA Motors auto company repeatedly stalled over exactly this issue, indicating how divisive the problem continues to be.

Freeing up labor markets requires a safety net and money for retraining redundant workers. Technical and financial assistance from international multilateral lenders would be very helpful in restructuring the labor market. Rather than general "policy stabilization loans," targeted lending to support retraining initiatives could prove extremely effective. Experience from both Western Europe and the United States in the 1980s and 1990s suggests that labor market reforms produce casualties. Some workers simply cannot or will not adapt to change. Having lost the security of lifetime employment, they need some form of social insurance on which they can rely.

As wrenching as these changes are likely to be, they pale in comparison to what will await a newly reunified Korean society that must incorporate a population from the North that is untrained and ill-adapted to a market economy.[10] The privation experienced by many in the former Soviet Union may prove a useful example. Russia abandoned an economically inefficient system of guaranteed housing and employment without adequately planning for the consequences.[11] Korea must begin to deal with these issues today if it is to have any chance of handling the millions of workers from the North and integrating them as productive members of society.

International lenders and investors have also worked vigorously to open up South Korea's markets to foreign goods and services, and more deregulation should be encouraged. Progress has been slower in the past two and a half years than most observers had predicted because *chaebol* management has proven very resistant to change and has successfully stymied efforts by President Kim's government to rationalize and deregulate.[12] Fortunately, the cold wind of free markets can have a wonderfully disciplining effect on even the most recalcitrant participants. The government's efforts to open markets and unfetter pricing by fiat in areas such as telecommunications and insurance have been very successful. More such reforms are needed.

Less successful to date have been efforts to reform the institutional framework of financial markets. This remains a crucial element to be addressed if Korea is to attract large amounts of foreign capital, especially in light of any effort to rebuild the North. It is not enough anymore for a country to offer low-cost land and large numbers of "docile" low-wage workers (the inducements usually cited in optimistic pronouncements about the process of rebuilding North Korea). Western investors simply have too many other options and have become extremely sophisticated at playing countries against each other in making such investments. Further, there is a recent trend by investors to force local capital to take the local risk: they are relying on contractual rather than investment relationships to capture the economic gains from manufacturing in emerging markets.

The old system is no longer tenable in South Korea and must be replaced with a market-driven economy that relies on price discovery and the discipline imposed by a rationing of capital determined by the expected return on investment. If South Korea's economy is to grow enough to hope to absorb the North, it must become fully integrated with the rest of the world economy. In planning for reunification, international institutions should focus their efforts on bringing South Korea up to international standards. Both the private and public sectors must be rigorously benchmarked against the best the world has to offer.

While South Korea pays much lip service to the market, international institutions can and must do more to pull the economy of the South into the twenty-first century. This is a difficult task in political terms. Restructuring an economy inevitably results in the loss of jobs, the displacement of bureaucrats, and the curtailment of careers. Typically, it is neither a pretty nor a pleasant process. Yet it is absolutely prerequisite if South Korea is to resume its growth path and be in a position to absorb the economic detritus of the North.

The rebound experienced by South Korea's financial markets in 1999 has had the unfortunate consequence of providing the illusion of restructuring. The trebling in share prices during the following twelve months and the resulting improvement in consumer and business confidence may have perversely enabled South Korea to avoid much-needed real reform. Seoul has been focused on ending the "IMF era" ("IMF *shidae*"). With the repayment of the last IMF credit in mid-September 1999, a collective sigh of relief could be heard throughout the financial and industrial sectors.

Yet the IMF *shidae* may have been the one opportunity to push through the sort of change that the South Korean economy must endure if it is to integrate successfully with North Korea in the future. Recent interviews and meetings with managers in various industries suggest that corporate South Korea is rapidly losing its zest for reform and is in danger of slipping back into comfortable old habits. There is a palpable sense that the crisis is past and that financial markets have validated choices and decisions made in the past 18 months.[13]

REFORM OF THE FINANCIAL SYSTEM:
LIQUIDITY AND SOLVENCY PROBLEMS

Unfortunately, the single largest problem—reform of the financial system—remains almost as intractable today as it was at the beginning of the IMF *shidae*. The South Korean government, afraid of the loss of confidence and the inevitable unemployment that must result if lasting structural reform is implemented, has dithered in the process of socializing the large losses in the financial system.

It took over nine months in 1999 for the government to conclude the sale of just one bank to a group of foreign investors.[14] But what of the rest of the banks? To a large extent, the government simply does not want to believe the magnitude of the problem. It has masked the severity to date by transferring the losses further from view. There is little enough transparency in the Korean banking system, but the investment trust sector (ITC) is nearly opaque. Appropriately enough, when liquidity in the banking system dried up, funds started flowing to the *chaebols* from the ITCs! And who controlled the ITCs? The *chaebols*.

Now the South Korean government faces a new problem, or rather a new manifestation of an old problem: a run on the "bank," except in this case the banks are the mutual fund companies, the ITCs. Korean retail investors, fearful of bank failures, despairing of falling bank rates forced down by a quasi-nationalized banking system, and lured by the promise of high returns, have poured trillions of won into the ITCs during the IMF *shidae*. This transfer of liquidity from the banking system froze the market for commercial bank lending but fueled a large increase in the institutional debt market, which in October 1999 was nearly half of South Korea's GDP, a staggering sum for a developing country.[15] While South Korea's external government debt gets all the headlines, it is the total indebtedness of the economy that counts. Korea now faces two problems: an immediate liquidity issue almost identical to the crisis that erupted in late 1997 and a longer-term solvency issue that stubbornly refuses to go away.

Many of the losses in the Korean financial system are only notional, in the sense that the transaction is not complete. That is, the banks may own a piece of property now that formerly was security on a loan. But until that property is sold no one knows the true extent of the loss. Korea must begin to consolidate and socialize the losses. They must make the losses explicitly part of the government budget and thus reveal to all the full extent of the problem. Only then will the economy begin to craft a solution.

In retrospect, it is clear that the IMF bailout of Korea, while giving the government and society time to work through its problems, addressed only the liquidity issue. It was hoped that the loans would "buy time" and allow society to tackle the much more difficult problems relating to solvency. Because all sides have been focused on liquidity, the solvency problem has become even larger. Korea has continuously sought to address the symptoms rather than the causes of the problem, and the IMF must shoulder some of the blame for this. The IMF focused on restoring liquidity, but liquidity without solvency is an empty sack. The Daewoo bankruptcy is a wonderful example of the law of unintended consequences at work in the financial system. The Korean government, intent on providing liquidity to the financial system, drove down interest rates and caused a massive outflow of retail deposits from the banking system. Investment trust companies, newly flush with cash, needed places to invest the money. The *chaebols* responded by refinancing themselves outside the banking system through the commercial paper market.

This inevitably led to new excesses, and the first manifestation of such excess has been the 1999 bankruptcy of the Daewoo *chaebol*, whose consolidated debt is thought to be *at least* $60 billion dollars and may be as high as $100 billion dollars.[16] According to government figures, total restructuring costs for Daewoo are expected to reach 7 percent of GDP.[17] Most observers believe that estimate is unrealistically low.[18] The losses in the life insurance industry may be that much again. To reiterate, the financial sector losses in Korea (in the banking, insurance, and mutual fund companies together) will constitute one of the worst on record—one that as a percentage of the GDP is many times greater in magnitude than the losses of the savings and loan institutions in the United States in the late 1980s and early 1990s.

In response to the Daewoo problem, the government instituted capital controls—though no one dares use that phrase—in the form of restrictions on withdrawals from ITC accounts by retail and other investors beginning in the summer of 1999. These restrictions were designed to prevent the ITCs from engaging in panic selling of Daewoo debt until a more comprehensive restructuring plan could be instituted. By early November 1999, two conclusions were obvious: the losses would be bad—worse than anyone in the government had admitted—and these losses could be masked through a massive injection of liquidity into the system. In effect, the Korean government agreed to purchase any and all Daewoo debt that came onto the market. By doing so, it hoped, paradoxically, that the debt would *not* be sold, simply because enough confidence had been restored among the holders.[19] In financial markets, holders of securities are always afraid of "not being able to get out" because of the sudden loss of liquidity that usually accompanies sudden price declines. One is much less likely to run for the exits if one knows there are plenty of open doors. A commitment by the government to buy constitutes a very large open door.

Losses of this magnitude are bad, but much worse are the distortions that have been introduced into the system by the failure to realize the loss. Korean investors should *not* be able to get out of their Daewoo debt positions. There is no market discipline in a system that allows investors to recklessly chase yield without suffering losses. This breeds not efficiency, but moral hazard. Over and over, the government has confused liquidity for solvency and has continued to adopt the Charlie Brown approach to problem-solving: "There is no problem so large that I can't run away from it!" Much of the blame for these distortions can be placed on the unwillingness of South Korea to adopt international accounting standards. Failing to do so has allowed the government and corporations to disguise the extent of the problem.

In the end, the government and the society have only ended up fooling themselves. The international bond market knows what the assets and liabilities of Korean banks and *chaebols* are worth. Or at least educated guesses can be made. But the South Korean government does not want its own people to know those figures.

Moreover, Daewoo is only a part of the problem. Little progress has been made in consolidating the losses from bad bank loans. The government may not wish to admit this, but it cannot hide from the facts indefinitely. Foreigners, who were so enamored of the opportunities in South Korea a year ago, are less eager to participate in the process as they realize how slowly matters have progressed. In November 1999, Moody's Investors Service rated the financial stability of South Korean banks 43 out of 46 countries—hardly the sort of performance one would associate with the "poster child of Asian economic reform."[20] South Korea has once again prevented a run on the bank but at a very large cost. As the debt of the banking and corporate entities has been transferred from the private to the public sector, the Korean government has lost much flexibility. Government debt, which was at very low levels going into the crisis, is now more than 80 percent of GDP.[21] More importantly, the total debt in the economy has not been significantly reduced since the crisis began—it has simply been moved off private sector balance sheets and onto that of the government.

Clearly, in retrospect a much larger emphasis on reform of financial institutions should have been part of the conditionality of the IMF bailout. Now, of course, multilateral lenders have lost most of their leverage and influence. International influence may come again if Korea requires large amounts of aid in order to absorb the North. We have already seen how Germany was able to spread the cost of absorbing East Germany throughout the European economy. An important part of that process was a willingness to recognize quickly that the assets were severely impaired and to move on to more productive tasks.

In merging the economies of North and South Korea, the government will face yet another large asset impairment and solvency issue. It will be far better if the society has already successfully navigated through one such crisis. A strict condition of any future flows of aid to Korea should be the insistence that the government and the private sector alike commit themselves to restructuring the economy by encouraging deregulation rather than red tape, transparency rather than opacity, and competition rather than protectionism.

WILL FOREIGN INVESTORS FINANCE REUNIFICATION?

A large component of the financing for reunification should come from foreign private sector investors. As things currently stand, this is unlikely to occur, at least in quantities sufficient to make a difference. The Korean distrust of foreign investors is real, palpable, and present at all levels of society. It may be the North that preaches *juche*, but all Koreans are skeptical of non-local capital. If reunification is to be successful, this must change. The experience of the Asian Development Bank (ADB) in other parts of Asia may provide a model. The ADB has invested in a variety of private sector projects using multiple sorts of structures: as an equity investor for its own account, as a hard lender, and as a soft lender. Private investors view the ADB's participation partly as validation of a project or a fund's investment merit and partly as insurance. The clear feeling among investors is that governments are much less likely to allow unfair or adverse judgments to stand against a group to which the ADB is party.

This is a simple model that can and should be emulated in Korea on a grand scale both before and during reunification. All sectors of Korean industry are ripe for restructuring and the fresh breeze of competition. Foreign capital and expertise, if allowed, can do much to stimulate growth and innovation in the economy. Participation by the ADB and the World Bank in individual private investment initiatives would serve two important roles: attracting foreign capital and serving as an honest broker to reassure locals that they are receiving impartial treatment and a fair deal. Koreans must learn to live up to the spirit as well as the letter of the law with respect to treatment of outside and minority shareholders—something they have been loath to do. It is much tougher to push around an entity like the World Bank than a mutual fund located a hemisphere away.

In addition to encouraging foreign capital investment, multilateral lenders must help Korea modernize its internal capital allocation mechanism. Economies allocate capital efficiently when prices are right. Prices become right when there is a free flow of information to all participants in the market. Transparent accounting, full disclosure, criminal sanctions against insider trading, and the legitimization of the concept of fiduciary duty are the key steps that need to be taken to begin to transform the Korean financial system from a casino-like system of crony capitalism into a modern, efficient market for pricing the riskiness of and return on investment. A serious first step would be to build up the network of independent institutional investors who can invest retail savings and corporate pensions. These investment strategies must replace the current structure of *chaebol*-controlled insurance firms and ITCs. They should be accountable both to stockholders and policyholders and should not be controlled by the large industrial combines. Such entities could and should invest in a wide range of corporate securities ranging from venture capital equity investments to senior secured debt. This system would provide local investors with a continuum of risk and return profiles and would allow corporate managers to begin to price capital intelligently. It would also wean corporate Korea from heavy reliance on bank debt. Again, multilateral lenders could "seed" this process by allocating sums of capital for professional managers to invest.

Korea's penchant for regulation extends deep into the pricing system, and the distrust of market forces allows the society to accept, without much comment, the imposition of additional controls at the sign of any problem or crisis. If the price of beer is controlled, why not the price of money? If firms can sell *soju*, Korea's national alcoholic beverage, only in certain regions and cannot transport it across the country, why then should capital be freely transferable? It is an easy trap to fall into. While the IMF has encouraged the government to change these policies, it will be much more effective if it invests on a regular basis in a series of ventures with contractual rights clearly established. And the IMF must invest in projects that are important enough that the government cannot afford to renegotiate terms later.

An important store of wealth in Korea today is in the form of land. Land needs to be made liquid so that the capital can be redeployed in other productive capacities. Multilateral lenders can help here too. They can establish real estate investment conduits to securitize and spread the ownership of land. New financial intermediaries should be established to provide more liquidity to the mortgage markets and to encourage private ownership of personal housing. The tax system ought to be amended to allow owners and lessees alike to transact in the property market in a direct and open fashion.

Korea needs to move aggressively to absorb the assets of the ailing *chaebols* and sell them off quickly. In addition, the government should continue to privatize assets quickly. Perhaps some form of voucher system, in which the government distributes ownership interests directly to citizens, could be implemented. Re-privatization of assets acquired by the government from bankrupt *chaebols* and banks could pave the way for the use of such programs in selling off assets in the North.

Further, spreading the ownership of private equity throughout the population can help to weave a tighter social safety net, which in turn could pave the way for reforming the labor market by allowing firms free reign in hiring and firing workers. Labor market mobility, real and perceived, is critical to increasing efficiency in the economy. Korea should learn from the examples of Scotland and Ireland, which have successfully attracted foreign capital that has led to the training and employment of workers previously laid off by sunset industries. They did so with the knowledge that they would not be sanctioned if they chose to lay off workers later. No such implicit bargain operates in Korea at present. And the trimming of the current workforce remains the single most problematic issue delaying more extensive restructuring of the Korean economy.

Foreign institutions, be they governments, bankers, or multilateral aid organizations, ultimately cannot "fix" what ails the Korean economy. The problems that manifest themselves today are the residue of decades of decisions and the unintended consequence of policies set, in many cases, long ago. South Koreans must change the South Korean economy, and they must do it quickly if they are to have a reasonable chance of absorbing the North. There is probably little that can be done by anyone at this point to change the minds north of the border. But in the South, Koreans must embrace competition and openness and help sweep away the inefficient system that exists today. South Koreans can be encouraged and led by the example of foreign governments and societies. They can be given economic incentives through investment programs and policies. But finally, they must stop deceiving themselves and get on with the job of instituting real economic reform.

NOTES

1. James Boswell, *The Life of Samuel Johnson*, cited from a letter from Johnson to Boswell dated September 19, 1777. The precise quote is: "Depend upon it, sir, when

a man knows he is to be hanged in a fortnight, it concentrates his mind wonderfully."

2. The examples of East Germany and Russia suggest that communist-era assets, when turned loose in a western-style market economy, turn out to be worth far less than the most pessimistic observers had assumed. In Russia, for example, western investors who bought assets "cheaply"—literally for pennies on the dollar, or kopecks on the ruble—have made little or no return on their investment, unless they were particularly nimble traders and were able to profit through the "greater fool theory"— the notion that one who makes a questionable investment will be able to sell at a higher price to another, more foolish investor.

3. For a good discussion of the issue, see Marcus Noland, "Some Unpleasant Arithmetic Concerning Unification," Institute for International Economics, *APEC Working Paper 96-13* (Washington, D.C.: Institute for International Economics, 1996). Noland estimates that reunification would have cost $500 billion to $750 billion in 1995 and that the figure would roughly double every five years, given the disparity in the growth rates between the North and South Korean economies. Thus a current figure of $1 trillion dollars does not seem unreasonable. This figure is more than twice South Korea's current GDP.

4. For that matter, the North Korean economy has also operated on a wartime footing. North Korea, however, has not enjoyed any success at it because experiments with such novel economic theories as *juche* have served mainly to squander resources.

5. It also produced innovative and quaint methods of bribery—such as the traditional Christmas box of fresh fruit in which the padding for the fruit was replaced with United States currency.

6. "Ponzi schemes" are named after Charles K. Ponzi, who ran such an operation in Boston in 1919–20. A Ponzi scheme is an investment program in which returns are paid to earlier investors entirely out of money paid into the scheme by newer investors. Many capital-intensive businesses, such as those favored by South Korean industry in the period of its rapid growth in the 1970s–1990s are essentially Ponzi schemes in that they produce no net economic profits for shareholders. Although dividends may be paid to shareholders, the funds are generated only through ever-increasing levels of indebtedness. This describes much of South Korean business even today.

7. In fairness, the banking system worked that way throughout much of Asia. And now many other countries are suffering through the whirlwind brought on by lack of disclosure and discipline. Thailand, for example, may now be going through

the single worst banking crisis in modern times. Its problems are more than an order of magnitude greater, in GDP terms, than the savings-and-loan debacle in the United States in the 1980s. Furthermore, the Korean system of allocating capital bears a striking resemblance to the system of state socialism instituted throughout Eastern Europe in the period of Soviet domination. The economist Janos Kornai in his analysis of the Hungarian economy has amply and brilliantly described this.

8. Psychic income is the non-monetary reward for holding an asset or engaging in an activity. Considerably less psychic income must have been available in 1998, as GDP contracted by 5.8 percent, private consumption by 9.6 percent, and fixed capital formation by an incredible 21.1 percent. These are the worst results since 1953. Bank of Korea news release, March 22, 1999.

9. Recent foreign investments and the presence of a large number of western "vulture investors" is evidence of this attraction. The author observed that it was very difficult to navigate through a hotel in Seoul during the spring of 1998 without running into an investment banker intent on "doing a deal." Most professed dissatisfaction with the Korean financial system but were attracted by the apparently high rates of return available by purchasing assets on the cheap.

10. The World Bank and the IMF have begun a pilot program to train members of the North Korean elite in law and economics by taking them on a tour of Australia. So far 60 individuals have participated. There is still much work to be done.

11. As an example, Russian male life expectancy has contracted by several years since the collapse of communism—a public health setback unprecedented in the twentieth century.

12. By October 1999, more than fifteen months after the Blue House promulgated its blueprint for *chaebol* reorganization—the so-called "Big Deal"—most of the parties were still negotiating and only a small amount of reorganizing had actually been accomplished. Meanwhile, Daewoo, one of the largest *chaebol*, had gone bankrupt. Local commentators have complained that President Kim had let economic policy "drift" while pursuing peace entreaties with North Korea. With the announcement in mid-October 2000 that President Kim would receive the Nobel Peace Prize, there was immediate speculation that the government's attention could turn back to managing the economy. Judging from the level of the stock market though, financiers are less willing to believe this time around.

13. Various comments made to the author in private interviews with business managers in a wide range of industries during September 1999 and again in September 2000 suggest that any lingering sense of crisis is well past in the Korean psyche.

14. One American investment banker, in a conversation with the author, described the painfully slow process of negotiating a transaction in Korea as "house-to-house combat."

15. Morgan Stanley Dean Witter, Inc, *The Investment Trust Companies and the Won*, October 8, 1999.

16. Jardine Fleming & Co., unpublished study on Korean *chaebol* asset quality, Hong Kong, 1999.

17. These figures, which seem conservative, have been picked up and repeated by numerous commentators (see note 18, below). The costs will not be realized at one time but will be spread over a period of years.

18. Namuh Rhee, "Get Ready for Year-End Rally," *Samsung Securities Market Strategy* (Seoul: Samsung Securities Co. Ltd., November 1, 1999). Rhee bases his estimate of a total cost to the economy of 30 to 40 trillion won (or 7 percent of current annual GDP) on the assumption promulgated by government officials that debt holders will recover 40 to 50 percent of their principal investment. Yet current private market transactions for Daewoo debt indicate that the private market is willing to sell debt at 20 percent of original face value, implying losses in the neighborhood of at least *50* trillion won, or around $40 billion. The losses from the Daewoo debacle will run approximately $1,000 for every man, woman, and child in South Korea—a high price indeed for one organization's financial folly.

19. To date, the Bank of Korea has promised to inject as much as 30 trillion won into a bond stabilization fund—about 5 percent of current GDP.

20. Digital [on-line] *Chosun Ilbo*, Nov. 7, 1999.

21. Bank of Korea, November 3, 1999. By contrast, in the United States, consolidated national government debt, as a percentage of GDP, is around 60 percent. In Japan it is over 80 percent. There is no "magic" number: every economy is different. Clearly, as the ratio increases, governments lose fiscal flexibility. The Korean government's ability to respond to future crises will be more limited because of this increased indebtedness.

STRATEGIC IMPLICATIONS

9

The Post-Korean Unification Security Landscape and U.S. Security Policy in Northeast Asia

Michael McDevitt

It is intellectually perilous to advance premises about the long term. The number of variables is too large, global changes are too rapid and diverse, and our imaginations are too limited. Who could have foreseen the world of 2000, or even 1990, in 1970? At one point or another during the last 15 years, expert opinion held that:

- The Soviet Union would never permit the reunification of Germany, much less permit a unified Germany to become a member of NATO.
- The Japanese economy was "number one"—the model for the rest of the world to emulate.
- North Korea, following the collapse of communist regimes in Europe and especially after the death of Kim Il Sung, would collapse by the mid-1990s.
- The Asian economic miracle was a "permanent" phenomenon because of the unique social and cultural characteristics of Asian nations.

This list could go on and on, but the point is that since the end of the

Cold War, expert opinion has had a dismal record in trying to forecast future outcomes.[1]

But what if we could foresee the future perfectly? In the area of security policy it would still be difficult to translate that vision into a future outcome. In security matters, diagnosis and prescription are not very closely aligned. All of the United States' war colleges instill in their students the strategic mantra of "matching ends, ways, and means." Yet the reality is that matching means and ends is always difficult. Frequently there are no optimum choices, only "less bad" ones. This is particularly true because the future does not always develop as we anticipate, and because national security planning and strategy is a *competitive business.*

National security strategy is not played out in a vacuum. It necessarily involves two nations or a group of nations in a dynamic interaction. For example, when the United States responds to perceived dangers from North Korea or tries to "shape" or hedge against uncertain outcomes, Pyongyang, as the object of these initiatives, will in turn adapt its stance in response to the actions of the United States. The point is that it is impossible to be correct all of the time. Instead one must constantly reassess the current situation and make changes accordingly.

This reality is not meant to imply that planning for the future is a waste of time. To the contrary, the very process of thinking about the future—which entails weighing alternatives, trying to understand relationships and linkages, appreciating that all actions have consequences, and trying to understand what these consequences may be—helps one to comprehend a range of plausible outcomes.

When thinking about the future of Northeast Asia there are many complex problems, but none so complex as attempting to speculate on the security implications of a reunified Korea. This chapter seeks to draw together a number of different themes related to this subject. They include: (1) the importance of the process of unification to the security policies a reunified Korea adopts; (2) the importance of history and current issues to the future of the strategic environment; (3) an analysis of the geostrategic landscape and how it may be a major post-unification concern for Korea; and (4) speculation on how U.S. security policy and presence in the region might evolve.[2]

NO SHORTAGE OF INFORMED SPECULATION

Korean Unification—A Cottage Industry

Ever since the early 1990s, when the government of the Republic of Korea and U.S. intelligence agencies seemed to be in a competition to see who could predict the precise date of North Korea's collapse, every respectable research institution and think tank that deals with East Asia has either sponsored a monograph, conducted a conference, or done both on this subject. The topic was normally approached in one of two ways. The first approach postulated and analyzed various scenarios of how Korean unification might unfold. In the broadest sense, this type of approach was captured by Kim Young Sam's airplane analogy of a hard landing or a soft landing. The second method skipped over the question of how reunification might take place and focused instead on the range of possible national security strategies that a unified Korea might pursue.

This outpouring of high quality speculation and assessment has left very few new things to say on either subject. What has not been addressed, however, is the importance of the *process* of unification in shaping the national security strategy of a unified peninsula. The bodies of work on unification and post-unification strategy are oddly disconnected. Work that focuses on unification scenarios normally does not go further than explaining and weighing the plausibility and likelihood of various scenarios. Similarly, studies that examine the range of post-unification issues normally start with the presumption of unification and proceed to abstractly evaluate the possible national security strategies a newly united Korean nation could pursue. These parallel intellectual tracks need to be connected because the process of unification, whether short and turbulent or protracted and peaceful, will be the most decisive influence on the range of plausible strategies a united Korea might implement.[3]

Reunification Scenarios

A review of mainstream opinion on reunification scenarios reveals that there are two prominent predictions: (1) a North Korean collapse or implosion that leads quickly to reunification (the German scenario) or (2) a drawn-out peaceful process of coexistence and gradual reunification. Other scholars and analysts go beyond these two opposing alternatives and present a richer range of alternatives that include three other outcomes in addition to the two aforementioned possibilities.[4]

The first of these is a war or lashing-out scenario. North Korea, for whatever reason—perhaps a final act of defiance, an incredibly incorrect evaluation of the correlation of forces, or a last ditch roll of the dice—starts a second Korean war by attacking the South. Although a difficult and bloody ordeal, the UN Command in the South manages to halt the attack, initiates a counterattack, and essentially conquers North Korea, eliminating it as a separate political entity. This, in other words, would constitute reunification by military conquest.

Another scenario postulates some sort of a loose Korean commonwealth in which North Korea comes to its economic senses, follows Beijing's advice, and puts in place "Deng-like" economic reforms while opening itself to the world. The result would be something along the lines of a "one Korea two systems" or federal Korea model that foreswore a total political reunification. Both sides surrender only a minimum of sovereignty to a Korean variant of the European Union. A scenario that today appears more plausible than even in late 1999.

A third outcome is no reunification at all—the two Koreas peacefully coexist, the threat of war is removed, and there is no desire on either side to politically reunify. An indefinite perpetuation of the status quo absent military confrontation. (Arguably, today all of the six parties with the greatest investment in the Korean Peninsula—the two Koreas, the United States, Japan, China, and Russia—would prefer this outcome, at least for the foreseeable future.) This scenario as well has gained in plausibility since the June 2000 summit between Kim Dae Jung and Kim Jong Il.

Whether the reunification scenarios one considers include all of the above possible outcomes or are reduced to the two canonical scenarios, they all imply an aspect of time, or process. In terms of the process of reunification there are really only two "time-line based" hypotheses—reunification that happens quickly or reunification that takes a long time. Unfortunately, the focus of the published intellectual effort has been only on the scenarios per se and the reactions of the interested regional powers, and not on the time-line and associated processes.

National Security Strategy Options for a United Korea

On the opposite side of the reunification scenario analysis are the mono-graphs and conferences devoted to post-unification Korean security strategy. These studies start with the presumption of unification. Either implicitly or explicitly, unified Korea is seen as a democracy led from Seoul with the option of selecting, from a menu of choices, a new Korean national security strategy. In general the options boil down to four alternatives:[5]

(1) *Continued alliance/alignment with the United States and the "West."* This is the unification scenario that most U.S. military analysts and security specialists hope for, as do the Japanese and, according to repeated assurances from President Kim Dae Jung, the current ROK government as well.

(2) *A return to the historic Sino-Korean pattern of a Korean state within China's "orbit."* This is Beijing's preferred choice, and Japan's night-mare.

(3) *Strategic independence.* A nonaligned Korea pursues an independent course looking after its own interests. This strategy—the choice of many Korean analysts—would include: a friendly relationship with all its neighbors; a Korea militarily robust enough to deter aggression (or at least to give any neighbor serious second thoughts before commit-ting to aggression); and a balanced military that consists of a capable air force and navy to complement the strong ROK army.

(4) *Neutrality.* Similar to strategic independence, with no bilateral alli-ances this option would, however, present a passive stance, implying a strict form of neutrality. Security would be underwritten by all the regional powers in return for a modest defense establishment. The Chinese would prefer this option if Seoul does not choose a Sino-centered security strategy. Japan, on the other hand, would not. To Japan, Korean weakness would be seen as a temptation to China to meddle in Korean affairs.[6]

CONNECTING SCENARIOS AND NATIONAL SECURITY
STRATEGIES: THE PROCESS OF UNIFICATION

Rapid Reunification through Absorption

The "rapid unification school," based on the scenario of a collapsed North Korea, began to be discussed publicly by ROK President Roh Tae Woo in 1991. Flush with the rapid succession of momentous and peaceful changes in the international system between 1989 and 1991—the Berlin Wall coming down, German reunification, the end of the Cold War, and the peaceful self-destruction of the Soviet Union—and with the success of his *Nordpolitik* with the Soviet Union and China, Roh predicted that North Korea would collapse in seven years (i.e., by 1998). Later, in the wake of Kim Il Sung's death in 1994, many experts in Seoul and Washington predicted that North Korea would collapse within six months. Others, more cautious, thought that in three years or so—by 1997—the DPRK would collapse and be absorbed by the Republic of Korea. John Deutch, director of the CIA, warned in congressional testimony that unless Pyongyang reformed, North Korea would soon collapse.[7]

Worried about being caught unprepared, the governments and military establishments of the United States and South Korea invested a great deal of effort in developing contingency plans that addressed a host of potential problems that might arise if North Korea were to collapse. Consideration was given to dealing with massive refugee flows, chaos, starvation, the possibility of combat with isolated pockets of recalcitrant KPA soldiers, and demobilization of the Korean People's Army, as well as to related problems associated with an impoverished North Korea becoming a ward of South Korea.

One of the great values in doing detailed contingency planning is that it forces the political and policy elite to focus on real problems. Although contingency planning almost by definition deals with hypothetical situations, the problems posed and addressed demand serious consideration. The point here is not to try and detail what those considerations and conclusions might be, but rather to imagine the cumulative impact of dealing with a collapsed DPRK on Korean security planners both in and out of uniform.

Undoubtedly, the experience was sobering. Even before the financial crisis severely damaged South Korea's economy, the enormity and economic impact of trying to absorb a collapsed North Korea made it clear that South Korea would be totally consumed with the problems of absorption for a number of years. Seoul could scarcely contemplate a dramatic departure from its current national strategy (such as becoming a strategically independent player) at the same time that it would be dealing with the aftermath of the collapse. Any dramatic shift in strategic approach and concomitant reshaping of the military to emphasize a more "regional" role, rather than peninsular defense, translates into a bigger navy and air force. But since air forces and navies are very expensive, that course would be out of the question. Whether Seoul and Beijing would welcome it or not, sustaining a U.S.-Korean treaty relationship would be a strategic necessity while the country and the ROK army were focused on internal matters. Financial assistance from Japan and the United States would be essential.

The bottom line is that a rapid collapse of North Korea, which would be even more difficult for the ROK today because of its weak economy, would make it probable that Seoul would maintain the current trajectory of its national security strategy even if it really wanted to embark on an independent course. If the nation were consumed by the crisis of absorption, it is hard to imagine that Seoul would decide to increase uncertainty, at home and regionally, by choosing to walk away from its alliance with the United States and asking that all U.S. forces leave the Korean Peninsula. To the extent that one can forecast, it seems more likely that a rapid process of reunification would result in a unified Korean national security strategy that comports closely with Seoul's current strategy—alliance with the United States and alignment with the West.

This is not to say that Chinese and perhaps Russian concerns over a unified Korea allied with the United States would not be heard. The Chinese have been quite clear in unofficial dialogue that while they can understand a U.S.-ROK alliance today, if the threat of a second Korean war were gone they would oppose as a matter of principle a continuation of the alliance and of a U.S. military presence in Korea. Nonetheless, in the rapid collapse scenario, Chinese leverage and ability to decisively influence Seoul's range of options might be reduced—but not eliminated.

Almost by definition, a rapid collapse is not "under control" and would unfold in an unpredictable manner. Among the many uncertainties would be China's reaction to this "uncontrolled" process unfolding before its eyes. Would Beijing feel compelled to militarily cross the Yalu and Tumen Rivers to create a buffer zone that would insulate it from chaos and refugees? While this prospect would depend on the circumstances at the time, the possibility of a buffer zone enforced by China's People's Liberation Army (PLA) cannot be ruled out. This temporary expedient could, like Israel's occupation of South Lebanon, become a longer-term proposition. The point of raising the question is to consider whether a rapid collapse in the North would provide China with greater leverage than it might otherwise possess in shaping Seoul's post-unification national security strategy.[8]

If China were to gain considerable leverage on the peninsula, would Seoul be more or less willing to jettison its relationship with Washington? Would People's Liberation Army occupation of a sliver of northern North Korea provide China a bargaining chip with which to press Seoul to forego its alliance with the United Sates, or would it have exactly the opposite effect? It seems likely that the people of what is now South Korea would be outraged at this new impediment to complete reunification and would not be willing to be "blackmailed" by Beijing into jettisoning their American anchor to windward at the very moment Seoul was facing the crushing burden of coping with a collapsed North Korea.

With Washington as Seoul's partner, this situation would raise the possibility of a direct U.S. confrontation with China to attempt to persuade the Chinese to withdraw. This prospect might cool enthusiasm in the United States for continued military involvement in Korea, but because of the damage that would result to America's position throughout East Asia if the United States failed to remain true to a long-time ally facing new difficulties, it appears unlikely that America would fail to stand by Korea's side.

The preceding discussion has only scratched the surface of the potential twists and turns that could accompany a rapid collapse of North Korea. But on balance it is hard to avoid the judgment that Seoul would conclude that its interests were best served by maintaining an alliance relationship with the United States. A period of rapid domestic change and economic and socially stressful circumstances seems unlikely to generate pressure for a complete overhaul of national security strategy, particularly since the most visible manifestation of the U.S. alliance, American forces, is likely to be reduced if the situation in the former North Korea were to stabilize and the risk of another Korean War were to permanently abate.

It seems probable that once the need to deter war in Korea fades, U.S. forces would begin a process of restructuring and downsizing, which would lead to a different sort of U.S. military presence in Korea. Even if the U.S. Department of Defense did not want to downsize the U.S. presence on the Korean Peninsula, it seems likely that Congress and the American public would pressure military officials to question seriously keeping forces where they were no longer required.[9]

Why the Interested Governments Do Not Want
Rapid Reunification by Absorption

The single greatest variable working against the collapse of the North Korean regime leading to a rapid reunification is that no interested power, not Pyongyang, Seoul, Beijing, Tokyo, Washington, or Moscow, wants this to happen. Today, all of these capitals are pursuing "two-Korea" policies with the aim of keeping Pyongyang afloat.

It would be foolish to expect that Pyongyang would be intentionally complicit in its own demise. The North Korean government has been quite clear in its comments regarding South Korean and American press speculation about reunification by absorption: "the question is not if there will be another war on the Korean Peninsula but when."[10] In fact, Pyongyang's nuclear and missile programs can only be understood as a cost-effective strategic equalizer and insurance policy for keeping the regime in place.

In Seoul, even before the financial crisis in late 1997, a change in both government policy and public attitudes about the costs and benefits of national unification had already taken place. Seoul has closely studied German unification by absorption and has come to the following conclusions:

• German unification came about largely by serendipity (the Gorbachev factor) and adroit U.S. diplomacy, and not incrementally. As such, it is not readily reproducible in the Korean case.

* It turned out that German national unity was not a solid foundation for the politics necessary for national reconciliation and reconstruction.

* Despite over $700 billion in subsidies in eight years, the east-west chasms remain as wide as ever before.

* Chancellor Helmut Kohl, the unifier of Germany, was voted out of office, with his singular achievement being one of the causes of his electoral defeat.[11]

Not only did the government learn these lessons, so too did the population of South Korea. An insightful piece in the *Washington Post* before the financial crisis reported that the more South Koreans learned about famine in the North and read speculation about collapse and absorption of the North by the South, the more they worried about the negative impact on their own lives. They became increasingly outspoken against unification by absorption, with the result that ROK government officials began to talk about some sort of continuing division of the two Koreas should the DPRK collapse. Unification would then only take place when the economic level of North Korea were raised and the results of a lifelong drumming of communist ideology into North Koreans were erased.[12]

Since that time, Kim Dae Jung has translated these concerns and apprehensions into official ROK policy. His "sunshine policy" and pledges not to undermine or absorb North Korea are a manifestation of both a realistic approach to the North and a response to public apprehension and concern about the economic impact of reunification. By officially abandoning notions of absorption and calling for peaceful coexistence, Kim Dae Jung is in effect drawing on one oft forgotten lesson from the German experience—the model of "one Germany, two states."[13]

Beijing does not desire Korean reunification. Despite lip service to peaceful unification, the central objective of Beijing's foreign policy is to create a nonthreatening external environment in Northeast Asia so continued economic development of China can receive undivided attention. Chinese leaders appreciate the strategic consequences of reunification by absorption following a collapse of the North, and as a result are willing, in a cost-effective way, to strengthen and support Pyongyang. Discussions with Chinese experts on North Korea make clear that they believe Pyongyang would rather fight than succumb to German-style unification.[14]

China has supported Pyongyang and the "Kim dynasty" in a number of ways, including: showing instant recognition and legitimization of Kim Jong Il as the paramount leader in the wake of Kim Il Sung's death; backing away from its requirement that Pyongyang pay for food and fuel; maintaining the 1961 military security treaty; being willing to provide as much food aid as necessary to help North Korea avoid a destabilizing famine; and supporting the extraordinary summit between the two Kims in June 2000.[15]

From Beijing's perspective, sustaining Pyongyang not only goes a long way toward precluding a second Korean war, it preserves a socialist buffer against the inroads of democratic theory (i.e., peaceful evolution) that the Chinese worry so much about. They also worry about a huge flow of refugees into China and the possibility that some two million Chinese Koreans in the Yanbian Autonomous Prefecture could develop nationalist sentiment and identification with a reunited Korea under the leadership of Seoul.[16]

The same concerns about another Korean war also inform United States, Japanese, and Russian policy toward North Korea. As a result, both Washington and Tokyo, despite their obvious distaste in dealing with the unscrupulous and murderous North Korean regime, help keep Pyongyang afloat.[17] North Korea has emerged, to the outrage of many, as America's largest aid recipient in Asia. Over the past five years, since the conclusion of the Agreed Framework for halting North Korean nuclear reprocessing at the Yongbyon site, the United States has pursued a de facto two-Koreas policy.

In Washington, the imminent collapse scenario so popular only a couple of years ago is today scarcely discussed. The resilience of the North Korean state, the massive infusion of aid, the recent summit, the fragile economic situation in the South, Kim Dae Jung's "sunshine policy," and the realization that China is willing to do whatever necessary to keep North Korea afloat have combined to create a new consensus in Washington. North Korea will not collapse; as a separate state it is going to be around for many years. The October 1999 report by former Secretary of Defense William

Perry, which was instigated by a Congressionally mandated review of U.S. policy toward North Korea, concluded that the United States must engage North Korea, live with it, and not hasten its demise. The Perry report represents mainstream, but certainly not all, opinion in Washington that the best policy is a step-by-step process that leads to normalized relations with North Korea in return for a North Korean roll-back of its long-range missile and nuclear program.[18] The October 2000 visit by a high-ranking North Korean official and subsequent visit by Secretary of State Albright to Pyonyang is the most recent and dramatic manifestation of this policy actually being implemented.

The same ambivalence that Washington has regarding dealing with North Korea exists in Tokyo as well. The Japanese remain outraged by the North Korean Taepo Dong missile that flew over Honshu in August 1998. They too worry about another Korean war, one in which North Korea would possess nuclear weapons and the means to deliver them to Japanese soil. In addition, the old vision of a united Korean peninsula (now, potentially with nuclear weapons) as a dagger pointed at Japan still informs Japanese strategists. So do worries that a united Korea would cast its lot with Beijing in an anti-Japanese coalition. According to one Japanese defense official, Tokyo's nightmare situation is where communist China is "superior" to Japan in terms of power (no matter how power is defined) and has influence over Korea. So for Tokyo, on balance, helping to sustain North Korea is the better of two bad choices.[19]

Of the four major regional powers, Moscow has the least influence in Korean affairs. This is a manifestation of its current weak state and of the mistaken decision early in the decade to put all of Russia's eggs in the South Korean basket by normalizing relations with Seoul in 1990. Pyongyang felt betrayed, and Moscow lost credibility and influence with the DPRK regime, and as a result has been on the sidelines in all the important geostrategic decisions regarding North Korea over the last decade.[20]

The goal of Russia's Northeast Asian policy is to ensure stability and a peaceful external environment for obvious domestic reasons. As a result, the Russians have also concluded that the least risky option is to pursue a two-Koreas policy and lend whatever succor they can to Pyongyang. The Russian attempt to regain some balance in their Korean relationships has been partially achieved, as evidenced by the March 1999 signing of a "Treaty of Friendship, Good Neighbor Relations, and Cooperation" by Pyongyang and Moscow, and by its initiative in July 2000 to seek an alternative that would end North Korea's ICBM program.[21]

Another factor has also crept into Russian calculations as U.S.-Russian relations have worsened—latent anti-Americanism in domestic Russian politics that seeks "revenge" for Moscow's defeat in the Cold War. Moscow is more inclined today to favor a nonaligned reunited Korea since a united Korea in alliance with the United States would represent another "American victory." Whether this return to a zero-sum assessment of Russian-U.S. interests will remain a feature of Russian domestic politics is difficult to predict. What is not difficult to predict though is that as long as Russia stays on the road of democracy, domestic politics will have an influence on Russian foreign policy.[22]

Finally, of all the external great powers concerned with Korea, only Washington would likely benefit if, without war or massive disruption, North Korea quietly sank.[23] Lifting the burden of having to deal with Pyongyang would be a great practical, strategic, and moral relief for the United States. This is not true today for Japan, China, Russia, and South Korea, who, even if the DPRK went away quietly, see bigger problems with that scenario than with the two Koreas peacefully coexisting.

Evolutionary Reunification and the Implications for
Korean National Security Strategy

One of the most interesting features of the analysis on unification that would come from a long-term evolutionary negotiated settlement is the willingness to assume, without question, that during the process of reunification the DPRK can be persuaded to acquiesce to a continuation of a U.S.-ROK alliance and some sort of U.S. military presence on the Korean Peninsula.[24]

There is no question that today these are declaratory positions of both Seoul and Washington. In Korea, President Kim Dae Jung has publicly stated on a number of occasions that a U.S. alliance and U.S. presence would be a welcome part of a unified Korea's security policy. On the U.S. side, officials including Secretary of Defense William Cohen have also indicated that America would welcome a continuation of a U.S.-ROK alliance and the opportunity to maintain some military presence in Korea.[25]

At the inter-Korean summit in June 2000 none of the agreed topics for future discussion dealt directly with the long-standing DPRK demand to remove U.S. forces from the peninsula. But, the issue of U.S. forces was raised at the summit. As President Kim Dae Jung has subsequently revealed, he advised North Korean leader Kim Jong Il of his views about the importance of a continued U.S. troop presence, not only for stability on the peninsula, but in Northeast Asia as a whole.[26]

Kim Jong Il allegedly expressed "understanding" of President Kim's views. Although many in South Korea and the United States remain skeptical about this apparent sudden shift in North Korean thinking on this issue, it is interesting that neither Kim Jong Il nor his government organs have found it necessary to publicly contradict President Kim's claimed espousal of continued U.S. military presence.[27]

So, one of the most dramatic developments in the blossoming North-South rapprochement is the apparent willingness of Pyongyang to countenance a U.S. military presence. On closer examination this central issue still involves a great deal of uncertainty. Pyongyang has not, as of this writing, positively endorsed a continued military presence—so its options remain open. Kim Jong Il's apparent acquiescence appears to be wise diplomacy. Rather than making U.S. troops a stumbling block to improved relations and the all important economic aid that he hopes it will yield by setting the issue aside, Pyongyang is free to raise it again in future negations about, first a peace treaty, and then eventually reunification. It is unlikely that we have not heard the last word on U.S. military presence in Korea from Pyongyang.

The desire of both Seoul and Washington to make clear a desire for U.S. presence over the long term is sensible. From Seoul's perspective, a U.S.-ROK alliance keeps its options open for both the present and the future. It gives Seoul leverage and something to bargain over with the North, and eases pressure from the ROK military for increased defense budgets. Moreover, rapprochement with Japan would be easier if the United States remains a common ally of both Korea and Japan. Finally, of course, sustaining a U.S.-ROK relationship guarantees help from the only nation in the world that could help Korea successfully resist Chinese military intimidation and pressure.

For Washington, an explicit desire to sustain the alliance is a hedge against an aggressive China. A unified Korea in some kind of trilateral relationship with Japan and the United States ensures that Northeast Asia will look to the United States rather than China as a force for stability. Keeping some military presence in a unified Korea ensures that Japan will not be the only nation in Asia that would have to host U.S. forces on its soil. Hopefully, the bases in Korea available to the United States today would remain available in the future for contingencies throughout East Asia. Beyond Japan and Korea, there are not many airfields available and accessible to the United States in East Asia. To employ air power on the scale demonstrated against Iraq and Serbia requires bases close to the scene of action that can accommodate a large number of land-based U.S. air force aircraft. Korea is one of the few places where a large number of tactical aircraft can be sent.

Sensible though these positions might be, they are also based on a heroic assumption and are more an expression of hope rather than a forgone conclusion. The assumption that at the end of the process of peaceful evolutionary reunification the U.S.-ROK alliance will survive more or less intact, or that a new treaty for the new situation can replace the old treaty, is simply not the only realistic alternative. Because both Seoul and Washington desire that this outcome should not foreclose thinking about other alternatives, one of which is presented here.

Peaceful reunification presumes the cessation of a military threat, ultimately leading to a unified Korean state. The process of integration assumes a political understanding or modus vivendi that includes agreement on a permanent peace mechanism as an interim measure prior to formal unification. Toward these ends, both Korean states would have to agree on very significant confidence-building measures associated with military withdrawal and reduction of tension. This, presumably, would be part of a gradual multiphased process of evolving and mutating through inter-Korean reconciliation and cooperation to a Korean commonwealth, and then to a single Korean nation-state. Another possibility is a confederation of two states, each with its own system and government, which some Koreans have dubbed the "one state, one nation, two systems, and two governments" formula. These processes may take years and will involve protracted and difficult negotiations.

Negotiations are the issue if one is concerned about preserving a U.S.-ROK alliance and all that it implies for an American presence in Korea and post-unification Korean national security strategy. Because a peaceful reunification will be negotiated rather than imposed, compromises on both sides will be required if the process is to proceed rather than stalemate. We already have decades of ample evidence of what tough negotiators the North Koreans are. One of their consistent negotiating points has been the withdrawal of U.S. forces from Korea. Even if it is now more possible to opine that U.S. presence would survive peace treaty negotiations, the next negotiating hurdle would be the unification negotiations.[28]

In addition, a number of Chinese sources have stated that once the threat of war abates in Korea, Beijing will oppose a united Korea that is aligned with the United States and the stationing of U.S. troops in Korea once peace has been achieved.[29]

It is possible that ROK and U.S. negotiations will be conducted so brilliantly that in the end North Korea and China will agree to a reunified Korea allied with the United States. It is also possible that retaining a modest U.S. military presence in Korea may also be an outcome. This is possible—but seems still to be a very long shot, particularly if Taiwan-PRC reunification remains unsettled. Beijing is not anxious to acquiescence in anything that would make it militarily easier for U.S. forces to intervene in Taiwan Strait crisis. The base structure in Korea would greatly aid in the deployment of U.S. land-based aircraft to East Asia in a Taiwan crisis.

It is more likely that even if the alliance and some of the U.S. presence survive the peace treaty negotiations, China and the DPRK would oppose preserving these two "artifacts" of the Cold War during the follow-up negotiations leading to reunification.

In addition, public opinion in South Korea will be a factor. If in the minds of South Koreans the U.S. alliance and presence remains a major impediment to successful reunification of the country, it is difficult to see how a South Korean democracy would allow that one point to stalemate the process. If the tradeoff is between a U.S. alliance and reunification, unification most likely would be the choice of the people of South Korea.[30]

What this implies is that despite the best intentions and desires of leaders and policymakers today, the process of making peace and then working toward reunification would almost certainly make the extension of the Republic of Korea's current national security strategy very difficult to achieve.

If Korea is not able to choose a strategy of continued alliance with the United States and the West, Korean leaders will have to choose among the other alternatives—either alignment with China, strategic independence, or neutrality. A China-oriented security posture is possible and in harmony with Korean historic tradition. However, as long as China remains a communist state with a strident nationalistic and bullying style of diplomacy, it is hard to imagine that Seoul would willingly cast its lot with Beijing before at least attempting to pursue a course of strategic independence. This is not to say that Seoul would go out of its way to provoke China, but the lure of being an "independent player" in Northeast Asia would seem rather irresistible. This would be a historic opportunity for Korea in the modern age, and one that would be hard to forgo.[31]

Certainly as Seoul pondered its choices there would be many variables at play. The strength of the Korean economy after many years of gradual progress toward unification would be an issue. The state of China's political evolution, the health of the Chinese economy, and the willingness of China to remain true to its currently expressed vision of a reunited Korea that is nonaligned and neutral would all be crucial variables. Assuming that Beijing did not object to an independent, nonaligned Korea, and that Korean public opinion also favored this option, it is difficult to foresee anything but grudging acquiescence and support by Tokyo and Washington. Taken together, this analysis leads to the conclusion that a very plausible strategic outcome for a Korea that "gradually" unifies will be either "strategic independence" or "neutrality."

UNIFIED KOREA AS AN INDEPENDENT PLAYER

When speculating about a reunified Korea that pursues an independent security policy, it is important to recognize the aspects of history and the present situation that are likely to be of continuing importance in the future. While we cannot make a "straight line" interpolation of today into the future, we must recognize that the future is never a clean slate. Certain features of today's geostrategic reality are going to be relevant in the future, including geography, the centrality and influence of a strong China, the continued influence of the United States in the region, and the importance of the U.S.-Japanese alliance in facilitating America's role in Asia.

Historical Context: A Tough Neighborhood

Since the Opium War era, rivalries over control of Northeast China and the Korean Peninsula have plagued this region. It is beyond dispute that the last century has been particularly bad for Northeast Asia in general, and Korea in particular. Since 1894, when the government of Imperial China intervened in Korea at the "request" of the Korean court to suppress the Tonghak movement, the region has been plagued with conflict. Japan seized upon the Chinese intervention as a pretext for a military intervention of its own, which then led to the Sino-Japanese War. This, in turn, helped to set in motion a remarkable sequence of events that has turned Northeast Asia into the region of the world most ridden with great power rivalry and conflict:

- The Russo-Japanese War over control of Manchuria and indirectly the Korean Peninsula;
- The 1905 Japanese occupation of Korea;
- The 1931 Japanese invasion of Manchuria from Korea;
- The 1945 Soviet offensive into Manchuria and North China;
- The post-World War II occupation and division of Korea by the Soviet Union and United States;
- The 1950 invasion of South Korea by the North;
- The Chinese intervention in Korea in 1950;
- The Cold War competition pitting the Soviet Union and China against

the United States and its allies;

- The U.S.-Chinese rapprochement based on a common antipathy to the Soviet Union;
- The continued armed stand-off across the DMZ, with a North Korean state probably armed with a nuclear weapon or two.

Almost any future would be better than this past.

A Unique Post-Unification Geostrategic Environment

Comparing the past with a prognosis for the future is revealing. It seems that none of the factors that created an unstable past will be present when a united Korea becomes part of Northeast Asia's future. After Korean unification, Northeast Asia will enter a period unique in its modern history. Most significantly China will not be weak; it will probably be unified and strong. Korea would be a far cry from the hermit kingdom of the late nineteenth century; ripe for imperialist plucking. Both Russia and Japan have left their imperialist predilections in the past, and it is hard imagine a twenty-first century return, even if democracy falters in Russia. The one constant seems likely to be U.S. presence in a militarily significant way.

By and large, all the states in the region will be territorially intact and reasonably well satisfied with their existing frontiers. In other words, there is a very good chance for this historically troubled region to be free of the prospect or reality of war for the first time since the mid-nineteenth century. The major remaining outstanding territorial issue in the region may be Taiwan. Taiwan will remain a regional stability issue if Korean reunification takes place in the near term; which will have an impact on Chinese attitudes toward U.S. presence. If on the other hand, Korean reunification comes about as a result of a slow negotiated process that unfolds over years, perhaps decades, then there is a reasonable possibility that some accommodation between Taipei and Beijing will have been reached. Such an accommodation would mean that Taiwan would no longer loom in the background of regional security issues.

Aside from the Taiwan issue, each of the regional powers are either satisfied with existing frontiers, or appear willing to be patient and seek a diplomatic solution to remaining problems.

When considering the distribution of conventional military power in the area surrounding Korea, it is interesting to note the reversal in military fortunes between China and Russia in the last century. Today Russia is the "sick man" of Northeast Asia. But unlike a century ago, when China was the "sick man," Russia's neighbors are not poised to bite off or compete with one another for the best portions of the Russian Far East. This is so because of contemporary diplomatic norms, but also because Russia's nuclear arsenal guarantees its continued territorial integrity. This also helps us understand why North Korea, despite—or rather because of—its enfeebled economy, appreciates the value of nuclear weapons.

The last century and a half also witnessed a fascinating evolution of power in Northeast Asia. China was dominant until the rise of Japan and western imperialism. By 1899, Russia, Great Britain, and Japan were the arbiters of security in Northeast Asia. Today, China and the United States share the role of arbiter: China on the mainland of Asia and the United States on edges of the continent. The two weakest in relative military terms a century ago are the strongest today.

In the past, it was the political and military weakness of Korea and China that created instability. Korea was unable to defend itself against its neighbors and when its great power patron, China, was also militarily enfeebled, Russia and Japan tried to impose their own brand of stability. As a result, Korea was either occupied or divided for the entire twentieth century. The fact is, today we have no empirical evidence on which to reach judgments about how a reunited modern Korea might behave. A united Korea that is well armed, militarily competent, and "strategically independent" would be a new feature on the modern Northeast Asian security landscape; whereas a united Korea that is "neutral" but militarily weak and dependent on the good will of its neighbors would have historically unpleasant resonance.

The record of U.S. diplomatic history is clear: throughout the twentieth century, the United States has been willing, diplomatically or militarily, to frustrate attempts by others to achieve regional hegemony. It is safe to assert that a fundamental strategic objective of the United States, starting with John Hay's Open Door Notes of 1899, has been to do whatever possible to avoid being excluded or frozen out of Northeast Asia. Furthermore, since Admiral George Dewey's victory at Manila Bay in 1898, the United States has been a militarily important factor in the Northeast Asian security calculus. U.S. presence in East Asia represents the longest period (interrupted for three years, between 1942 and early 1945, when the Japanese occupied the Philippines) of overseas military deployment in American history. It is not rash therefore to predict continued U.S. military involvement in the region after Korea reunites, even if there are no U.S. forces stationed on the Korean Peninsula.

The Impact of Today's Realities on the Future

Turning from history to the present, the other factor that will help to determine how a reunited Korea would fit within Northeast Asia is the likely persistence of many of today's realities into the future. In the geostrategic realm, projecting today's alliances, partnerships, and friendly relationships into the future helps focus analysis of how future interstate relations might develop. What seems apparent when considering the diplomatic record of the past decade is that everyone in the region, including North Korea in its own, often unsophisticated fashion, is trying to improve relationships with neighbors. A list of the existing interstate relationships and recent diplomatic activity makes the point:

- The Kim Dae Jung and Kim Jong Il summit in June 2000
- the Sino-Russian strategic partnership
- the U.S.-Japan Alliance
- the U.S.-ROK Alliance
- Russo-Japanese rapprochement
- Japanese-ROK rapprochement
- the PRC-DPRK "alliance"
- Russia-South Korea normalization and the recent successful attempts to repair the Russo-DPRK alliance.
- PRC-ROK normalization
- And whatever replaces the now moribund U.S.-China strategic partnership

This flurry of diplomatic activity is based on uncertainty. Uncertainty exists concerning China's rise, the process of Korean reunification, and how a reunited Korea will elect to ensure its own security.

Today, every power in Northeast Asia is jockeying for position and influence in order to guarantee its long-term strategic interests. This concern with long-term interests is translated into diplomatic initiatives all aimed at hedging (i.e., keeping options open), or putting in place understandings that will be important if things do not turn out as each power might wish: or conversely, to help ensure that the future unfolds as each wishes. Korea and its future are a central focus of this activity. Korea will become the wild card as the United States, China, Japan, and to a degree Russia, all compete to ensure that at a minimum Korea does not assume an antagonistic posture toward them, as unrealistic as this might appear currently.

To a surprising extent, Korea has already become a cockpit for diplomatic competition between the great powers of Northeast Asia. Beijing courts Seoul, and the Koreans reciprocate. Beijing continues to support Pyongyang. Russia tries to work its way back into the good graces of Pyongyang while maintaining a good relationship with Seoul. Japan works assiduously to improve the Tokyo-Seoul relationship while being poised to improve relations with Pyongyang if it finally stops threatening Japan. And finally, Washington and Pyongyang are rapidly improving relations. If this is what takes place today when reunification increasingly seems a distant dream, consider for a moment how active the competition could become during an evolutionary reunification process following a peace treaty.

It is also reasonable to speculate on whether the network of bilateral relationships with varying degrees of formality might evolve into a multinational Northeast Asian security organization. That is an oft-expressed goal for many, including the Clinton administration. But so far, efforts to convince Pyongyang to participate in even track two unofficial contacts have been futile. Another more serious impediment is United States, Japanese, and South Korean insistence that any multinational framework not be at the expense of the current U.S. alliances with Japan and Korea. This important reservation makes it more difficult to forecast a positive Russian and Chinese response. Baring a major change in policy it is likely that Beijing and Moscow would want a supercession of U.S. bilateral alliances before buying into a multilateral security structure.

The PRC's insistent—and consistent—view has been that U.S. alliances in the region are not compatible with Beijing's long-term vision. This is spelled out clearly in China's "New Concept of Security," given voice by Foreign Minister Tang Jiaxuan during his September 22, 1999 address to the UN General Assembly. China's concerns about United States unilateralism, NATO expansion, strengthening of the U.S.-Japan alliance (which Beijing likens to NATO expansion), and development of a North Pacific theater missile defense system seem unlikely to change in the near term.

Neither is the United States likely to conclude that U.S. security interests in the region can be sustained without the U.S.-Japan alliance. Without Japanese bases, particularly if Korean reunification results in an American military departure from the peninsula, it would be impossible to sustain a reasonable military presence in East Asia. As long as the United States believes its military presence is important, and China thinks it is an intrusion, these opposing perceptions about the value and importance of bilateral alliances are likely to remain. This suggests that for the foreseeable future multilateral security in Northeast Asia will remain stuck at the unofficial, track two level.

How does the U.S. military presence in Korea fit into the reunification picture? The actual process of reunification will be decisive in answering this question. The hypothesis is straightforward. A quick reunification set in motion because of a North Korean collapse would have the least impact on the avowed aims of Seoul and Washington to preserve the U.S.-ROK alliance and on the continued presence of some U.S. forces on the peninsula. On the other hand, a slow, evolutionary process of reunification that involves negotiation, with its attendant compromises, probably dooms chances for sustaining any U.S. forces in Korea and makes a continuation of some sort of U.S.-ROK alliance highly problematic.

U.S. FORCE STRUCTURE CONSIDERATIONS

The current U.S. presence in Korea, and in Japan as well, is rationalized by the fact that there is no peace in Korea, only an armistice. Therefore, U.S.

troops are necessary to deter a renewed outbreak of conflict. In any evolutionary scenario for Korean reunification, it is safe to posit that a peace treaty would be the first step in the process. On the other hand, a collapse leading to rapid reunification could come either before or after a peace treaty, but once it happened and the initial turmoil had been stabilized, the nature of the U.S. military presence in Korea would almost certainly have to evolve. While at first glance the U.S. presence in Korea can be analyzed in a vacuum, in reality Korea is the rationale behind the size and nature of U.S. forces in Asia, and if that rationale is removed, an entirely new justification would have to be developed.

Today, of course, the United States remains committed to sustaining the current posture of about 100,000 U.S. military personnel permanently assigned in East Asia. This was unequivocally stated in November 1998 when the Department of Defense published a report on U.S. strategy for East Asia. The report reaffirms the 1995 decision to stabilize the presence at 100,000 personnel and argues that this figure is not arbitrary. Rather, it is based on an analysis that shows that the strategic environment, both now and in the immediate future, will not change significantly, and as a result there is no need for a macro-level change in the U.S. posture.

These few rather unremarkable sentences in a 60-odd page report are central to any consideration of how U.S. force posture in East Asia might evolve. The crucial point is that the only factor that will precipitate a major change, either up or down, to the 100,000-person baseline is a major change in the strategic environment. There are a number of potential crisis spots in East Asia that could have military ramifications, but clearly the possibility of either war or peace in Korea is the most significant independent variable that could precipitate change in U.S. presence in East Asia.[32] Were war to break out in Korea, U.S. presence in the region would dramatically increase, since virtually 50 percent of America's entire military power would flow rapidly from the United States to the Korean Peninsula and bases in Japan.

Thus Korea is the most important factor in shaping the military mix and overall strength of U.S. forces permanently assigned in Asia. As long as the requirement to *deter* North Korea exists, there will be little change in the overall size and composition (the balance of army, air force, navy, and marine corps) of the U.S. presence in the region. However, it would not require the reunification of Korea to create the circumstances for a major change in U.S. force structure. A peace treaty that included a mutual pullback from the DMZ and other verifiable confidence-building measures that made the prospect of North Korean aggression remote would be sufficient to trigger a major reevaluation of the roles and missions of U.S. forces in East Asia.

In fact such a reevaluation would encompass the whole of U.S. military strategy. Ever since the 1992 defense review conducted at Secretary of Defense Les Aspin's direction, America's armed forces have been sized and organized to be able to respond to two nearly simultaneous "major theater wars"—a characterization intended to capture the idea of a conflict on the scale of Desert Storm. Korea has, from the beginning, been considered one of the two-theater-war planning cases, and fully 50 percent of U.S. military power is earmarked for Korea if conflict breaks out. (Conflict in the Persian Gulf is the other canonical scenario.) Absent another plausible theater-war scenario, and there could be one, peace in Korea would surely have a dramatic impact on the size and composition of the entire U.S. military.[33]

The post-peace reevaluation of the U.S. military presence in Korea would necessitate a publicly coherent case for a continued presence that makes sense in capitals throughout Asia as well as in Washington. Declared U.S. policy would no longer include deterring conflict in Korea, nor, presumably, containing China. Addressing security concerns about China becomes a difficult case in public diplomacy and declaratory policy. U.S. presence in East Asia clearly hedges against an assertive and potentially destabilizing China. But, it is difficult to publicly make the hedging case without conjuring up visions of a China "containment" policy; which would not necessarily be the intent. The reality is that U.S. presence balances China's military influence in the region. Finding the best way to publicly articulate this is more problematic.

A possible approach to such a new rationale could be called "regional stability." Actually, sustaining stability is not a new idea or rationale for U.S. presence. Preserving stability has long been an avowed rationale when discussing America's military role in East Asia. What would be new is that sustaining regional stability would be the sole mission focus and would no longer share pride of place with the easily comprehended mission of deterrence in Korea, or during the Cold War containing the Soviet Union.

It is fair to pose the following question: why could not the rationale include *deterring conflict* in other potential hot spots in East Asia, especially across the Taiwan Strait and in the South China Sea? Without becoming entangled in a long digression about deterrence, the difference between deterrence in Korea and deterrence across the Taiwan Strait is in declared U.S. policy. In Korea the United States has a treaty obligation and a firm commitment to respond to a North Korean attack with overwhelming force. No such treaty or explicit obligation exists regarding Taiwan or the South China Sea. The United States has been insistent that these issues be resolved peacefully, but for good reasons has not elected to commit to a guaranteed military response. Without such a commitment, an openly stated and openly planned deterrence mission in these two cases is simply not possible, and would almost certainly introduce an aspect of military confrontation into the U.S. relationship with China.

To put the idea of regional stability as the primary mission for forward deployed forces into context, a brief review of how the Department of Defense has explained U.S. military presence in East Asia since the collapse of the Soviet Union is in order.

The U.S. Military Presence in the First Post-Cold War Decade

Over the past decade, the question of U.S. forces stationed in East Asia—the so-called forward presence—has been a central, if not the central, focus of U.S. security policy in the region. Two interrelated issues—whether there should be any permanent forward presence at all, and if so what the number and military nature of those forces should be—have been the thematic centerpiece of U.S. regional strategy and dialogue with East Asian nations.

A U.S. forward presence acts as both a force for stability and deterrence because it blends multi-service capabilities well-tailored to address the three most dangerous security uncertainties found in Asia today: the possibility of war in Korea, the possibility of military conflict over Taiwanese independence, and the conflict over sovereignty claims in the South China Sea. This important point bears emphasis. Forward-deployed forces are relevant because they have the proper blend of capabilities to deal with the most credible military problems in the region—not *all* of the problems, but the most likely problems.

A quick survey of the major elements of U.S. forces illustrates this point. The ground forces in East Asia, located in Korea (army) and Okinawa, Japan (marine corps), are largely oriented toward Korea. In addition to their major role in any Korean contingency, the marines stationed in Okinawa also play a regional crisis response role when they are embarked in the Amphibious Task Force located in Sasebo, Japan. The U.S. Seventh Fleet, whose flagship and aircraft carrier battle group are in Yokosuka, Japan, would also play a key role in any Korean contingency. However, because of the maritime nature of the vast East Asian region, the inherent mobility of the fleet results in a decidedly regional rather than peninsular operational orientation. The numbered U.S. air forces in Northeast Asia, the seventh in Korea and the fifth in Japan, are largely focused on Korea as well. Air forces also are inherently very mobile, and the tactical aircraft located in Japan could be employed region-wide.

Because this combination of capabilities packs real combat potential, U.S. forces are welcomed by most of the countries in the region as a balancing or countervailing presence to a China that is modernizing its military and as a hedge against the remote possibility of a militarily assertive Japan. Since they are well suited in size and capability for the military tasks they might be called upon to perform, these forward forces already underwrite much of the continued political stability of East Asia.

Stability and the Balance of Power

Over the past few years, especially since the Clinton administration began to consider multilateralism complementary to traditional bilateral arrangements, balance-of-power considerations have been the subject of considerable debate between foreign policy and security practitioners on the one hand, and academics and intellectuals on the other. Unquestionably, the 1990s saw a dramatic growth in nonmilitary sources of power and influence. That growth, however, has not been at the expense of military power as a force for stability in the region. Rather, it has been a complement to military presence. In fact, military power is still a very important aspect of politics in Asia. According to Australian strategist Paul Dibb, "statesmen in Asia are still inclined to a realist, state-centric perception with a primary concern for sovereignty, national interest and state influence. Changes in relative power continue to be important because a state's relative position is by definition relative to that of other states. . . ." in the region.[34] Dibb best describes the broad definition of a balance of power that is relevant to the evolution of U.S. presence when he states that it means that "nation-states will ensure that no one power is in a position to determine the fate of others."

The Department of Defense's East Asia Strategy Initiative of 1990 clearly spells out that America's security interests include "maintaining the balance of power to prevent the rise of any regional hegemony. . . ."[35] A second East Asia Strategy Report, issued in 1992, repeated this fundamental stance. The report discussed maintaining regional stability and specifically stated that one of the reasons that the United States maintains its military forces in East Asia is to "discourage the emergence of regional hegemony."[36] Finally, in a 1995 report, the policy of "preventing the rise of any hegemonic power or coalition" was again prominent as a permanent U.S. interest in Asia.[37]

Balance-of-power considerations have been central to contemporary strategic concepts for East Asia not simply for American strategists but for specialists in virtually every country in the region. There is general public recognition almost everywhere in Asia, with the exceptions of China and North Korea, that the United States is the single most important country in sustaining the strategic equilibrium that has been preserved in Asia over the last two decades. This is not simply because of the overall strength of the U.S. military, but also because a large component of that strength is physically present in the region.[38] That leading U.S. officials such as the secretary of defense have routinely referred to the U.S. role by such phrases as a "balance wheel" is a perfect illustration of how familiar and congenial the idea of participating in an Asian balance of power is to American strategists and policymakers.

The Two Central U.S. Military Missions: Deterrence and Stability

The two concepts, or missions, of stability and deterrence have been used together for so long and with such frequency in policy and strategy statements that it is easy to forget that in practice they are different missions. Deterrence is narrowly focused in practical terms on Korea, whereas stability is thought of on a region-wide basis. Looking to the future, it is important that the idea of stability be more clearly transformed from a broad concept to a well-articulated military mission so that U.S. forces in Asia can be sustained on militarily defensible logic.

As practiced today in Korea, the military mission of deterrence combines a militarily credible land and air force in Korea with the promise of swift and massive reinforcement from the United States. It also counts on having a small but militarily significant force elsewhere in the region to diminish the possibility that a surprise attack could succeed before reinforcements from the United States would arrive.

When trying to differentiate between the missions of deterrence and regional stability on the Korean Peninsula, I do not mean to convey the idea that deterring a North Korean attack does not also contribute to overall regional stability. Of course it does, for war in Korea would profoundly affect stability in Asia. Nor should one conclude that the mission of regional stability does not also implicitly include a military capability to deter certain forms of aggression—because it does. But the difference between a specified mission and an implied capability is very different for the commanders who are responsible for training and otherwise preparing their forces.

Conceptually, as a general proposition almost all military forces are fungible in that they can be shifted between missions. The reality is different, however. Primary mission tasking commands the bulk of training time and readiness focus. In Korea, for example, a virtually single-minded preparation for war is manifested by established lines of communication, in-place logistics support, administrative arrangements that include integration of ROK draftees into U.S. units, and command relationships that include integrated ROK and U.S. staffs. It would be very difficult, if not impossible, to employ U.S. forces in Korea on an off-peninsula regional basis, even if all political and policy-level impediments and treaty obligations could be overcome.

On the other hand, forces that are tasked with maintaining regional stability must have flexibility in administrative and support arrangements. The main criteria are:

- They must not be tethered to specific crisis scenarios so they can quickly respond throughout East Asia.
- They must have the political or policy freedom from the host country that permits them to use bases for contingencies not directly associated with the defense of the host country.
- They must be agile enough to be able to carry out a wide range of tasks anywhere in the region. This agility is a combination of characteristics of the force themselves as well as their training and command arrangements.

Because they are not tethered to a Korean contingency, it is the forces located in Japan—particularly the navy, the U.S. Army Special Forces in Okinawa, some of the marines, and some of the air force—that perform the regional stability mission today.

WHAT IS STABILITY?

To help in understanding what a primary mission organized around stability really means, it is necessary to shift to the conceptual level. Abstractly, the term "stability" is clear; it connotes "equilibrium" or "balance" or "making a system resistant to change"—words that in a geostrategic construct conjure up a notion of balance of power. Power vacuum is the term most frequently used to describe an East Asia without a militarily significant U.S. force. The clear implication is that other countries, presumably China and perhaps Japan, or in the distant future Russia, would compete to fill the vacuum, and in the process of competition introduce instability to the entire region.

One of the tools for executing the mission of stability, and in fact the most important one, is forward presence. It is important to not define the mission of stability too broadly. It would be foolish to argue that the U.S.

military presence could be the panacea for every form of misfortune that might befall the countries of East Asia. Clearly, the U.S. military presence had little effect one way or another in arresting or preventing the recent economic instability. On the other hand, U.S. forces have contributed to the long peace that permitted the economies to flourish in the first place. Today the absence of conflict permits nations to single-mindedly focus on solving economic problems and to not fear the slashing of military budgets.

Furthermore, when we think about internal political instability in East Asia, the U.S. military presence is not a major preventative factor. One need only consider the recent changes in Indonesia, or the coups or putsches in Thailand, Burma, and Cambodia that have taken place during this decade despite the U.S. presence in the region. Except for their involvement in thwarting one of the many coup attempts against the Aquino government in the Philippines in the early 1990s, it is safe to say that the presence of U.S. forces in the region has had little direct impact on internal political change.

But the opposite side of the same coin is also true: by contributing to overall stability, forward presence has helped contribute to the process of democratic change by eliminating the pretense of defending against external aggression as a justification for military rule.

What forward presence does accomplish is to prevent militarily induced instability, more commonly called aggression. Military presence plays a significant role in East Asia by dampening the military dimension of historic animosities and rivalries. It inhibits the use of military power to change boundaries or resolve territorial disputes.

However, U.S. military power is not omnipotent throughout East Asia. There are imaginable situations in which the United States would simply not be able to prevent aggression or to nullify the outcomes of aggression by means short of nuclear war or unacceptably widening a conventional conflict. The location of conflict and its distance from the centers of U.S. power and proximity to the aggressor's power centers impose limits on what the United States is militarily able to do. Simply put, "you have to be able to get there." This is not new. For example, during the Cold War, America's inability to prevent the Soviet Union from crushing either the Hungarian or Czech revolutions was due among other things to the limits imposed by geography: distance from the center of U.S. power and proximity to Soviet power. The same sorts of geostrategic constraints limit U.S. power in Asia.

The Centrality of China to Considerations of Stability

Today in East Asia, even with the unresolved flash points of Korea, Taiwan, East Timor, and the South China Sea, the region is at peace and is considered to be militarily stable. When the prospect of another Korean war no longer poses a threat, any discussion about stability in East Asia must start with China. This is not because of China's rising power, although that is an issue on the minds of most Asian strategists and security planners, and not because China is bent on regional conquest. The discussion starts with China because of its geographic centrality, its physical size, the size of its population, and its historic position as the Middle Kingdom. The Chinese themselves spend considerable effort trying to determine or calculate "comprehensive national power," factoring in such things as territorial expanse or size, population, economic development, and military potential.

When carrying out calculations about China, certain geostrategic facts become evident. One cannot escape the conclusion that China is the dominant conventional military power on the continent of Asia. China's central position in Asia allows it to command internal lines of communication throughout the continent. The military protection afforded by mountains and deserts, its improving militarily useful infrastructure (roads, airports, communications), its large modernizing army, and the PLA's combat history of being able to absorb tremendous punishment and keep on fighting all contribute to this judgment. China's guerrilla—or people's war—tradition, which makes a virtue of overcoming more technically advanced foes, is also a factor. The enormous population, strong sense of nationalism, and historical record combine to suggest that China is not casualty-adverse in the pursuit of its strategic objectives.

Consider the military potential of nations with which China shares a common land frontier: North Korea, Vietnam, Laos, Burma, Bhutan, Nepal, India, Pakistan, Tajikistan, Kyrgyzstan, Kazakhstan, Mongolia, and Russia. Although Vietnam gave China a bloody nose in 1979, the fighting capabilities of the Vietnamese and Chinese armies are going in opposite directions.

If China chose to invade and to pay a heavy price, Vietnam would lose. It is hard to imagine China and India, separated by the Himalayas, finding enough suitable terrain to be able to get at one another in a militarily decisive way. They can punish one another, but not conquer one another. Russia's conventional military is a shadow of its former self and, given the dismal state of Russia's armed forces, China is conventionally superior to its northern neighbor. This is not to suggest that China has any intention to use this superiority to occupy neighboring countries. This is extremely unlikely. But China has a history of using the PLA to teach lessons and intimidate neighbors that pursue policies Beijing believes are not in China's interests. PLA actions against India in 1962, Russia in 1969, and of course Vietnam in 1974, when they seized the Paracels, and in 1979, when they demonstrated—at great cost—the capability of invading, are all examples of the use of the PLA on China's periphery. A united Korea is the one country with the potential to hold off a Chinese attack. If the Korean army were well dug in along the Yalu and Tumen Rivers, with the United States as an ally, preventing an invasion or a PLA attempt at intimidation begins to seem credible.

Clearly, China need not fear an invasion from any of her continental neighbors, whereas those neighbors, with the exception of India and perhaps as mentioned Korea, are vulnerable to an overland Chinese invasion. Faced with this continental preeminence, short of threatening nuclear war, it is difficult to see how any U.S. forward-presence force in East Asia would pose a credible deterrent to the use of the PLA against a continental neighbor (excepting Korea).

The point is not to paint the Chinese as ten feet tall, but to attempt to illustrate the very real limits of U.S. power when considering the utility of U.S. forward-presence forces in halting or rolling back aggression on the Asian continent. Since World War II, the United States has fought two land wars in Asia, both with the advantage of superiority in the air and on adjacent high seas, and the best it could do was a draw in Korea.

China's continental dominance is a fact of life today—an accepted feature of the East Asian strategic landscape that is not considered destabilizing. Throughout modern history, the successful domination of Europe by a single power has been seen as very destabilizing and worth fighting unlimited wars to prevent. China's implicit domination today, however, generally is greeted with equanimity—certainly in the United States. The fact that China is the dominant military power on the Asian continent has not triggered an arms race. Continental neighbors following the withering of communist solidarity have not sought collective security regimes to balance China's dominance.

The conclusion to be drawn is that a U.S. force structure whose mission is to sustain stability need not have a capability to preserve stability on the Asian mainland. First, it is not militarily feasible; and second, the existing Chinese dominance, which is likely to persist, is not inherently destabilizing. In the foreseeable future, it simply is not credible to create scenarios that postulate any other power wresting control of the Asian mainland from China. In the 1930s and 1940s Japan tried for eight years and failed. There is no reason to believe things will change.

A Condominium of Stability in East Asia

In Roosevelt Hall, home of the National War College in Washington, D.C., an enormous map of the world hangs in the main stairwell. Below this map is a plaque with a cautionary reminder for potential strategists. It reads, "Everything changes but geography." Applying that wisdom to Asia, one must visualize and then reflect upon Asia's distinctive geography. The three most strategically striking features of Asia's geography are: (1) the geographic centrality and physical enormity of China; (2) the number of significant states that are totally, or very nearly, surrounded by water (Japan, Korea, Taiwan, the Philippines, Indonesia, Singapore, Malaysia—connected to the continent only by the slender Isthmus of Kra—Australia, Papua New Guinea, and New Zealand); and (3) the vast distances involved.

Just as there are limits to U.S. power in East Asia, so too is China's power limited. Beyond the Asian landmass, China has serious shortcomings. While China can project impressive military power against continental neighbors, it cannot do so against any country that is not contiguous to China. One recent U.S. Department of Defense report on the Chinese military, for example, concluded, ". . . the PLA is still decades from possessing a comprehensive capability to engage and defeat a modern adversary beyond China's boundaries."[39]

This shortfall in power-projection capabilities is not limited to China. Throughout Asia, the ability of any country to project decisive force beyond its immediate neighbors is almost nonexistent. The sort of military capability that would be required for a projection mission, principally naval and air forces, are in most cases either rudimentary, obsolete, too small, or nonexistent. Forces to control the sea and airspace around and over a noncontiguous objective, lift large numbers of troops by sea or air, surveil "maritime Asia," and conduct sustained long-range bombardment from the air (China's conventional ballistic missile force is too small to provide a sustained bombardment capability) are not in today's regional military inventories. Not only are they not available in Asian inventories, but the U.S. presence, because of strong naval and air force components, is particularly well suited to counter and defeat attempts to project power.

In effect a condominium of military power exists in East Asia. China dominates the continent, and the United States and its allies dominate the rimland. This division of the region into de facto spheres of military influence has produced a certain kind of stability.

Because so many of Asia's most important nations lie beyond both China's and one another's reach, the action that would most upset this condominium would be an attempt by China or any other power to become militarily superior on both the continent and the rim of Asia. Were China to make a choice to become truly serious about developing a region-wide projection capability, those countries currently beyond China's reach certainly would attempt to restabilize the situation through the development of counterprojection military capabilities (e.g., submarines, surveillance, air defense, and local air superiority, or through alliance with the United States).

We see hedging by rim and maritime Asian nations in this direction today. But realistically, it is important to appreciate that it would take decades for either China or anyone else to develop such a capability. Security analysts must be able to differentiate between token Chinese military capabilities intended for prestige and flag waving, such as a single medium-size aircraft carrier that has no real strategic weight, and an attempt to create a truly dominant projection force.

China has apparently decided not to take this destabilizing road. This may be because it has no desire to seek such a military predominance, but also presumably because it appreciates that due to the proper mix of U.S. forces in the region, rimland and maritime Asia will always have the ability to keep ahead or at least keep pace with projection capability and therefore be able to "trump" regional projection attempts.

The insight to be drawn from this discussion is that once there is peace in Korea, and thus no longer a need to worry about deterring a North Korean invasion of the South, the main role for U.S. and allied forces in East Asia will be to prevent *militarily induced instability* by defeating attempts to project power over the high seas or through the air.

Throughout this discussion, the example of China has been used to make the point about what kind of military capability is either stabilizing or destabilizing. China was used because it is the most demanding case, but the general proposition applies to any of the other countries of East Asia. Specifically, any country that obtains a capability for force projection that endangers the territorial integrity and continued sovereignty of its neighbors is potentially destabilizing. To remove the threat of instability, that capability must be compensated for either by individual countries or within a coalition with other regional powers and U.S. forward-deployed forces. In other words, to sustain stability in the future, U.S. force structure would have as its primary combat focus defeating power projection anywhere beyond the East Asian littoral. For want of a better term we could call this anti-power projection. *In the future, anti-power projection ought to be the concept of operations for forward-deployed U.S. forces.*

Translating the Stability Mission into an Anti-Power-Projection Force

An important point of clarification: anti-power projection is not equivalent to taking preemptive action. What is important is not the ability to prevent the development of power-projection forces by any country in the region, but the ability to defeat or "trump" those forces by U.S., allied, and friendly forces in the region. Certainly, an objective for U.S. diplomacy and overall security policy ought to focus on discouraging or dissuading acquisition of a serious power-projection capability by any country in Asia. But U.S. forces ought to be shaped with the assumption that diplomatic persuasion may not work.

In fact, at the conceptual level one could argue that it is not inherently destabilizing if a country develops a power-projection capability such as a long-range bomber force, carrier battle groups, a large amphibious assault force, or a multidivision airborne (paratroop) force. Destabilization occurs only when there is no other force in the region that can thwart this capability. Remembering that a threat consists of both capability and intent, as long as the United States and its allies can frustrate intent by defeating capability, stability should continue. In other words, as long as power-projection forces and anti-power-projection forces rise together on the same tide, the region will remain stable. By the same token, once it becomes clear that a determination to keep pace with projection developments exists, the incentive for their development in the first place could be removed.

A force structure with stability as its primary mission (accomplished by being an anti-power-projection force), given the geography of the region and the central position of China, would be based on the *ability to control the sea and air space around the periphery of Asia.*

More specifically, when a peace treaty with North Korea and the associated draw-down of forces from the DMZ takes place, or North Korea collapses and the inevitable restructuring of U.S. forces in the region occurs, the best option to pursue would be a U.S. force optimized for regional stability. By the very nature of the mission and the geography of East Asia, it would necessarily be composed primarily of air and naval forces. Ground forces, so important in deterring war in Korea, would be less relevant under these new circumstances. Certainly some permanent ground-force presence would be required for essential nonstability missions (operations other than war) such as military engagement and training with friends and allies in the region, noncombatant evacuation operations, humanitarian assistance, peace-keeping, search and rescue, and special operations. But this presence need not number more than 3,000 to 5,000 soldiers and marines or a combination of both.

The U.S. air force has an important role to play in a stability-creating anti-power-projection force. The force structure that remains in East Asia must be a comprehensive mix of air to air, air to ground, surveillance, and tanking, along with earmarked U.S.-based airlift capacities. Because of the nature of the anti-power-projection mission, the current composition of U.S. navy forces in the region is unlikely to change. A carrier battle group, a robust submarine presence, and an amphibious ready group would remain at the heart of naval capability, which is perfectly suited for this new mission.

Basing and Command Considerations

The first thing to appreciate about this hypothetically reshaped U.S. presence in the region is that the return of most of the soldiers and marines to the United States would greatly reduce its overall size, perhaps by as much as 60 percent. This remaining force can be accommodated at U.S. facilities in Japan alone. This is an important consideration because, as mentioned, U.S. forces might no longer be welcomed or permitted in Korea, depending on how reunification actually plays out.

If a U.S. presence is not prohibited or is not politically impossible in a reunited Korea, then positioning some of the residual U.S. forces—probably air power—in Korea would be helpful. It would permit more tactical aircraft to be moved into the region in times of tension, and Korean basing would help in preserving continued U.S. access to bases in Japan. Most experts believe it is politically important that the people of Japan realize that other Asian nations also share the burden of a U.S. military presence on their soil.

A modification in force structure occasioned by a change in the situation on the Korean Peninsula would also trigger an adjustment in the command structure for forward-deployed U.S. forces. Command arrangements are intended to reflect and be optimized to deal with the reality of the strategic situation at the time. The reasons that there has been so little evolution in command arrangements in Korea is the strategic situation has been more or less frozen in time since 1953. It is almost a certainty that the strategic situation in Korea does change as well. Both the UN Command and Combined Forces Command will probably not survive in their present form, if they survive at all. This is not bad. Command structures and arrangements must be flexible and adaptive.

If some U.S. forces should remain in Korea, their mission would be the same as U.S. forces located in Japan—preserving stability through counter-power projection. Because the notion of "unity of command" is ingrained in the U.S. way of war, forces in both Japan and Korea should be under the operational command of a single individual who is located in East Asia. The real strength of the stability force is the synergy provided by combining appropriately tailored forces from all the services—hence, a joint headquarters should command the forces in East Asia. Optimally, this would be commanded by an officer of three-star seniority who would report to the Commander in Chief of the Pacific Command.

CONCLUSION

The process of Korean reunification is critical to the strategic outlook that a reunited Korea adopts. All the best intentions and hopes expressed by Seoul and Washington about the desire to preserve a U.S.-Korea treaty relationship and to continue to station U.S. forces in Korea could easily be irrelevant to the real outcome if the process of reunification is evolutionary and negotiated. While today that is the preferred alternative for all parties concerned, there appears to be a plausible contradiction between the hopes for a continued alliance and a less satisfactory outcome of negotiated reunification. This is not to say that Seoul and Washington should prematurely concede that a continued relationship after reunification will be too hard, or abandon policies that are aimed at creating the circumstances for an evolutionary reunification. Indeed what is required is greater consideration of the impediments that stand between declared intentions for a future relationship and their realization. Those impediments center around Chinese concerns about continued U.S. alliances and presence in Asia in general (and on the Asian mainland in particular) and Korean public opinion. Will the latent resentment toward the United States for a whole range of real and perceived sins dating back to the 1905 Taft-Katsura Agreement burst into the open and make a continued relationship with the United States a political impossibility? Will Seoul choose to go it alone even if a relationship with the United States after reunification is possible? These are questions that deserve serious consideration even as the prospects for a rapid reunification by North Korean collapse in the next few years grow increasingly dim.

Militarily, when the threat of war in Korea finally abates, it will be necessary to rethink the roles and mission of U.S. forces in the region. As the U.S. military presence evolves following changes in Korea, it will be important that the size and makeup of the force structure remain relevant to the nature of the military challenges of the region. As long as the force is expected to do more than "show the flag," it has to possess significant combat capability that is tailored for both the most likely military problems of the region and the most potentially destabilizing.

Whether the U.S. Department of Defense chooses to label it as such or characterizes the mission in different terms, the only mission for these forces that makes sense will be to preserve regional stability. The concept of regional stability as spoken and written about today is at once general in conception and vague in scope. It will be the job of American military planners to translate the conception into more precise terms that recognize the realities of power and geography in East Asia. This chapter postulates a coherent way of thinking about stability as a military mission, differentiating between what is militarily possible and what is not. It also suggests a general template of how a specific force might be tailored to provide stability by being optimized to defeat attempts to project power beyond the Asian heartland or from one maritime state to another.

I have not attempted to translate this force into a hard number or be overly precise about its specific composition, which will take detailed military planning. It does seem clear, however, that once deterrence in Korea ceases to be a military mission requiring forward-deployed forces, a stability mission could be conducted with far fewer than today's 100,000-person benchmark.

NOTES

1. Historian Donald Kagan captures this perfectly when he writes, "...the one great truth of history is that there is always one other possibility besides all the ones that you imagine, no matter how clever you are. What usually happens in history is in the category of 'none of the above.' If one examines the predictions made in the area of international relations over the centuries, most of the time, most of the people get it wrong—even the most learned, experienced and intelligent people." *Survival*,

Summer 1999, p. 142. A marvelous piece that helps make this point is Robert G. Kaiser, "Ten Years Later, It's Obvious That Nothing at All Was Obvious," *Washington Post*, November 7, 1999, p. B1. Kaiser examines the inaccurate predictions made by experts shortly after the fall of the Berlin Wall to illustrate just how intellectually hazardous prognostication can be.

2. These observations are based on the author's experience in long-range planning, three assignments totaling seven years, and the introduction to a short monograph by Richard Danzig, *The Big Three: Our Greatest Security Risks and How to Address Them* (New York: Center for International Political Economy, 1999), p. 6.

3. In their study *Preparing for Korean Unification: Scenarios and Implications* (Santa Monica, Calif.: RAND, 1999), p. 85, Jonathan Pollack and Chung Min Lee correctly conclude that issues surrounding the nature of the U.S.-ROK alliance and the future of the U.S. military presence in Korea will be contingent on the character and consequence of the unification process, the U.S.-China relationship at the time, and the influence China has and wishes to use in the process. But these issues are not explored in detail because they were beyond the scope of the current chapter.

4. For additional details about reunification scenarios, see chapter 2, "Conflict and Cooperation: The Pacific Powers and Korea," by Chae-Jin Lee in this volume. A comprehensive assessment of reunification scenarios also is found in a paper by Byung Joon Ahn, "Let's Engage North Korea with Contingency Planning: Security Implications of Korean Unification and the South Korean-U.S. Alliance," in *Managing Change on the Korean Peninsula*, ed. by Kim Kyung Won and Han Sung Joo (Seoul: Seoul Press, 1998), pp. 83–122. See also, William J. Taylor, et al., *Great Power Interests in Korean Reunification,* the report of a Center for Strategic and International Studies (CSIS) Project (Washington, D.C.: CSIS, 1998), pp. 41–47. Author's notes of a discussion by Dr. Robert Scalapino at CSIS on November 18, 1998, at which Dr. Scalapino discussed the scenarios subsequently included in the CSIS report.

5. A good, brief summary is found in Robert A. Manning and James J. Przystup, "Asia's Transition Diplomacy: Hedging Against Futureshocks," *Survival*, Autumn 1999. See also, Robert Scalapino, "The Role of Unified Korea in Northeast Asia" (paper prepared for the conference, *Restructuring the Korean Peninsula for the 21st Century*, Seoul, September 29–30, 1998); Narushige Michishita, "Regional Aspects of Korean Unification—Focusing on Strategic Issues," (paper prepared for the European Union Policy Seminar, Brussels, Belgium, October 13, 1998); Zbigniew Brzezinski, *The Grand Chessboard: American Primacy and its Geostrategic Imperatives* (New York: Basic Books, 1997), p. 190; and William Drennan, "Prospects and

Implications of Korean Reunification," Northeast Asia Peace and Security Network (NAPSNET), no. 9, August 22, 1997.

6. Today the ROK military is overwhelmingly army-dominated and ground-force heavy. This is not surprising given the experience of invasion from North Korea in 1950, and since the armistice, the subsequent threat of invasion. Not only is this logical, it has been the advice of a parade of U.S. army four-star commanders; again for a good reason. First, as the overall commanders of the U.S.-ROK forces, these officers have understood that the capability of the ROK army would determine their success or failure in defending South Korea if another war broke out. A second reason is because U.S. strategists and policymakers believed—as they do today—that it was entirely appropriate for the ROK army to bear the brunt of the fighting in the defense of their country.

In the decades immediately after the Korean War, the issue was not whether the ROK army should do this, but whether *they could do* it. Today there is no question that the ROK army will and can perform this mission. For its part, the United States, has over time agreed to offset the obvious capabilities imbalance in the ROK military establishment by providing the lion's share of the air and sea power necessary to defend Korea.

The South Korean navy is still more of a coastal defense force than a force capable of conducting sea control in the area around Korea, although as funds permit, it is gradually expanding its open ocean capability. Similarly, the ROK air force is oriented to air defense and close air support—although it is in the middle of a major F-16 upgrade—the bulk of their tactical fighters are Vietnam War vintage F-4s and F-5s. For all practical purposes the U.S. air force is South Korea's long-range strike and interdiction force, and the U.S. Seventh Fleet is the ROK's sea-lane and regional protection and projection force. To U.S. planners this represents a reasonable division of labor.

In Seoul, however, once the idea of reunification became commonplace, military planners began to wrestle with post-reunification scenarios and it became clear to them that a reunified Korea would face the major powers in the region with a military that was too dependent on the army. As a result, over the last 10 years or so the ROK Joint Staff and Ministry of Defense have been so confident about their ability to defeat a North Korean invasion that they have begun to divert defense dollars to improving the ROK navy and air force. This diversion was over the objections made by U.S. commanders who worried that the ROK planners were too blasé about the North Korean threat. This point is raised not to enter the debate over whether this is a wise course of action. Rather, it is to highlight the fact that ROK planners recognize that if a reunited Korea elects to pursue a national security strategy of "strategic independence," it will require greater long-term investment in air and sea power while maintaining a sizable army (they will share a frontier with China.) Other national security strategic options put less pressure on the defense budget because of alliances or friendships.

When addressing post-unification scenarios, analysts often assume that a strategically independent Korea will require nuclear weapons. It is not entirely clear to me why this is so. There is no reason to believe that a reunified Korea, even if it inherits intact whatever capability the North possesses, would elect to "go nuclear" with the attendant international opprobrium associated with renouncing the Nuclear Nonproliferation Treaty unless an incredibly hostile environment confronted Seoul. That does not seem likely. There is no reason to believe that Seoul's efforts to maintain good relations with all of its neighbors will not continue to be the primary objective of South Korea's foreign policy. Unlike Israel's neighbors of just a few years ago, Korea's neighbors do not seem inclined to make the destruction of the unified Korean state an avowed goal. There are no irredentist claims against Korea. Japan does not hunger for a new Korean colony. China is not interested in absorbing Korea. Russia does not seek a Korean sphere of influence. The quickest way to undermine and possibly lose U.S. support for a reunited Korea would be for Korea to become a nuclear power. Korea would appear to have more to lose than gain by pursuing the nuclear option.

Finally, should things turn bad, South Korea would have the resources available to quickly become a nuclear weapon state. More important than a possible nuclear inheritance from the North, a reunited Korea would have in hand the missile technology necessary to translate nuclear options into credible delivery systems in short order.

7. President Roh's statements on the collapse of the DPRK within seven years come from the author's recollection from his period (1990–1992) as Director of the East Asia and Pacific Region Office on the Secretary of Defense's staff (OSD/ISA). John Deutch, Director of Central Intelligence, testimony before the Senate Select Committee on Intelligence, February 22, 1996; and Larry Niksch, "The Prospect of Relations between the United States and North Korea Beyond the 1994 Nuclear Accord," (paper presented at the Annual International Security Symposium of the Korean National Defense University, Seoul, August 1996).

8. Pollack and Lee, *Preparing for Korean Unification*, pp. 75–81.

9. This point will be explored in depth later in this chapter.

10. North Korean first vice minister of the People's Armed Forces, cited in Samuel Kim, "Images and Realities of Korean Unity: Wither Inter-Korean Relations?" (paper prepared for a conference on "The Republic of Korea after 50 Years," Georgetown University, October 2–4, 1998), p. 12.

11. Ibid., pp.13–14.

12. Mary Jordon, "Second Guessing Korean Unification," *Washington Post*, March 4, 1997, p. A1.

13. Ministry of Unification, Republic of Korea, "Policy Towards North Korea for Peace, Reconciliation and Cooperation" (Seoul: ROK Ministry of Unification, 1999); and Kim, "Images and Realities of Korean Unity," p. 15.

14. Conferences attended by the author in Tokyo, November 1997, in Shanghai, October 1998 and May 1999, and in Honolulu, July 1999.

15. Kim, " Images and Realities of Korean Unity," p. 21.

16. Scott Snyder, *North Korea's Decline and China's Strategic Dilemmas*, U.S. Institute of Peace Special Report (Washington, D.C.: USIP, October 1997), pp. 7–9.

17. Referring to the behavior of North Korea, the unclassified version of the Perry report says, ". . . many aspects of its behavior will remain reprehensible to us even if we embark on this negotiating process." William J. Perry, *Review of United States Policy Toward North Korea: Findings and Recommendations*, October 12, 1999.

18. Ibid.

19. Author's interview with a Japanese official, July 1999. For more on the Japanese perspective, see also chapter 5, "Japan and the Unification of Korea: Challenges for U.S. Policy Coordination," by Michael Armacost and Kenneth Pyle in this volume.

20. Don Oberdorfer, *The Two Koreas: A Contemporary History* (Reading, Mass.: Addison-Wesley, 1997), pp. 197–228.

21. Sergei Grigoriev, "How the Korean-US Security Alliance is Viewed by the Russians," (paper presented at the 14th Annual Conference of The Council on U.S.-Korean Security Studies, Arlington, Virginia, October 28–29, 1999). See also chapter 6, "Russia, Korea, and Northeast Asia," by Herbert J. Ellison in this volume.

22. Grigoriev, "How the Korean-US Security Alliance is Viewed by the Russians," p. 13.

23. See Armacost and Pyle, "*Japan and the Unification of Korea.*"

24. See for example the excellent 1995 RAND study by Jonathan Pollack and Young Koo Cha, "*A New Alliance for the Next Century: The Future of U.S.-Korean*

Security Cooperation" (Santa Monica, Calif.: RAND, 1995). Another example is Pollack and Lee, "Preparing for Korean Unification," p. 55. The authors write, ". . . the peaceful unification scenario also assumes that the North will choose to drop its decade-long demand for the withdrawal of U.S. forces from the ROK, and that the two Koreas will be able to come to terms with respect to the deployment of U.S. forces after unification." The other alternative—that the ROK might be forced to sacrifice the U.S. presence for reunification—receives one sentence and no further analysis: "Conversely, a unified Korean government could decide to terminate all U.S. military deployments on the peninsula, or agree to a substantially smaller U.S. presence."

25. Kim Hyoung-min, "Kim calls for Continued Presence of US Forces After Reunification," *Korea Times,* January 23, 1998.

26. President Kim Reaffirms Kim Jong Il's Approval of U.S. Troops Here, *" Korea Times*, August, 17 2000

27. Stephen Noerper, "Looking Forward, Looking Back," Pacific Forum CSIS, Comparative Connections, 2nd Quarter, 2000, p 5.

28. The definitive work on negotiating with North Korea is Chuck Downs, *Over the Line: North Korea's Negotiating Strategy* (Washington, D.C.: AEI Press, 1999).

29. A recent example was a bilateral (U.S.-China) conference held in Shanghai in May 1999, cosponsored by Pacific Forum-CSIS and Fudan University. The conference topic was "Asian Security: Looking Forward to the 21st Century." Chinese participants included members from Beijing think tanks (China Institute of Contemporary International Relations and the Chinese Academy of Social Sciences). The Chinese view was that following unification Beijing wants a nonaligned "neutral" Korea. They believe that the process of reunification will result in the withdrawal of U.S. forces.

30. Taylor et al., *Great Power Interests in Korean Unification*, p. 12.

31. Scalapino, " The Role of a Unified Korea in Northeast Asia," p. 16. William Drennan, "Prospects for a United Korea and What it Would Mean" (paper presented at the 13th Annual Conference of The Council on U.S.-Korean Security Studies, Seoul, November 4–7, 1998), pp. 8–10.

32. Department of Defense, *United States Security Strategy for the East Asia-Pacific Region*, Office of International Security Affairs, November 1998.

33. In 1992 then-Secretary of Defense Les Aspin instituted a "Bottom-up Review (BUR)" of United States military strategy and force structure. One of the results of this review was the decision that the size of the U.S. military should be dictated by the need to be able to fight and win "two nearly simultaneous major regional contin-

gencies (MRCs)." The nature of the threat the United States might face in these MRCs was defined as a pre-Desert Storm Iraq. Hence it would take four to five army divisions, five to six aircraft carrier battlegroups, ten to eleven air force tactical fighter wings, and most of the U.S. marine corps, plus appropriate support to fight a single MRC. At the outset of the second Clinton administration, Congress mandated a similar review to be conducted every four years. The first Quadrennial Defense Review (QDR, as it is now known), concluded the same: the U.S. military should be large and capable enough to fight in two different places in the world, nearly simultaneously. Instead of calling these hypothetical conflicts "contingencies" they have been redubbed "wars." Hence the current term of art is "major theater war (MTW)."

34. Paul Dibb addresses this entire point with great clarity in *Toward a New Balance of Power in Asia*, Adelphi Paper No. 295 (London: Oxford University Press, 1995), pp. 6–7.

35. *A Strategic Framework for the Asia Pacific Rim*, Department of Defense Report to Congress, April 1990, p. 1.

36. *A Strategic Framework for the Asia Pacific Rim*, Department of Defense Report to Congress, September 1992.

37. Department of Defense, *United States Security Strategy for the East Asia-Pacific Region*, Office of the Assistant Secretary of Defense for International Security Affairs, February 1995.

38. Virtually the entire focus of the 1995 report is on this very point. This is the report that makes the 100,000 person "guarantee."

39. *The Security Situation in the Taiwan Strait*, Department of Defense Report to Congress, February 1999. For a more recent and comprehensive analysis of the Chinese military, see *Annual Report on the Military Power of the People's Republic of China*, Department of Defense Report to Congress, June 2000.

10

Negotiating Korean Unification: Options for an International Framework

Robert L. Gallucci

In 1997 the topic of an international framework for Korean unification would have entailed an examination of the four-party talks, perhaps with a focus on whether they should be expanded to six or more, or turned into a bilateral engagement. A second fundamental question would have concerned the future of the Agreed Framework—whether it needed to be subsumed into a broader deal or allowed to stand as is. Also among the principal concerns would have been the future of the Korean Peninsula Energy Development Organization (KEDO), to ask if this specialized international organization could be the vehicle to carry a substantial burden on the road to reunification.

Three years ago, when the Agreed Framework was three years old, the situation was quite different from today. Compliance with the Agreed Framework on nuclear matters was good: the International Atomic Energy Agency was generally satisfied with its inspections; the spent fuel was in the process of being re-canned; ground had been broken for the light water reactor project; heavy fuel oil was being delivered; and KEDO was managing to stay funded and to complete negotiations of critical documents. The concern about North

Korean development and export of medium-range ballistic missiles, not explicitly mentioned in the Agreed Framework, was the subject of U.S.-DPRK negotiations. And perhaps most significantly, the United States was hard at work calculating the virtues and routes to various varieties of "hard" and "soft" landings for North Korea, none doubting that the only question was when, not whether there would be a landing.

There were then three questions that seemed particularly relevant. First, would the Republic of Korea do what was necessary with respect to its own domestic economic and financial situation so that when the collapse of the DPRK came, South Korea would be in a position to provide sufficient support for the people in the North to avoid massive flows of refugees south? Second, what role might Japan play, particularly with respect to the reparations that had been contemplated? And finally, would the passing of then-South Korean President Kim Young Sam from the scene fundamentally change the atmosphere between North and South?

Now, six years after the signing of the Agreed Framework, a series of developments have fundamentally redefined the situation. While most of what has happened is hardly helpful to advocates of near-term, peaceful reunification, one development clearly falls into the good news category: the election of Kim Dae Jung as president and his dogged commitment to the so-called "sunshine policy" toward the North.

Yet for advocates of peaceful reunification, three negatives stand out. The first is the nuclear issue. After it was revealed that there was at least one underground site in North Korea where construction apparently was under way related to a secret nuclear program, advocates of the Agreed Framework had to contend with the real possibility that the North was cheating on its commitments. The news raised questions about whether the North Koreans ever intended to give up their nuclear weapons program and exactly how far along they were in regenerating it. Now that the North has been persuaded to accept an on-site inspection, KEDO remains viable, as does the Agreed Framework. What we learned is just how quickly we could be driven back to "June 1994," when the imposition of UN sanctions had Washington preparing to enhance the U.S. military posture in Northeast Asia to deal with a possible DPRK military reaction to sanctions. Whatever happens in the coming months and years, it is clear that if concern about a secret nuclear program rises again, financing for the light water reactors and heavy fuel oil will be in deep trouble and KEDO's survival will be at stake.

A second issue is the development and export of medium-range ballistic missiles. The West regretted the nuclear weapons tests by India and Pakistan in 1998. But these tests were made all the more threatening to stability on the Asian subcontinent by Pakistan's test of a medium-range ballistic missile, developed with assistance from North Korea and actually very similar to the DPRK's No Dong missile. Later, another medium-range ballistic missile was tested, this time by Iran. It was also very similar to a No Dong, following assistance supplied to Iran by the North Koreans. Finally, to add insult to injury, the North chose the last day of August in 1998 to test-fire a multistage Taepo Dong missile over the main island of Japan and in the general direction of Hawaii. This occurred on a day when U.S.-DPRK bilateral talks were going on in New York, and Tokyo was about to announce its billion-dollar commitment to the light water reactor project. So we then had a situation in which North Korea had created a linkage between its ballistic missile activities and the ability of at least Tokyo and Washington to fund the KEDO projects. Now, presumably as a result of former Defense Secretary Perry's mission and the discussions with the DPRK conducted by Ambassador Charles Kartman, U.S. Special Envoy for Korean Peace Talks, there is a moratorium of sorts on ballistic missile tests by the North. The future, with respect to exports, tests, and deployment is unclear.

The third issue revolves around the deterioration of the economic situation in Asia. Most relevant here is perhaps the incongruity, at least in the near term, of Seoul seriously contemplating the assumption of the economic burdens associated with reunification. South Korean economic recovery is variously projected to be in the three- to five-year time frame. Although the diagnosis is different, the impact on a Japanese role in helping to finance peaceful reunification is obvious: it may happen, but it won't happen soon.

In addition to these issues that have emerged over the last year, we also have to consider the strategy of the United States toward Korean reunification. That strategy may be captured with a phrase taken from game theory: mini-max. To mini-max is to forgo the very best outcomes in order to guard against the risk of having to accept the very worst outcomes. It is now clear that the American enthusiasm for a "soft landing" only revealed half a policy. The United States would not only prefer to see North Korea fail peacefully over time, as compared to pushing it to a violent, early collapse, but it would also prefer to see the DPRK continue flying indefinitely to guard against a collapse that might precipitate a bloody war on the peninsula. While not all South Koreans would agree that the North Korean regime should be perpetuated, it is important that the Chinese would enthusiastically agree, and have provided significant food aid to help sustain the North during the worst years just past.

This, then, raises a question: If the United States and China work to avoid a catastrophic situation from emerging in the North, and the regime itself continues to pursue limited openings for investment that marginally improve conditions, what will motivate or impel North Korea toward unification? Even if concerns about nuclear weapons and ballistic missiles were resolved, an obstacle would be removed but no road would be paved.

The question now is whether there is a way forward to serious talks between North and South Korea that could lead to reunification over time. There is a way, but it is a less plausible path for all to follow than it would have been two years ago. First, to get to that path, the DPRK will have to accept on-site inspections as necessary and resolve concerns about nuclear developments whenever they are raised. Second, ballistic missile talks will have to lead to an end to testing and perhaps to exports as well. Third, the U.S. Congress will have to be persuaded to continue support for KEDO and the Agreed Framework.

Following those preliminaries, we could look for some developments that would be intrinsically important and together create a new atmosphere. For example, North Korea could cease all provocations by land, sea, and air of the kind we have become accustomed to. The two sides could also begin to implement selectively earlier agreements that were left unfulfilled, including perhaps mutual inspections of nuclear sites. Finally, confidence- and security-building measures have long been discussed that would be important to creating a better atmosphere: the pullback of forces from the demilitarized zone; notification of military exercises; the exchange of observers during exercises and of data on forces; and the institution of a hotline.

The talks could follow any number of models. The four-party talks could actually address a new peace arrangement and evolve into a dialogue that would encompass elements of political or economic integration. It is, however, just as probable that a new set of talks would follow the peace talks or begin in parallel. This line of thinking leads one away from the expectation that the Agreed Framework or KEDO will be a model or vehicle for serious political talks between North and South. Indeed, if we are not bound by existing structures, it is easier to imagine new arrangements that take account of the need to include regional players in addition to the principals.

Ultimately, we can expect talks that settle the future of the Korean Peninsula to involve not only North and South Korea, but the United States, Japan, Russia, and China. That involvement will come at different times and in separate ways, but the outcome, if it is to stick, should emerge from an inclusive process. It is plausible to envision a tiered structure in which the negotiations between the ROK and DPRK are at the core, China and the United States moving between them and holding bilateral discussions at the same time, with consultations pursued with Japan and Russia by the other four in order to ensure their support for the process and its outcome.

Whatever structure for reunification talks is created, we can expect the objectives of the parties to differ substantially in geopolitical and other terms. Briefly, we can expect China, whatever level of real enthusiasm for reunification it may have, to work to eliminate the U.S. military presence from the peninsula and to limit American influence in the Asia-Pacific region as much as it can. Japan is likely to be focused on the military capability of a reunited Korea, hoping to prevent it from becoming a nuclear-weapon state, limit its development and deployment of ballistic missiles, and contain its conventional military force-projection capability. Russia will seek recognition as a great power, specifically a Pacific power, and attempt to use its residual influence with the North Koreans as leverage with the ROK and the United States. A reunified Korea will attempt to get out of negotiations with its options open with respect to military posture and perhaps its nuclear weapons status, beginning early on to play China off against the United States and reserving the highest level of mistrust for Japan. The United States can be expected to promote its continued presence in Northeast Asia as the best guarantor of stability, arguing for a reconfigured U.S. military presence on the peninsula and for continuing alliances with a reunited Korea and Japan in which both allies maintained their nonnuclear weapon status.

All this cannot be expected to happen soon, whether it happens this way or not. In the meantime, it will be important for the United States, Japan, and South Korea to: (1) contain the North Koreans, using the Agreed Framework if it can be preserved; (2) prevent ballistic missile exports from increasing instability in the Middle East and South Asia and prevent tests from undermining improved political relations with Japan and the United States; (3) avoid circumstances that could lead to conventional war on the peninsula; (4) continue to push a negotiating track—four-party talks or whatever works; and (5) continue looking for economic openings in the North that will help produce the economic and political evolution that the United States seeks.

11

A Policy Agenda for
Achieving Korean Reunification

Douglas H. Paal

Since the death of Kim Il Sung in 1994, Korean and other analysts have struggled to identify scenarios and timelines for the reunification of the Korean Peninsula. These have ranged from a rapid decline and disintegration of the North Korean state followed by reunification with the South Korea on its terms, to "muddling through" for an indefinite period. No one to date has credibly predicted regime regeneration and long-term survival for a North Korea independent from the South. Some envision a violent, or at least a messy, transition to a unified Korean state.[1]

Since 1993, United States policy toward the Democratic People's Republic of Korea has, with varying degrees of consistency and cooperation, sought to form a common front with the Republic of Korea and Japan, and on an issue-by-issue basis with the People's Republic of China. Initially, the policy thrust was to limit and dismantle the DPRK's observed nuclear weapons capacity. This was embodied in the October 1994 Agreed Framework, in which the United States, Japan, and South Korea agreed to finance and build two light water reactors in the North, with the United States meanwhile providing 500,000 tons of heavy fuel oil annually to support the North's ailing industry. In return, Pyongyang was to permit the International Atomic Energy Agency to dismantle and remove the DPRK's plutonium generating and reprocessing facilities. At the time, members of the United States Congress were encouraged in background briefings by Clinton administration officials to believe that there was a high likelihood that the North Korean regime would cease to exist before reactors would be completed there.

Subsequently, North Korea's dire economic situation—produced by a combination of inappropriate policies and the dual losses of its former benefactor in the Soviet Union and the barter market of the Council for Mutual Economic Assistance in the former socialist world—led to chronic food shortages. In 1995 North Korea requested rice from the South and was rewarded with 150,000 tons by then-president Kim Young Sam. That donation, gracelessly received by the North though it was at the time, when Pyongyang humiliated the crew of the delivering ship, inaugurated a stimulus-response pattern in which the North leverages its capacity to threaten others, or to not cooperate with them, into nourishment for the regime to survive.

In 1998 and 1999, grain donations and agricultural assistance were made in payment for North Korean attendance at meetings of the "four parties" (North Korea, South Korea, China, and the United States) seeking a "peace mechanism" for the peninsula; for DPRK participation in bilateral North-South talks; and for U.S. "site visits" to suspected nuclear facilities. Most recently, the United States suspended much of its trade embargo—imposed on North Korea since the Korean War began in 1950—in exchange for a unilateral DPRK statement of its intent not to test a provocative long range Taepo Dong-II missile.

The election of South Korean President Kim Dae Jung in 1997 did much to legitimize a pattern of generosity toward North Korea. Kim had spent decades refining his thinking about reunification and came to believe that engagement, or what he called initially the "sunshine policy," rather than confrontation, would be an effective means to coax the DPRK into opening to outside influence and ultimately cooperating with the ROK. The economic crisis that wracked South Korea in 1997 contributed to public acquiescence to and support for Kim's approach, since opinion widely held that the ROK could ill afford the costs of a rapid reunification amidst its own troubles.

The use of economic incentives to induce specific policy objectives with the DPRK has had the advantage, so far, of producing identifiable results that can be used to define the policy's success. Supporters of this approach refer to the "fruits of engagement": the North Koreans are showing up at the meetings for which they are rewarded, and they are not doing what supporters of engagement feared they would do to undermine support for the policy, such as visibly constructing a new nuclear weapons facility or conducting provocative missile launches.

Critics of engagement, however, view the policy as one of "payment for process," "extortion," or—as described in this chapter—conditional appeasement. At the heart of the critique are four judgments. First, the limited interaction with the DPRK and the mounting aid bill (the DPRK is the largest U.S. aid recipient in Asia) are not producing observable positive change in the way the DPRK is ruled. Second, the security concessions from North Korea are either merely temporary or are so difficult to verify as to render them negligible. Third, by temporizing, the western coalition is compromising itself as the North continues to engage in human rights outrages and exploitation of the population. Fourth, in light of the first three, it will not be possible to sustain public and legislative support for assistance to the DPRK beyond that defined in the Agreed Framework, if at all.

This analysis begins by adopting a critical stance toward the engagement policy as a long-term approach to managing the reduction of conflict on the Korean Peninsula, the North's disappearance, and ultimate reunification. It will offer as an alternative a series of modest policy adjustments intended to end the counterproductive cycle of conditional appeasement, which has had the pernicious effect of encouraging North Korea to develop new means to threaten the United States and its allies in order to extract new concessions. The analysis is not intended to signal a radical or sudden departure from Clinton administration policy that would leave American allies in the lurch and the North cornered desperately. It does anticipate that late Clinton era efforts to solidify gains with North Korea through high level exchanges are likely to be illusory.

DETERRENCE AGAINST NONPROLIFERATION

Since the Agreed Framework was first announced—just days before the 1994 mid-term Congressional elections that replaced Democratic with Republican majorities in both houses of Congress—Clinton administration supporters have argued frequently that no one has presented an acceptable alternative to the Agreed Framework approach to dealing with North Korea's nuclear capability, imperfect though that approach may be. Policy choices were framed as two: either mobilize international sanctions and forces against Pyongyang under a United Nations Security Council mandate, with a clear expectation that military conflict would result; or, reward North Korea for surrendering its declared nuclear facilities with two light water reactors and 500,000 tons of heavy fuel oil annually.

What had actually occurred, however, in the effort to wrestle with a thorny problem posed by a viperous state, was that nonproliferation goals began to supercede the traditional deterrence that had prevented new war on the peninsula since 1953. The avenue that was apparently not explored, or was deemed insufficient, in policy deliberations in 1994 was reliance on deterrence by Korean and American forces and the threat of retaliation if deterrence were to fail. Instead deterrence was supplemented by an activist approach. By joining in the Agreed Framework, the United States was to achieve a positive, concrete result in the dismantling of the North's declared nuclear facilities without a resort to force. As noted above, this was thought likely to contribute to the regime's rapid collapse while promoting the American nonproliferation agenda. Dismissed at the time were arguments that rewarding DPRK efforts to terminate particular nuclear activities would actually promote the further development and proliferation of nuclear capabilities. The "demonstration effect" of rewarding North Korea for pressing against nonproliferation norms would not be lost on would-be proliferators elsewhere.

At the time, the tilt by the Clinton administration toward priority for nonproliferation objectives instead of reliance on deterrence alone seemed relatively low cost, especially under the expectation that South Korea and Japan would bear the brunt of the price tag for the light water reactors. So little was thought of the annual obligation of the United States to provide heavy fuel oil that no specific existing legal authority was cited in the documents associated with the Agreed Framework, nor was any sought, as the administration chose not to seek Congressional approval of the agreement.

The nuclear weapons tests in India and Pakistan in 1998 and the failure so far to discourage steps toward nuclearization on the Indian subcontinent have raised new doubts that further undermine the basic assumption of the Agreed Framework—that states have more to gain than to lose by abandoning proliferation. The August 31, 1998, launch of the Taepo Dong I multistage missile over Japan and the September 1999 Berlin understanding that the United States would lift its embargo so long as North Korea does not test the Taepo Dong II missile gave potential missile proliferators a new incentive to develop those capabilities, knowing that their development of these capabilities could draw U.S. sanctions and thereby provide leverage for a bargaining process. In the end, therefore, the push to limit proliferation has actually undermined the region's security.

Thus, the stated choice between two policy courses since 1994—open conflict versus conditional appeasement under the Agreed Framework—played down a third option: reliance on effective deterrence. Washington might well have instructed the commander of U.S. forces in Korea to take effective measures to bolster deterrence against the North's new capabilities instead of invoking the provisions of the Nuclear Nonproliferation Treaty that would lead to a UN Security Council vote (for which China's approval or abstention could prove highly problematic), active international sanctions against North Korea, and a build-up of U.S. forces in Korea and the region. If deterrence had been chosen, no additional provocative measures would have been needed to damage Pyongyang, in the absence of offensive moves by the North, or to reward it. (As Michael McDevitt writes in chapter 9, the capabilities of U.S. forces in Korea are very limited when it comes to other goals besides deterrence of a North Korean invasion of the South.)

From a nonproliferation perspective, deterrence would be a less-than-optimal outcome. From the perspective of regional security, however, this approach would leave North Korea unrewarded for its proliferation activity. The DPRK's isolation and economic weakness would continue to diminish its conventional military threat. Reasonable people can certainly disagree about whether even a relatively small number of nuclear weapons can be tolerated in the hands of the Pyongyang leadership, especially given the assumption of worsening circumstances in the North. This assessment, however, should be made with the understanding that even with a successful Agreed Framework, it will be years before a scientifically based judgment can be made on the possible number of nuclear weapons North Korea may already possess. (One can easily imagine the bargaining that might then result, and the consequent demonstration effect on other would-be proliferators.)

Practically speaking, realignment of U.S. and allied policy to a concept based solely on deterrence that seeks to break the cycle of "threat and reward" in dealing with the DPRK will not be a simple matter. For one thing, the Agreed Framework is an international undertaking of the U.S. government, and as such should be honored to the letter, unless North Korea first breaches its terms. Yet paradoxically, as support flags in Seoul, Tokyo, and Washington for bearing the costs of assistance to Pyongyang for its participation in international meetings, its consent to site visits to suspected nuclear facilities, etc., confining the obligations to those of the Agreed Framework may in fact make the agreement more palatable.

President Kim Dae Jung has centered much of his policy on generosity toward North Korea—for example, encouraging assistance and investment there. But shifting popular attitudes toward the North in light of subsequent perceived provocations (e.g., the naval skirmish over the Northern Limit Line in June 1999), have moved Kim toward an increasingly conditional and reciprocal approach to Pyongyang. As South Korea continues its economic recovery from the nadir of 1997–98, it is likely that the Korean public will be less fearful of the consequences of the fall of the Northern regime. Meanwhile, President Kim's honeymoon political phase has ended, and criticism by hard-liners of his policy toward the DPRK is on the rise. By early 2001, it is possible, even likely, that Seoul's leaders will be more receptive to a less generous, more demanding tack in dealing with Pyongyang.

Japanese opinion has also shifted—most dramatically after the Taepo Dong I launch in August 1998 and a subsequent intrusion by presumed North

Korean spy ships into Japanese waters—toward a more demanding approach to Pyongyang. Even so, a sudden shift of policy gears would not be welcome in Tokyo, but a gradual disengagement from deals that amount to conditional appeasement of Pyongyang would be well received. Here too, by reducing the range of contributions to North Korea and relying on robust deterrence, policymakers may find more support for continued funding of the Korean Peninsula Energy Development Organization that is building the light water reactors in North Korea.

One country that benefits directly from the current course of policy is China. Outside assistance to North Korea reduces the burden on China to feed and fuel its sister regime. Beijing is clearly not eager to see the peninsula reunified under Seoul, with the likely prospect of a military alliance between the ROK and United States extending right up to China's border with northern Korea.

Beijing may also have an interest in North Korea developing weapons of mass destruction, despite rhetoric claiming an identity of views with the ROK, Japan, and the United States against such a development. A North Korea with such capabilities will presumably be less subject to U.S. military pressure than, say, Serbia, which lacked means to fight back against NATO forces in Kosovo. China is noisily eager to ensure that interventions similar to that in Kosovo not occur in Asia. A possible policy straddle for Beijing would be to encourage the DPRK to develop its missile capabilities through ground testing, computer simulation of system performance, and possible testing in a second country. At the same time, Beijing would encourage Pyongyang not to test overtly at home, which would only feed the region's appetite for theater missile defense and other measures that could degrade China's own offensive capabilities. What is more, by not testing while continuing to develop missiles, North Korea will garner new economic opportunities to help perpetuate the regime.

As China's reactions to a harder allied line toward North Korea unfold, it is possible that fundamental differences over the future of the peninsula will emerge more clearly than heretofore. For its part, China will have to weigh the costs and benefits of, alternatively, publicly supporting a regime of North Korea's character, somehow adopting a more neutral posture, or—least likely—

joining a serious allied effort to counter DPRK threats. Being North Korea's last backer will carry the unappetizing burden of taking responsibility for Pyongyang's actions, something Beijing would presumably be loath to do for long.

For the United States, entering a new phase in dealing with the DPRK is likely to be less destabilizing if the U.S. posture toward China is not uniformly confrontational. As a general rule in East Asia, regional problems are easier to work out when the United States and China have an effective relationship. It does not have to be at the level of "strategic partnership." Just normal relations, where cooperation builds to further cooperation and confrontation encounters the same, should be enough.

In sum, regional reactions by the key players to a shift in U.S. policy would be at best uneven at first. Over time, however, most regional states should be prepared to let North Korea live or die by its own efforts to reform itself, not by its capacity to threaten its neighbors. Redirecting policy toward not rewarding Pyongyang should be both increasingly sustainable in the legislatures concerned and more likely to produce the desired change in the DPRK regime. Meanwhile, maintenance of robust deterrence should reduce the prospect of North Korean miscalculation while leaving South Korea and the United States better prepared if deterrence somehow fails.

A second aspect of a new approach to North Korea would be to front load the opportunities for regime transformation. In the policy package presented by former Secretary of Defense William Perry to North Korea in 1999 in his capacity as Congressionally mandated coordinator for policy toward the DPRK, the United States offered to reduce the scope of its trade and investment embargo on North Korea if the regime meets a long list of American security concerns. As in the case of the Agreed Framework, the Perry proposal is intended to reduce the North's threatening behavior while planting the seeds of internal reform through heightened economic and personal interaction with the outside world. While explicitly grounded in the reality of the many security problems posed by North Korea, the Perry package differs at its core little with the announced engagement policy of the Clinton administration. Its advantage lies in detailing areas for sustained attention to the North by an administration whose attention wandered.

An alternative approach would be to reduce nonstrategic barriers to trade and investment with North Korea at the outset. Among the goals of doing so up front would be to set as much pressure for regime transformation in motion as possible, rather than doling it out bit by bit. By conditioning progress to economic well-being on meeting international norms of conduct, the opening would undermine the foundations of a secretive and exclusionary regime. Additionally, this policy would recognize that the Pyongyang authorities maintain their military machine as their last resort for survival and would be unlikely to trade away core capabilities in any event. Better to undermine those military priorities with an alternative incentive structure founded on economic survival. If North Korea subsequently were to persist in threatening behavior, the allies would have something to deny Pyongyang, rather than to reward it.

Humanitarian assistance for starving Koreans should not be discontinued. One of the unfortunate aspects of recent food and medical assistance to North Korea has been that despite a clear humanitarian need for help for children, the elderly, and other groups not enjoying official North Korean favor, the assistance has been used for policy objectives with Pyongyang. This has the perverse result of tainting both the humanitarian and the policy mechanisms.

Moreover, the regime has at least the theoretical capability to worsen the appearance of a humanitarian crisis so as to stimulate greater donations for other purposes, and international aid agencies have an understandable institutional bias to seek higher levels of aid. The United States got into the aid business in part because nongovernmental organizations and the Congress are eager to provide agricultural assistance, but Congress is unwilling to appropriate other forms of incentives for North Korea. The administration, therefore, learned to manipulate aid programs to achieve its goals.

The beginning of the end of the threat-reward cycle will be to establish clear criteria for humanitarian assistance, insulate it from policy objectives, and demand North Korean transparency and the capacity to monitor distribution. Here again, one goal is subtle pressure for regime transformation through greater opening to the outside world on terms other than Pyongyang's.

Given North Korea's downward economic trajectory through the 1990s and, so far, mere tinkering with reforms, denial of conditional appeasement as a path to survival should impel Pyongyang to take up the opportunities that greater trade and investment offer. Theoretically, the DPRK should be able to harness economic benefits similar to those China procured through reform and opening of the country without suffering an immediate threat to its survival. As Kim Jong Il and authoritative editorials have repeatedly indicated, however, the DPRK does not seem to see this theoretical possibility; hence, the special appeal of gaining wherewithal from the United States and its allies on terms that do not imply genuine efforts at opening the society to outside influence.

Using this observation as a guide to policy, the allies should first reduce the existing barriers to nonstrategic trade and investment, block the alternative channel of conditional appeasement, prevent the distortion of humanitarian assistance, and compel North Korea to confront its need to change. The explicit underlying assumption is that this will more likely than not lead to the disintegration of the North Korean regime, a disintegration that could follow the paths of a number of scenarios, from peaceful to violent, slow to swift, internal to multinational.

In anticipation of regime transformation, allied policy should lay the groundwork for eventual reunification. Jonathan Pollack and Chung Min Lee, as well as David Reese, have written on the implications for the powers concerned in seeking stability and security for the Korean Peninsula in the aftermath of the transformation of the DPRK. The existing four-party talks are a small step in the right direction organizationally, although only in a latent sense up to now. Reaching an international agreement to guarantee the security of the Korean Peninsula after reunification will require the involvement of at least the six powers concerned: North and South Korea, China, Russia, Japan, and the United States. A new forum will be required, although it may not prove acceptable to all concerned parties until the last possible moment. For this reason, extensive preliminary consultations will be necessary at various official and unofficial levels to establish common vocabularies and test the concerns of the various parties. Some of this has begun, but there is considerable scope for further exploration and preparation.

The United States will need to have done serious thinking at home first, then among its allies, then with the Chinese and Russians, about what it views as its vital interests on the peninsula and in the region. For example, the United States would probably prefer to maintain a military alliance with Korea after unification. According to Kim Dae Jung, Seoul wants to maintain a U.S. alliance, but another president may have different priorities.

Washington will need to listen equally carefully to what the other capitals say and to be prepared to accommodate them to some extent in the interest of Korea's long-term security. Beijing, for example, may have objections or conditions it would insist upon regarding Korea's security arrangements, perhaps attempting to limit the deployment of U.S. forces on the peninsula. Washington would do well to know China's bottom line beforehand.

The economic implications of reunification similarly beg early consultations among the parties concerned and the international financial institutions that may be called upon to help the South rebuild the North. Some of this has started already, but pressure by the United States and South Korea will be needed to ensure maximum preparation is carried out.

Washington should also seek ways to support or encourage greater educational and training opportunities for North Koreans in the United States and elsewhere. Australia is already directing a small program, and private citizens are training North Koreans in law in Beijing. It will be important to maintain the criterion for study abroad that the students are chosen by a process of mutual agreement on the candidates, not by a one-sided North Korean decision.

An American administration contemplating taking a tougher approach to North Korea's threatening behavior while simultaneously evoking movement toward reform to undermine the regime will be walking a policy tightrope. Close coordination within the U.S. government will require strong leadership by an individual designated to take the helm of the interagency process. A small group under this person's leadership could provide effective management of the implementation of a policy shift and the process of reunification that may follow it.

In addition to harnessing resources to induce regime transformation from within, the leader and the small group should be prepared to enforce discipline on the North Korea's behavior from without. If the North Korean leadership decides change is too risky to venture, the team can present Pyongyang with contact information, should it change its mind. If life becomes unendurable for Pyongyang, the leaders there can call Seoul or Washington and ask for a negotiation; if they choose to threaten instead, they can face an effective deterrent capability. Effective deterrence—not running after Pyongyang with new offers for greater cooperation—will remain in the end the allies' greatest asset.

NOTES

1. Three recent works stand out in the analysis of reunification scenarios: Jonathan D. Pollack and Chung Min Lee, *Preparing for Korean Reunification: Scenarios and Implications* (Santa Monica, Calif.: RAND, 1999); Marcus Noland, *Stumbling Toward the Apocalypse: Economic Turmoil on the Korean Peninsula* (Washington, D.C.: Institute for International Economics, 2000); and David Reese, "The Prospects for North Korea's Survival," *Adelphi Paper*, no. 323 (1998).

12

Assessing Interests and Objectives of Major Actors in the Korean Drama

Nicholas Eberstadt and Richard J. Ellings

In this concluding chapter, we focus on "national interests" of the major state actors in today's unfinished Korean drama, some of the possible strategies by which they might attempt to advance their respective positions in the years ahead, and the implications of such interactions for the United States.

The Korean Peninsula's eventual political future—in terms of both internal domestic arrangements and the sort of regional order in which Korea finds itself embedded—remains at this juncture highly uncertain. Dramatically different scenarios can be plausibly spun out today—some of them full of promise, others almost unspeakably tragic. Momentous stakes are on the table—and not only for Koreans. For each of the great powers of the Pacific, the nature of the ending that ultimately unfolds for Korea's long "Cold War" could either promote their country's prosperity, national security, and international influence—or alternatively could compromise these quantities, quite possibly severely. Moreover, it is not self-evident that the outcomes and scenarios most pleasing to American sensibilities will be considered optimal by the other major actors who share an intimate concern with Korea's future.

At the end of the twentieth century, the prospects for great power cooperation in East Asia are more favorable than at almost any point in the past hundred years. On the other hand, we must also recognize that nowhere on earth is there more potential for great power conflict in the new century than in East Asia. The major schisms in this part of the world derive from unresolved issues from World War II and the Cold War (and more broadly from an unfortunate history that permeates the region with deep mistrust) and from the rise of a dissatisfied China enamored with the notion of replacing the United States as the preeminent power in East Asia (or again more broadly: from the varying levels, rates and directions of political and economic development that have been altering the relative capabilities of state actors within the region). Statesmen attempting to craft an effective national strategy for their country's engagement in East Asia must perforce contend with the swirling mix of these factors—and in their calculations, as so many times in the past, will find Korea at the vortex.

The pivotal question on the Korean Peninsula itself, of course, is the future of the DPRK. Economically failing and politically calcified, the long-term viability of the present North Korean polity is open to serious doubt—and under the pressure of events, systemic changes in North Korea in the years to come may well be radical and discontinuous rather than gradual and evolutionary. A fundamental alteration of the Korean equation at this date presupposes major changes in the North rather than the South. The ultimate disposition of the DPRK will shape, and possibly recast, the entire East Asian regional order—and the disposition of this troublesome, failing state lies in the hands of South Korea, the United States, China, Japan, and Russia. Factors within North Korea may be consequential in determining, for example, whether the process of systemic change is inclined to be orderly and peaceful or wracked by violence, yet the ROK and the great powers will ultimately determine the DPRK's future and its place in history through their complex relations and unilateral actions.

Today North Korea is, quite obviously, strategically important because of the danger its armed forces pose to peace in the region and because hostilities that it might provoke could lead to great power conflict. Yet ironically, North Korea's strategic importance also derives from the fact that it has served (albeit inadvertently) as a buffer between wary states that have a modern history of warfare with one another. North Korea forms a buffer between South Korea and its erstwhile Korean War enemy China, and between China and its World War II enemy Japan. The country's military power and location, therefore, dominate strategic thinking regarding North Korea in all capitals of Northeast Asia—aside from modest mineral deposits and a potential pool of disciplined low-wage labor, there is really little else in the country at present to attract foreign interest. As long-term strategic thinkers in these capitals contemplate the related effects that dramatic transformation in North Korea could have on the balance of power and the role of the United States in the region, they will appreciate that while the country's military potential may change greatly in the years to come, its location will not.

INTERNATIONAL RELATIONS THEORY APPLIED TO NORTH KOREA

The task of this chapter is arguably the oldest form of analysis in international relations, with roots in Thucydides's *History of the Peloponnesian War* and Machiavelli's *The Prince*. It is, in short, an endeavor to analyze what the foreign-policy leaders of states value in their relations with other states: that is, their conceptions of national interests and their ability to pursue those interests.

"National interest" is a term that must be used carefully. As Joseph Frankel has observed, "'national interest' is a singularly vague concept"[1]; James N. Rosenau has underscored its inescapably subjective foundations.[2] Yet despite its inherent norm-dependence and consequent resistance to value-neutral specification, and the poor odor the term has taken on among thinkers who hope for a declining importance of nation-states as actors on the international stage, the conception of the national interest remains powerful—even catalytic—in relations in the international arena. Assessment of national interests is in fact integral to, and implicit in, the formulation of external strategy and international policy for any modern mass society. The obligation is unavoidable: the only question is how well any such assessment succeeds in reflecting more objective realities.

For the United States, attention to national interests has a special historical significance, for it is deeply fused into the American political tradition.
Indeed, explicit and extended consideration of the national interest—its nature and its particulars—was devoted by America's Founding Fathers in the
framing of the U.S. political experiment, and the notion of charting American foreign policy against the compass of national interests has remained
deeply resonant with the American public ever since.[3]

In response to the unprecedented scale of violence in the twentieth century, modern political science tackled the question of national interest in
extraordinary "realist" scholarship: by E. H. Carr, who assessed the naiveté
of international diplomacy during the interwar period in *The Twenty Years'
Crisis*; by Hans Morgenthau, who wrote the definitive realist text *Politics
among Nations*; and by Klaus Knorr, who examined the military, political,
and economic means by which nations seek to exert influence in *The Power
of Nations*.[4] Realists prefer to define interest in terms of power, and thus are
concerned with the distribution of power among states and the relationship
between a nation's policy and its capacity to pursue that policy.

Realism as an intellectual approach and guide to statesmen has retained
its allure even in the post-Cold War era, but other theoretical perspectives
have developed over the past century as numerous scholars and practitioners
have attempted to "solve" once and for all the central problem of international relations—the scourge of war. Liberalism produced the notion of collective security, which is grounded in the belief in a global "collective interest" in stopping aggression through universally imposed economic isolation
or, in a later variant, through universal military response. Core to most
liberal theories is the belief that economic interchange and cultural and political interaction create conditions of interdependence such as those enjoyed
in the U.S.-Canadian relationship, in which war seems obsolete as a way of
resolving even the most vexing issues.[5] As conditions of interdependence
spread, according to this view, nations lose their penchant for waging war to
solve problems with other states. The historical record, unfortunately, does
not give us clear guidance, for nations that have enjoyed robust economic
relations have frequently fought. The more interactions one nation has with

another may lead, in fact, to resentment rather than empathy.

The nature of governments may be more important than patterns of international interactions, as evidenced by the remarkable peace that has existed thus far among established democracies—and the proliferation of democratic systems in the last two decades of the twentieth century.[6] Thus far, it seems that governments that are legally based and electorally accountable on a regular basis do not fight each other. There is, in other words, a growing "democratic zone of peace."[7]

More ably than perhaps any other contemporary theorist, Robert Gilpin has endeavored over his career to judge the value of the realist school and its competitors and to synthesize from them explanations of the salient features of international relations, including the balance of power, what drives foreign policies of states, and the causes of war.[8] The relative weight of these theoretical approaches varies among cases, but in explaining the likely alternative fates of the Korean Peninsula, one is struck by the primacy of power and the compelling plausibility of a realist interpretation of events. As Gilpin argues, the major challenge in maintaining peace (without capitulation) is the need for states to adjust to change: to the relative economic and military growth or withering of nations that alter the balance of power. Northeast Asia presents a potent blend of high rates of change since World War II by almost any measure—economic growth of Japan, South Korea, and China; the collapse of the Soviet empire; the plunge of the Russian and North Korean economies—together with being the locus of the world's greatest regional concentration of power. Diplomatic focus on questions of power in fact intensified in Seoul, Tokyo, and Washington in the mid- and late 1990s over issues of weapons development in North Korea and China.

Other factors must be considered as well, particularly the contrast between the governmental systems in China and North Korea versus those of Japan, South Korea, and the United States. Closed communist regimes are naturally distrusted by open democratic states, and vice versa, as communist rulers rightly fear free presses and competitive elections. The recurrent debate in Washington over "China's intentions" (who can assess intentions confidently when decisions are made behind closed doors by the few?) and Beijing's recurrent campaigns to quash dissent and discredit "foreign ideas" exemplify the inherent tensions and contradictions between contrasting systems of political organization.

Nor, perhaps, should one overlook the political import of the patterns of economic interdependence in Northeast Asia. Japan, South Korea, and the United States share abiding interests in their significant trade relations, but these commercial ties end abruptly at the North Korean border. On the other side of that border is a failed autarky that has been playing a high stakes game of international extortion to survive. And beyond the DPRK is China, a giant but fragile state with one foot in the international economy and one still in its command economy past. Whether viewed from realist, domestic political, or liberal perspectives, contemporary Northeast Asia exhibits strong potential for instability.

U.S. INTERESTS AND OBJECTIVES IN KOREA

U.S. interests in Korea were deemed sufficient by President Truman and the U.S. Congress to warrant sacrificing the lives of 54,000 American soldiers in the Korean Peninsula in the early days of the Cold War. The disposition of the peninsula may be no less vital to U.S. interests today, half a century later, although the threats are rather less immediate and distinctly more complex.

In 1950, the threat was a North Korea openly hostile to the United States, supplied by Stalin's USSR and supported by Maoist China, poised to unify the Korean Peninsula on its own terms. Today, the North Korean army remains ready to attack the force of 37,000 American soldiers stationed near the Demilitarized Zone. (The DMZ, contrary to its name, is the most heavily militarized place on earth.) But North Korea today enjoys no military guarantees from any great power. Its economy lies in ruins; by most reasonable measures, it qualifies as a failed society. At the dawn of the twenty-first century, unconditional unification of the Korean Peninsula on Pyongyang's terms looks like an utterly impossible contingency.

Why, then, does the United States keep its alliances with the ROK and so many soldiers in harm's way long after the demise of the USSR? Part of the answer lies in the concentration of power and deep mistrust among the countries of Northeast Asia. Asia's surge in economic growth since the Korean War has transformed America's stake in the region, which had previously been informed by more classical security concerns. America's trade with China and Japan grew from 0.6 percent of U.S. GDP in the early 1960s to 3.3 percent by the late 1980s.[9] South Korea, which had no exports to speak of in 1950, is now America's seventh largest trading partner. Northeast Asia is now a region of major global economies, with Japan and China ranking second and third largest in the world and the ROK eleventh. Further relative economic advance is anticipated for the region: the Chinese economy is frequently said to be on a course to exceed the size of America's (perhaps before the middle of the twenty-first century); South Korea's economy, according to some prognosticators, could be the world's seventh largest by 2010—even without unification with the North.

Military power in the region is no less consequential. Currently North Korea, Russia, and China maintain three of the five largest armies on the planet[10]; China and Russia have nuclear arsenals, and the DPRK may possess nuclear weapons as well. Japan and the ROK, also impressive military powers, could quickly develop nuclear forces; they are also potential partners with the United States in developing theater missile defense. The PRC is modernizing all of its forces and has the potential for building Asia's dominant military.

What makes this concentration of productivity and military power especially worrisome is the deep legacy of mistrust and enmity that pervades bilateral relations in the region. The burdens of history—of recurrent bitter wars and cruel occupations, and particularly of Japan's twentieth-century invasions of Korea and China—are still palpable today. (Thus the Japanese are routinely criticized by their neighbors for flirting with "militarism," irrespective of how prudent their efforts to develop a reasonable self-defense capacity may actually be.) The burden of history is made all the more onerous by a sobering contemporary fact: the established communist regimes in North Korea and China. The "democratic zone of peace" ends at the thirty-eighth parallel and the East China Sea. Given the intrinsic potential for instability in the region, a U.S. presence there appears critical to preventing arms races and possibly a horrific war.

For the moment, the threat posed by the DPRK is the principal justification for America's forward presence in Asia, including its forces on the ground in Japan as well as in Korea. Absent the North Korean threat, the United States, South Korea, and Japan would have to face the issue squarely of justifying American troops and bases in Asia. Without the DPRK, would the justification be balancing China or "restraining" Japan? The longer the DPRK manages to last, the longer the question can be postponed. But the question can only be deferred—and it must be answered.

The central challenge in any post-DPRK reconfiguration of the Korean Peninsula is how afterward to ensure a stable Northeast Asia that is as democratic as possible, that is open to free trade and international investment, that participates constructively in world organizations, and that is friendly to the United States.

Long-term U.S. goals in the reunification of Korea can be succinctly summarized as the development of a Korean Peninsula that: 1) is unified; 2) has a stable and democratic government; 3) maintains an open market economy throughout the peninsula, and one friendly to private international investment; 4) achieves social integration between the North and South (a presumed condition for long-term political stability on the peninsula); 5) fields a strong but non-threatening defense; and 6) foreswears weapons of mass destruction. With respect to the region as a whole, long-term U.S. objectives may be described as a Northeast Asia that: 1) is marked by cooperative relations and low levels of tension among the United States, China, Japan, Russia, and Korea; 2) remains anchored by the 1954 Mutual Defense Treaty between South Korea and the United States, or by a contemporary variant; 3) allows the retention of some U.S. forces on the Korean Peninsula as a symbol of American commitment; 4) adjusts to allow for the full integration of Korea into the regional and international economies and regional and international economic and political institutions; 5) is further anchored by the U.S. alliance with Japan and a U.S. base presence in Japan; and 6) witnesses normal constructive relations between the United States and China and between the United States and Russia.

In an arena no longer concerned with the "North Korean threat," the principal strategic question facing the United States and its Northeast Asian allies would most likely revolve around the means of coping with any significant growth of Chinese power. We should expect over time, should its relative power expand, that Beijing might wish to woo or threaten the ROK into splitting off from the U.S. security architecture. One can imagine this kind of effort reaching its crescendo during a Korean reunification process, when China, the United States, and Japan might all be maneuvering strenuously to establish a security arrangement on the peninsula that accorded with their own distinct conceptions of vital self-interests. Given Beijing's ambitions and its evident dissatisfaction with the regional status quo, a process of reunification on the Korean Peninsula could easily prove difficult and contentious—it could qualify as an international problem, not merely a Korean problem.

From either the U.S. or the Japanese perspective, one terribly menacing variant of Korean reunification can be envisioned: namely, a united Korea aligned with a hostile China (and perhaps supported by a resentful Russia), bifurcating East Asia and raising the possibility of a new cold war, or worse, in the region. That such a result would seriously compromise American interests requires no explanation. U.S. strategic planners, consequently, must not only concentrate upon avoiding war in the Korean Peninsula, but upon avoiding this sort of a peace.

As this discussion has underscored, apprehending Beijing's own perceived interests in Korea's future, and anticipating the strategies it may employ to advance them, will likely be an especially weighty factor in any serious American forward thinking about Korea. The Chinese calculus in the Korean Peninsula will be thoroughly examined in the following paragraphs. First, however, it is necessary to review prospects for the other major states that would be interacting in a post-DPRK Korea.

ROK INTERESTS AND OBJECTIVES

The vision is powerful: a united, democratic, economically strong, and secure Korea, in 25 years approaching the size of Japan in both population and wealth. One can argue the scenarios for realizing this vision, but most South Koreans at the moment worry more about the costs and possible dangers in getting there. Cynics, in fact, may argue that the tortured status quo—Korea's "Cold War"—has actually served the ROK rather well.

Even more than the other surrounding powers, Seoul's immediate concern must be its security—deterring an attack from the North or, conversely, avoiding the violent chaos that could attend the DPRK's collapse. Not far behind is concern over the financial burden that would be borne significantly by the ROK in absorbing North Korea's population should the DPRK suddenly collapse. The German experience, as has been noted frequently, may have been mishandled but the challenge was, comparatively speaking, not nearly so daunting as the challenge that looms before the Korean people.

The Asian financial crisis was particularly sobering for South Koreans. Their "economic miracle," while not unraveled by the events of 1997 and 1998, was nonetheless shown to be vulnerable to external shock. Reunification would be an even greater external jolt, and might therefore threaten the economic achievements of an enterprise that in barely a generation lifted the ROK from one of the world's poorest countries into the ranks of the OECD. Not surprisingly, in the near term, avoiding military conflict and preventing political implosion in the North are at the top of Seoul's priority list.

President Kim Dae Jung's "sunshine policy" aims to avoid most of the dangers and costs of relations with North Korea by attempting to engage Pyongyang skillfully, thereby reducing tensions and beginning a daunting, long-term process of bringing the two sides closer, so that reunification becomes "thinkable" and eventually feasible. The sunshine policy augments a strong defense policy by offering aid, investment, private contacts, and talks to induce the DPRK to open up and to reform—implicitly, to become more like the ROK. Seoul seeks a process of integration that ends in a "soft landing" with as few costs to South Koreans as possible.

Yet the sunshine policy itself may contain serious costs. To the extent that it fails to alter DPRK policy or plant seeds of routine change in North Korean society, it simply assists the DPRK to survive by providing other previously unavailable capital that the DPRK leadership can funnel to threatening military programs or use to quell disaffection among cadres. In other words, the policy may have effects opposite to its purpose.

The ROK seeks to minimize its dependence on China, Japan, and the United States, but understands the importance of the region's great powers in protecting its security and in dealing with the North. This posture reflects a very old tradition in Korean foreign policy, developed out of necessity over the centuries to deal with a succession of attempts by China, Japan, and Russia to gain hegemony over the peninsula. While Seoul's defense is bolstered through its alliance with the United States, and nuclear weapons issues are addressed with leadership from the United States, it recognizes the extraordinary role of China in other dealings with the North (particularly political matters such as defections, North-South meetings, and contacts with Koreans living in China near the North Korean border). If some Koreans feel more comfortable with the Chinese than with the Japanese due to the latter's more recent invasion and mistreatment of Koreans, the perception is nonetheless strong among public and policy circles in South Korea that China is a rising power with ambitions and grievances that may conflict with vital Korean interests.

The Korean relationship with Japan is deeply ambivalent. It is, on the one hand, plagued by memories of Japanese imperialism in the first half of the twentieth century. On the other hand, it is also framed by an important mutuality of interests. The ROK's economy and political structure were influenced by the Japanese colonial experience and, later, by Japan's remarkable economic development from the 1950s to the 1980s. The two countries' very close financial and commercial relations proved sufficient to ensure intense cooperation as both sought to ameliorate the effects of the financial crisis of 1997–98. And South Korea-Japan strategic cooperation has expanded impressively since North Korea's provocative missile test in August 1998, including unprecedented summits and ministerial meetings in the autumns of 1998 and 1999 along with plans for long-term coordination. (The framework for their cooperation, called the Joint Declaration on a New ROK-Japan Partnership, was signed during President Kim Dae Jung's historic visit with Prime Minister Keizo Obuchi in October 1998.) So while some South Koreans persist in distrusting Japan, Seoul may nevertheless build upon an old tradition of strategic pragmatism to work with Japan in accordance with economic circumstances and security interests.

In fact, strategic coordination is essential from the ROK's perspective. Without outside help, South Korea cannot, for instance, easily absorb the North in the event of a collapse. It will need strategic support from the United States, acceptance by China, UN assistance with refugees, and international economic aid and investment from Japan and others to commence the long process of integrating the North's primitive economy into the South's.

To the extent China or the DPRK are perceived as a threat, the ROK's continued natural ally is the United States, along with Japan. Following reunification, however, and in the event of friendly Sino-Korean and Japanese-Korean relations, an alliance with the United States may seem to make little sense to Seoul. Calls within Korea for the removal of U.S. troops from the ROK are likely to be voiced. If the Washington-Seoul military alliance is to continue beyond the tenure of the DPRK, both American and Korean statesmen will have to be able to convince their publics that the relationship continues to have a persuasive rationale.

JAPAN'S INTERESTS AND OBLIGATIONS

Japan's interests in the Korean Peninsula must be understood first and foremost from the perspective of the country's increasing strategic concerns, and in the context of Asians' vivid memories of its often brutal colonization of Korea from 1910 to 1945.

Focused mostly on economic development since World War II, Japan is witnessing a major transformation in the configuration of power in Northeast Asia. As it struggles to lift its economy out of a seemingly interminable recession, Russia staggers in a dramatically weakened condition while China's economy continues to grow, and its PLA to modernize. Japanese leaders face the simultaneous difficulties of revitalizing their own economy, responding to the long-term challenge of a rising China, and countering the immediate threat posed by North Korea's development of weapons of mass destruction. They can, further, see on the horizon the economic and military potential of a united Korea.

Two decades ago, Tokyo may have been enthused by talk of "Japan as

Number One" and a forthcoming "Japanese century"; Japan's future now appears much more problematic. From the Japanese perspective, the creation on the peninsula of a powerful and united Korean state would not necessarily brighten the strategic picture—for a united Korea that was disconnected from the U.S. security architecture, or positively aligned with China or Russia, would constitute a serious new challenge to the nation's security.

Japan's economic interests complement larger strategic ones. The ROK and Japan have developed close commercial ties, with Japan having provided key ingredients in South Korea's economic miracle: an economic model; substantial aid, investment, and technology; and a market. The two economies are interdependent today, with South Korea serving as Japan's second largest trading partner. During the depths of the Asian financial crisis in 1997–98, Tokyo provided the ROK with substantial cash outlays to support its economy (and to keep loan payments flowing to weak Japanese banks). At the same time, the prolonged recession in Japan depresses ROK exports. Should the two Koreas reunify, Japan will count on its neighbor's economic health and openness to trade and investment, just as Korea will have an interest in Japan's recovery and further opening of its market. A happy Japanese-Korean symbiosis, of course, is by no means a foregone conclusion following reunification. Korea's future political configuration and the manner by which that configuration is reached are of critical interest to Japan's economic future.

In the final analysis, we would argue, Japan shares most of the short- and long-term interests of the United States with regard to a Korean reunification. Because of the legacy of Japan's colonization of Korea and domestic policy constraints, Japan is not able to muster the leadership required to shepherd the reunification process. It is a necessary supporter of that process, however. As Michael Armacost and Kenneth Pyle conclude in chapter five,

If the North succumbs to acute political instability, Japan can help the United States cope with uncertainties and humanitarian crises. If the North's collapse leads to its eventual absorption by the South, Japan's assistance will be critical to the economic revival of a unified Korea. And if the outside world is to find ways of helping Seoul draw North

Korea into a more constructive involvement in the affairs of the Northeast Asian region, Japan has a large role to play in that endeavor.

The "Japan question," for all too poignant historical reasons, was addressed quite differently after World War II by America's allies in Asia than was the "German question" in Western Europe. The Federal Republic of Germany came to be viewed by its neighbors as a "normal country"; multilateral security networks enmeshing Germany, the United States, and other local American allies consequently flourished. Northeast Asia still lacks such deep relationships. We believe that an analogous network of security relationships is self-evidently in the Japanese national interest. For Japan to foster such a network, however, it is imperative that Tokyo embark on the final steps to becoming viewed as a "normal country" by its prospective peers in the region. More perhaps than for any other major capital, it is therefore incumbent upon Tokyo to deal with its "burdens of history," and for reasons of rank self-interest. This therapeutic process promises to be liberating, not debilitating. And it offers the specific, tangible prospect of a reward that might evoke the benefits that accrued from Germany's extraordinary postwar rapprochement and entente with France: a sturdy Japan-ROK axis at the heart of Northeast Asia.

RUSSIA'S INTERESTS AND POLICIES

The days of Soviet influence on the Korean Peninsula are now a distant memory, the result of a reorientation of policy by Gorbachev near the end of his leadership of the Soviet Union. Russia now wields little influence in Korean affairs due to its own severe political and economic difficulties, which are likely to last for some time. As Herbert Ellison points out in chapter six, "Many of the high hopes that accompanied the Russian revolution of 1989–91 have been shattered, and the vision of a new Russian role in Northeast Asia is among them."

Gorbachev's initiatives toward Korea in 1990 were aimed at reducing the costs of underwriting DPRK security and economic well-being while opening a robust relationship with South Korea that would help modernize the

Soviet economy. What influence the Soviets wielded at the time in North-east Asia derived from the threats that emanated from propping up and arming the DPRK and from its bases in the Russian Far East. Gorbachev had little to offer besides goodwill (and virtually nothing in the economic sphere) through which to build a new set of interests. By withdrawing So-viet implicit military support for Pyongyang and abrogating Moscow's treaty with the DPRK, while at the same time recognizing the South and position-ing Moscow as supplicant by seeking financial aid from Seoul, he all but gave up the Soviet claim to a role on the peninsula.

This abrupt turn by Gorbachev forced North Korea to cooperate more than it had with South Korea, China, and the United States. No less impor-tantly, Moscow's *volte face* may have spurred the DPRK in its pre-existing quest for its own nuclear capability.

Current Russian interests in a Korea reunification derive from security concerns related to the balance of power in Northeast Asia. Fearful that the Russian Far East is vulnerable to the powerhouses of East Asia, Moscow's interest would appear to be in a stable balance of power that protects exist-ing borders and prevents the chaos that could result in Korean or Chinese refugees flooding into Russia (or that could serve as the pretext for interven-tion by China or others). To cover its bases and perhaps recover some influ-ence, Moscow has been reaching out to the DPRK; the recent Putin-Kim Jong Il concordance on the dangers of a prospective U.S. program of na-tional missile defense, and the almost simultaneous ratification of a new Moscow-Pyongyang friendship treaty, indicate that leadership of the Rus-sian Federation believes that it shares some important interests with the North Korean regime.

Even so, Russia may still share the long-term ROK and U.S. interest in reunification (albeit with greater emphasis on a united Korea's emerging as an independent actor). A unified Korea could be a stabilizing factor in the region, helping to balance the powers of China and Japan. It could offer Russia new opportunities to forge the kind of economic ties envisioned in 1990, and to engage the region as a diplomatic participant because of the more complex balance of power. For example, Russia could view a united, powerful Korea as a logical ally against an aggressive China or Japan—or as a flywheel against an imperious Washington. On the other hand, a united Korea allied with either Beijing or Tokyo and unconstrained by the United States would be a recipe for disaster in the Far East from a Russian standpoint. The geopolitical dynamics necessary for such adverse outcomes, however, would be profound—and would also be largely beyond Moscow's control. On balance, a prospective Korean reunification therefore may not look as dangerous from the Russian perspective as from Tokyo's, or more importantly, Beijing's perspectives.

Expanded economic opportunities for Russia could emerge in a Korea unified under an open, fast-growing system like the ROK's. Unification could accelerate development of the Tumen River Basin and encourage the import of Russian forest and mining products, and of Russian oil and gas. (In the short term, an effort to revive some of North Korea's Soviet-era factories could also create a market for Russian supplies and spare parts.)

Russia has a role to play in a Korean reunification process: it could facilitate the process, or, given its residual military and diplomatic power, it could complicate the process, perhaps consequentially. It is hard to imagine that Russia will never again be a force to contend with, but its weakness for the foreseeable future means that it must cooperate with the United States, Japan, South Korea, and China to protect its security interests on the peninsula. This should be seen as an opportunity by the United States in view of its long-term interests in maintaining good relations with Moscow. The Russian Federation, for its part, is clearly a work in progress; as it evolves, its government's assessments of the country's national interests—and its objectives in the Korean Peninsula—will predictably undergo some change as well.

From an American standpoint, one potentially crucial facet of interactions with Moscow—both in the Korean Peninsula and beyond it—could be diplomacy to prevent a Russian *mis-assessment* of the country's national interests. History is replete with examples of national directorates that made fatefully bad choices when better options were available to them. When and where Washington and Moscow share interests, it may be incumbent upon American statesmen to persuade their Russian counterparts of the fact, so as to prevent resentful sentiment from standing in the way of mutually beneficial cooperation.

CHINA'S INTERESTS AND OBJECTIVES

Fifty years ago, China demonstrated in blood that it indeed had vital interests on the Korean Peninsula.[11] The legacy of the Korean War and the importance of the Korea question to China have remained lasting influences on Beijing's perceptions of U.S. intentions toward Korean reunification. The Korean War was costly to the young People's Republic of China—not only in lives lost, but in chances lost as well. Because of the Korean War, China quite probably postponed a "final campaign" against the Chinese nationalists who had retreated to the island of Taiwan, by transferring the best troops of the invasion force from South China to Manchuria.[12] The fledgling PRC lost indefinitely the chance of an invasion of Taiwan when President Harry S Truman ordered the U.S. Seventh Fleet into the Taiwan Strait in response to the North's invasion of South Korea. Many senior officers of the People's Liberation Army fought in Korea against the United States: even today, at least four members of the small, seven-man CCP Central Military Commission, China's highest-level politico-military decisionmaking body, fought in the Korean War.[13] For Americans, whose memories are sometimes short, it is essential to understand that the Korean War shaped the context for many of the core problems that remain sources of tension in U.S.-China relations today.

In spite of the end of the Cold War and Asia's economic ascent, China's basic interest in the Korean Peninsula has changed little since the Korean War. This interest is centered on security concerns due both to the continued division of the peninsula and to the resilience of the U.S.-led alliance architecture in the region. As in the 1950s, a communist-led China still faces the U.S.-Japan and U.S.-ROK alliances to its east. China's priorities over the quarter-century since the death of Mao Zedong have reinforced this evaluation of the peninsula. China's "core" priorities under Deng Xiaoping and his successors to date have been the advancement of national strength through the "four modernizations" program (in industry, agriculture, science, and defense); the preservation of China's territorial integrity and sovereignty; and the prevention of regional hegemonism. To advance those interests effectively, PRC leaders have stressed regional stability with their neighbors and have given up their earlier goal of assisting communist revolution around the world. Focused first and foremost on developing national strength, they have attempted to limit potential costly involvements outside Chinese territory while pursuing relatively low-cost policies to achieve progress on the subsidiary goals of reunifying with Hong Kong, Macao, and Taiwan and limiting U.S. and Japanese power in the region.

One of the greatest threats to this strategy would be a series of events on the Korean Peninsula requiring, from Beijing's perspective, Chinese intervention to prevent the establishment of a united, democratic Korea aligned with the United States and Japan. Although to Washington's way of thinking a continued U.S. troop presence on the Korean Peninsula does not constitute "domination," Beijing seems to take the position that it does. In its July 1998 "White Paper" outlining military and security policies, the PRC complained that "the enlargement of military blocs" has tended to destabilize—rather than stabilize—the Asian continent.[14] Many factors will determine Chinese policy toward any U.S. military presence on the peninsula following a Korean reunification, chief among them being the perception of Chinese leaders of their country's capabilities and will relative to those of the United States, Korea, and Japan.

For reasons both psychological and strategic, PRC leadership places value on the existence of an old-fashioned "buffer zone"—however geographically small—between China and possibly hostile neighbors on the Korean Peninsula. Today, China continues to regard North Korea as a strategic buffer providing some distance from the freewheeling, democratic South with U.S. forces stationed there. Beijing should be expected to remain extremely wary of any circumstances that might allow a U.S. troop presence above the thirty-eighth parallel. Perpetuating the division of the Korean Peninsula sustains the buffer (and also defers a possible crisis entailed in a DPRK collapse, the subsequent turmoil and costs of reunification, and/or enhanced economic competition from a united Korea).

At a time when China's overwhelming focus is on maintaining as peaceful an international environment as possible so it can attend to its immense internal challenges of modernization, stability and predictability are attractive. Consequently, China fears developments on the Korean Peninsula that threaten the status quo. It fears nuclear proliferation and has been support-ive of the Agreed Framework to cap North Korea's weapons program. China's position on the nuclear issue, however, reveals the tension between China's concern over the intervention of outside powers and its worries over the North's reckless behavior. DPRK brinkmanship over the nuclear and mis-sile issues is a frustrating annoyance to PRC leaders. At the same time, these leaders are wary of any significant bilateral or multilateral security regimes that might be established under U.S. and/or Japanese control.

As a far-flung empire embracing many distinct peoples within its periph-eries, China cannot help but be concerned with the security implications of the "Korean question" for its own internal reasons. According to official PRC statistics, there are about two million ethnic Koreans in China, largely located in the Yanbian Korean Autonomous Prefecture along the DPRK border in Jilin Province. As Korean issues spill into the world's headlines, Beijing may be increasingly concerned that its ethnic Korean population not develop loyalties that conflict with loyalties to the PRC.

Since ROK-China diplomatic normalization in 1992, there has been a steady rise in individual visits between South Korea and China that appear to have supported economic exchange. Ethnic Korean Chinese minorities have sought both legal and illegal entry into South Korea to earn money in low-end jobs. South Korean tourists have traveled to China and particularly to the Yanbian Korean Autonomous Prefecture, site of Mount Paektu, the mythological birthplace of the Korean people. The ROK attempted, effec-tive July 1999, "to allow ethnic Koreans in the PRC and Russia with long-term resident visas to freely enter and exit the ROK for the duration of their visa,"[15] but the PRC government reportedly raised objections, arguing that the ethnic Koreans living in the PRC were full Chinese citizens and should therefore not be treated differently from their ethnic Chinese compatriots. Yet the chief concern for Chinese leaders is a massive flow of refugees from North Korea in the event of a collapse of the DPRK or other catastrophic event such as war or famine. The costs of such an inflow would be large and numerous, ranging from financial outlays for food, housing, security, and administration, to potential political problems as a consequence of a major population increase of an ethnic minority. In addition, a major refugee problem would attract international attention and, very likely, United Nations involvement. Accordingly, Chinese policy has stressed stability on the Korean Peninsula and economic reform in the North to bolster the DPRK's capacity to survive and maintain control of its population.

To achieve its development goals rapidly, China's interests would seem to be in a continuation of investment from, and in fruitful trade ties with, the ROK. Reunification would redirect South Korean and some other international investment to North Korea. For South Korean and multinational companies, the North might develop as an important alternative for cheap, educated, and disciplined labor to China's still underdeveloped interior population (although Marcus Noland and Gifford Combs, in chapters seven and eight, are skeptical about the attractiveness of North Korea as a source of cheap labor).

Over the long term, China has economic reasons to question Korean reunification under Seoul. As an economic powerhouse approaching the size of Japan, a united Korea in perhaps 20 years could transform the strategic calculus in Northeast Asia.

For Beijing, the Korean question is in part a question regarding national or theater missile defense. China has already signaled to the United States and its allies that it opposes a theater missile defense system in East Asia, and that regional instability and arms races may result should Washington go ahead with proposed plans to speed up development of a TMD system that incorporates its regional allies.[16] (This has become an increasingly contentious issue between the PRC and United States, especially since Japan agreed to fund joint development of a TMD system.) Ironically, the Japanese decision to join America on TMD development, after years of equivocating, was largely the result of North Korea, China's "friend," testing a missile over the Japanese mainland.[17] The official Chinese government position is that the United States has exaggerated the Asia security threat, and that TMD is too "advanced" for DPRK missiles and is in fact designed to thwart China.

In any crisis on the Korean Peninsula that threatens regional security, estimating Chinese intentions and capabilities will be the central issue for U.S. strategists. The United States and its allies cannot afford to repeat their miscalculations made during the Korean War.

China's capability to disrupt missions on or around the peninsula by the United States and its allies is gradually increasing. So too is China's intercontinental strategic capability. Progress in its short- and medium-range missile forces; the acquisition of Russian Su-27s, Sovremenny destroyers, and Kilo-class submarines; and advancements in its nuclear arsenal simply mean that China will have to be taken more seriously as a regional and strategic player than ever before. China's border with the DRPK and still substantial PLA ground forces (in spite of recent downsizing), mean that China retains the option of direct intervention on the peninsula, whether to stabilize the DPRK in a preemptive occupation or to counter a U.S.-ROK effort to secure a collapsing North.

Since July 11, 1961, the PRC has had a "Treaty on Friendship, Cooperation and Mutual Assistance" with the DPRK, although there apparently is quite a bit of confusion regarding the current validity of the treaty. The second article of the agreement stipulates that both countries agree to

... take all measures to prevent either Contracting Party from being attacked by any other country. If either of the Contracting Parties should suffer armed attack by any country or coalition of countries and thus find itself in a state of war, the other Contracting Party shall immediately extend military and other assistance with any means at its disposal.[18]

The PRC reportedly told the ROK government prior to the August 24, 1992 normalization of relations between the two countries, however, that its treaty obligation to the DPRK was "practically invalid" and was not a justification for the deployment of troops.[19]

So long as North Korea's buffer status is stable, China can treat the ROK as a normal economic partner. What remains to be seen is if China and the ROK can build on their years of normal relations to allow for the peaceful incorporation of the North into the ROK. In this respect, Beijing is not promising anyone anything. During the important visit to Beijing of Kim Yong Nam, head of the DRPK Supreme People's Assembly and second in line in the ruling Korean Worker's Party, Li Peng reiterated Chinese policy of supporting "both sides of the peninsula in a peaceful reunification without external interference."[20] Jiang Zemin stated that:

> In the current complicated and changeable international situation, improving this bilateral traditional friendship is in the interest of the people of the two countries. . . . China also supports the DPRK to improve relations with the United States, Japan, and the European Union, and ultimately normalize bilateral relations.[21]

Some observers believe that because of its past "friendship" with North Korea and skilled diplomacy with the Republic of Korea, China may play a key brokering role in the transformation of the peninsula. Past policies aside, because of its geographic position, the growth of its power, and its flexible diplomacy, China will exert influence. And it will likely retain influence with the DPRK, so long as that entity survives, as the DPRK's only potential friend with any power. Even if China opts not to intervene with troops should North Korea teeter, we should assume that China may influence the North's leadership by providing emergency aid and, in the end, safe haven.

The U.S. needs to take into account how China might respond to different unification circumstances. The role of U.S. troops is an especially touchy subject. The question of what form a post-Cold War East Asian order will take is still largely unanswered. The interests of the United States, South Korea, and Japan lie in the continuation of the present alliance system, but this will become increasingly difficult with a continued rise of China. A more powerful China is unlikely to want to remain subject to, or become part of, a U.S.-led security system.

It is important to keep in mind that the unification of the Korean Peninsula is likely to be played out with China positioning itself for long-term goals as well as immediate bargaining advantage. Therefore, throughout the unification process, it will be imperative that Chinese interests and options are clearly understood. These interests will vary according to many factors. What kind of regime is in power in Beijing, and how secure is it? Is the Chinese economy dependent upon U.S. trade and investment, or upon IMF or World Bank loans? What are the international circumstances? If led by an insecure communist party whose overriding, popular appeal is nationalism, China will fear a unified and democratic Korea hosting U.S. troops on its soil, and will suspect that any trilateral security arrangement or series of bilateral alliances among Korea, the United States, and Japan will be for the purpose of containing it. No matter who sits atop the leadership, China will seek progress on major strategic goals during reunification, and it should simultaneously be expected to attempt to enhance its bargaining position through maneuvering that may seem creative or crude to outsiders, but not surprising.

Accordingly, in the drama of a collapsing North Korea and perceiving victory by a U.S.-ROK-Japan coalition, China could intervene with PLA forces in the North and seek to divert U.S. attention and forces by challenging them directly or by striking deals with others to stir up trouble for American commitments in other regions. It may even seek sufficient advantage to attempt a grand bargain, such as the withdrawal of U.S. security guarantees for Taiwan—in other words, Chinese reunification—for some sort of Korean unification scheme. The acquisition of Taiwan would not only serve the sentimental interest of reunification and economic interests, it would also provide the PRC with a strategic outpost in the Pacific, and in the process cut a major slice out of what it perceives as a U.S.-led encirclement of China. The PRC could push the Taiwan "button" in the midst of a crisis on the Korean Peninsula by engineering a crisis with Taiwan to complicate and weaken the U.S. strategic position and thereby gain the upper hand in negotiations over the future of North Korea.

One can conjure up a Eurasian-Pacific strategy to include a crisis coordinated with Iran, an attempt to split ASEAN over the Spratly Islands and other issues, a build-up of forces in Fujian Province together with air and naval clashes in the Taiwan Strait, PLA forces crossing into North Korea, and a flurry of diplomatic initiatives with Russia against Japan igniting a crisis over the "Northern Territories," all in the effort to stretch the U.S. Seventh Fleet from the Strait of Hormuz through the Indian Ocean and South China Sea to the Taiwan Strait, Sea of Japan/Eastern Sea, and the Sea of Okhotsk. One cannot overemphasize the potential for China to "play the

Taiwan card" in particular. China may calculate that the stakes are worthwhile and perceive that its power and strategic capabilities relative to those of the United States are sufficient to risk the expenditure of much diplomatic capital, if not war. Any appearance of U.S. indecisiveness or naiveté upon a collapse of the DPRK could serve as a further invitation to more nationalistic factions in China to initiate a Taiwan crisis or attempt to orchestrate a Eurasian-Pacific strategy.

The United States can do much to prepare for dealing with an aggressive China (if one were to develop) in anticipation of Korean reunification. Everything America can do in a prudent way to bolster its alliances, strengthen its forces, and communicate its resolve would be a start. Contingency planning must be based on the assumption of simultaneous, numerous challenges by China (and the DPRK, for that matter) working with possible collaborators in different parts of the world—even terrorists. (One must remember the terrorist history of the DPRK and that Chinese strategic thinking reflects the teachings of Sun Tzu. That thinking emphasizes a balance of power view of the world, the importance of dispersing the enemy's forces so that those of China are superior where the goals are dear, and making the costs high to the enemy in order to break his will.) America must have sufficient working relations with, and a better deal to offer, Russia or Iran, or a credible threat that a hostile Iran, for example, could not help but appreciate.

In the heat of a full-fledged crisis in North Korea in which China nonetheless attempts to gain leverage through a Taiwan or Eurasian-Pacific (or global) strategy, the United States will have to provide China with clear alternatives that make playing out such a game to its logical conclusion unacceptably costly. China could probe America's will, and thus would have to be confronted rapidly by a broad counterstrategy in which economic, security, and political incentives were quickly compelling.

The further China went down the road of an aggressive strategy, the harder it would find backing out with dignity (saving face), so a counter-strategy must be established early in the game, with its basic elements crystal-clear.

Such a counter-strategy ought to incorporate all three elements of national power. First, China will need to understand that its status in the international economy would be threatened if it acted irresponsibly. (This is listed first because of the importance of the U.S. and other international markets to China). Second, China would need to appreciate the capacity of the United States and its allies and friends to answer military challenges in the Pacific—to respond simultaneously to multiple threats to sea lines of communication and to Taiwan while dealing with a debacle on the Korean Peninsula, the one part of the Asian mainland where the United States is committed to using ground forces. Finally, China would find itself confronted by a broad and effective diplomatic initiative that offers China two alternatives: (1) be constructive with regard to a Korean reunification and be rewarded with an appropriate role to play in world and regional institutions and arrangements dedicated to managing economic relations and stability; or (2) act brazenly and irresponsibly, and be left outside the zone of free trade and peaceful relations among (mostly) democratic states—and outside the leadership of many international institutions.

U.S. policy has to be realistic about the difficulty of isolating China diplomatically, or even economically, over the long term. In the short and medium term, however, much of the Chinese economy is extraordinarily vulnerable. China's impoverished banking system and still large state-owned enterprise sector are propped up by the good faith deposits Chinese citizens keep pouring in from their earnings in a growing economy, fueled by sales to an open and rich international market. China teeters on the edge of a financial crisis of potentially historic proportions, which should give pause even to those in Beijing prone to reckless policy. An investor panic could send the Chinese economy crashing into a very deep chasm.[22]

America must keep its guard up and be as prepared as possible for such contingencies, while the nation's goal should be a positive one that requires the patience and dedication of leaders and diplomats whose job it is to build an acceptable order in Northeast Asia. Indeed, China should be part of the solution, not left outside so that the day of reckoning with this dissatisfied power has simply been postponed.

U.S. policy with regard to the disposition of North Korea must be driven by America's core, long-term interests, which means policy must be thought through before a crisis, when short-term considerations may be overwhelming. American statesmen will need to understand the capabilities, perspectives, and vital interests of each of the surrounding powers, foremost among them South Korea and China. Most of the challenges that could derail a Korean reunification or some other peninsular settlement attend the policies or politics of these two:

1) Will China prop up North Korea with economic and military aid indefinitely in order to retain a buffer between itself and a vibrant, democratic South Korea? Would China intervene militarily if the DPRK collapses and U.S. and ROK forces move to assist refugees or secure weapons of mass destruction, key units of the Korean People's Army, strategically important infrastructure, etc.? In other words, would China risk war with America and South Korea to maintain North Korea as a buffer?

2) Will South Korean economic policy toward the North, should reunification occur, attract international investment or favor the *chaebols*—to the exclusion of foreigners? In other words, will South Korean policy encourage or discourage the flow of international capital required to absorb and rebuild the North Korean economy? This question bears on another: namely, following reunification, will South Koreans wish to retain their strategic link with the United States for the ultimate guarantee of their security, or opt to build an independent defense strategy based on powerful conventional or nuclear forces?

The United States and the ROK should prepare the answers to these challenges now, so they do not have to be addressed hurriedly in the midst of crisis. Not to wrestle with these prospective policy problems now, we believe, would eventually appear to be terribly shortsighted.

NOTES

1. Joseph Frankel, *National Interest*, (New York: Praeger Publishers, 1970), p. 15.

2. James N. Rosenau, "National Interest," in David L. Sills, *International Encyclopedia of the Social Sciences*, (New York: Macmillan Company and the Free Press, 1968), vol. 11, pp. 34–39.

3. For background on the special significance of the concept of "national interest" in U.S. foreign policy, consult Charles A. Beard, with the collaboration of G. H. E. Smith, *The Idea of National Interest: An Analytic Study in American Foreign Policy*, (New York: Macmillan Company, 1934).

4. E. H. Carr, *The Twenty Years' Crisis*, (New York: St. Martin's Press, 1961); Hans Morgenthau, *Politics among Nations*, (New York: Knopf, 1960); and Klaus Knorr, *The Power of Nations*, (New York: Basic Books, 1975).

5. See for example Robert Keohane and Joseph Nye, *Power and Interdependence: World Politics in Transition*, (Boston: Little, Brown, 1977).

6. Samuel P. Huntington, *The Third Wave: Democratization in the Late Twentieth Century*, (Norman, Okla.: University of Oklahoma Press, 1991); and Larry Diamond, Juan Linz, and Seymour Martin Lipset, ed., *Democracy in Developing Countries*, (Boulder, Colo.: Lynne Reinner, 1988–1998), vols. 1–4.

7. See, for example, Michael Doyle, "An International Liberal Community," in Graham Allison and Gregory F. Treverton, ed., *Rethinking America's Security: Beyond Cold War to New World Order*, (New York: Norton, 1992), and Max Singer and Aaron B. Wildavksy, *The Real World Order: Zones of Peace, Zones of Turmoil*, (Chatham, N.J.: Chatham House Publishers, 1996). For democratic peace theory applied to Asia, see Aaron Friedberg, "Ripe for Rivalry: Prospects for Peace in Multipolar Asia," *International Security*, Winter 1993, pp. 5–34.

8. See, for example, Robert Gilpin, *War and Change in World Politics*, (Cambridge: Cambridge University Press, 1981).

9. Richard J. Ellings, "The Leadership Imperative in U.S. Relations with East Asia," *Asian Journal of Political Science*, vol. 2, no. 1 (June 1994), pp. 169–96. See Table 1, p. 190.

10. U.S. Department of State, Bureau of Verification and Compliance, "World Military Expenditures and Arms Transfers 1998", released August 21, 2000, available <http://www.state.gov/www/global/arms/bureau_vc/wmeat98fs.html> (accessed December 8, 2000). In 1998, according to this report, the countries fielding the largest armed forces were, in order, China, the United States, the Russian Federation, India, and the DPRK.

11. This section of the chapter has benefited enormously from the comments of William B. Abnett.

12. William W. Whitson, *The Chinese High Command*, (New York: Praeger, 1973), p. 94. According to Whitson, two of the best army groups of the PLA (the Ninth, under Song Shilun and the Thirteenth, under Li Tianyu) were moved from South

China to Northeast China by late August 1950.

13. The men are Minister of National Defense Chi Haotian, Chief of the PLA General Staff Fu Quanyou, Wang Ke, and Yu Yongbo. Their biographies are found in Huang Chen-hsia, *Zhongguo Junren Minglü [Mao's Generals]*, (Hong Kong: Research Institute of Contemporary History, 1968).

14. "China's National Defense," Defense White Paper Published by the Information Office of the State Council of the People's Republic of China, Beijing, July 1998.

15. Myoung-jin Kim, "Special Status for Ethnic Koreans from China, Russia," *Chosun Ilbo*, Seoul, May 2, 1999.

16. Michael J. Green and Toby F. Dalton, "Asian Reactions to U.S. Missile Defense," *NBR Analysis*, vol. 11, no. 3, November 2000, pp. 32–34.

17. Ibid., p. 15. See also "Theater Missile Defenses in the Asia-Pacific Region," Henry L. Stimson Center Working Group Report No. 34, June 2000.

18. Cited in Chae-Jin Lee, *China and Korea—Dynamic Relations*, (Stanford, Calif.: Hoover Institute Press, 1996), p. 60.

19. Kay Möller, "China and Korea: The Godfather, Part Three," *Journal of Northeast Asian Studies*, vol. 15, no. 4, pp. 36 and 43 (footnote 6).

20. "China, North Korean Talks Cover Bilateral Ties, NATO, Regional Security," *Xinhua News Agency*, June 3, 1999.

21. "China: President Calls on North Korea to Improve Relations with USA, Japan, EU," *Xinhua New Agency*, June 4, 1999.

22. See, for example, Gerrit Gong, Robert Kapp, Nicholas Lardy, Greg Mastel, Dwight Perkins, and Edward Steinfeld, "China into the Abyss?" *Washington Quarterly*, Spring 1999, pp. 27–36; and Nicholas Lardy, "China and the Asian Contagion," *Foreign Affairs*, July–August 1998, pp. 78–89.

About the Editors and Contributors

Nicholas Eberstadt is Henry Wendt Chair in Political Economy at the American Enterprise Institute, visiting fellow at the Harvard Center for Population and Developmental Studies, and senior research associate at The National Bureau of Asian Research. He has served as consultant to the Departments of State and Defense, the U.S. Information Agency, the Census Bureau, the Congressional Budget Office, and the World Bank. Dr. Eberstadt has published extensively in scholarly and foreign policy journals, and is the author of many books, including *Prosperous Paupers and Other Population Problems* (2000), *The End of North Korea* (1999), *The Tyranny of Numbers: Mismeasurement and Misrule* (1995), *Korea Approaches Reunification* (1995), *The Population of North Korea* (with Judith Banister, 1992), and *The Poverty of Communism* (1988).

Richard J. Ellings is president and cofounder of The National Bureau of Asian Research. His areas of focus are national strategy, the international political economy of East Asia, and Chinese foreign relations. He is the editor of *Southeast Asian Security in the New Millennium* (with Sheldon Simon, 1996), and has authored *Private Property and National Security* (with others, 1991) and *Embargoes and World Power* (1985). Dr. Ellings has recently led projects and conducted studies on comparative national strategies, U.S. strategic options, and the history of U.S. strategy in the Asia Pacific. He has served as a consultant on Asia policy to the Departments of State and Defense and to the U.S. Information Agency, and as a legislative assistant in the U.S. Senate.

Michael H. Armacost is president of The Brookings Institution. During his twenty-four years in government, he served as the U.S. Ambassador to Japan, the U.S. Ambassador to the Philippines, and Under Secretary of State for Political Affairs. He has also held senior policy responsibilities in the National Security Council and Department of Defense. From 1993 to 1995 he was distinguished senior fellow and visiting professor at Stanford University's Asia/Pacific Research Center. Ambassador Armacost has published three books, including an analysis of Japan and the United States in the post-Cold War world. He is the recipient of the President's Distinguished Service Award, the Defense Department's Distinguished Civilian Service Award, and the Secretary of State's Distinguished Service Award.

Gifford Combs is the founder and managing general partner of the global hedge fund, Chemin de Fer Limited. He served as partner in the Pacific Financial Research money management firm from 1985 to 1994. Mr. Combs was awarded the Stevenson Prize in Economics for his dissertation on food import policies and price stabilization in developing economies.

Chuck Downs is a consultant in Asian affairs, and until his retirement in June 2000 was senior foreign and defense policy advisor for the House Policy Committee. From 1996 to 1998 he served as associate director of Asian studies at the American Enterprise Institute. He has held numerous positions with the Department of Defense, including deputy director for regional affairs and congressional relations, East Asia and Pacific region; country director for Indonesia, Malaysia, Singapore, Brunei, Australia, New Zealand, the Philippines, and the Pacific Islands; and assistant to the director for foreign military rights affairs. He has also held positions in the Department of the Interior, Senate staff, and Congressional Research Service. Mr. Downs is author of *Over the Line: North Korea's Negotiating Strategy* (1999), coeditor with James Lilley of *Crisis in the Taiwan Strait* (1997), and author of numerous articles on America's strategic role in Asia.

Herbert J. Ellison is professor of history and Russian studies in the Henry M. Jackson School of International Studies at the University of Washington and founding director of Eurasia Policy Studies at The National Bureau of Asian Research. Previously, Professor Ellison has served as the director of the Kennan Institute for Advanced Russian Studies at the Woodrow Wilson International Center for Scholars and as a consultant to the Department of State and the Foreign Affairs Committee of Congress. He has led numerous major projects on Russian relations with Japan, China, and the two Koreas, including as chief consultant for the PBS and BBC documentary series *Messengers from Moscow*. Relevant publications written by Professor Ellison include: *The New Russia and Asia: 1991–1995* (1996), "Political Transformation of Communist States: Impact on the International Order in East Asia" (1995), and "Superpower Arms Control and the Future of Korean-American Security Ties" (1991).

Robert L. Gallucci is dean of Georgetown University's School of Foreign Service. He was previously Ambassador-at-Large with the Department of State, during which he served as the principal U.S. negotiator for the 1994 Agreed Framework between the United States and the DPRK. In his 21 years of government service, Ambassador Gallucci was also the Assistant Secretary of State for Political-Military Affairs and the deputy executive chairman of the UN Special Commission overseeing the disarmament of Iraq. He has authored a number of publications on political-military issues.

Chae-Jin Lee is BankAmerica Professor of Pacific Basin Studies, professor of government, and director of the Keck Center for International and Strategic Studies at Claremont McKenna College. He has done extensive research on the interactions of the United States and major Asian powers in regard to the Korean Peninsula. Professor Lee has authored a number of prominent works in the field including *North Korea after Kim Il Sung* (1998) and *China and Korea: Dynamic Relations* (1996). He serves on the board of advisors for The National Bureau of Asian Research.

Michael McDevitt is a retired rear admiral of the United States Navy and senior fellow at the Center for Naval Analyses Corporation, a non-profit research and analysis center focusing on national security issues, primarily those involving the Navy and Marine Corps. His research interests include security issues in East Asia and U.S. security policy throughout the region. Rear Admiral McDevitt's military career spanned 34 years, during which he served in several positions, including director of the East Asia policy office for the secretary of defense during the Bush administration; director for strategy, war plans, and policy for the commander of the U.S. Forces, Pacific; and commandant of the National War College in Washington, D.C.

Marcus Noland is senior fellow at the Institute for International Economics. Dr. Noland's most recent publication is *Avoiding the Apocalypse: The Future of the Two Koreas* (2000). In addition, he has written numerous articles addressing Korean unification with the Institute for International Economics, and one which appeared in *Foreign Affairs*, "Why North Korea Will Muddle Through." He is also a coauthor of several volumes on the international economic relations of Japan and other East Asian states.

Douglas H. Paal is president of the Asia Pacific Policy Center, a non-profit institution in Washington, D.C. The Center promotes education and information on Asia Pacific trade and investment as well as defense and security ties throughout the region. Mr. Paal's past positions include special assistant to Presidents Reagan and Bush for national security affairs and senior director for Asian affairs at the National Security Council. He has also served on the State Department policy planning staff and as a senior analyst for the CIA.

Kenneth B. Pyle is professor of history and Asian studies in the Henry M. Jackson School of International Studies at the University of Washington, and founding president of The National Bureau of Asian Research. He specializes in Japanese foreign policy and diplomatic history. Dr. Pyle is the author of numerous books and articles on Japan, including "Japan: Opportunism in the Pursuit of Power" in *A Century's Journey: How the Major Powers Shaped the World* (1999), *The Making of Modern Japan* (1996), and *The Japanese Question: Power and Purpose in a New Era* (1992). He has served as chairman of the Japan-U.S. Friendship Commission, director of the Henry M. Jackson School of International Studies, an advisor to the Departments of State and Defense, and has frequently testified on Japanese affairs before Congressional Committees.

Robert A. Scalapino, arguably the dean of Asian studies in America, is Robson Research Professor Emeritus of Government at the Institute of East Asian Studies at the University of California-Berkeley, where he formerly served as director. His research interests include Northeast Asian politics and foreign relations as well as U.S. policy toward China, Japan, and Korea. Professor Scalapino is editor emeritus of *Asian Survey*, and his numerous publications include "The Major Powers and the Korean Peninsula" in the *Korean Journal of Unification Studies* (1994), *The Last Leninists: The Uncertain Future of Asia's Communist States* (1992), *Internal and External Security Issues in Asia* (with Seizaburo Sato and Jusuf Wanandi, 1986), *Asia and the Road Ahead: Issues for the Major Powers* (1975), and *Communism in Korea* (with Chong-Sik Lee, 1972). He serves on the board of advisors for The National Bureau of Asian Research.

Index